Didascalia Apostolorum

Ancient Texts and Translations
K. C. Hanson, Series Editor

Robert William Rogers
*Cuneiform Parallels to the
Old Testament*

D. Winton Thomas, editor
*Documents from
Old Testament Times*

Henry Frederick Lutz
*Early Babylonian Letters
from Larsa*

Robert Francis Harper
The Code of Hammurabi

G. R. Driver and John C. Miles
The Babylonian Laws (2 vols.)

Albert T. Clay
*Babylonian Epics, Hymns,
Omens,
and Other Texts*

G. R. Driver and John C. Miles
The Assyrian Laws

Daniel David Luckenbill
The Annals of Sennacherib

A. E. Cowley
*Aramaic Papyri of the
Fifth Century B.C.*

G. R. Driver
*Aramaic Documents of the
Fifth Century B.C.*, rev. ed.

Adolf Neubauer
The Book of Tobit

August Dillman
The Ethiopic Text of 1 Enoch

R. H. Charles
The Book of Enoch

The Book of Jubilees

R. H. Charles
*The Testaments of the
Twelve Patriarchs*

The Apocalypse of Baruch

H. B. Swete
The Gospel of Peter

R. Hugh Connolly
Didaskalia Apostolorum

Didascalia Apostolorum
The Syriac Version

R. Hugh Connolly

Translated and Accompanied by the Verona Latin Fragments
With an Introduction and Notes

New Foreword and Bibliography by
K. C. Hanson

WIPF & STOCK · Eugene, Oregon

DIDASCALIA APOSTOLORUM
The Syriac Version Translated and Accompanied by the Verona Latin
Fragments, with an Introduction and Notes

Ancient Texts and Translations

Copyright © 2009 Wipf and Stock Publishers. All rights reserved. Except
for brief quotations in critical publications or reviews, no part of this book
may be reproduced in any manner without prior written permission from
the publisher. Write: Permissions, Wipf and Stock Publishers, 199 W. 8th
Ave., Suite 3, Eugene, OR 97401.

Wipf & Stock
An imprint of Wipf and Stock Publishers
199 W. 8th Ave., Suite 3
Eugene, OR 97401

ISBN 13: 978-1-55635-669-8

Cataloguing-in-Publication data:

Didascalia Apostolorum. English.

   Didascalia apostolorum : the Syriac version translated and
accompanied by the Verona Latin fragments, with an introduction and
notes / by R. Hugh Connolly, with new Foreword and Bibliography by K.
C. Hanson.

   Ancient Texts and Translations

   ISBN 13: 978-1-55635-669-8

   cix + 280 p. ; cm.

   English and Latin on opposite pages.

   1. Church orders, Ancient. I. Connolly, R. Hugh (Richard Hugh),
1873–1948. II. Hanson, K. C. (Kenneth C.). III. Didascalia apostolorum.
Latin. IV. Didascalia apostolorum. Syriac version. English.

BV761.A46 A2 2007

Manufactured in the U.S.A.

CONTENTS

Series Foreword / ix

Foreword / xiii

Select Bibliography / xv

Introduction / xviii

Preface / xxiiii

Abbreviations of Books Quoted / xxv

Abbreviations / xxxiv

Supplement to Thesaurus Syriacus / 1

HOC QUALECUMQUE OPUSCULUM
NON QUOD DIGNUM SED QUOD PRAESTO EST
MEMORIAE DEDICO
PII PARITER IN CHRISTO PATRIS
ATQUE AMICI PRETIOSI

RR. DD. LEANDRI RAMSAY

DIE XIV MARTII AN. MDCCCC XXIX DEFUNCTI
ABBATIS NUPER S. GREGORII MAGNI DE DOWNSIDE
EIQUE DOMUI
OB PIETATEM SIMUL SINGULAREM ET MERITA EGREGIA
INTER ALUMNUS CLARIORES
SEMPER COLENDI

SERIES FOREWORD

THE DISCOVERIES OF DOCUMENTS from the ancient Near Eastern and Mediterranean worlds have altered our modern understanding of those worlds in both breadth and depth. Especially since the mid-nineteenth century, chance discoveries as well as archaeological excavations have brought to light thousands of clay tablets, stone inscriptions and stelae, leather scrolls, codices, papyri, seals, and ostraca.

The genres of these written documents are quite diverse: receipts, tax lists, inventories, letters, prophecies, blessings and curses, dowry documents, deeds, laws, instructions, collections of proverbs, philosophical treatises, state propaganda, myths and legends, hymns and prayers, liturgies and rituals, and many more. Some of them came to light in long-famous cities—such as Ur, Babylon, Nineveh, and Jerusalem—while others came from locations that were previously little-known or unknown—such as Ebla, Ugarit, Elephantine, Qumran, and Nag Hammadi.

But what good are these remnants from the distant past? Why should anyone bother with what are often fragmentary, obscure, or long-forgotten scraps of ancient cultures? Each person will answer those questions for herself or himself, depending upon interests and commitments. But the documents have influenced scholarly research in several areas.

It must first be said that the documents are of interest and importance in their own right, whatever their connections—or lack of them—to modern ethnic, religious, or ideological concerns. Many of them provide windows on how real people lived in the ancient world—what they grew and ate; how they related to their families, business associates, and states; how they were taxed; how and whom they worshiped; how they organized their communities; their hopes and fears; and how they understood and portrayed their own group's story.

They are of intense interest at the linguistic level. They provide us with previously unknown or undeciphered languages and dialects, broaden our range of vocabularies and meanings, assist us in mapping the relationships and developments of languages, and provide examples of loan-words and linguistic influences between languages. A monumental project such as *The Assyrian Dictionary*, produced by the Oriental Institute at the University of Chicago, would have been unthinkable without the broad range of Akkadian resources today.[1] And our study of Coptic and early gospels would be impoverished without the Nag Hammadi codices.[2]

The variety of genres also attracts our interest in terms of the history of literature. Such stories as Athra-hasis, Enumma Elish, and Gilgamesh have become important to the study of world literature. While modern readers may be most intrigued by something with obvious political or religious content, we often learn a great deal from a tax receipt or a dowry document. Hermann Gunkel influenced biblical studies not only because of his keen insights into the biblical books, but because he studied the biblical genres in the light of ancient Near Eastern texts. As he examined the genres in the Psalms, for example, he compared them to the poetic passages throughout the rest of the Bible, the Apocrypha, the Pseudepigrapha, Akkadian sources, and Egyptian sources.[3]

---

1. I. J. Gelb et al., editors, *The Assyrian Dictionary of the Oriental Institute of the University of Chicago* (Chicago: Univ. of Chicago Press, 1956–).

2. James M. Robinson, editor, *The Nag Hammadi Library in English*, 3d ed. (San Francisco: Harper-SanFrancisco, 1990).

3. Hermann Gunkel, *Einleitung in die Psalmen: Die Gattungen der religiösen Lyrik Israels,* completed by Joachim Begrich, HAT (Göttingen: Vandenhoeck &

While the Akkadian and Egyptian resources were much more limited in the 1920s and 1930s when he was working on the Psalms, his methodology and insights have had an on-going significance.

History is also a significant interest. Many of these texts mention kingdoms, ethnic and tribal groups, rulers, diplomats, generals, locations, or events that assist in establishing chronologies, give us different perspectives on previously known events, or fill in gaps in our knowledge. Historians can never have too many sources. The Amarna letters, for example, provide us with the names of local rulers in Canaan during the fourteenth century BCE, their relationship with the pharaoh, as well as the military issues of the period.[4]

Social analysis is another area of fertile research. A deed can reveal economic structures, production, land tenure, kinship relations, scribal conventions, calendars, and social hierarchies. Both the Elephantine papyri from Egypt (fifth century BCE) and the Babatha archive from the Judean desert (second century CE) include personal legal documents and letters relating to dowries, inheritance, and property transfers that provide glimpses of complex kinship relations, networking, and legal witnesses.[5] And the Elephantine documents also include letters to the high priest in Jerusalem from the priests of Elephantine regarding the rebuilding of the Elephantine temple.

Ruprecht, 1933). ET = *Introduction to the Psalms: The Genres of the Religious Lyric of Israel,* trans. James D. Nogalski, Mercer Library of Biblical Studies (Macon, Ga.: Mercer Univ. Press, 1998).

4. William L. Moran, *The Amarna Letters* (Baltimore: Johns Hopkins Univ. Press, 1992).

5. Bezalel Porten et al., editors, *The Elephantine Papyri in English: Three Millennia of Cross-Cultural Continuity and Change,* Documenta et Monumenta Orientis Antiqui 22 (Leiden: Brill, 1996); Yigael Yadin et al., *The Finds from the Bar Kokhba Period in the Cave of Letters,* 3 vols., Judean Desert Studies (Jerusalem: Israel Exploration Society, 1963–2002) [NB: vols. 2 and 3 are titled *Documents* instead of *Finds*].

Religion in the ancient world was usually embedded in either political or kinship structures. That is, it was normally a function of either the political group or kin-group to which one belonged. We are fortunate to have numerous texts of epic literature, liturgies, and rituals. These include such things as creation stories, purification rituals, and the interpretation of sheep livers for omens. The Dead Sea Scrolls, for example, provide us with biblical books, texts of biblical interpretation, community regulations, and liturgical texts from the second temple period.[6]

Another key element has been the study of law. A variety of legal principles, laws, and collections of regulations provide windows on social structures, economics, governance, property rights, and punishments. The stele of Hammurabi of Babylon (c. 1700 BCE) is certainly the most famous. But we have many more, for example: Ur-Nammu (c. 2100 BCE), Lipit-Ishtar (c. 1850 BCE), and the Middle Assyrian Laws (c. 1150 BCE).

The intention of Ancient Texts and Translations (ATT) is to make available a variety of ancient documents and document collections to a broad range of readers. The series will include reprints of long out-of-print volumes, revisions of earlier editions, and completely new volumes. The understanding of ancient societies depends upon our close reading of the documents, however fragmentary, that have survived.

—K. C. Hanson
Series Editor

---

6. Florentino García Martínez, *The Dead Sea Scrolls Translated: The Qumran Texts in English*, 2d ed., trans. Wilfred G. E. Watson (Grand Rapids: Eerdmans, 1996).

FOREWORD

R. Hugh Connolly (1873–1948) was born in Carcoar, a small town in the "Central Tablelands" of New South Wales, Australia, but was educated in England at Downside Abbey and Christ's College, Cambridge. He joined the Benedictines and was ordained a priest in 1899. He was Head of Benet House, Cambridge from 1904 to 1916.

At Cambridge, Connolly became a leading patristics scholar, specializing in Syrian Christianity. His most enduring legacy has been his editing, translating, and interpreting Syriac texts from the third through the tenth centuries.

Among Connolly's publication are:

Connolly, R. Hugh. *The Liturgical Homilies of Narsai.* Texts and Studies: Contributions to Biblical and Patristic Literature 8/1. Cambridge: Cambridge University Press, 1909. Reprinted, Eugene, OR: Wipf & Stock, 2004.

———. *The So-Called Egyptian Church Order and Derived Documents.* Texts and Studies: Contributions to Biblical and Patristic Literature 8/4. Cambridge: Cambridge University Press, 1916. Reprinted, Eugene, OR: Wipf & Stock, 2004.

———. *Sixth-century Fragments of an East-Syrian Anaphora.* Sonderabdruck aus Oriens Christianus 12. Leipzig: Harrassowitz, 1925.

———. *Some Dates and Documents: For the Early History of Our House. Our Establishment as a Community at Douay.* Worcester, UK: Baylis, 1930.

———. *The De Sacramentis: A Work of St. Ambrose.* Bath, UK: Downside Abbey, 1942.

———. *The Explanatio Symboli ad Initiandos: A Work of St. Ambrose.* Texts and Studies: Contributions to Biblical and Patristic Literature 10. Cambridge: Cambridge University Press, 1952.

———. *Anonymi Auctoris Expositio officiorum Ecclesiae.* 4 vols. Edited by R. Hugh Connolly. Corpus scriptorum christianorum orientalium 64, 71, 72, 76. Louvain: Durbecq, 1953–54.

———, and H. W. Codrington, editors. *Two Commentaries on the Jacobite Liturgy.* London: Norgate, 1913.

McCann, Justin, and Hugh Connolly, editors. *Memorials of Father Augustine Baker and Other Documents Relating to the English Benedictines.* Catholic Record Society Publications 33. London: Whitehead, 1933.

—K. C. Hanson

Select Bibliography

Achelis, Hans, and Johannes Flemming. *Die ältesten Quellen des orientalischen Kirchenrechts.* Vol. 2: *Die syrische Didaskalia.* Texte und Untersuchungen zur Geschichte der altchristlichen Literatur 25/2. Leipzig: Hinrichs, 1904.

Bartlett, James Vernon. *Church-Life and Church-Order during the First Four Centuries: With Special Reference to the Early Eastern Church-Orders.* Birkbeck Lectures 1924. Oxford: Blackwell, 1943.

Bradshaw, Paul F., Maxwell E. Johnson, and L. Edward Phillips. *The Apostolic Tradition.* Hermeneia. Minneapolis: Fortress, 2002.

Brent, Allen. "The Relations between Ignatius and the *Didascalia*." *Second Century* 8 (1991) 129–56.

Brock, Sebastian, and Michael Vasey, editors. *The Liturgical Portions of the Didascalia.* Grove Liturgical Study 29. Bramcote, UK: Grove, 1982.

Cox, James J. "Studies in the Determination and Evaluation of the Dominical Logoi as Cited in the Original Text of the Greek Didascalia Apostolorum." Ph.D. dissertation, Harvard University, 1973.

―――. "Prolegomena to a Study of the Dominical Logoi as Cited in the *Didascalia Apostolorum*." *Andrews University Seminary Studies* 13 (1975) 23–33; 249–59; 15 (1977) 1–15; 97–133.

―――. "Some Prolegomena and Addenda to a Study of the Dominical Logoi as Cited in the *Didascalia Apostolorum*." In *Studia Patristica* 16.2:82–87. Berlin: Akademie, 1985.

Fonrobert, Charlotte. "The *Didascalia Apostolorum*: A Mishnah for the Disciples of Jesus." *Journal of Early Christian Studies* 9 (2001) 483–509.

Funk, Franciscus Xaverius. *Didascalia et Constitutiones Apostolorum.* 2 vols. Paderborn: Schoeningh, 1905. Reprinted, Torino: Bottega d'Erasmo, 1959.

Gamber, Klaus. "Die frühchristliche Hauskirche nach *Didascalia Apostolorum* II, 57, 1–58, 6." *Studia Patristica* 10:337–44. Berlin: Akademie, 1970.

Gargano, Guido Innocenzio. "L'immagine dell'ape laboriosa di Prov 6, 8abc e la *Didascalia* trasmessa dai Padri cristiani." In *La Tradizione: Forme e Modi: XVIII Incontro di studiosi dell'antichita cristiana, Roma, 7–9 Maggio*

1989, 266–82. Studia ephemeridis "Augustinianum" 31. Rome: Institutum Patristicum "Augustinianum," 1990.

Gibson, Margaret Dunlop. *The Didascalia Apostolorum in English*. Horae Semiticae 2. London: Clay, 1903.

———. *The Didascalia Apostolorum in Syriac*. Horae Semiticae 1. London: Clay, 1903.

Hauler, Edmund. *Didascaliae Apostolorum Fragmenta Ueronensia Latina*. Leipzig: Teubner, 1900–.

Holzhey, Karl. *Die Abhängigkeit der syrischen Didaskalia von der Didache*. Fribourg: Saint Paul, 1898.

Lagarde, Paul de, editor. *Didascalia Apostolorum Syriace*. Göttingen: Dieterich, 1911.

Methuen, Charlotte. "Widows, Bishops and the Struggle for Authority in the *Didascalia Apostolorum*." *Journal of Ecclesiastical History* 46 (1995) 197–213.

———. "'For pagans laugh to hear women teach': Gender Stereotypes in the *Didascalia Apostolorum*." In *Gender and Christian Religion: Papers Read at the 1996 Summer Meeting and the 1997 Winter Meeting of the Ecclesiastical History Society*, edited by R. N. Swanson, 23–35. Studies in Church History 34. Woodbridge, UK: Boydell, 1998.

Maclean, Arthur John. *The Ancient Church Orders*. Cambridge Handbooks of Liturgical Study. Cambridge: Cambridge University Press, 1910.

Metzger, Marcel. "The *Didascalia* and *Constitutiones Apostolorum*." In *Eucharist of the Early Christians*, edited by Willy Rordorf, 194–219. Translated by Matthew J. O'Connell. New York: Pueblo, 1978.

Nau, F., translator. *La didascalie, c'est-a-dire l'enseignement catholique des douze apotres et des saints disciples de Notre Sauveur*. Ancienne littérature canonique Syriaque 1. Paris: Lethielleux, 1902.

O'Leary, De Lacy. *The Apostolic Constitutions and Cognate Documents, with Special Reference to Their Liturgical Elements*. Early Church Classics. London: SPCK, 1906.

Saxer, Victor. "La tradizione nei testi canonico-liturgici: Didaché, Traditio apostolica, Diascalia, Constitutiones apostolorum." In *La Tradizione: Forme e Modi: XVIII Incontro di studiosi dell'antichita cristiana, Roma, 7–9 Maggio 1989*, 251–63. Studia ephemeridis "Augustinianum" 31. Rome: Institutum Patristicum "Augustinianum," 1990.

Schöllgen, Georg. *Die Anfänge der Professionalisierung des Kerus und das kirchliche Amt in der syrischen Didaskalie*. Jahrbuch für Antike und Christentum Ergänzungsbad 26. Münster: Aschendorffsche Verlagsbuch-handlung, 1998.

Tidner, Erik. *Sprachlicher Kommentar zur lateinischen Didascalia Apostolorum*. Stockholm: Wahlström & Widstrand, 1938.

———. *Didascalia Apostolorum, Canonum Ecclesiasticorum, Traditionis Apostolicae Versiones Latinae*. Texte und Untersuchungen zur Geschichte der altchristlichen Literatur, Bd. 75. Berlin: Akademie, 1963.

Torjesen, Karen Jo. "The Episcopacy—Sacerdotal or Monarchical? The Appeal to Old Testament Institutions by Cyprian and the *Didascalia*." In *Papers Presented at the Thirteenth International Conference on Patristic Studies held in Oxford, 1999*, edited by M. F. Miles and E. J. Yarnold, 3:387–406. Studia Patristica 36. Leuven: Peeters, 2001.

Vööbus, Arthur. *The Didascalia Apostolorum in Syriac*. Corpus Scriptorum Christianorum Orientalium 401, 402, 407, 408. Louvain: Secrétariat du CorpusSCO, 1979.

INTRODUCTION TO THE 2009 EDITION

THE ENGLISH BENEDICTINE COMMUNITY of St Gregory the Great began at Douai in Flanders in 1606 and settled at Downside in Somerset in 1814 following the disruption of the French Revolution. Its apostolate was the provision of priests for its scattered mission among the Roman Catholics of England and Wales and its school. Scholarly monks were the exception rather than the norm. In the second half of the nineteenth century both Downside's religious community and school began to prosper and in 1899 St Gregory's attained abbatial status. It was Dom Hugh Connolly's good fortune to be at Downside during its period of transformation from a quiet backwater to a powerhouse of "godliness and good learning."

This change was made possible by the movement towards a more monastic self-understanding within the community. This was encouraged in particular by a gifted trio of scholars: Aidan Gasquet (1846-1929), Edmund Bishop (1846-1917) and Cuthbert Butler (1858–1934). Gasquet, who was to become a cardinal in 1914, was a historian whose expertise was in the late Medieval English Church and the Reformation. He was a prolific if not always meticulous writer. Bishop, a layman whose library provided a centre for research at Downside, was a pioneering student of the liturgy. Butler, who became second Abbot of Downside was an editor of early monastic texts and an authority on al things Benedictine. All three, influenced by the new freedom on Catholic studies associated with Pope Leo XIII, looked to origins and precedents.

Connolly, the equal of Bishop and Butler as a clear-minded and original thinker, benefited from this context that made his career possible. Richard Joseph Connolly, Hugh was his religious name, was born on 12 July 1873 (he was to die in 1948) at Werajel, near Carcoar, in New South Wales. The English Benedictines had established the Catholic archdiocese of Sydney and were known to his parents. He arrived at Downside School in 1888 and excelled, after a slow start owing to his deficient education, on arrival, both in his studies and in the game of cricket. He entered the monastic community in 1891 and was ordained priest in 1899.

Cambridge, like Downside, had a number of scholars who appealed to his developing interests and languages and Christian origins. These included James Bethune-Baker (1861–1951) editor of *The Journal of Theological Studies* and a leading liberal churchman, Francis Burkitt (1864–1935), the authority on the *Didache* and J. Armitage Robinson (1858–1933), the founder of *Texts and Studies*. Armitage Robinson, a Fellow of Christ's College, was chiefly responsible for cementing the relationship between that college and Downside, which was to flourish for over sixty years and, with his appointment as Dean of Wells in 1911, became a near neighbour of Connolly and Downside for several decades.

Connolly graduated through the Theological Tripos in 1899 as a member of Christ's, the first Catholic cleric to take a Cambridge degree since the Reformation. After a short period in the school, as a teacher of what would now be called Religious Studies, he returned to his research in Cambridge, which centered on Hebrew and Syriac texts. The "Modernist Crisis" meant that Patristics had become a relatively safe field for Catholic academics who wished to avoid the theological opprobrium associated with more speculative studies. He was superior (in succession to Cuthbert Butler) of Benet House, the Downside residence in

INTRODUCTION TO THE 2009 EDITION xxi

Cambridge, from 1904–1916. In 1911 he became lecturer in Syriac at Christ's College and was an examiner in the Oriental Languages Tripos. With the temporary closure of Benet House owing to the Great War, he returned to Downside where he was to remain until his death. He served as editor of *The Downside Review* for two periods, from 1917–20 and from 1925–29.

His reputation rests not on his monastic life or on his occasional teaching (at school and university) but on his scholarly output in the field of Patristics, especially in his studies of Syriac authors. He made many important contributions to *The Journal of Theological Studies* as well as publishing several books. His first published volume was *The Liturgical Homilies of Narsai* (1909), in the Cambridge *Text and Studies* series; but perhaps his greatest work was *The so-called Egyptian Church Order and Derived Documents* (1916). *The Didascalia Apostolorum* (Oxford, 1929), based on a complete text available only in Syriac, showed his mastery of the Syriac language and a profound knowledge of what seemed to be a third-century text claiming apostolic authority. It appeared in the context of the collaborative work he had been undertaking with Armitage Robinson on the dating and status of the *Didache*.

Connolly, withdrawn in later life (he felt much bereaved by the death of Downside's third abbot, Leander Ramsay, a scholar of Cyprian in 1929) and possessed of a somewhat mordant wit, remained dedicated to the end to his studies and to Downside. He had edited Edmund Bishop's liturgical studies for publication as well as pursuing continuing (and fundamentally important) research into the history of his monastery and the revival of English Monasticism. This bore fruit in a series of articles in *The Downside Review*, work for The Catholic Record Society (in co-editing the Society's 1933 volume on English Benedictines) and the privately published *Some Dates and Documents* (1930).

A monk in the great scholarly tradition of the Maurists, he combined great linguistic gifts with a methodical and highly accurate approach to his research. His pioneering contribution to Syriac studies makes him a still useful commentator as well as a painstaking editor of texts that were, before his work, unavailable to the English language reader. In his opening up of Patristic Studies he revealed the crucial importance of the Fathers in a proper understanding of Christian origins.

—Dom Aidan Bellenger
Abbot of Downside

PREFACE

THE writer who has given us the fullest and most careful study of the *Didascalia*, Dr. Hans Achelis, has characterized this third-century book in words which are to this effect: that there is no other ancient Christian writing which provides us with anything like the same detailed information concerning the life, in all its aspects, of an early Christian community.

If this approaches at all to a just appreciation, the *Didascalia* should be a document well worth the study of any one who takes an interest in the early history of the Church. But however the case may stand with the scholar or the expert, it can hardly be said that the ordinary English-speaking student has had, up to the present, any convenient means of access to this important relic of antiquity. This is due primarily to the form in which the *Didascalia* has survived. If it were extant in Greek, the language in which it was written, it would long ago have been edited and re-edited, and translators would not have been wanting to make its contents available to all. But no manuscript of the work in its original language has yet been discovered. It is true that considerable portions of the Greek lie imbedded in the first six books of the fourth-century *Apostolic Constitutions*; but the compiler of that work dealt so freely with his source, making perpetual additions, omissions, and alterations, that we can seldom feel sure that he has left a sentence exactly as he found it; and of course we could not know what he had taken from his source in any form, or even what that source might be, without an independent knowledge of the *Didascalia* itself. This knowledge is supplied in the first place by an early, and on the whole a very faithful, Syriac translation, the only form in which the document is preserved in its entirety; and secondly by considerable fragments of an ancient Latin version.

The Latin fragments have been edited, and may be read by those who possess a copy of the edition or are able to consult a library which contains one. The Syriac version has also been edited; but that hardly places its contents within the reach of many. How then can the student find his way to the complete document? Only in modern translations. He can read it in the French of Mgr. Nau, or in the German of Dr. Flemming. There is also the English translation of Mrs. Dunlop Gibson; but this has at least two serious defects: it is incomplete, omitting the long final chapter which in many respects is the most interesting and important part of the whole book; and it is based upon a corrupt and defective manuscript. Probably the text most commonly consulted by English students is that of Dr. F. X. Funk in his great edition of the *Apostolic Constitutions*. But even this requires to be supplemented: it is a composite text, containing in a modern Latin translation only so much of the Syriac as is needed to fill the lacunae of the old Latin fragments. Where the old Latin supplies the text Funk gives only a selection of variants from the Syriac, so that a notable portion of the latter is quite inadequately represented. And even the old Latin is not given exactly as it stands, but its readings are often set aside in favour of improvements suggested by the Syriac or the *Apostolic Constitutions*; and the grammar and orthography are for the most part standardized. If we take a passage from Funk's edition under the impression that we are quoting the very words of the old Latin version, there is always a danger that we may be caught tripping. Funk's main task was the edition of the *Constitutions*, and the text of the *Didascalia* which he provides (a very good one for its purpose) is chiefly designed to illustrate the other document.

What is offered in the present volume is a complete translation of the Syriac with the Latin fragments printed opposite as they occur. This as a general plan will, I hope, commend itself to nearly all who may use the book. But I must point out that the present work does not aspire to be a final and comprehensive edition of the *Didascalia*, and that its limits have made it impossible for me to quote in the notes more than a very small proportion of all the parallel matter in the *Apostolic Constitutions*. What is aimed at here is to enable students, or at least English-speaking students, to read and study in a convenient form the two ancient versions in which alone the work is preserved in its original form and content, and from which all study of it must begin. Those who desire to reconstruct as much as may be recovered of the author's Greek must still be referred to Funk's edition of the *Constitutions*, where they will find much of the preliminary work already done; but for the remainder of their task they will find that the only safe check upon the elusive methods of the ' Constitutor ' lies in the Syriac and Latin versions.

For encouragement and help while this volume was in the making my thanks are due pre-eminently to the Dean of Wells, Dr. Armitage Robinson, to whom I am also indebted for many valuable criticisms and suggestions. To the Clarendon Press I am under particular obligations, not only for accepting the book for publication, but also for allowing the text and notes to be advanced to page form before the rest was presented: a concession which greatly eased the labour of reference in writing the Introduction.

R. H. C.

DOWNSIDE ABBEY,
March 1929.

CONTENTS

	PAGE
INTRODUCTION	xi
1. The Text	xi
The Syriac Version	xi
The Latin Version	xviii
The Apostolic Constitutions	xx
Editions and Translations of the Syriac	xxi
2. The Document	xxvi
Title	xxvii
Contents in outline	xxviii
The Didascalia *a unity*	xxxvi
The Ministry	xxxviii
Theological standpoint	xlv
Baptism	xlviii
The Eucharist	l
Penitential Discipline	liv
The Problem of the Old Law	lvii
The Author's use of Scripture	lxix
The use of Apocrypha	lxxv
The use of other writings	lxxix
Traces of the Didascalia *in early writings*	lxxxiv
3. Place and Date	lxxxvii
ABBREVIATIONS AND SIGNS EMPLOYED IN NOTES AND TEXT	xcii
TRANSLATION OF THE SYRIAC WITH THE LATIN FRAGMENTS	1
Chapter I (= Funk i. 1-2)	2
II (,, i. 3-7)	8
III (,, i. 8-10)	20
IV (,, ii. 1-6)	28
V (,, ii. 6-11)	37
VI (,, ii. 12-18)	40
VII (,, ii. 18-24)	55
VIII (,, ii. 24-25)	78
IX (,, ii. 26-36)	85
X (,, ii. 37-43)	101
XI (,, ii. 44-56)	109

			PAGE
XII (= Funk ii. 57–58)	. . . . . .	119
XIII (,, ii. 59–63)	. . . . . .	124
XIV (,, iii. 1–4)	. . . . . .	130
XV (,, iii. 5–11)	. . . . . .	132
XVI (,, iii. 12–13)	. . . . . .	146
XVII (,, iv. 1–4)	. . . . . .	152
XVIII (,, iv. 5–10)	. . . . . .	156
XIX (,, v. 1–6)	. . . . . .	161
XX (,, v. 7–9)	. . . . . .	167
XXI (,, v. 10–20)	. . . . . .	178
XXII (,, iv. 11)	. . . . . .	193
XXIII (,, vi. 1–10)	. . . . . .	194
XXIV (,, vi. 11–13)	. . . . . .	202
XXV (,, vi. 13–14)	. . . . . .	210
XXVI (,, vi. 15–23)	. . . . . .	216
ADDITIONAL NOTES	. . . .	261
INDEX LOCORUM	. . . .	271
GENERAL INDEX	. . -	275

INTRODUCTION

1. The Text.

WRITTEN in Greek, the *Didascalia* has reached us in a complete form only in an early Syriac translation. But in addition to this we have extensive fragments of an ancient Latin version, which cover about two-fifths of the whole text and include both the beginning and the end. And further, though no manuscript of the original Greek has yet been found, considerable portions of the Greek text are recoverable (if, too often, only in an approximate form) from the fourth-century *Apostolic Constitutions*, the compiler of which made the *Didascalia* the basis of his first six books.

We must now consider these sources of the text; which done, we may pass on to notice the modern editions or translations in which it has been made available for students.

The Syriac Version.

The Syriac version is preserved, wholly or in part, in four principal manuscripts.

1. Codex Sangermanensis (S). This is now MS. Syr. 62 of the Bibliothèque Nationale, Paris, and is said to be of the eighth or ninth century. It contains the whole of the *Didascalia*, and as it is the oldest, so without doubt it is the most trustworthy authority for the Syriac version. By good fortune it was from this copy that the text was first edited by Lagarde in 1854. The evidence of the Latin version and of the *Apostolic Constitutions*, where it is available, gives us assurance that S preserves the Syriac version in a pure form, at least in the sense that it contains a text which has not been subjected to editorial manipulation. But this MS. appears to be very faithful also in matters of detail. The scribe who wrote it certainly made mistakes, and particularly many mistakes of omission; but his copy was afterwards carefully corrected both in the body of the text and in the margins. I have not examined the MS. personally, but

Lagarde has been at pains to record all corrections by placing them in square brackets, printing those which are made in the text in smaller type to distinguish them from those made in the margin. When these corrections are considered in themselves and in comparison with other authorities for the text it is found in almost every case that they contain true readings, and there is good reason for believing that they were derived from the parent copy and not from a collation of other MSS. Of the corrections made in the margins practically all, so far as I have noticed, supply words, or groups of words, accidentally omitted: corrections of the written text are not made in the margins.

Over and above the omissions which are made good in the margins of S, and which appear to be due to the scribe of this MS., there are several which can be supplied from one or more of the other MSS. (exclusive however of the third, B, which here omits with S).[1] The latter class in all probability existed already in the copy from which S was taken. A few further omissions, some of which may be due to the translator himself, are revealed and supplied only by the Latin version.[2] In one case in which the Syriac seems to be defective, and where the Latin is not available, the *Apostolic Constitutions* may preserve the substance of a missing passage.[3] In regard to all the omissions in S, it is to be observed that they are short and that most of them can be recognized at once as being of a purely accidental character.

Before passing on, a word needs to be said about the marginalia of this MS. in general, for there are many more besides those which clearly proclaim themselves as textual corrections. Lagarde tells us that the marginalia are in three hands. (*a*) By far the most numerous are those in the hand of the scribe who made the copy. But only a few of these are of the nature of corrections; some are short headings, or 'captions', added within the chapters to help the reader;[4]

---

[1] See notes to pp. 24 l. 11, 163 l. 17, 179 l. 24, 226 l. 19, and the Additional Notes referring to pp. 78 l. 2-4, 122 ll. 21 and 30.
[2] These are marked in the translation by pointed brackets ⟨ ... ⟩.
[3] See p. 131 ll. 21-2, and the note there.
[4] A few more similar 'captions' are found rubricated in the text itself.

others are glosses on individual words; a few contain short explanatory notes on the text; three or four in ch. xxi appear to be addressed to scribes (e.g. 'Pay well attention here').
(*b*) Lagarde mentions eight marginalia which are in another (he does not say in a later) hand.[1] All of these are real corrections of the kind already described, all receive independent support from the MS. next to be mentioned (H), and all appear, whether independently or not, in the text of our third MS. (B). (*c*) To a third hand are assigned about half a dozen notes, only one of which was possibly intended as a correction. The purpose for which these details are mentioned will appear under no. 3 below.

2. Codex Harrisianus (H). Some thirty years ago Dr. Rendel Harris found a Syriac manuscript of the *Didascalia* in Mesopotamia and procured a copy of it. The original was written in 1036. In 1903 the copy was edited by Mrs. Dunlop Gibson with a full collation of cod. S. Mrs. Gibson's edition deserves the highest praise for care and accuracy, especially as the work of collation must have been an extremely trying one. I cannot enter here into any detailed comparison of the texts of S and H, but there can be no doubt as to the conclusion to which such a study would lead. H cannot be regarded as a straightforward copy of the *Didascalia*; it deserves rather to be called an edition, and a late edition, produced by some Syrian canonist who had other aims than the mere preservation of our document. Not only is this MS. characterized by innumerable and often lengthy omissions, but it is evident that many of these were deliberately made, and probably with the definite object of shortening the document. This appears not only from a comparison of the other MSS., but also from the Latin version and the *Apostolic Constitutions*, which lend no support to the shorter text of H. It has been shown also that the absence of certain passages contained in the other MSS. and wanting in H interferes with the sequence and produces an inferior sense.[2]

[1] In giving these lists Lagarde does not profess to be exhaustive, for he adds: 'de ceteris notis marginalibus aut nihil adnotaui aut tutius credo tacere'. The number of marginal *corrections* alone is somewhere about fifty.   [2] See Flemming, *Die syrische Didaskalia*, pp. 253 ff.

But the peculiarities of H do not end with its omissions; it has also a number of extensive additions in the shape of interpolations from extraneous sources which can easily be identified. To begin with, it has a preface of about a page in length wherein the book which follows is said to have been sent for delivery 'by the hand of Clement our comrade'. This is the same preface which introduces the Ethiopic and Arabic versions of the *Didascalia*, which are based on the first six books of the *Apostolic Constitutions*. Then, after ch. iii, is inserted a whole series of documents, as in the note below.[1] These larger insertions, it is true, do not affect the text of the *Didascalia*; but they do not stand alone, for the editor was not content with simple omissions and additions but has taken liberties with the text itself.[2] And even in regard to mere variants it would be easy to show that some of them are editorial in character, and that the text of H in general is much inferior to that of S. Flemming, who has dealt at some length with the relative merits of these two MSS., rightly concludes that H can be used only as a subsidiary aid in any edition of the Syriac version.[3]

This, however, is by no means to say that H is devoid of value. It has an appreciable number of good readings where S appears to be at fault; and in particular it enables us to make good several omissions in S which are not supplied in the margins of that MS. Further, where it is available it

---

[1] Extracts from the *Testamentum Domini* i 20–5, but taken probably from the first book of the Syriac collection known as the Clementine Octateuch.—A portion of the *Apostolic Church Order*, which forms the third book of the same Octateuch.—A piece answering to the *Apost. Const.* viii 34, or bk. vi ch. 5 of the Octateuch.—The Edessene Canons, equivalent to the document published by Cureton as 'The Doctrine of the Apostles'.—A list of prohibited degrees. The addition of all this extraneous matter offers a ready explanation of the shortening of the *Didascalia* itself.

[2] For example: at p. 44 l. 5 (of the present volume) after the words 'his seed was cursed' H adds 'because he made sport of his father'. At p. 72 l. 8 after 'led him away to Babylon' H adds 'in a *zodion* of brass' (as to which see the Additional Notes). The account of Simon Magus (pp. 200–2) is much embellished. The passage 'those heretics ... goes forth for them', at p. 212 l. 29 to p. 214 l. 4, is replaced by the words 'and say that the Holy Spirit does not rest upon the (water of) baptism, nor upon the Body and Blood of Christ'.

[3] *Op. cit.* pp. 245–56.

often lends support to marginal or other corrections in S, thus giving us additional assurance that these are true readings. It is to be observed also that the omissions in H are not distributed over the whole book, but begin systematically only in ch. xvi. Then in ch. xvii they are few and slight, but from ch. xviii to the end they are constant and extensive. A long omission in ch. xi is evidently accidental and probably due to mutilation of the MS.

3. Codex Borgianus (B). This is now MS. Borg. Sir. 148 of the Vatican Library, containing (foll. 1–61) a complete copy of the *Didascalia*.[1] The date of the writing, which is in a firm and neat Jacobite hand, is not easy to determine, but I fancy it can hardly be earlier than the thirteenth century. The MS. was first made known by Mgr. F. Nau in 1902, in the additional notes to his translation of the *Didascalia* (p. 161). He drew attention to its close affinity with the Paris MS. (S); and indeed, apart from certain omissions in B which may be credited to the scribe of this copy, the differences between B and the corrected text of S are even less than might appear from Nau's account. Especially remarkable is the agreement between the two MSS. in the matter of marginal annotation. The marginal *corrections* of S do not appear in the margins of B, as they are incorporated in the text; but in other respects the marginalia of the two MSS. are nearly identical. The question therefore arises whether B is not a mere copy, or at least a lineal descendant, of S. So far as I can judge there is nothing positively to exclude such a view, for a scribe copying from S would have little difficulty in distinguishing between the corrections and the other marginalia. Yet it must be mentioned that there are a few points in which B agrees with H against S. The most noticeable are three of its omissions; but here the coincidence with H loses some of its force when we remember the large part that omission plays in H, and observe also that in each of the three cases there is a tempting homoeoteleuton which would render independent omission in B quite possible. It is certain at least that the parent copies of S and B were

[1] I have been able to examine this MS. by means of photographs.

almost identical in text and marginalia; and it follows that B, which is an uncorrected copy and has a number of errors due to its own scribe, can have little independent value, though without S it would be our best authority for the Syriac version. Mrs. Gibson made use of this MS. in her edition of cod. H, but she has recorded only the readings which are peculiar to it. Where B is not quoted beside S in the notes to the following translation it may be assumed that it agrees with the latter.[1]

4. Codex Cantabrigiensis (C). This is MS. 2023 of the Cambridge University Library, and is said to be of the thirteenth century. It contains (foll. 169-204) a large number of extracts from the *Didascalia* extending from the first chapter to the twentieth. While Mrs. Gibson's edition of cod. H was passing through the press she became aware of the existence of this other MS. The printing of her text had then advanced as far as p. 104, so that the readings of C up to that point could only be given separately in an appendix; thereafter they are placed below the text together with the variants of S. The text agrees predominantly with that of S and B, but in not a few cases it departs from them and agrees with H. To the distinctive peculiarities of H, however, it lends no support. I have not found that it contributes very much towards the establishment of the Syriac text, and I have been able to adopt only a couple of readings on its sole authority.

The Syriac is on the whole a very good and intelligent, though not by any means a literal, translation. Setting

---

[1] Another Vatican MS. (Lat. 5403, foll. 1-72) contains a copy of *Didasc.* in Syriac with an interlinear Latin translation which was made for the Spanish scholar Frances Peña in 1596. The Syriac copy is believed to be of about the same date as the Latin and to have been made from either B or S. See Funk *Didasc. et Const. Apost.* i p. viii, and A. Baumstark in *Oriens Christianus* iii (1903) 211 ff.

The *Nomocanon* of Bar-Hebraeus (saec. xiii) contains a few short extracts from *Didasc.*; but they are all more or less paraphrastic and contribute nothing to the criticism of the text.

Here also it may be mentioned that *Didasc.* ch. xii has found its way in a modified and shortened form into the Ethiopic version of the so-called 'Egyptian Heptateuch'. The passage is to be found in G. Horner's *Statutes of the Apostles* pp. 194 l. 29-196 l. 17. The corresponding text in the present volume is at pp. 120-4.

himself to turn the Greek into his own language and idiom, the translator was often obliged to deal somewhat freely with Greek constructions. This was the way of the older Syriac translators, and indications are not wanting that our version was made at a comparatively early date, Still, where we can compare it with the Latin version or the Greek in the *Apostolic Constitutions*, the Syriac is usually found to have kept the form as well as the sense with sufficient accuracy. A feature common to most Syriac translations is the tendency to put two words (usually nouns or adjectives, but occasionally verbs) for one in the original.

As to the date of the Syriac version, Flemming has expressed the opinion that it may be earlier even than the Latin, which has been assigned to the latter end of the fourth century. In this view I am tempted to concur, and for several reasons. The character of the translation marks it as early, and there appears to be nothing in the Syriac itself that would require a date later than the time of Aphraates (*fl.* 337–45). There are indeed certain points of vocabulary which definitely suggest antiquity. Thus the translator never employs the word *meṣ‘āya*, which is invariable in the Syriac New Testament for μεσίτης. For 'mediator' he uses instead *tĕlīthāya*, 'a third', in the sense of a third party or go-between. This use of the word seems to be quite archaic; the only parallel I have been able to find is in Aphraates, who twice describes Haman as 'the *tĕlīthāya* of the king', that is, I suppose, his grand vizier or confidential officer, through whom he would issue his commands and through whom alone he could be approached.[1] In the margins of cod. S the term has been glossed by the common word for 'mediator'. Another familiar word which the translator appears to have been unacquainted with is *‘ālmāya* (*saecularis*), 'a layman'; he used instead the compound 'son of the world' or 'son of the people', but the single term is usually supplied in the margin. Then for a 'fold' he twice uses *daira*; but as this

---

[1] Compare the Hebrew *shălīsh* in 2 Kings vii 2, ix 25, xv 25, and the Aramaic *taltī* in Dan. v 7. But in none of these places does *tĕlīthāya* appear in the Syriac Bible.

term came to denote almost exclusively a 'monastery', it is glossed by the unambiguous word *ṭĕyāra*. Another indication of early date is found in the renderings of quotations from the Gospels, from which it is clear that the text with which the translator was familiar was of the Old Syriac type, not the Syriac Vulgate which dates from the early years of the fifth century.

Thus internal evidence points to a date not later than the end of the fourth century. Can it be fixed more precisely? In the notes to the translation I have cited a number of parallels to the *Didascalia* from the Homilies of the early Syriac writer Aphraates. These, while they are sufficiently close to attract attention, would hardly prove that Aphraates knew the *Didascalia*; but taken together with two longer passages which are given in the Additional Notes (see pp. 265 f., 269 ff.) they create in my mind a strong impression that he must have known and used our document. It seems to me possible therefore that the book was translated into Syriac between the years 300 and 330.

The Latin Version.

Cod. LV (53) of the Chapter Library of Verona contains the *Sententiae* of St. Isidore in a hand of the eighth century. It consists of 99 leaves, of which 41 are palimpsest, the remains of a much older MS. written in a semi-uncial hand of an ancient type. It has been estimated that the older book, when complete, consisted of thirteen gatherings of 4+4 leaves, or 104 leaves in all. Those preserved in the present MS. are not all consecutive, but range, singly or in groups, from the beginning to near the end of the original book. A Latin translation of three ancient documents formed the contents: the *Didascalia*, which occupied 86 folios; the *Apostolic Church Order*, covering a little over four folios; and the *Apostolic Tradition* of Hippolytus (as it is now recognized to be), covering nearly thirteen folios. Of the surviving leaves the fragments of the *Didascalia* occupy 32, so that about two-fifths of this document are preserved. The first leaf of all was not devoted to the text of the *Didascalia*, but upon it is inscribed, in uncial characters, a list of consuls from A.D. 439 to 486, and the list was continued in another hand to the year 494. Hence it may be inferred with some confidence that the MS. was written in 486 at the latest, and perhaps some years earlier.

The translation itself is believed to be a century older than the MS., being assigned by expert authorities to about the age of St. Ambrose. The translation of all three documents appears from internal evidence to come from the same hand, and the translator must have had before him a Greek copy in which they already formed a collection—the earliest collection of this 'Church Order' literature which is known to have existed. The fragments were deciphered with great patience and skill by Edmund Hauler of Vienna and published by him in 1900.[1]

In character the Latin version, in contrast with the Syriac, is studiously literal, and herein lies its special value. Disregarding elegance of form the translator attempted no more than to give a plain and unsophisticated rendering of the Greek. In its present state the translation is by no means free from difficulties, but there can be no doubt that a good many of these are due to faults of transcription. As regards the orthography of the MS. also, it is impossible (at least for any but the expert) to say how far it is that of the translator or that of later scribes. The Latin, however, often reflects Greek influence, and here we must recognize the hand of the translator.[2] While the language of the palimpsest offers a plentiful field of investigation to expert scholars, any such philological discussion is beyond my competence, and it would exceed the scope of this work. What it is of present interest to note is that these Latin fragments provide us with a valuable standard by which to measure the more free and

---

[1] *Didascaliae Apostolorum fragmenta Veronensia latina; accedunt Canonum qui dicuntur Apostolorum et Aegyptiorum Reliquiae.* Primum edidit Edmundus Hauler (Leipzig, 1900). For an account of the MS. see, besides Hauler's preface, C. H. Turner in the *Church Quarterly Review* for Oct. 1917, p. 88 ('The Church Order of St. Hippolytus'), and A. Wilmart in *Recherches de Science Religieuse*, t. x, 1921, pp. 65 ff. ('Le texte latin de la *Paradosis* de Saint-Hippolyte').

[2] To quote a single example, we find *regnare* construed with a genitive: 'rex corporis solius regnat, ... Episcopus autem et animae et corporis regnat' (p. 97 ll. 10-12).

literary Syriac version; or perhaps it may be said rather that they help to bring out more clearly the real merit of the Syriac, for though the Latin constantly helps us to control the Syriac, yet when the two versions are in conflict the advantage is far from being always on the side of the Latin.

From a comparison of the two versions and the *Apostolic Constitutions* one important conclusion may confidently be drawn, viz. that the original *Didascalia* had suffered no serious modification during the fourth century. The document lay before the two translators and the author of the *Constitutions* in the same form, and substantially in the same text. It may be that individual copies had received an additional touch here and there, but there is no evidence that anything like a new edition of the work had been produced earlier than, or other than, that which the 'Constitutor' himself has given us. The later Ethiopic and Arabic *Didascaliae*, so called, are radically nothing else but separate editions of the first six books of the *Constitutions*, with some additional matter.

The Apostolic Constitutions.

The compilation known as the *Apostolic Constitutions* is generally believed to date from about the year 375, though Funk places it about 400. The author (I hold it for certain that the eight books are all from the same hand) was probably, to some degree at least, an Arian.[1] The first six books are based on the *Didascalia*, the seventh begins with a version of the *Didache*, and the chief known source of the eighth is the *Apostolic Tradition* of Hippolytus. These earlier documents are all subjected to a more or less drastic process of edition and revision. The author's treatment of the *Didascalia* varies a good deal for different parts of the book; in some passages, and chiefly in the earlier part, the editorial process is comparatively slight, but in others, and notably towards the end, it becomes so destructive that hardly anything is left of the

---

[1] So C. H. Turner (*Journal of Theol. Studies* xvi 54 ff. Oct. 1914). This conclusion rests mainly on the text of cod. Vat. 1506 (Funk's b) of the *Constitutions*. But Prof. Turner has made it appear very probable that the Arianizing forms of certain passages in this MS. are original.

original work. Some general notion of the compiler's method and its results may be formed by merely turning over the pages of Funk's edition, in which all purely additional matter is marked by underlining; but this tells us nothing of what has been omitted, and even the absence of underlining is no guarantee that the original text has been let alone. Thus the extraction from the *Constitutions* of the residue of the Greek *Didascalia* is a delicate task. We must always be suspicious of the 'Constitutor' when his text shows any departure from the versions. Still, the *Constitutions* do preserve a considerable amount of the original text; and hence they frequently afford valuable help to a better understanding of the versions, by showing us the Greek which the translators have been but partially successful in representing.

A Greek fragment of the *Didascalia* itself was published in 1917 by Dr. Vernon Bartlet in the *Journal of Theological Studies* (vol. xiii pp. 303 ff.). It corresponds to pp. 133 l. 4–134 l. 7 of the present volume, and is from ch. xv, on widows. It is in a very mutilated condition, but has been carefully restored by Dr. Bartlet with the help of the Syriac version and the *Apost. Const.* The only notable variants are (1) that after p. 133 l. 10 a quotation is added from Prov. x 19: $\overline{\epsilon(i\pi\epsilon\nu\ \gamma\grave{\alpha}\rho)\ \overline{\kappa s}\ \dot{\epsilon}\kappa\ \pi o\lambda\langle v\lambda o\gamma i\alpha s\rangle\ o\dot{v}\kappa\ \dot{\epsilon}\kappa\phi\epsilon\acute{v}\langle\xi\eta\ \dot{\alpha}\mu\alpha\rho\rangle\tau\acute{\iota}\alpha s}$, and (2) that for 'the other Mary' (*ib.* ll. 19–20) the fragment seems to have had $\tau\grave{\eta}\nu\ \Sigma\alpha\lambda\acute{\omega}\mu\eta\nu$. Neither reading, in my opinion, is original: the text from Prov. is really inappropriate; and Salome, who is mentioned only in Mk., does not appear elsewhere in the *Didascalia* (cf. pp. 148 and 183).

Editions and Translations of the Syriac.

As already said, the Syriac version was first edited, anonymously, by Paul de Lagarde (then Paul Bötticher) in 1854, from the Paris MS. (S).[1] The method by which the corrections and marginalia of the MS. are represented has also been described above (pp. xii f.). Apart from a very few typo-

---

[1] *Didascalia Apostolorum Syriace.*—'L'ouvrage n'a été tiré qu'à cent exemplaires'. — Lipsiae. B. G. Teubnerus formis suis expressit et venumdat. 1854.

graphical errors of a common sort, the edition leaves little room for improvement and is altogether worthy of the great reputation of the editor.

At the end of his preface Lagarde announced that he had already essayed to reconstruct a Greek text with the aid of the Syriac. This work appeared in the same year, 1854, and fills most of the second volume of Bunsen's *Analecta Ante-Nicaena*. Here Lagarde printed in the first place a Greek text of the first six books of the *Apostolic Constitutions*, distinguishing by larger type the portions represented in the Syriac version. Then followed a separate reconstruction of the '*Didascalia purior*', that is to say, a translation into Greek of the Syriac version except for such portions as were adopted from the *Constitutions*. Here no distinction of type was employed. Unfortunately in this reconstruction many passages of the Syriac were omitted, and where the same matter was differently presented in the Syriac and the *Constitutions* the secondary and depraved text of the latter was too often followed.[1] In this curiously misleading form the *Didascalia* was first presented to other than Oriental readers, and for nearly fifty years this was the only form in which it could be studied.

In 1902 Mgr F. Nau published a French translation of the Syriac (the first to appear in any modern language) with a very brief Introduction and a few footnotes.[2] A second edition was issued in 1912, with an enlarged Introduction and more copious annotation.

In 1903 appeared Mrs. Gibson's edition of cod. H already mentioned.[3] It was followed by an English translation, which, however, did not include the final chapter (xxvi). This serious omission was occasioned by a quite tentative suggestion

---

[1] See Funk, *Die Apost. Konstitutionen* (1891) pp. 26-7 and 41 ff., also *Didasc. et Const. Apost.* I, pp. viii–ix, and Hauler *op. cit.* p. ix.

[2] *La Didascalie c'est-à-dire l'Enseignement Catholique des douze Apôtres et des saints Disciples de notre Sauveur.* Traduite du Syriaque pour la première fois par F. Nau. Paris. (Extrait du *Canoniste contemporain*, février 1901 à mai 1902.)

[3] *The Didascalia Apostolorum in Syriac.* Edited from a Mesopotamian Manuscript with various readings and collations of other MSS. by Margaret Dunlop Gibson. ('Horae Semiticae' No. I.) Cambridge. The translation is 'Hor. Sem.' No. II (*The Didasc. Apost. in English*).

thrown out by Nau (1st ed., p. 166) to the effect that the last chapter is possibly a later addition—a view which, very properly, has found no favour, and which is tacitly abandoned by Nau in his second edition. Besides this defect, Mrs. Gibson's translation is based upon the inferior text of cod. H, and though the chief lacunae in this MS. are supplied from Lagarde's edition, and though its longer interpolations are easily distinguishable, yet the translation reflects many faults of the underlying text; and as a translator Mrs. Gibson hardly reached the standard set in her edition of the Syriac.

The next year, 1904, saw an important work on the *Didascalia*. This was a German translation by Dr J. Flemming and, based upon it, a valuable study of the document by Dr Hans Achelis.[1] The translation, which is of a high order, is followed by eighty pages of textual notes in which account is taken of the MSS. C and H and of the Latin version and the *Constitutions*. Then there are eleven more pages containing a useful conspectus of Syriac readings and proposed emendations. The ensuing pages (243–57), in which the character of the Syriac version and the relative merits of the MSS. are considered, are also by Flemming. The essay of Achelis which follows (pp. 257–387) is the most thorough and instructive study of the *Didascalia* that I have seen. Yet one general criticism suggests itself: the author's language and meaning are discussed almost exclusively on the basis of the Syriac version, even where reference to the Latin or the *Constitutions* would have been possible and desirable. The only real exception to this occurs in the section on the New Testament.

Finally, there is the text provided by Funk in his great edition of the *Apostolic Constitutions*.[2] As already noted in the Preface, this is a composite text consisting of the Latin fragments supplemented by a modern Latin translation of the Syriac, both Latin and Syriac being emended so as to represent as far as possible the original *Didascalia*, but not necessarily the original text of either version. Hence, while Funk's text

---

[1] *Die syrische Didaskalia* übersetzt und erklärt von Hans Achelis und Johs. Flemming. Leipzig. ('Texte u. Untersuchungen', N.F. x 2.)

[2] *Didascalia et Constitutiones Apostolorum*. Edidit Franciscus Xaverius Funk. Paderborn, 1905 (2 vols.).

may be taken as a very good reconstruction of the document, it is hardly satisfactory for those who wish to follow clearly the evidence of the versions and compare it *for themselves* with the Greek in the *Constitutions*. The translation of the Syriac was made by Albert Socin and then turned into Latin by Funk, being afterwards compared with the versions of Nau, Mrs. Gibson, and Flemming, especially the last ' quae ceteris multo praestat '.

For the present translation cod. S, in Lagarde's edition, has been taken as the basis, but a number of corrections have been introduced from other MSS. Only such emendations have been adopted as seemed sure and necessary, and when emendation has been resorted to the object in view has been to restore the Syriac of the translator, not to correct his translation. Evident mistranslations, of which there are not many, are usually obelized in the text and corrected in the notes; but in a few instances it seemed preferable to correct them in the text, marking the correction with asterisks and pointing out the translator's mistake in the notes. The division into chapters has been retained, though there is no trace of it in the Latin, and even in the Syriac it is no doubt later than the translation.[1] For the chapter headings codd. S and B are followed ; those in H are usually more elaborate and appear to be later. No account has been taken of certain subordinate headings, or short labels, which appear sporadically in the margins, or as rubrics in the text of the MSS. ; there appears to be no system in the employment of these 'captions', and their insertion would serve no useful purpose.[2]

As for the translation, I have done my best to make it accurate, but without striving to be painfully literal or to keep always the same English for the same Syriac words—a method which I believe would make for ambiguity more than for accuracy. Of previous translators I have received most help

---

[1] Thus ch. xx (p. 167) really breaks a sentence in the Syriac; while ch. v (p. 37) does so in the Greek, and ch. viii (pp. 78–9) in the Greek and Latin.

[2] There is a whole series of them in ch. xv, that on widows, and hardly more than half-a-dozen in all the rest of the work. They are omitted by Funk but translated by Flemming.

from Flemming, whom I have constantly consulted; but I have not felt it necessary to compare his translation throughout with my own, and I have not specified in the notes every point in which I have ventured to differ from him. I have also derived much help from his textual notes and from the conspectus of readings which follows them, and if I have not sufficiently recorded my obligations to him elsewhere I desire to cover all omissions here by the fullest possible acknowledgement. Some details regarding the evidence of the MSS. which were overlooked in the notes are supplied in the Additional Notes.

In presenting the text of the Latin fragments I have thought it best to keep closely to the orthography of the palimpsest, and in all cases where this rule has been departed from the original spelling is given in the notes. For the philological student Hauler's edition must remain indispensable; yet it seemed desirable to put the reader in touch with the MS. as far as the scope of the present work would permit. A feature of this and many other early MSS. is the frequent interchange of the letters *e* and *i*, *b* and *u*, and sometimes of *o* and *u*. But from such alternations ambiguity can seldom arise except in regard to the tenses of verbs, and even here the reader who is once on his guard will rarely be put to serious trouble: the context will usually show him at once, for example, whether *conseruabit* is not for *conseruauit*, *manducauit* for *manducabit*, or *dimittis* for *dimittes*, and so forth, while in cases of real ambiguity he must necessarily be left in a position to make his own decision. In some cases, however, it seemed that the reader, whose attention is here directed to the substance of the Latin version rather than to its accidental form, was entitled to receive some help, or at least to be relieved of unnecessary distraction in following the text. Hence I have sometimes departed from the MS. and adopted normal forms:—thus I have printed *egeret* for *egerit* (p. 223 l. 9), *excidit* for *excedit* (p. 49 l. 11), *consolatur* for *consulatur* (p. 49 l. 31), *habet* for *auet* (p. 33 l. 9), *meretricis* for *meletricis* (p. 19 l. 14), *pacificus* for *pacificos* (p. 31 l. 22). In a matter of this kind it is difficult not to fall into some inconsistency: however, by glancing at the footnotes on each page the reader will easily see whether any change has been introduced in the text above. The mere addition or omission of letters is sufficiently indicated in the text itself: in cases like *ora* for *hora* and *honera* for *onera* I have printed ⟨*h*⟩*ora* and [*h*]*onera*. Final *e* for *ae* is retained, but final *ae* (in adverbs) for *e* is printed [*a*]*e*.

Only those emendations have been adopted absolutely in the text which seemed to admit of no doubt, as 'Ei enim' for 'etenim' at p. 65 l. 23. Others have been suggested only in the notes, including a few which might perhaps have been safely introduced into the text. Apparent mistranslations and suspected corruptions are usually obelized. Emendations involving only the addition or omission of words are suggested in the usual way by their inclusion in brackets, ⟨. . .⟩ or [. . .]. For slight and obvious emendations no reference is made to previous editors or writers; in other cases I have had to be content with referring to Hauler or Funk, though some of Funk's emendations were derived, he tells us, from other scholars. When a suggestion is made in the notes without such reference, it may generally be assumed that it is offered here (to my knowledge) for the first time (see for examples the notes to p. 227 ll. 9–11).

2. The Document.

The *Didascalia* is recognized on all hands as being a work of the third century, though opinion differs as to whether it is to be assigned to the first or the second half of the century.[1] It professes to have been compiled by the Apostles at Jerusalem immediately after the council described in the fifteenth chapter of the Acts. This apostolic claim, however, though it is put forward boldly enough at certain points in the book, does not go very deep, and lends no serious air of unreality to the author's work as a whole. The general impression that we get from reading him is that the writer is looking out upon his own age and environment and is occupied for the most part with matters of his own experience.

The book has naturally been classed with that family of documents which we know as the Church Orders, among which

---

[1] See p. lxxxix ff.

it forms a third in point of time to the *Didache* and the *Apostolic Tradition* of Hippolytus. In its aims, however, and in the character of its contents it stands apart from most of the other documents of this class, for it deals hardly at all with formal legislation. The *Apostolic Tradition* of Hippolytus, to take what is probably the nearest contemporary example, might fairly be described as a rudimentary Ordinal or Sacramentary, providing as it does set rules and forms for the ordination of ministers, the celebration of the Eucharist, and the administration of baptism. But any such description would be quite inapplicable to the *Didascalia*, which is much more an elementary treatise on Pastoral Theology. While the author does not come before us here as a theologian in the strict sense of the term, neither does he appear in any sense as a canonist, or one who formulates ecclesiastical rules on the basis of custom or tradition. His interest is engaged with other matters, with personal conduct, and with ecclesiastical discipline only in its wider aspect, as it affects the daily life of the community at large. His subject is a comprehensive one, and his treatment of it is ample, indeed we must say diffuse. He carries out to the full the injunction: 'Preach the word: be instant in season, out of season: reprove, rebuke, exhort'. Yet with all his insistence and abundance of repetition he is far from being unreadable. The matter of his discourse provides variety, and his handling of the many topics that present themselves has about it a directness and force which suggest that behind it all there is life and reality.

The *Didascalia* would provide matter for perhaps a score of lengthy dissertations; but here it is not possible to do more than indicate and briefly discuss a selection of points which appear to be of chief importance or interest. Before this is attempted, however, it may be helpful to sketch in bare outline the contents of the document, pausing first for a moment to consider its title.

Title.

The title as it appears in the Syriac version may be reproduced exactly in Latin thus: 'Didascalia id est Doctrina catholica duodecim apostolorum et discipulorum sanctorum

Saluatoris nostri'. Earlier translators (Nau, Flemming, and Funk) have divided this so as to mean: 'Didascalia, that is catholic doctrine, of the twelve Apostles and holy disciples of our Saviour'. But to explain the Greek word 'Didascalia' all that the Syriac translator needed to insert, and did insert, was 'that is Doctrine'; for 'catholic', as will be seen, was already attached to 'Didascalia' in the Greek title. Also 'holy', standing after 'Apostles and Disciples', is naturally to be taken with both words, which indeed appear to denote the same group of persons.

Whatever else the original title contained, it seems certain that it began with either Διδασκαλία καθολική or, perhaps more probably, Καθολικὴ διδασκαλία. So it is three times called in the book itself; see pp. 204–5: 'this Catholic Didascalia' (Syr.) ,'catolicam ⟨hanc Doctrinam⟩' (Lat.), τὴν καθολικὴν ταύτην διδασκαλίαν (Ap. Const.). So at pp. 210–11 (Syr. and Lat.—Ap. Const. here omits): 'this Catholic Didascalia', 'catholicam hanc Doctrinam'. And again at pp. 214–15 (Syr., Lat., and Ap. Const.): 'this C. D.', 'hanc c. D.', τήνδε τὴν καθολικὴν διδασκαλίαν. Moreover Ap. Const., after its general title, has before bk. i the sub-title Καθολικὴ διδασκαλία περὶ λαϊκῶν. The once rubricated title in the Latin palimpsest has now entirely vanished: Hauler suggests 'Doctrina Apostolorum', but has overlooked the passages in which 'catholica' occurs.

The full title therefore may have been something as follows: Καθολικὴ διδασκαλία τῶν δώδεκα ἀποστόλων τοῦ σωτῆρος. The choice of *Didascalia* was determined, we may surmise, by the fact that the more obvious word for doctrine, *Didache*, was already in requisition for the title of an older work. Whether 'catholic' is to be understood in the sense of universal, as addressed to the Church at large, or as denoting orthodoxy, I do not attempt to decide.

Contents in outline.

The work opens in lofty and somewhat grandiloquent style with an address to the Church, that is to all faithful Christians, 'the elect', calling upon them to hear the 'holy Didascalia' which by the Saviour's command has been set forth in harmony with His own glorious utterances. Then follows, in ch. i,[1] a selection of maxims from the Sermon on the Mount, which show also some influence of the *Didache*, i. 2–3.

The next two chapters are addressed to the laity, ch. ii to men, ch. iii to women. The dominant note here is fidelity in the married state and the avoiding all occasions which might endanger it, as meretricious personal adornment, idleness, promiscuous bathing. Long passages are quoted from the book of Proverbs to enforce this lesson.

Then we have a lengthy treatise on the episcopal office, covering eight chapters. Chapter iv lays down the qualifications required in one who is to be entrusted with the bishopric. Chapters v–vii treat of the bishop's powers and obligations in relation to his people, and especially in his character of judge in the place of God. Closely bound up with this, and running all through these four chapters, is the author's teaching on repentance and forgiveness, which will presently be considered more particularly. In ch. vi Ezekiel xviii is quoted in full, and in ch. vii the whole of Ezekiel xxxiv is recited, then the story of Manasseh with apocryphal additions: and the exhortation to gentleness and mercy closes with an appeal to Our Lord's example as shown by His treatment of the sinful woman in the famous 'Pericope de adultera'.

Chapter viii insists that bishops (and presumably the other clergy), like the priests and Levites of the Old Covenant, have a right to be supported by the gifts and offerings of the people. Numbers xviii is cited at length. Chapter ix addresses the laity on the same subject, reminding them of their obligations in this regard. The bishop requires their help especially for the relief of the needy; and in this connexion there is incidental mention of the Agape (pp. 88 ff.).

Chapters x and xi are concerned with 'judgements', or lawsuits between the brethren. Christians may not go to law before the heathen: all causes are to be tried by the bishop

---

[1] In this survey I follow the Syriac division into 26 chapters, which on the whole is a very intelligent attempt to mark the transitions from one subject to another.

with his presbyters and deacons. Careful instructions are given with a view to securing just decisions. Judgements are to be held on Monday, that there may be time to settle all differences before the following Sunday.

Chapter xii, in order to the seemly conduct of divine worship, describes how the clergy and people are to be disposed in the church. It has a special interest as being the earliest notice of the kind that has come down to us. The bishop has his throne at the eastern end of the building, where he sits surrounded by the presbyters. Mention is made of two deacons: the one remains 'by the oblations of the Eucharist'; the other at first acts as a sort of usher or verger, marking those who enter and seeing that they take their appointed places; but when all are assembled and the service begins, he joins his companion in attendance, as it seems, on the bishop: 'and afterwards, when you offer, let them minister together in the Church' (p. 120). Of the laity, the men have their place nearest to the presbytery, and behind them are the women. It is implied that seats were provided for the elder folk, but not for all, since those who are young are directed 'to sit apart, if there be room, and if not to stand up'. Visitors from another diocese ($\dot{\alpha}\pi\dot{o}$ $\pi\alpha\rho\text{οικίας}$) are to be received with all courtesy. A visiting bishop is to be invited to address the people and to offer the Eucharist.

Chapter xiii exhorts the people to be constant in their attendance at church, and to avoid heretical assemblies as also the theatre, fairs, and all festivities of the heathen. This brings us to the end of the second book according to the *Apostolic Constitutions*, and to almost exactly the middle of the whole document.

Chapters xiv–xv are devoted to widows, their appointment, their status and duties, and their characteristic failings. The picture which the author gives of them is very lifelike, and it is evident that as a class these good women provided the bishop with a difficult problem. We shall have to return to them anon.

Chapter xvi is on deacons and deaconesses. The services of women deacons are required especially for the anointing of women at their baptism; but also because 'there are houses whither thou canst not send a deacon to the women, on account of the heathen, but mayest send a deaconess'. Then the qualifications and duties of a deacon are described.

Chapter xvii directs that orphan children be adopted into Christian families. A girl should be adopted by one who has a son, so that when she is of marriageable age she may be given to him to wife. Before or after this chapter would be the natural place for what in the Syriac forms ch. xxii (on the upbringing of children), which in the *Apostolic Constitutions* is placed after ch. xviii (of Syr.). In both xvii and xxii marriage is taken for granted, and in xxii early marriage is recommended: there is no mention of virgins or virginity in the *Didascalia*.

Chapter xviii strictly forbids the bishop and the deacons to receive contributions for the support of widows and orphans from the heathen, from persons of evil life, or those who follow any disreputable calling. A list of such persons and occupations is given.

Chapter xix is on martyrs and martyrdom. Christians must help and refresh by all means in their power those who are in prison for the faith, and if possible ransom them. All are exhorted to face persecution and death bravely for the name of Christ. They are encouraged to do so by the thought of the resurrection.

Chapter xx completes a sentence begun in ch. xix (see note to p. 167), and continues with the subject of the resurrection. Some lines are quoted from the Sibyl, and the story of the Phoenix is adduced.

Chapter xxi is on the Pascha, or more precisely on the paschal fast. The subject is introduced rather oddly by a discourse of a couple of pages in which Christians are warned against profane speech and swearing. The transition is made thus: 'Therefore it is not lawful for a believer to swear, ... nor to make mention with his mouth of the name of idols; nor to utter a curse out of his mouth ...; and especially in the days of the Pascha, wherein all the faithful throughout the world fast' (p. 180). The author's purpose is evidently

INTRODUCTION

to show reason why the fast before Easter should extend over the whole six days, from Monday to Saturday. To this end he adopts, and probably invents, a strange chronology of Holy Week for which there is no shadow of authority in the Gospels. The fast should coincide with our Lord's passion; but His passion extended, in a sense, over six days, thus: on Monday, the 10th of the moon, Judas arranges with the priests to betray Him; in the evening of Tuesday, the 11th, He ate the Passover with His disciples (the priests having maliciously published a false date for the Feast, anticipating the true one by two days), and in that night He was seized and taken to the house of Caiaphas. All Wednesday and the following night He was kept in ward in the high priest's house. On Thursday He was brought to Pilate; and He was kept in ward by Pilate till the beginning of Friday. On Friday morning He was judged and condemned (Herod, not Pilate, passing the sentence). Incidentally we are given also a curious explanation of the 'three days and three nights' that our Lord was 'in the heart of the earth': they are obtained by counting (apparently) the period of His trial as the first day, and also counting the three hours of darkness and the ensuing hours of light as a night and a day.[1] Besides the paschal fast of six days there is prescribed a weekly fast on Wednesday and Friday. The week of the paschal fast is to be determined by observing when the Jews keep the Passover. There is much confusion of thought and treatment in this chapter, but an attentive study of it will show that the main end in view is to defend, or establish, the practice of a six-days' fast before Easter.

Chapter xxii. See under ch. xvii.

Chapter xxiii is on heresies and schisms. The evil of schism is exemplified by the fate of Korah, Dathan, and Abiram. The first heretics were Simon Magus and Cleobius. The former follows Peter to Rome, where he seduces many by his magic arts. He is finally discomfited while attempting to fly in the air. The chief errors of the early heretics were,

---

[1] For a remarkable parallel in the Syrian writer Aphraates, see Additional Notes, p. 265 ff.

the rejection of the Law and the Prophets, the denial that God is almighty, and disbelief in the resurrection. Others taught that men should not marry, that it was necessary to abstain from eating flesh, or at least swine's flesh, and to be circumcised according to the Law.

It is, to my mind, very doubtful whether this particular list of heresies is to be taken seriously as a summary of errors which our author had encountered in an acute form in his own locality. It strikes one rather as being of an antiquarian character, the fruit of the author's reading rather than of his own experience: the first three items are probably taken from the apocryphal letter of the Corinthians to St. Paul (see p. lxxviii), and the foundation of the rest may well be 1 Tim. iv. 3, 'forbidding to marry, (and commanding) to abstain from meats'.[1] The author's real polemic is directed against certain practices which he represents as, at least *in radice*, Jewish (see ch. xxvi), while the present list is in the main non-Jewish. He was, of course, acquainted with many forms of heresy, at any of which he might deal a blow in passing; but the object of his main attack is to be found, I have no doubt, in the last chapter of his book.[2]

Chapter xxiv explains the steps taken by the Apostles to meet the danger of heresy. They assemble at Jerusalem, hold their council there, as in Acts xv, and dispatch their letter; after which they remain in the city for some time taking counsel for the common good and 'writing this Catholic Didascalia'.

Chapter xxv: the Apostles disperse to their several provinces, leaving instructions that those who have erred and repented are to be permitted to remain in the Church, but those who are obstinate are to be expelled; leaving also 'this Catholic Didascalia rightly and justly to the Catholic Church for a memorial and for the confirming of the faithful'.

[1] I do not suggest here that in the first of these groups Marcionism, and in the second encratism, or Tatianism, may not have been in the author's mind. It is probable that he had both these heresies in view; but as he is writing in the name of the Apostles, he must necessarily have behind him documents which he believes to be apostolic.

[2] The present list of heresies reappears in ch. xxvi (p. 240), but only in a general warning against *all* heretics.

At first sight it may seem strange that the circumstantial fiction of apostolic authorship elaborated in chapters xxiv–xxv should be placed near the end of the book instead of at the beginning. That the *Didascalia* is the work of the Apostles has already been intimated plainly enough, but still only indirectly; it is only when the author approaches the subject of false teachings that he formally asserts it. The reason appears to be, that he has now come to a point where he feels it necessary to have behind him the full weight of the apostolic authority, the point namely where he is about to launch into his great polemic in the last chapter.

Chapter xxvi. With the artificial *mise-en-scène* of the last two or three chapters the author has prepared the way for a formal treatment of a matter which he has touched upon already, and which for him is evidently of practical and vital interest: the relation of Christianity to the ceremonial legislation of the Old Testament, or in his peculiar terminology, to the *Deuterosis* or 'Second Legislation'. To this he now addresses himself in full earnest. His polemic has for its object certain Judaizing tendencies which it seems impossible not to recognize as a real and present danger in the community to which he belonged. He begins with an exhortation to those 'who have been converted from the People', that is to Jewish converts, not to continue in their former conversation by observing the vain obligations (*or* bonds, *uincula*) of the ceremonial Law—purifications, separations (ἀφορισμοί), baptismal aspersions, and distinctions of meats. Then follows a long discussion (pp. 216–33) in which 'the Law' is distinguished from the *Deuterosis*. As some pages are devoted to this subject elsewhere,[1] it will be enough to say here that 'the Law' is defined to be the Decalogue and 'the Judgements',[2] while the *Deuterosis* embraces the whole ceremonial legislation of the Old Testament. Pp. 233–9 deal with the Sabbath. On p. 240 there is a general warning against all heretics, and the list of false opinions given under ch. xxiii is repeated. I have already expressed the opinion that this

---
[1] See pp. lvii ff.
[2] See p. lxvii note.

list is largely artificial; it is evident at least that several of the items in it can have no connexion with the *Deuterosis*.

It is on p. 242, and after, that we seem to get to the root of the trouble and the reason for the whole of this impassioned attack on the *Deuterosis*. It lay in certain practical abuses which the author traces to the influence of the Jewish Ceremonial Law:[1] 'But if there be any who are precise (*or* fastidious) and desire, after the Second Legislation, to observe the wonted courses of nature and issues and marriage intercourse: first let them know that, as we have already said, they affirm the curse against our Saviour and condemn themselves to no purpose'. There were men and women who for such causes refrained themselves 'from prayer and from receiving the Eucharist, or from reading the Scriptures', supposing themselves to be unclean, and deeming it necessary either to absent themselves from church for a season or to have recourse to ceremonial 'baptisms'. To such persons the author propounds this dilemma: during those periods of ceremonial purification either they still possess the Holy Spirit, received in baptism, or they are devoid of the Holy Spirit. If the former, then there is no ground for abstaining from the fruits of the Holy Spirit; but if the latter, then (as they have committed no sin) the assertion that they have not the Holy Spirit amounts to a denial of the power and lasting effect of their baptism. Christians therefore are to take no notice of these supposed defilements: 'And do not observe these things, nor think them uncleanness; and do not refrain yourselves on their account, nor seek after sprinklings, or baptisms, or purification for these things. For in the Second Legislation, if one touch a dead man or a tomb, he is baptized; but do you, according to the Gospel and according to the power of the Holy Spirit, come together even in the cemeteries, and read the Holy Scriptures, and without demur perform your ministry and your supplication to God; and offer an acceptable Eucharist, the likeness of the royal body of Christ, both

---

[1] These were alluded to at the very beginning of the chapter, before the general discussion of the *Deuterosis*, and their being placed there in the forefront is another indication of their paramount importance.

in your congregations and in your cemeteries and on the departures of them that sleep' (p. 252).

At p. 256 the Apostles excuse and defend themselves for the seeming austerity of their teaching in the *Didascalia*; and then the book ends with a remarkable doxology, which appears to embody a number of clauses from the author's Creed (pp. 258, 259).

The Didascalia *a unity.*

There is no need to dwell at any length upon this question. It has already been pointed out (p. xx) that in the fourth century the document lay before the Syriac and Latin translators and the author of the *Apostolic Constitutions* in the same form. The internal indications of unity are equally strong: the same language and ideas are constantly reappearing in different parts of the book, as also certain quotations.[1] It would be difficult to find an ancient document in which the marks of single authorship are more pronounced. Considerations of this kind have satisfied such careful scholars as Funk, Achelis, Nau, Bardenhewer, and others that the Greek lying behind the Syriac and Latin version was that of the original author. I include Mgr Nau's name because, although in the first edition of his translation (p. 166) he suggested that the last chapter was possibly a later addition, in his second edition he lets that suggestion drop and discusses the author's treatment of the *Deuterosis* on the basis that ch. xxvi is genuine (Introd. p. xxviii). Harnack[2] was of opinion that the Greek copy used by the Syriac translator represented a slightly revised form of the original *Didascalia*. Some parts of the treatment of penance, which he regarded as definitely anti-Novatianist, he thought were added later. He speaks of these passages as being absent from the *Apostolic Constitutions*; but the pieces which would lend themselves most easily to an anti-Novatian interpretation (viz. p. 44, ll. 7–18, and p. 50, ll. 1–10 of the

---

[1] e.g. the words referred to Numbers (xxiv 9) at p. 6 and recurring pp. 144, 145, 250; also Mt. xi 28–30 (in whole or part) pp. 14, 98, 207, 226.
[2] *Altchristl. Lit.* (1st ed., 1893) i 517; cf. ed. 2 (1904), ii 488–501.

present volume) are duly represented not only in *Apost. Const.* but also in the Latin version. In fact in the whole of chapters vi–vii, which deal most particularly with the treatment of penitents, *Apost. Const.* omits singularly little, the author being apparently in full agreement with the sentiments expressed in the *Didascalia*. Bardenhewer also thinks that chapters v(?)–vii are directed against Novatianism;[1] but Achelis,[2] in discussing Harnack's view, states it as his own impression that the adversaries directly aimed at by our author are not any sect outside the Great Church, but the members of the community for which he is writing. This I believe to be a true observation, and true of the *Didascalia* as a whole.

Those who have read the discussions of the *Didascalia* which have appeared since 1901 will inevitably have met with the name of C. Holzhey. It seems necessary therefore to mention the two theories which he has propounded. (1) The first of these, put forward in 1897, is that the *Didascalia* is merely an enlarged and improved edition ('eine erweiterte, vermehrte und verbesserte Ausgabe') of the *Didache*.[3] (2) The other, formulated in 1901, is that the *Didascalia* as we have it has passed through three stages of development, thus: as a document of small compass it was known to Dionysius of Alexandria (*Didasc.* A); Dionysius, towards the end of his literary career, or a disciple of his after his death, subjected it to a fundamental revision (*Didasc.* B); a little later it was worked over and interpolated in a Jewish-Christian sense by some third hand (*Didasc.* C).[4] Neither of these two theories has been taken very seriously; and are they not mutually exclusive?[5] As to (1) it is generally recognized that the

[1] *Altkirchl. Lit.* ii (1903) 259. He does not suggest that they are later than the rest.   [2] *Die syrische Didaskalia* p. 259.
[3] 'Compte rendu du quatrième Congrès scientifique des Catholiques à Fribourg (Suisse), 1898', sect. i pp. 249–77. I had occasion to offer some remarks on this paper, and on the parallels between *Didasc.* and *Didache* there collected, in the *Journal of Theol. Studies* for Jan. 1923, p. 147.
[4] *Theologisch-praktische Monatschrift*, Passau, 1901, pp. 515–23. Like Achelis, I have not been able to see this publication, and have had to depend on Nau *Didascalie*, 1st ed. p. 165, and Bardenhewer *op. cit.* ii 260.
[5] The parallels on which (1) is based are drawn from *Didasc.* in its present form: are they only relics of the first edition, or was the use of the *Didache* carried on by all three editors?

author of the *Didascalia* knew and made a limited use of the *Didache*; and that is the utmost that can be said. As to (2), Funk[1] and Bardenhewer[2] find no reason to suppose that Dionysius was acquainted with the *Didascalia* at all, and certainly I can see none. The three stages of development are purely fanciful, and can claim no more consideration than any other process of evolution which might be imagined.

The Ministry.

The ministers of whom we hear in the *Didascalia* are bishop, presbyter, deacon, subdeacon, and lector; and there are besides two classes of women, the deaconess and the widow, to whom certain ministerial functions are assigned.

The bishop. We have seen that no less than eight chapters (iv–xi) are devoted to the bishop. He is indeed the centre and pivot of the whole community. He holds the place of God in relation to his people; he is their father after God, their mediator with God, their high priest, their leader and king. He is judge of all causes *in utroque foro*, with heavenly power on earth to bind and loose both soul and body. He is the guardian of the poor and needy, of the widow and the orphan, and the dispenser of all alms offered for their support. He is also the people's guide and teacher in the faith, the minister of God's word and the expounder of His holy Scriptures. In a word, the bishop within his province is supreme. We are reminded of the teaching on the bishop in the letters of St. Ignatius, which our author had read; but here it is intensified and applied in far greater detail.

There is no attempt to define the bishop's relation to other bishops, nor any word suggestive of a hierarchy within the episcopate, whether of dignity or authority. Nor is there any allusion to apostolic sees or churches, from which we might deduce a distinction between these and other churches not founded directly by the Apostles. But in a work ascribed to the Apostles themselves this tells us very little as to the author's own position in regard to such questions; and from

---

[1] *Didasc. et Const. Apost.* vol. i p. iv.   [2] *Op. cit.* ii 260.

his silence we can hardly conclude that Antioch, for example, was held by him to have no sort of pre-eminence or authority over the lesser churches in its neighbourhood. Still less should we be justified in concluding, as Achelis does, that this author, writing in the third century, had no conception of an apostolic origin of the episcopate itself,[1] merely because he makes no express mention of it. History, and the position occupied by the bishop in the *Didascalia*, alike suggest that this is improbable.

The bishop's qualifications are described in ch. iv; but, in conformity with the general lack of ritual detail in the book, nothing is said of the manner of his election or ordination. In age he is to be not less than fifty years; but in a small church in which a suitable person of mature age is not to be found, a young man may be appointed: for were not Solomon, Josiah, and Joash but boys when they began to reign? He must also be 'the husband of one wife', and satisfy other conditions laid down in the Pastoral Epistles. In conduct he is to be a model and pattern to his flock, even as he himself has Christ for a pattern. He must not be rough and churlish with his people, and above all his treatment of sinners should be guided by the law of mercy.

The presbyters. Presbyters are mentioned in the *Didascalia* only as it were by the way. There is no formal discussion of their qualifications and duties such as we find in the case of the bishop, deacon, deaconess, and widow, and what we can learn of them is to be gathered only from incidental allusions. They are appointed by the bishop,[2] and their characteristic function is to be the bishop's counsellors, or the council of the Church.[3] In church they have their seats about the bishop's throne at the eastern end.[4] Along with the deacons they assist the bishop in all cases of judgement which come before him.[5] Following St. Ignatius, the author compares the bishop to Almighty God and the deacon to Christ, while the presbyters are likened only to the Apostles.[6] This might suggest

---

[1] *Op. cit.* p. 270. The idea, he says, is simply unfamiliar to the author.
[2] p. 96.   [3] pp. 90, 96.   [4] p. 119.
[5] p. 111.   [6] pp. 88, 90.

INTRODUCTION

a subordination of the presbyters to the deacons; and for such a view another passage might be cited, in which the presbyters are mentioned after the widows as if almost by an afterthought: 'But if any one wish to honour the presbyters also, let him give them a double (portion), as to the deacons'.[1] But the analogies in question are hardly to be pressed: the presbyters, as a collective body, must needs have a collective counterpart. The deacon represents Christ in His aspect of minister only;[2] and the presbyters are not the counsellors of the deacons but of the bishop, and as such stand above the ministers, the deacons, though their functions bring them less before the public eye. In a small church, such as the *Didascalia* appears to contemplate, in which public worship was regularly conducted by the bishop, the presbyters would find no independent role as preachers or celebrants, and as a mere *collegium* they would stand for the most part in the background.[3] They had no administrative or pastoral work to bring them into prominence.

The deacon. Unlike the presbyter, the deacon figures prominently in the *Didascalia*. He is the bishop's right-hand man and his trusted agent and go-between with the people. Much of the bishop's directly pastoral work appears to have been delegated to him; and accordingly he should be such a man as to deserve the bishop's fullest confidence: he is to be 'the hearing of the bishop, and his mouth and his heart and his soul; for when you are both of one mind, through your agreement there will be peace also in the Church'.[4] The bishop and his deacon are to be 'of one counsel and of one purpose, and one soul dwelling in two bodies'.[5] The deacon holds the place of Christ, and his relation to the bishop is to be like that of Christ to the Father; and hence when the

---

[1] p. 90.
[2] Cf. p. 148, where Mt. xx 28 is quoted: 'even as the Son of Man came not to be ministered unto, but to minister'; and compare p. 150, where Christ's washing the feet of His disciples is adduced.
[3] Cf. Achelis, *op. cit.*, p. 272. At Rome as late as the end of the fourth century we still find the presbyters overshadowed by the more select and influential body of deacons. See in the *Quaestiones ueteris et noui test.* the section on 'The airs of the Roman deacons' ('de iactantia Romanorum leuitarum': *Quaest.* ci), and comp. St. Jerome's letter to Euangelus (*Ep.* cxlvi). [4] p. 109. [5] p. 148.

laity wish to bring any matter before the bishop, they are to do so through the deacons: 'For neither can any man approach the Lord God Almighty except through Christ. All things therefore that they desire to do let them make known to the bishop through the deacons, and so do them.'[1] The deacons have their appointment from the bishop,[2] and their number is to be in proportion to the size of the community.[3] In church we hear of the ministry of two deacons: 'But of the deacons let one stand always by the oblations of the Eucharist; and let another stand without by the door and observe them that come in; and afterwards, when you offer, let them minister together in the Church', etc.[4] In the *Didascalia* we meet for the first time in Christian literature with a formula to be uttered by the deacon in church: 'Wherefore, O bishops, that your oblations and your prayers may be acceptable, when you stand in the Church to pray let the deacon say with a loud voice: Is there any man that keepeth aught against his fellow?'[5]

Subdeacon and lector. These two orders receive each but a single passing mention in the *Didascalia*. On p. 90 we find that at an Agape the perquisites of a lector are the same as those of a deacon and a presbyter. Here subdeacons are not mentioned; and chiefly on this account Achelis regards their appearance on p. 96 as a later insertion.[6] They are found there, however, in the Latin as well as the Syriac version (in *Apost. Const.* the whole passage is omitted), and I am not disposed to reject the evidence of these two authorities without stronger reasons than Achelis has alleged. Of the status and functions of subdeacons before the end of the third century we really know very little, and that little suggests that originally they were hardly more than the servants, $\upsilon\pi\eta\rho\acute{\epsilon}\tau\alpha\iota$, of the deacons. In the *Apostolic Tradition* of Hippolytus the institution of subdeacons is described after that of widows, lectors, and virgins, and their duty is said to be to 'minister to the deacons'.[7] So in the *Didascalia* it is

---

[1] p. 90. [2] pp. 96, 146. [3] p. 148, cf. 96.
[4] p. 120. [5] p. 117. [6] *Op. cit.* p. 265.
[7] So the Ethiopic and Arabic texts (Horner, *Statutes of the Apostles*,

probable that the subdeacon is quite an inferior person to the lector, and therefore his omission on p. 90, where the lector is mentioned, is no matter for surprise. Nor do I find difficulty, as Achelis appears to do, in the fact that the subdeacon is not mentioned on p. 120, where the ministrations of the deacons in church are described.

The deaconess. Deaconesses are mentioned at pp. 88 and 146–8. The office of a woman deacon is required, we are told, chiefly for two reasons: first that she may visit Christian women who are isolated in heathen households, where a deacon's ministrations would be open to hostile comment; secondly, and especially, that she may assist women at their baptism and administer the anointing to them. The anointing in question was apparently one of the whole body, and doubtless took place before the actual baptism.[1] But as regards baptism itself, it is evident that the deaconess comes under the general prohibition against the conferring of this Sacrament by women.[2] In the analogies drawn between the Christian ministry and the heavenly hierarchy the deaconess is likened to the Holy Spirit;[3] which is probably an indication of the oriental associations of the *Didascalia*, since 'spirit' in Semitic languages is feminine. Achelis expresses some misgiving as to whether the passages mentioning the deaconess are to be considered part of the *Didascalia* in its original form,[4] but on the whole he seems inclined to regard them as such. I can see no sufficient ground for hesitation. The deaconesses were appointed by the bishop,[5] and it seems probable that they were selected from the order of widows, though this is not indicated.

Widows. The section on widows (chapters xiv–xv) is one of the most lively and telling passages in the whole of the *Didascalia*. The account of them has been summarized, not unfairly, thus: 'The Widows were a numerous and somewhat troublesome body of Church pensioners. Among their besetting sins were grumbling at their fellow-widows who

pp. 147, 248); the Sahidic version (*ib.* p. 309) places the subdeacon before the widow and the virgin, but still after the lector.

[1] See p. xlix, and note to p. 146 ll. 20 ff. [2] p. 142.
[3] p. 88.   [4] *Op. cit.* p. 265.   [5] p. 146.

happened to receive larger doles, and making begging expeditions instead of being content with the supplies that reached them in the normal way. They had to be reminded that " the Altar of God does not go running about, but is fixed in one place ".'[1] Widows of this sort are summed up by our author in two words with a Greek pun: they are not χῆραι but πῆραι, not 'widows' but 'wallets'.[2]

Chapter xiv begins with a virtual quotation from 1 Tim. v. 9: 'Appoint as a widow one that is not under fifty years old'. But the age limit is here reduced by ten years, for St. Paul says, not under sixty years old. In the *Apost. Const.* the biblical reading 'sixty' reappears; but though the Latin version is not available there seems no reason to question the evidence of the Syriac MSS. It is evident that not every woman who had lost her husband was reckoned *ipso facto* as a widow in the technical sense; there was an 'order' of widows, though the age of fifty was possibly the only absolute qualification for membership : ' But let not young widows be appointed to the widows' order.' The author goes on, however, to commend the younger widows very particularly to the bishop's care, and especially with a view to their continuing in widowhood. After the words just quoted he continues: 'Yet let them be taken care of and helped, lest by reason of their being in want they be minded to marry a second time.'[3] . . . Wherefore assist those who are young, that they may persevere in chastity unto God.' Though there is no word about virginity in the *Didascalia*, yet the author sets a value on the continency of widowhood, and is averse to second marriages.

Widows and orphans are supported by the charitable donations of the faithful, which are allotted to them according to their individual needs by the bishop. The donors are not to make these gifts directly to this or that widow;[4] and even

---

[1] Dr. Armitage Robinson, in his Appendix to Miss C. Robinson's book *The Ministry of Deaconesses*, p. 176.
[2] p. 134.
[3] Cf. 1 Tim. v. 11, contrasting *v.* 14—if the latter should refer to young widows and not to young women in general.
[4] p. 131, cf. 88.

when one of the brethren provides an Agape, it rests with the bishop to choose and send widows to it at his discretion.[1] Following St. Polycarp (*Phil.* 4) the author likens the widows (sometimes joined with the orphans) to the very altar of God; and hence the bishop may not receive contributions on their behalf from any but the faithful brethren. At p. 158 there is a long list of persons of disreputable occupation from whom he is absolutely forbidden to accept such offerings. When a widow receives an alms through the bishop she is to be told the name of the giver, that she may pray for him;[2] but on no account is she to disclose the name to others, lest another widow hearing of it should fly off and scold the bishop, or the deacon, or the donor, saying: 'Knewest thou not that I was nearer to thee and in more distress than she?'[3]

The proper duty of widows is to pray and fast for their benefactors and for the whole Church. There is mention also of certain active ministrations, as visiting the sick, praying with them, and, which is remarkable, laying hand upon them.[4] But such things are to be done only with the permission of the bishop or of a deacon, lest through ignorance a widow should communicate with one who is expelled from the Church.[5] Widows are forbidden to teach, except only 'in refutation of idols and concerning the unity of God'; they are not to speak of the mysteries of the Incarnation: 'For when the Gentiles who are being instructed hear the word of God not fittingly spoken, as it ought to be, unto edification of eternal life—and all the more in that it is spoken to them by a woman—how that our Lord clothed Himself in a body, and concerning the passion of Christ, they will mock and scoff, instead of applauding the word of doctrine.'[6] They are forbidden also to baptize.[7]

As already observed, there is no mention in the *Didascalia* of an order of virgins, or of virginity at all. On the contrary, parents are warned to have their children married at an early age to save them from the dangers of incontinency. See

[1] p. 88. [2] p. 131. [3] pp. 143-4.
[4] pp. 138-40. [5] p. 148. [6] pp. 132-3. [7] p. 142.

THE DOCUMENT lxiii

especially chapters xvii and xxii. The contrast here with western ideals will be appreciated by all who have examined the writings of Tertullian, Hippolytus, and St. Cyprian.

Theological standpoint.

It will not be necessary to tarry long over the author's theology or his teaching in regard to the Sacraments. He is not writing here as a theologian, but as a preacher; and his allusions to the Sacraments are quite incidental. By recourse to the General Index the reader will easily be able to collect the more important passages. It is now generally recognized that the author's theological outlook was entirely Catholic, and that he writes as a champion of the Great Church as opposed to all manner of heresy and schism.

In the Syriac version we find here and there a tendency to introduce divine epithets in regard to Our Lord where they appear to have been absent in the original work. But a comparison with the Latin version will show that there are still many passages in which such epithets were fearlessly used by the author himself.[1] So far is he from any suggestion of adoptionism, that Achelis has called him 'a naïve modalist',[2] though this also is a characterization which it would be hard to justify from the pages of the *Didascalia*. But though he quotes from St. John's Gospel, and was probably acquainted with the writings of St. Justin, our author makes no use of the Logos doctrine to explain the divine pre-existence of the Son. Only in one place (if I understand the text there aright) does he speak of Christ as 'the Word of God'.[3]

As regards the Holy Spirit we may note especially the following passages.

1. 'And we have established and set down therein (*sc.* in the *Didascalia*) that you worship God Almighty and Jesus Christ and the Holy Spirit' (p. 204).

The Latin version, very unfortunately, breaks off just before

---

[1] In the Latin cf. pp. 77 l. 13, 149 l. 19, 151 ll. 6-7, 217 l. 2, 251 l. 19. For the Syriac, where the Latin is not extant, cf. pp. 63 l. 20, 133 l. 16, 167 l. 6.
[2] *Op. cit.* p. 378.
[3] See p. 193 and note, also Additional Notes p. 268.

this sentence. The Arianizing compiler of the *Apostolic Constitutions* gives the sentence another turn, but the sort of turn we should expect from him if confronted by a text like that just quoted: God Almighty alone is to be worshipped, 'through Jesus Christ our Lord, in the all-holy Spirit' (see note *in loc.*, p. 205).

2. At p. 102 the author asks: 'Now why, brethren, is it required that a testimony be established at the mouth of two or three witnesses?' and he answers: 'Because the Father and the Son and the Holy Spirit bear witness to the works of men.' Here again the Latin is wanting, and again the author of *Apost. Const.*, misliking the passage, has altered the text, this time by substituting quite other words. The context here precludes any suspicion that the mention of the Holy Spirit is of later introduction. The reader should compare also the parallel from Irenaeus which is quoted in the notes.[1]

3. At pp. 86-9 the author, in a single context, likens the bishop to Almighty God, the deacon to Christ, and the deaconess to the Holy Spirit. The Latin is extant here, and the author of the *Constitutions*, as we might expect, has readily adopted these analogies, with their *prima facie* suggestion of the subordination of the Son and the Holy Spirit to the Father.

Besides these three trinitarian passages we may consider the evidence of certain doxologies in the *Didascalia*, five in number.

1. The first is at p. 4, l. 9. There is no mention of the Holy Spirit here in any of our authorities for the text, as the doxology is one of Christ alone.

The next four all include reference to the Holy Spirit in the Syriac version. It is regrettable that the Latin is extant only for the last.

2. At p. 20, l. 13, the inclusion of the Holy Spirit is not borne out by *Apost. Const.*, and we must reckon with the possibility that it is not original.

3. At p. 156, l. 17, we have: 'through His beloved Son and

---

[1] Add also Tertullian *de Bapt.* 6.

His Holy Spirit: to whom' (sing.), etc. In the *Constitutions* this becomes: 'through His beloved Son Jesus Christ our Lord, through whom (is) glory to God in spirit and truth'—a peculiar form which is apt to suggest that an original reference to the Holy Spirit has been tampered with.

4. P. 167, ll. 3–5: 'while we believe in our Lord Jesus Christ and in His Father, the Lord God Almighty, and in His Holy Spirit,—to whom' (plur.), etc. Here the author of the *Constitutions* has altered, with insertion of other words where the Holy Spirit is mentioned in the Syriac, thus: πιστεύων τῷ ἑνὶ καὶ μόνῳ ἀληθινῷ θεῷ καὶ πατρὶ διὰ 'Ιησοῦ Χριστοῦ [τοῦ μεγάλου ἀρχιερέως καὶ λυτρωτοῦ τῶν ψυχῶν καὶ μισθαποδότου τῶν ἄθλων], ᾧ ἡ δόξα, κτλ.

5. In the great doxology at the end of the work (pp. 258–9) it seems evident, from the consensus of the Latin and *Apost. Const.*, that the mention of the Holy Spirit in line 26 of the Syriac is an interpolation.

From the symptoms of *Apost. Const.* I am inclined to infer that the Holy Spirit was originally mentioned in 3, and perhaps in 4; but the evidence is far from conclusive. It is an unfortunate accident that, in regard to the Holy Spirit, the evidence of the Latin version is missing in so many places, sometimes for the want of only a few additional lines.

On p. 244 and the following pages we are told of some of the special operations of the Holy Spirit. Through the Holy Spirit prayer is heard (or accepted), and the Eucharist is sanctified; and the Scriptures are the words of the Holy Spirit. Then (pp. 244–9) there is a very curious and striking passage which is to this effect: All baptized persons, receiving the Holy Spirit at baptism, have Him dwelling in them continually as long as they 'do good works'. Correspondingly the heathen are filled with evil spirits; and a Christian also, if he drive away the Holy Spirit by sin, is forthwith invaded by unclean spirits: 'For all men are filled with their own spirit'[1]—'A believer is filled with the Holy Spirit, and an unbeliever with an unclean spirit: and his nature does not receive an alien spirit.'[2] The whole passage should be read

[1] p. 246 l. 21.   [2] *Ibid.* ll. 13–15.

and compared with the beginning of the fifth *Mandate* of Hermas (§§ 1–2).[1] And here again we seem to catch echoes of the *Didascalia* (unless it be of Hermas himself) in the early Syriac writer Aphraates. Sections 14–17 of his sixth Homily or 'Demonstration' are almost a treatise on the Holy Spirit, and will repay careful study on the part of students of Christian doctrine. They may be read in Parisot's Latin version[2] or in an excellent English translation by Dr. John Gwynn in vol. xiii of *Nicene and post-Nicene Fathers* (pp. 371 ff.).

For the first three centuries, and longer still, the Church was preoccupied theologically with the defence of Our Lord's divinity and true humanity against a variety of heretical opinions. As regards the doctrine of the Holy Spirit there is, generally speaking, a lack of positive treatment during this period; and we do not look for precise definition in a non-theological work like the *Didascalia*. The most significant and important passage is that already quoted from p. 204, and I see no reason to doubt that the Syriac here represents what the author wrote.

Reference to the Index *s.v.* 'Church' will suffice to show that the author had a full conception of the universal Church as distinguished from 'the churches'. She is 'the Catholic Church', 'the holy Catholic Church', one alone, and 'the receptacle of the Holy Spirit'.

Baptism.

Of the ritual of baptism we gather certain details from pages 146–7, where it is prescribed that women at baptism should be anointed by a woman, and preferably by a deaconess. After this general direction we read (p. 146, ll. 16 ff.): 'but with the imposition of hand do thou anoint the head only. As of old the priests and kings were anointed in Israel, do thou in like manner, with the imposition of hand, anoint the head of

---

[1] At p. 252 we have the curious statement that Elisha's dead body 'was holy and filled with the Holy Spirit'.

[2] In *Patrologia Syriaca*, pars prima, tomus primus (Paris, Firmin-Didot, 1894), col. 291 seqq.

those who receive baptism; and afterwards—whether thou thyself baptize, or thou command the deacons or the presbyters to baptize[1]—let a woman deacon, as we have already said, anoint the women. But let a man pronounce over them the invocation of the divine Names in the water. And when she who is being baptized has come up from the water, let the deaconess receive her', &c.

Here, I have no doubt, we have the rite of baptism described according to the actual order of the ceremonies used; and it is very remarkable when compared with the ritual which we are generally familiar with in East and West alike. The order of the *Didascalia* is: first, an anointing of the head only by the bishop, with 'imposition of hand'; secondly, an anointing (evidently of the whole body [2]) by the minister, or by a woman where women are being baptized; thirdly, the baptism itself with pronouncing of the trinitarian formula. That the actual baptism closed the ceremony is plainly indicated by the last sentence quoted above. There is thus no anointing after the baptism, such as we find in Tertullian,[3] Hippolytus,[4] Cyprian,[5] Cyril of Jerusalem,[6] and the *Apostolic Constitutions*.[7] Moreover, what we recognize as the distinctively post-baptismal acts —the anointing on the forehead by the bishop and the imposition of hand—here precede the baptism. Is the rite of the *Didascalia* then quite peculiar and isolated, or is the account given of it merely confused and the order of events disturbed? I believe the right answer is: Neither the one nor the other.

Twenty years ago I pointed out that the rite as described in the *Didascalia* is in agreement with the practice of the early Syrian, or Syriac-speaking, churches as represented in documents of the third, fourth, and fifth centuries.[8] The evidence

---

[1] Cf. Tertullian *de Bapt.* 17: 'Dandi quidem habet ius summus sacerdos, qui est episcopus; dehinc presbyteri et diaconi, non tamen sine episcopi auctoritate'.
[2] Compare Cyril of Jerus. *Myst.* ii § 3.
[3] *De bapt.* 7, and *de Res. carnis* 8.
[4] *Apost. Trad.*, ed. Hauler p. 111.
[5] *Ep.* lxx.
[6] iii 16 (= *Didasc.* iii 12 in Funk's arrangement), where the words καὶ μετὰ τοῦτο ὁ ἐπίσκοπος χριέτω τοὺς βαπτισθέντας τῷ μύρῳ are added to the the account in *Didasc.*   [7] *Myst.* iii.
[8] See *The Liturgical Homilies of Narsai* (Cambridge 'Texts and

then collected need not be gone over again here, but of one document special mention must be made. The Syriac *Acts of Judas Thomas* are not only of native Syriac composition,[1] but they are also assigned to the third century, and may thus be nearly contemporary with the *Didascalia*. They contain no less than five accounts of the conferring of baptism. In one of these there is no express mention of oil; in the other four the rite consists of an anointing followed by baptism in the name of the Father, Son, and Holy Spirit. Two of these four cases involve the baptism of women; and here we have an exact reproduction of what is prescribed in the *Didascalia*: Judas 'casts' oil upon the head, then the women are anointed by other women, and finally they are baptized by the Apostle.[2]

Though women might, and should, perform the anointing of other women at baptism, they are forbidden to baptize: 'For if it were lawful to be baptized by a woman, our Lord and Teacher Himself would have been baptized by Mary His mother' (p. 142). At p. 178 it appears to be implied that the effect of baptism—the complete forgiveness of all former sin—is supplied by martyrdom, and this even if baptism has already been received.[3]

The Eucharist.

There are a good many passing allusions to the Eucharist in our document, but nothing approaching to a description of the rite of its celebration. At p. 86 we read that the sacrifices which were in the Old Law are now 'prayers and petitions and thanksgivings' (εὐχαὶ καὶ δεήσεις καὶ εὐχαριστίαι, *Ap. Const.*); and that the firstfruits, tithes, and other gifts are now 'the

---

Studies', viii 1, 1909) pp. xlvii ff., and for the Syriac version in general pp. xlii-xlix.

[1] See Prof. F. C. Burkitt's notes in the *Journal of Theol. Studies* i 280-90, ii 429 and iii 94. I may add that a subsequent study of the question has confirmed my conviction that he is right, and that the Greek version of the *Acts* is a translation of the Syriac.

[2] See W. Wright, *Apocryphal Acts of the Apostles*, vol. ii p. 258 (the baptism of Mygdonia) and p. 289 (the baptism of Vīzān and others). In the second case, after the Apostle has 'cast' the oil on the heads of all, we read: 'And he commanded Mygdonia to anoint them (the women), and he himself anointed Vīzān'.

[3] So Tertullian *de Bapt.* 16: 'Hic est baptismus qui lauacrum et non acceptum repraesentat et perditum reddit'.

oblations (προσφοραί) which are offered through (διά) the bishops to the Lord God'. These 'oblations', or 'offerings' appear not to be eucharistic, but to be merely the contributions made by the faithful for the support of the clergy, widows, and orphans, &c. The preceding εὐχαριστίαι, on the contrary, no doubt contain a reference to the Eucharist. At p. 94 we meet in the Syriac with the expression 'the holy Eucharist of God', the original of which was probably τῆς ἱερᾶς εὐχαριστίας, as in the *Apost. Const.*

On pp. 252-3 there is an interesting passage in which, after warning Christians against the ceremonial law of the Old Testament, the writer goes on: 'For in the Second Legislation, if one touch a dead man or a tomb, he is baptized; but do you, according to the Gospel and according to the power of the Holy Spirit, come together even in the cemeteries, and read the holy Scriptures, and without demur perform your ministry and your supplication to God; and offer an acceptable Eucharist, the likeness (ἀντίτυπον, *Apost. Const.*) of the royal body of Christ, both in your congregations and in your cemeteries and on the departures of them that sleep—pure bread that is made with fire and sanctified with invocations— and without doubting pray and offer for them that are fallen asleep.'[1]

The application to the Eucharist of ἀντίτυπος, or ἀντίτυπον as a substantive, is first met with to my knowledge in the *Apostolic Tradition* of Hippolytus:

'Et tunc iam offeratur oblatio a diaconibus episcopo, et gratias agat panem quidem in exemplum, quod dicit Grecus antitypum, corporis Christi: calicem uino mixtum propter antitypum, quod dicit Graecus similitudinem, sanguinis quod (*sic*) effusum est pro omnibus qui crediderunt in eum.'[2]

In addition to the text answering to the *Didascalia* above, the same usage is found in two other passages of the *Apost. Constitutions*,[3] and it is met with also in the Liturgy of

---

[1] Cf. Tertullian *de Corona* 3: 'Oblationes pro defunctis, pro nataliciis, annua die facimus'.
[2] Hauler p. 112 (see also p. 118 *ad fin.*).
[3] See v, 14 § 7 and vii. 25 § 4, according to Funk.

INTRODUCTION

St. Basil.[1] In the liturgy of Serapion we have ὁμοίωμα, and in Latin we meet with such terms as *figura*,[2] *imago*, *similitudo*.[3]

There appears to be no example of similar terminology before Tertullian; certainly it is not met with in the eucharistic passages of SS. Ignatius, Justin, and Irenaeus. And Tertullian uses *figura* hardly as a directly eucharistic term, but to show that the Eucharist bears out his interpretation of an Old Testament 'figure' of Christ's (natural) body. A discussion of the early history and the significance of such terms as applied to the Eucharist can find no place here; and I can do no more at present than express my conviction that their employment by early writers is no proof that those writers conceived of the Eucharist as being the Body and Blood of Christ only in some relative or metaphorical sense; the passages in which they occur require to be read side by side with others which suggest a different conclusion.

In the passage quoted from p. 252 we read further that the Eucharist is 'sanctified with invocations' ('per inuocationem', Lat.); and twice on p. 244 it is said to be sanctified by the Holy Spirit. Some readers accordingly will doubtless be led to find in the *Didascalia* an Invocation, or Epiclesis, of the Holy Spirit as the form of consecration. It may be that this is a legitimate inference; but for my part I should hesitate thus to put two and two together.[4]

The correct translation of a passage on p. 190, from which Achelis inferred that the Eucharist of the *Didascalia* 'still had the form of a meal', is discussed in the Additional Notes *ad loc.*

On pp. 122–3 it is enjoined that if a bishop come from another church, the local bishop is to request him to address

---

[1] Brightman, *Liturgies*, p. 329 l. 24.
[2] Tertullian *adv. Marc.* iii 19, iv 40; and in the Canon of the Mass as quoted in the *de Sacramentis*.
[3] Cf. Pope Gelasius I, Tract. III, *adv. Eutychem et Nestorium*, c. 14 (Thiele *Epp. Rom. Pont.* i p. 541): 'Et certe imago et similitudo corporis et sanguinis Christi in actione mysteriorum celebrantur'. With which is to be compared the Mozarabic prayer in the *Liber Ordinum* (ed. Férotin) coll. 321–2: 'quae est imago et similitudo corporis et sanguinis Ihesu Christi'. The prayer is evidently built up of old Roman pieces.
[4] For my reasons I may perhaps be allowed to refer to a paper in the *Journal of Theol. Studies* for July 1924, pp. 337 ff., '"The Meaning of ἐπίκλησις": a Reply'.

the people, and then is added (according to the Latin version):
' Et in gratia agenda ipse dicat. Si autem, cum sit prudens et honorem tibi reservans, non uelit,[1] super calicem dicat.' How are we to explain the cup here alluded to? Is it the eucharistic cup? I am inclined to think not. What the visitor is offered as a mark of respect is evidently the celebration of the Eucharist,[2] and it is this that he wisely and tactfully declines as pertaining in the highest degree to the rights of the local bishop. We are led to expect accordingly that what is offered him in lieu of this will be something else, not something that is virtually the equivalent; and hence I take the cup in question to be that which is offered at the Agape. There is evidence from the beginning of the third century that the giving thanks over a cup was the first act at a religious supper which is certainly to be identified with the Agape. Thus we read in the *Apostolic Tradition* of Hippolytus: ' Before any taste and drink anything whatsoever, it is proper for them to take the cup and give thanks over it, and (then) drink and eat.'[3] St. Cyprian also, contrasting the evening *cena* with the morning Eucharist, asks : ' An illa sibi aliquis contemplatione blanditur, quod etsi mane aqua sola offerri videtur, tamen cum ad cenam venimus mixtum calicem offerimus?'[4] Coming to a later date, we read in the 25th canon of the Council of Laodicea: ὅτι οὐ δεῖ ὑπηρέτας ἄρτον διδόναι οὐδὲ ποτήριον εὐλογεῖν. Whatever may be said of the ' bread ' which these minor clerics are forbidden to ' give', a special order against their attempting to ' bless ' the eucharistic cup seems quite out of the question ; but both the bread and the cup are no doubt those of the Agape, which forms the subject of the 27th canon.[5]

---

[1] The Syriac and *Apost. Const.* add ' to offer'.
[2] Compare the story of Anicetus and Polycarp told by Irenaeus (Euseb. *H.E.* v 24) : see note on p. 123 after.
[3] Cf. G. Horner, *Statutes of the Apostles*, p. 158 l. 2 (Ethiopic) ; for the Sahidic and Arabic texts see *ibid.* pp. 321 l. 11, 257 l. 22 ; and for the juncture of these texts with the Latin fragment (Hauler p. 113) see *The so-called Egyptian Church Order and derived Documents* (Cambridge ' Texts and Studies ' viii 4) p. 189.
[4] *Ep.* lxiii 16. The words above represent a pretext put forward by those who use only water at the morning Eucharist, but a mixed cup at some form of Agape in the evening.
[5] There is little likelihood that this Council refers to the ' Signing of

An Agape, in the sense of a charity supper given by one of the faithful, is mentioned in the *Didascalia* at pp. 80–91. If the host desires to invite widows, the bishop is to select and send those whom he knows to be in special need of relief. At these suppers fixed portions are set aside for the widows, the bishop, and the clergy.

Penitential Discipline.

Chapters vi and vii of the *Didascalia* contain the author's teaching on repentance and forgiveness and constitute an important section of the book. The general trend and tone of these chapters, the strong condemnation of puritanical austerity in dealing with sinners which is to be met with in several passages, and the striking examples of the divine mercy quoted from the Scriptures all combine to produce the impression that the writer was a conscious opponent of the older rigorism, and that like Pope Callistus—whose practice gave such offence to Tertullian and Hippolytus[1]—he would have been ready to re-admit to communion, after penance performed, any sinner whatsoever. Thus, after quoting Ezekiel xviii *in extenso*, he comments:

'You see, beloved and dear children, how abundant are the mercies of the Lord our God and His goodness and loving-kindness towards us, and (how) He exhorts them that have sinned to repent. And in many places He speaks of these things; And He gives no place to the thought of those who are hard of heart and wish to judge strictly and without mercy, and to cast away altogether them that have sinned as though there were no repentance for them' (pp. 48–50).

And before this he has said: 'It behoves you not therefore to hearken to those who desire (to put to) death, and hate their brethren and love accusations, and are ready to slay on any pretext' (p. 44). Further on the whole story of Manasseh and his repentance is recited with apocryphal additions, and the moral is drawn without hesitation: 'You have seen, beloved children, how Manasseh served idols evilly and bitterly, and

the Cup', or Mass of the Presanctified, which is found later among the Syriac Jacobites.

[1] Tertul. *de Pudicit.* 1; Hippol. *Philos.* ix 12 (λέγων πᾶσιν ὑπ' αὐτοῦ ἀφίεσθαι ἁμαρτίας).

slew righteous men; yet when he repented God forgave him, albeit there is no sin worse than idolatry. Wherefore, there is granted a place for repentance' (p. 74). This is followed presently by another remarkable example, Christ's treatment of the woman taken in adultery, as to which we read:

'But if thou receive not him who repents, because thou art without mercy, thou shalt sin against the Lord God; for thou obeyest not our Saviour and our God, to do as He also did with her that had sinned, whom the elders set before Him.... In Him therefore, our Saviour and King and God, be your pattern, O bishops, and do you imitate Him' (p. 76).

The woman's sin is not specified in the *Didascalia*, but there can be no doubt that the author understood it to be adultery. In these two examples, therefore, instances are adduced of the forgiveness of idolatry, murder, and adultery; and these examples are set before the bishops for their imitation. From this it may seem inevitable to conclude that even such sins were remissible by the Church, and their perpetrators capable of being restored to communion—unless indeed the author has considerably over-reached himself in his argument. Achelis is confident that the author 'knows of no sin which cannot be atoned for; nay more, he has never heard of particular cases that are too serious to be dealt with by the bishop's authority: the Roman rule which excepted mortal sins did not prevail in Syria'.[1]

I am inclined on the whole to the view that the author would himself have been ready to rehabilitate any sinner upon his doing penance; yet I cannot repress a certain misgiving on this point. There are passages which suggest at least that he was still under the influence of another discipline. Thus in ch. v we read:

'For we believe not, brethren, that when a man has (once) gone down into the water he will do again the abominable and filthy works of the ungodly heathen. For this is manifest and known to all, that whosoever does evil after baptism, the same is already condemned to the Gehenna of fire' (p. 38: for the last sentence the Latin has: 'quoniam notum est omnibus quod, si quis peccauerit iniquum aliquid post baptismum, hic in gehenna condemnatur').

[1] *Op. cit.* pp. 306-7.

It may be that we are to understand here the condition, 'unless he repent', which is inserted in the *Apost. Const.* But the Syriac does not suggest this, and still less does the Latin.

Again, commenting on Ps. xxxi (xxxii) 1, 'Blessed are they whose iniquity is forgiven', &c., the writer says:

> 'To every one therefore who believes and is baptized his former sins have been *forgiven*; but after baptism also, provided that he has not sinned a deadly (*or* mortal) sin nor been an accomplice (thereto), but has heard only, or seen, or spoken, and is thus guilty of sin' (p. 178). The Latin is not available at this point, and in *Apost. Const.* the passage is quite altered.

The distinction here drawn between mortal and lesser sins committed after baptism is emphasized by the next words, which appear to abolish such distinction in the case of martyrdom, this being equivalent in its effects to baptism: 'But if a man go forth from the world by martyrdom, *blessed* is he; for brethren who by martyrdom have gone forth from this world, of these *the sins are covered.*'

I will not insist on the strong language used at p. 163 about those who have lapsed under persecution, or on the harrowing picture of an apostate's death which is drawn at pp. 165-6; for, as Achelis says, these things may be set before the reader only as possibilities, to frighten him. There is, however, another passage which is apt to suggest that the forgiveness and reconciliation of penitents, so earnestly enjoined, are intended for cases which involve less than the most heinous sins. The passage is on p. 52; and there, without other indication of the gravity of the sin, the bishop is told to receive the penitent back into the Church and 'appoint him days of fasting according to his offence, two or three weeks, or five, or seven'. This strikes one as being a very mild penitential code. Can it possibly cover such sins as idolatry, murder, &c.?[1] And if not, does the author legislate at all for these sins as remissible by the Church? It must suffice to state both sides of the question, leaving it to students to arrive at their own conclusions.

---

[1] Contrast the long years of penance prescribed by the 11th canon of Nicaea for those who have lapsed under persecution.

The Problem of the Old Law.

The reader will meet many times in these pages with the terms 'Second Legislation' and, in the Latin version, *secundatio* or *secundatio legis*. The Greek word of which these are renderings was δευτέρωσις, as is shown by passages retained in the *Apostolic Constitutions*. This *Deuterosis* was something about which our author had cause to be deeply concerned, and about which also he has much to say. An attempt must be made therefore to trace the use of the term, to explain in what sense it is here employed, and to indicate the part it plays in the author's exegesis of the Old Testament. For its Hebrew or Aramaic background I can do little more than follow what Schürer and other writers have to tell us, as I have no direct acquaintance with the Rabbinic literature.[1]

We are familiar with the word Mishna (properly *mishnāh*, fem.) as the general title of certain post-biblical Jewish treatises of a legal character. It is formed from the verb *shānāh*, to do something a second time, repeat. But the kind of repetition commonly implied by this verb (at least in its Aramaic form *tĕnā*) was the oral repetition employed in teaching or learning; and hence it came to mean simply to teach or to learn.

The substantive *mishnāh* correspondingly denoted oral teaching, and particularly that of the traditional law as distinguished from the *miḳrā*, that which was read, the Scripture text. But it also denoted the tradition itself, or what is called in the Gospel 'the tradition of the elders'. This tradition, codified and reduced to writing somewhere between 160 and 220 A.D., is the Mishna. 'The Mishna', says Dr. Schechter, 'meaning a "teaching", a "repetition", is a designation most appropriate for the work generally looked upon as the main depository of the contents of the Oral Law, which (in contradistinction to מקרא, reading matter, or the Scriptures) could be acquired only by means of constant repetition'.[2] He tells us, however,

---

[1] For this I make use especially of Schürer, *Geschichte des jüdischen Volkes im Zeitalter Jesu Christi*; H. Hody, *De bibliorum textibus originalibus* (1705); Schechter's article 'Talmud' in the extra volume of Hastings's *Dictionary of the Bible*; and Stephanus's *Thesaurus* under δευτέρωσις, δευτερόω, δευτερωτής. [2] *Op. cit.* p. 60.

INTRODUCTION

in a footnote that there is another explanation of the name, also represented in Rabbinic literature, which connects it with the masculine noun *mishneh*, a double or second, and that according to this the Mishna is 'second to the Torah'—in other words, as I understand it, a second or secondary Law. And this explanation, he says, is supported by the patristic rendering δευτέρωσις.

The Greek verb answering to *shānāh* was δευτερόω, which also means to do or say a second time, to repeat. And in technical Jewish language it meant particularly *to teach the traditions*. The substantive corresponding to *mishnāh* was δευτέρωσις (more often found in the plur.), which likewise denoted especially an oral teaching *of the traditions*, or the traditions themselves. And a teacher of the traditions was a δευτερωτής. These meanings were fixed and clear before the end of the fourth century A.D. They admit of abundant illustration, chiefly from the writings of SS. Jerome and Epiphanius, but the following examples may suffice for the present purpose.

1. Δευτερόω.—' Uidetur igitur obseruationes Iudaicae apud imperitos et uilem plebeculam imaginem habere rationis humanaeque sapientiae. Unde et doctores eorum σοφοί, hoc est sapientes, uocantur. Et siquando certis diebus traditiones suas exponunt discipulis suis, solent dicere οἱ σοφοὶ δευτεροῦσι, id est, Sapientes docent traditiones' (Jerome).[1]

2. Δευτέρωσις.—' Quantae traditiones Pharisaeorum sint, quas hodie uocant δευτερώσεις, et quam aniles fabulae, euoluere nequeo' (Jerome).[2]

' Hic (Papias) dicitur mille annorum Iudaicam edidisse δευτέρωσιν' (Jerome).[3]

Αἱ γὰρ παραδόσεις τῶν πρεσβυτέρων δευτερώσεις παρὰ τοῖς Ἰουδαίοις λέγονται (Epiphanius).[4]

' Nescit (sc. adversarius) habere praeter scripturas legitimas et propheticas Iudaeos quasdam traditiones suas, quas non scriptas habent sed memoriter tenent et alter in alterum transfundit, quas *deuterosin* uocant' (Augustine).[5]

[1] *Ep.* cxxi 10, ad Algasiam.
[2] *Ibid.*
[3] *De uiris illustr.* xviii.
[4] *Haer.* xxxiii. 9.
[5] *Contra adversarium Legis et Prophetarum* lib. ii c. 1 § 2.

3. Δευτερωτής.—Ναὶ μὴν καὶ τῶν πρώτων μαθημάτων δευτερωταί τινες ἦσαν αὐτοῖς (Eusebius).[1]

'Ιουδαίων αἱρέσεις ἑπτά· γραμμάτεις, οἵτινες νομικοὶ μὲν ἦσαν καὶ δευτερωταὶ παραδόσεων τῶν παρ' αὐτοῖς πρεσβυτέρων, κτλ. (Epiphanius).[2]

'Audiui Liddae quemdam de Hebraeis, qui sapiens apud illos et δευτερωτής uocabatur, narrantem huiusmodi fabulam' (Jerome).[3]

Many more passages are cited by Hody (pp. 233 ff.), Schürer and Stephanus, but no reference is given to any writer earlier than Eusebius. In Rufinus's translation of Origen's Commentary on the Canticle, however, I find the following :

'Sed et illud ab eis accepimus custodiri, quoniamquidem moris est apud eos omnes scripturas a doctoribus et sapientibus tradi pueris, simul et eas quas δευτερώσεις appellant, ad ultimum quattuor ista reseruari' (sc. the beginning of Genesis, the beginning and end of Ezekiel, and the Canticle).[4]

It seems improbable that the use of δευτέρωσις to denote the oral traditions of the Jews was only a development of the fourth century; and hence there can be little doubt that the author of the *Didascalia* was familiar with that sense of the term. It is surprising therefore to find that he gives it an entirely different content. He does not employ it to describe any 'tradition of the elders', whether written or oral, but comprises under it the whole ceremonial legislation of the Pentateuch—as to sacrifices, the Sabbath, circumcision, clean and unclean animals, ceremonial defilement and purification.

Moreover, the *Deuterosis* of which he speaks is distinctly a 'second legislation': it is not the Law, but was added after the Law. The Law 'is that which the Lord God spoke before the People had made the calf and served idols, which consists of the Ten Words and the Judgements. But after they had served idols, He justly laid upon them the bonds, as they were worthy.'[5] The *Deuterosis* was added as a punishment for sin, and laid as a grievous yoke upon those who had shown them-

---

[1] *Praep. euang.* xi 5.
[2] *Rescript. ad Acacium et Paulum*, Migne *P. Gr.* xli 172 A.
[3] *In Habac.* ii 15.   [4] Berlin ed., vol. viii p. 62.
[5] p. 14; cf. 224.

selves unfaithful. It was not this that Christ came to fulfil, but only the moral Law enshrined in the Decalogue, in which He had set His own Name: for *Iota* stands for *ten*, and is also the first letter of the Name of Jesus.[1] 'For in the Gospel He renewed and fulfilled and affirmed the Law; but the Second Legislation He did away and abolished. For indeed it was to this end that He came, that He might affirm the Law and abolish the Second Legislation.'[2] The abrogation of the *Deuterosis* was foretold by the prophets: 'If, then, even before His coming He made known and revealed His coming, and the disobedience of the People, and spoke of the abolition of the Second Legislation, much more, being come, did He fully and completely abolish the Second Legislation.'[3]

It was for a punishment, then, that the *Deuterosis* was laid upon the People, as a bondage and a burden and a hard yoke: 'Therefore the Lord was angry; and in His hot anger—(yet) with the mercy of His goodness—He bound them with the Second Legislation, and laid heavy burdens upon them, and a hard yoke upon their neck'.[4] But not even so were they brought to obedience, and there was added to them further a blindness and hardening of their heart: 'For because of manifold sins there were laid upon them customs unspeakable; but by none of them did they abide, but they again provoked the Lord. Wherefore He yet added unto them by the Second Legislation a blindness worthy of their works, and spoke thus: *If there be found in a man sins worthy of death, and he die, and ye hang him upon a tree; his body shall not remain the night upon the tree, but ye shall surely bury him the same day: for cursed is every one that is hanged upon a tree*; that when Christ should come they might not be able to help (?) Him, but might suppose that He was guilty of a curse. For their blinding therefore was this spoken.'[5] And again: 'Hence also the word aforesaid in the Second Legislation was for the blinding of a blind people, to wit: *Cursed is every one that is hanged upon a tree....* Wherefore... that word was set down for the blinding of the People; and it was a bar that they might not

---

[1] pp. 216-19. [2] p. 224. [3] p. 226; cf. 224-5.
[4] p. 222. [5] *Ibid.*

believe and be saved. ... For by this word, because of their works, their eyes were blinded, and their ears made deaf like Pharaoh's.'[1] To this text of Deuteronomy (xxi 23 : cf. Gal. iii 13) the author returns again and again. A Christian who meddles with the *Deuterosis*, imagining himself to be bound by any of its ordinances, is said to 'affirm the curse against our Saviour', that is to deny Christ, and to take upon himself the idolatry for which the Second Legislation was imposed: 'for if thou take upon thee the Second Legislation, take (*or* thou takest, Lat.) also idolatry, for because of idolatry the Second Legislation was imposed'.[2]

The author's treatment of the problem of the Old Law is doubtless influenced by St. Paul, and especially by the Epistle to the Galatians. But he is more daring and explicit in his formulation of it. St. Paul would not indeed have included the moral precepts of the Decalogue in 'the Law' which he rebukes the Galatians for clinging to: by 'the Law' or 'the works of the Law' he means the ceremonial ordinances; but he does not expressly draw the distinction. The author of the *Didascalia*, on the other hand, sharply divides the ceremonial from the moral law, and brands it with a distinctive and ominous name. But he differs more widely from St. Paul in his estimate of the purpose and value of the ceremonial law. It would probably be unjust to him to say that he had no conception of the formative purpose of that legislation, as a factor and stage in the spiritual education of the race; but this aspect of it is not developed, and is barely even indicated, in the *Didascalia*. Moreover, the emphasis on the punitive and repressive character of the *Deuterosis* is here so strong that it hardly leaves place for the thought that the Law, even in its ceremonial ordinances, was 'our tutor unto Christ', or part of a progressive revelation which was to reach its goal in the Gospel and the Church. It may almost be said that in the author's mind the *Deuterosis* was nothing more than an interim measure, forced as it were on the Divine Legislator, and no part of His own plan. It admitted of no fulfilment or perfection, and waited only to be clean swept away. A *praeparatio*

[1] p. 230.   [2] p. 250.

evangelica is to be sought only in the Law properly so called and in the Prophets.

I do not think this is too strong a statement of the case. And yet it is probable that some allowance is to be made for the practical issues with which the author was faced, and for the fact that he speaks in the *Didascalia* as a preacher rather than as a theologian. We must note also that he allows a typical or figurative value to certain institutions of the Old Law—the tabernacle with its ministry and sacrifices, the Sabbath and circumcision. Whether for him these institutions formed a special subdivision of the *Deuterosis* there is no means of telling: we shall see that they constituted a separate class of *typica* in at least one Gnostic discussion of the Law. Yet when all is said, we cannot resist the impression that our author's attitude to the ceremonial law of the Old Covenant was one of hostility rather than of piety and reverence.

How different is his tone, and his whole treatment of the problem, from that which we are accustomed to in the reverent words and solemn periods of the Epistle to the Hebrews. ' The writer of the Epistle to the Hebrews [I cannot do better than quote the words of Dr. Armitage Robinson] addressed himself to Jewish readers, who had accepted Christianity, but under the pressure of some great crisis were looking wistfully back to the religion of their fathers. With passionate earnestness he warned them against apostasy. And he brought them a great message of hope. He bade them see that the Christ was more than they had ever supposed, even in the enthusiasm of their first acceptance of Him. He was the Fulfiller of the past —that sacred past in which fragments of the eternal truth had been enshrined in temporary ordinances, whose only abrogation lay in their complete fulfilment. One great thought he was inspired to give them—the Eternal High-priesthood of Christ. The sacred past was theirs because it was taken up and fulfilled: to honour the record of it was a part of their loyalty to the Fulfiller.'[1] To the author of the *Didascalia* the *Deuterosis* was something of which the only fulfilment lay in its complete abrogation. He definitely excludes it from fulfilment.

[1] *Barnabas, Hermas and the Didache* (S.P.C.K., 1920), p. 3.

Another early effort to grapple with the same problem is found in the 'Epistle of Barnabas'. This is an obscure and disorderly treatise, and its root idea is that a special *gnosis* or spiritual enlightenment is needed to understand the ceremonial ordinances of the Law. It is not merely that the things commanded had a spiritual as well as a literal meaning: some at least of them were not even spoken in a literal sense, but were parabolic utterances which required to be spiritually translated before they could be obeyed at all.[1] In a word, the Law needed to be allegorized from the first. Unlike the author of the *Didascalia*, 'Barnabas' makes no distinction of higher and lower standards within the Law; all its ordinances are high and spiritual, but the Jews had not the spiritual endowment to discern their true meaning.

The Catholic writer who in his treatment of the Law comes nearest to the ideas expressed in the *Didascalia* is St. Irenaeus. And this is but natural, for I have no doubt at all that our author used and was much influenced by him. Irenaeus too makes a clear distinction between the Decalogue and the ceremonial Law: there were on the one hand the 'naturalia praecepta' given directly by God Himself, eternal, and needing only to be 'fulfilled', that is developed, extended, enlarged by Christ (*superextendi, augeri, dilatari*); and on the other hand there were the 'uincula seruitutis' which were afterwards delivered through Moses and imposed upon the People for sin, and which when they had served their purpose had perforce to be abrogated and removed ('necesse fuit auferri'). Irenaeus's formal discussion of the Law is to be found in the fourth book of the *Heresies*, chapters xxiv–xxix, from which I have quoted some phrases in the notes. There is one feature, however, in Irenaeus's treatment of the ceremonial Law which finds no parallel in the *Didascalia*, and which the author has either neglected or rejected as unsuited to his own purpose. As already said, the *Didascalia* seems to leave no room for the *Deuterosis* as a factor in the spiritual education of the People:

[1] See especially the tenth chapter, in which the author deals with the distinction of clean and unclean animals; and compare also the fifteenth, on the Sabbath, a chapter which I have no doubt was used by the writer of the *Didascalia*.

it was a punitive measure, and whether intended at first to be corrective or not, it proved in effect to be the opposite. The People went from bad to worse, until (apparently as a second instalment of the *Deuterosis*) that word in Deuteronomy, 'Cursed is every one that is hanged upon a tree', was set down 'for their blinding' and as a positive obstacle, that when Christ was come they might not be able to recognize Him but should suppose that He too was one of the accursed. We must say, I think, that the author finds no place for the *Deuterosis* as an educative factor. It is otherwise with Irenaeus, as two passages will suffice to show:

> Etenim lex, quippe servis posita, per ea quae foris erant corporalia animam erudiebat, uelut per uinculum attrahens eam ad obedientiam praeceptorum, uti disceret homo servire Deo. Uerbum autem liberans animam, et per ipsam corpus uoluntarie emundari docuit. Quo facto necesse fuit auferri quidem uincula seruitutis, quibus iam homo assueuerat et sine uinculis sequi Deum (IV xxiv 2).

And again:

> Sic autem et populo tabernaculi factionem et aedificationem templi et Leuitarum electionem, sacrificia quoque et oblationes et mundationes,[1] et reliquam omnem legis statuebat deseruitionem. Ipse quidem nullius horum est indigens; ... facilem autem ad idola reuerti populum erudiebat, per multas uocationes praestruens eos perseuerare et seruire Deo: per ea quae erant secunda ad prima uocans, hoc est per typica ad uera, et per temporalia ad aeterna, et per carnalia ad spiritalia, et per terrena ad caelestia.... Per typos enim discebant timere Deum et perseuerare in obsequiis eius. Itaque lex et disciplina erat illis et prophetia futurorum (IV xxv 3).

The contrast here with the *Didascalia* is striking; but we must not forget the different situations in which the two writers were placed. Irenaeus had to defend the Church's view of the Old Testament against the heretic Marcion, who rejected it as unworthy of the Supreme God and as the work of some inferior Being. The author of the *Didascalia* had to meet a danger from the opposite side, and to remind Christians that for them

---

[1] The current text has 'et monitiones'; but Dr. Armitage Robinson informs me that the Armenian version has 'and purifications', which is far more suitable in the context, and from which I venture to adopt the above emendation—I do not know whether the form 'munditiones' would be possible.

the ceremonial ordinances of the Old Law are gone irrevocably, and may not under any pretext be revived. It was natural for him therefore to stress, and even over-stress, the short-comings of the *Deuterosis*, and, representing it as historically a failure, to ascribe the failure, not indeed to its Author, but to the circumstances which made such a legislation possible and necessary.

I am coming to feel that the author of the *Didascalia* was not quite so unsophisticated and isolated a writer as parts of his book are apt to suggest, indeed that on the whole, and for his time, he was well informed and well read. Since, then, the great question of the Old Law was one to which he had evidently given much attention, it seems that we ought to reckon with the possibility that his reading on this subject had led him beyond the circle of Catholic writers, and that his unfriendly attitude to the *Deuterosis* may be due in part to an unconscious bias derived from other influences. Whether this be so or not, it will not be out of place here to give some account of yet another early attempt to solve the problem of the Law—the attempt this time of a writer who was not of the Church. The Letter of Ptolemaeus to Flora (a lady otherwise unknown) has the unique interest that it gives us at some length, and in the form of a complete document, the *ipsissima verba* of a member of one of the great Gnostic sects. The writer was of the Italian branch of the Valentinian school of Gnostics, and his letter is thought to have been written about the year 160.[1]

After a short introduction he explains to Flora that the whole legislation of the Pentateuch needs first to be sorted out into three component parts: (1) that which comes from God; (2) those things which Moses set down of his own authority and devising (as the permission of divorce); and (3) the additions of the Elders (Corban is cited as an instance). Then, passing over (2) and (3), he further explains that even (1), the portion of the Law which comes from God Himself, is likewise

---

[1] The letter is preserved by Epiphanius, *Haer.* xxxiii, and may be read in Migne *P. Gr.* xli 555. There is a handy edition by Harnack in Lietzmann's *Kleine Texte* (Bonn), no. 9.

to be distinguished into three elements. First there is the pure Law unmixed with evil, 'which also is properly called the Law' and which the Saviour 'came not to destroy but to fulfil'. Secondly there is that which has an admixture of evil and unrighteousness, which the Saviour abolished as being foreign to His own nature. And thirdly there are certain things which are merely typical and symbolical, being ordained as figures of better and spiritual things.

The first of these elements consists of the Decalogue, the Ten Words disposed on the two tables. These, though pure and unmixed with evil, yet came short of perfection, and had need therefore of fulfilment ($\pi\lambda\eta\rho\omega\sigma\epsilon\omega s$) by the Saviour. As examples of the second element are adduced the *lex talionis* and the command to slay a murderer. As to the latter, the writer says that He who has condemned murder by the command 'Thou shalt not kill', by making a second law ($\delta\epsilon\upsilon\tau\epsilon\rho o\nu$ $\nu\acute{o}\mu o\nu$) that the slayer should be slain shows that He has allowed Himself to be forced into inconsistency. To the third, or typical, element belong the laws regarding sacrifices ($\pi\rho o\sigma\phi o\rho\alpha\acute{\iota}$), circumcision, Sabbath, fasting, Passover, unleavened bread, and the like. 'All these, being images and symbols, were changed when the truth was made manifest'; that is to say, their outward and material observance was abolished, but in their spiritual content they were carried on, the names remaining the same, but the things undergoing a change: 'For the Saviour also commanded us to offer oblations, but not by means of dumb animals or with incense of this sort,[1] but with spiritual praises and doxologies ($\delta o \xi \hat{\omega} \nu$) and thanksgiving, and by liberality and beneficence towards our neighbours.' And the other *typica* are similarly explained.

Then the writer comes to the crucial question: 'Who then is this God who gave the Law?' It could not be the Perfect God, for the Law at its best was not perfect; neither could it be the Devil. It must therefore have been one who stood midway between, and who, being neither good nor bad, nor yet unjust, may properly be called Just and the arbiter of such

---

[1] $\mathring{\eta}$ τούτων τῶν θυμιαμάτων. Harnack notes: 'τούτων looks strange; we expect an adjective like κοσμικῶν.'

justice (or righteousness) as is according to himself. And this is the Demiurge and maker of this universe with all that is in it, who is still other in nature than the universe itself.

Whether or no the author of the *Didascalia* had read this letter it is impossible to say; but it is likely enough that he was acquainted at first hand with analogous discussions of the Old Law. Thus he speaks of 'those who blaspheme the Holy Spirit, those who lightly and in hypocrisy blaspheme God Almighty, those heretics who receive not His holy Scriptures, or receive them ill, in hypocrisy with blaspheming, who with evil words blaspheme the Catholic Church which is the receptacle of the Holy Spirit':[1] words which have every appearance of being aimed at Marcion or other heretics who either rejected the Old Testament or refused to regard it as coming from God Himself. It may not be altogether idle therefore to note that there are one or two points in the language of the letter of Ptolemaeus that are apt to recall the *Didascalia*. When the writer says of the best portion of the Law, the Decalogue, that it is that 'which also is properly called the Law' ($\mathring{o}s$ καὶ κυρίως νόμος λέγεται), we are reminded of a puzzling expression in the *Didascalia* (pp. 218–19) where the Latin reads: 'Lex ergo est decalogus et iudicia ... Nam lex uocata est specialiter propter iudicia.' For 'specialiter' the Syriac has 'truly', but I suspect that these are both renderings of κυρίως. The original therefore may have been νόμος γὰρ κυρίως λέγεται διὰ τὰς κρίσεις.[2] Now our author has said again earlier (p. 14) that the Law consists of 'the Ten Words and the Judgements', and I take these 'Judgements' to mean the formally legal enactments in Exod. xxi–xxiii, which in the LXX are called the δικαιώματα, but in the Hebrew simply 'the judgements'.[3] The *Didascalia*, then, pointedly

---

[1] p. 212.
[2] In *Apost. Const.* the passage is re-written: νόμος δέ ἐστιν ἡ δεκάλογος ... οὗτος δὲ δίκαιός ἐστιν, διὸ καὶ νόμος λέγεται διὰ τὸ φύσει δικαίως τὰς κρίσεις ποιεῖσθαι.
[3] But the word used in *Didasc.* was apparently not δικαιώματα but κρίσεις, as in *Apost. Const.*; the former would more probably have been rendered 'iustificationes' in the Latin. The note on p. 14 is therefore to be read with this qualification: though in that passage *Apost. Const.* omits 'and the Judgements'.

attaches these laws to the Law proper and excepts them from the *Deuterosis*. But by Ptolemaeus they are expressly classed with that portion of the Law which has an admixture of evil, being thereby distinguished from the Decalogue; and from them he takes his two examples of this inferior element in the Law, viz. the law of retaliation and the command to slay the murderer. Thus it seems possible to read the above words in the *Didascalia* as a direct retort against Ptolemaeus and his assertion that the Decalogue alone 'is properly called the Law'. Not only is the command to slay the murderer good, but it is a necessary sequel to the commandment 'Thou shalt not kill'; this and the other 'Judgements' in fact justify the term 'law' as applied to the moral precepts of the Decalogue, which are not strictly legal in form and content.

Again, the writer of the Letter admits that the sacrificial ordinances of the Law were figures of the 'spiritual praises and doxologies and thanksgiving'[1] which were the oblations that the Saviour commanded His followers to offer. And in the *Didascalia* (p. 86) we read: 'instead of the sacrifices which then were, offer now prayers and petitions and thanksgivings'.[2]

If it be asked what parts of the Pentateuch constituted the *Deuterosis*, the answer is not easy to give; nor do I imagine that the author himself could readily have supplied it. Large portions of Exodus, Leviticus, Numbers, and Deuteronomy ought logically to be excluded from 'the Law'. But Law and *Deuterosis* were interwoven, it would seem, in all the books, and we are told that it is one of the first qualifications of a Christian bishop to be able to separate the one from the other: 'But before all let him be a good discriminator between the Law and the Second Legislation, that he may distinguish and show what is the Law of the faithful, and what are the bonds of them that believe not' (p. 34).

The word δευτέρωσις at first puzzled the Latin translator. On its first appearance (see p. 13, l. 14) the clause containing it is passed over, though perhaps only by a clerical error.

---

[1] πνευματικῶν αἴνων καὶ δοξῶν καὶ εὐχαριστίας.

[2] εὐχαὶ καὶ δεήσεις καὶ εὐχαριστίαι *Apost. Const.*, without 'offer' (and so Lat.).

Then at l. 17 we find an untranslatable 'bis', representing only part of the word, i.e. δευτερωσ. A few lines on (l. 20) there appear 'secunda legatio' and 'repetita alligatio' (? for 'legatio'). But on p. 15, l. 7, we meet with 'secundatio legis'; and this, or 'secundatio' alone, is henceforth regularly employed.

The Syriac translator has no hesitation: he adopts from the outset *tenyān nāmōsa*, 'repetition (*or* double) of the Law'. This is really the Syriac title of the book of Deuteronomy, which was taken no doubt from the Greek δευτερονόμιον.[1] He nowhere uses *tenyāna* alone in the way the Latin translator uses 'secundatio'; and indeed it would hardly be intelligible in Syriac. I have adopted the rendering 'Second Legislation', not because it is a real translation of the Syriac, but because it conveys to the reader with fair accuracy the author's own interpretation of the *Deuterosis*.

The Author's use of Scripture.

The Old Testament. As Achelis has said, the author had a 'highly respectable' knowledge of his Bible. Of the books of the Old Testament he quotes most freely from the Psalms and Proverbs, Isaiah, Jeremiah, and Ezekiel. From Proverbs and Ezekiel he makes lengthy excerpts, once or twice to the extent of a whole chapter. Of books outside the Jewish Canon he shows acquaintance with Wisdom, Ecclesiasticus, Susanna, and possibly Tobit. His single quotation from Daniel has the distinction of following the LXX, not the more widely used version of Theodotion. But for Ezekiel he employed a version which had the nature of a revision of the LXX, and his text shows many readings that are to be found only in hexaplaric codices.

There are several apparent quotations from unknown sources, of which those at pp. 109, 152, and 234, l. 10, are the most

---

[1] In the Hebrew the fifth book of Moses is called by the words with which it begins, 'These are the words'. The Greek name Deuteronomy appears to have been derived by misunderstanding from a phrase in xvii 18, where it is directed that the future king 'shall write him a *copy* (*mishneh*, not *mishnāh*) of this law in a book'. This is rendered in the Greek καὶ γράψει αὐτῷ τὸ δευτερονόμιον τοῦτο εἰς βιβλίον.

singular. One text attributed to Isaiah has not been identified, but bears some resemblance to a Targum on Deut. xxviii (p. 128). The author also knows and reproduces, after 2 Chron. xxxiii. 11, an apocryphal story of the repentance of Manasseh which has a parallel in the Targum at the corresponding place;[1] and he is our earliest authority for the Prayer of Manasseh, which he quotes in full (p. 72). After the account of Manasseh he adds also some details about Amon which may have been drawn from the same source (pp. 74–7). His application of Scripture is generally simple and straightforward, but at times he allows himself to be drawn into fanciful interpretations, as at p. 220. His attitude to the ceremonial legislation of the Old Testament, which he designates by the term *Deuterosis*, is discussed elsewhere (see pp. lvii ff.).

Certain forms of citation are noteworthy as marking the early associations of the *Didascalia*. The Psalms are regularly cited as 'David', and the Proverbs most frequently as 'Wisdom', though 'Proverbs' is also used (see p. 16, l. 4, and note). Passages from the Minor Prophets are three times referred collectively to 'the Twelve Prophets' (see p. 36, and note). Malachi is 'Malachi the Angel' (p. 216, and note) or 'Malachi who was called the Angel' (pp. 217, 254–5). Twice we find 'the holy word' coupled with a reference to 'Wisdom' (pp. 16, 24: ὁ ἅγιος λόγος, and ὁ θεῖος λόγος, in *Apost. Const.*): with which compare St. Clement of Rome, xiii. 3, φησὶν γὰρ ὁ ἅγιος λόγος, introducing words from Isaiah. Chronicles has the Greek name Paralipomenon coupled, apparently, with an abbreviated form of the Hebrew title 'The Words (Acts) of the Days' (see notes to pp. 68, 69).

The New Testament. The author makes use of all four of our Gospels. His main source of quotation is St. Matthew, but St. Luke is well represented. Traces of St. Mark are naturally much less prominent, but are to be recognized in the form of certain quotations: 'He eateth with publicans and sinners' (p. 104); 'two mites, which is one dinar' (p. 138); 'to-day, in this night' (p. 181); 'they accused him much' (p. 182). Apart from certain echoes of the language of St. John's Gospel

---

[1] See pp. 72–5, and the Additional Notes.

there are at least two plain allusions to it: the washing of the disciples' feet (xiii. 4-5) is introduced with the words 'And again in the Gospel you find it written' (p. 150); and at p. 120 it is said that 'our Lord likened the Church to a fold', implying John x. References to 'the Gospel' are numerous; but only once is a separate book named, 'the Gospel of Matthew' (p. 182), and I suspect that the passage in which this occurs was originally a marginal gloss which has crept into the text.

The *Didascalia* is remarkable as containing the earliest known citation of the famous *Pericope de adultera* (or the section after John vii. 52).[1] The author does not refer to 'the Gospel', but he introduces it without hesitation or apology, as if he expected that it would be known to his readers. He cites only a few words of the actual text and does not specify the woman's sin; but from the indications given there can be no reasonable doubt that he knew the Section nearly in the form with which we are familiar. Eusebius (*H. E.* iii. 39. 16), to quote Westcott and Hort, 'closes his account of the work of Papias (Cent. II) with the words "And he has likewise set forth another narrative (ἱστορίαν) concerning a woman who was maliciously accused before the Lord touching many sins (ἐπὶ πολλαῖς ἁμαρτίαις διαβληθείσης ἐπὶ τοῦ κυρίου), which is contained in the Gospel according to the Hebrews". The notice is vague and the language is probably that of Eusebius himself: but it is natural to suppose that the narrative referred to by him was no other than the Section'. In view, therefore, of the almost complete absence of Greek evidence for the Section in St. John's Gospel until a comparatively late date, it is open to us to suppose that the author had read it

---

[1] See p. 76. On the documentary evidence for the Section the reader may consult Westcott and Hort's 'Notes on select readings', p. 82 and ff. of the Appendix to their edition of the N.T. (1881); but on p. 85 we should now read (instead of 'in the Apostolic Constitutions') 'in the Didascalia and in the parallel text of the Apostolic Constitutions'. Indeed, from the manner in which the reference is introduced in the *Constitutions*, we may suspect that the Section was not known to the author independently of the *Didascalia*; and so Funk notes: 'Animadvertas, iam Didascaliam pericopen... cognitam habere, nec demum Constitutiones.' After quoting Luke vii 47, the 'Constitutor' goes on: ἑτέραν δέ τινα ἡμαρτηκυῖαν κτλ. (See notes at p. 76.)

either in Papias or in the Gospel according to the Hebrews. Achelis favours the latter alternative (*op. cit.*, pp. 329–30).

From the Acts there are some lengthy extracts (pp. 204 ff.) which are made to provide the occasion for the writing of the *Didascalia* by the Apostles. There is, naturally, no reference to a written source, as the *Didascalia* affects to have been compiled immediately after the events described in Acts xv, and therefore many years before the book of the Acts was written.

In a work ascribed to the Apostles we cannot look for formal quotations from the Epistles; but while the author shows a suitable reserve in this matter, he is not afraid to let the Apostles speak on occasions as they have spoken elsewhere. Hence he uses freely the language of 1 Timothy and Titus in speaking of bishops, deacons, and widows; and there is a reminiscence of 2 Timothy on p. 28. Of the other Pauline Epistles there are clear traces of Ephesians (pp. 20, 116) and 2 Thessalonians (p. 129), while the influence of Romans xvi. 35 is unmistakable at p. 258. The words 'whose god is their purse' (pp. 136–7) no doubt imply Philippians iii. 19, and the Syriac version accordingly adds 'and their belly'. There appear also to be reminiscences of 1 and 2 Corinthians, Galatians, and 1 Thessalonians. It is probably safe to assume that the author had a full collection of the Pauline letters, with exception perhaps of the Epistle to the Hebrews: though in one place our Lord is called 'the true High Priest' (p. 86).

Turning to the Catholic Epistles we find clear evidence of the use of 1 Peter (pp. 2, 86, 145, cf. 32). The words 'for even the demons, trembling before His name, lauded His advent' (p. 176) may carry an allusion to James ii. 19, and the passage beginning at p. 122, l. 29, recalls James ii. 2. At p. 176–7 there is a passage which is suggestive of 1 John i. 1, though the verb 'concibauimus' in the Latin ($\sigma\upsilon\mu\phi\alpha\gamma\acute{o}\nu\tau\epsilon\varsigma$ in *Apost. Const.*) shows that Acts x. 41 must also have been in mind. On p. 118 it is said to be God's will 'that no man should perish, but that all men should believe and be saved': which appears to combine 2 Peter iii. 9 and 1 Timothy ii. 4.

THE DOCUMENT

Of the remaining Catholic Epistles I have not observed any traces.

A phrase in which the Church is described as 'the bride adorned for the Lord God' (p. 86) is rather more suggestive of the Apocalypse xxi. 2 than of the similar text in Isaiah lxi. 10.

There are a few extra-canonical sayings, or Agrapha, which appear also in other early Christian writings: cf. pp. 38–9, 101, 198, 234. Besides these there is a very remarkable version of our Lord's words from the cross (cf. Lk. xxiii. 34), which appears twice over: 'My Father, they know not what they do (*or* have done), neither what they speak: (but) if it be possible, forgive them' (pp. 52, 212–3). No doubt the author often quotes from memory, but nowhere else in the *Didascalia* is there any parallel to this strange elaboration of a familiar text, and the fact that the words are cited twice in almost identical form strongly suggests that there was a document behind them other than our Gospel of St. Luke.

At p. 256 we find the Syriac and Latin versions of the *Didascalia* concurring in a distinctively 'Western' reading for Mt. xxv. 41, and we must therefore conclude that it stood in the original Greek. Again, at p. 93, the context seems to imply the presence of the words, 'Thou art my son: I this day have begotten thee' (Ps. ii. 7), in connexion with the account of our Lord's baptism: and therefore probably the 'Western' reading in Lk. iii. 22. But at Acts xv. 20 there is no trace in the Syriac (the Latin is wanting here) of the famous Western' reading, nor in the Syriac or the Latin of the similar reading at xv. 29 (see pp. 207 and 208–9).

As regards the Latin version, it may be assumed that the translation of biblical quotations has been influenced to some extent by the Latin text familiar to the translator. To identify or classify that text (which may have varied in character for the different books, or groups of books, of the Bible) is a work which must be left to those who have made a special study of the Latin Bible: but it may be said summarily that the translator was accustomed to a pre-Vulgate version for both the Old and the New Testament.

Dom Wilmart has remarked that the renderings of familiar passages, where memory would be most active, 'ont une forme décidément occidentale, sans trace marquée d'influence africaine'.[1]

As for the form of (Syriac) biblical text lying behind the Syriac version, the question is a practical one only in the case of the Gospels. Of the Old Testament only one Syriac version is known to have been in use, which was made from the Hebrew at an early date. For the rest of the New Testament the early history of the Syriac text is still obscure, and we can hardly use the terms 'Old Syriac' or 'Syriac Vulgate' in regard to it. We are confined therefore to the Gospel quotations. And here the reader needs to be reminded that 'as a general rule ... translators render the quotations afresh from the original without paying much heed to the current version of the words', and that 'it is only from striking agreements with other texts, agreements either too particular or too extensive to be accidental, that we are able to draw our inferences'.[2] But at least one of these criteria, that of particularity, is not wanting in the Syriac version of the *Didascalia*. Besides many lesser points of agreement with the MSS. of the Old Syriac against the Syriac Vulgate we find certain renderings which seem almost to forbid the idea that the translator could have had any knowledge at all of the Vulgate text. Three examples may suffice.

p. 218. 'One Yod letter shall not pass away from the law' (Mt. v. 18). This remarkable rendering of $ἰῶτα\ ἓν\ ἢ\ μία\ κεραία$, κτλ agrees exactly with that found in the Sinaitic MS., and its characteristic feature is found also in the early Syriac writers Aphraates and St. Ephraim. The Curetonian MS. adds 'or one horn' after 'one Yod letter'. The Syriac Vulgate has 'one Yod or one line'.[3]

p. 148. 'Mary Magdalene, and Mary the daughter of James and mother of Jose, and the mother of the sons of Zebedee.' This again is, in the Syriac, word for word with the Sinaitic

---
[1] *Recherches de science religieuse*, t. x p. 66.
[2] F. C. Burkitt, *Evangelion Da-Mepharreshe*, vol. ii p. 166.
[3] See Prof. F. C. Burkitt's note in his *Evangelion Da-Mepharreshe*, vol. ii p. 117, also the note at p. 218 hereafter.

MS. at Mt. xxvii. 56, except that the latter has 'Joseph' for 'Jose'. Syr. Vulg. has '... and Mary the mother of James and of Jose', etc. Everywhere in the *Didascalia* the second Mary appears as the *daughter* of James: and so in all extant passages in the Old Syriac.[1]

p. 150. 'Wash-basin' in l. 12 (= Joh. xiii. 5) is literally 'dish (λεκάνη) of washing', as in the Sinaitic MS. and in Aphraates. The Syriac Vulgate has a single word which denotes a vessel for washing in. The word in the Greek is νιπτήρ. This employment of one Greek word to translate another is curious but not unexampled in the Old Syriac Gospels.[2]

The use of Apocrypha.

That the author made some use of at least one apocryphal Gospel seems almost certain. On p. 183 we read that after His appearance to Mary Magdalene and Mary the 'daughter' of James, our Lord, on the first day of the week, 'went in to (the house of) Levi; and then He appeared also to ourselves'. The only known document which offers a possible explanation of this singular statement is the *Gospel of Peter*, the surviving fragment of which ends thus: 'But we, the twelve disciples of the Lord, wept and were grieved: and each one grieving for that which was come to pass departed to his home. But I Simon Peter and Andrew my brother took our nets and went away to the sea; and there was with us Levi the son of Alphaeus, whom the Lord ...'.[3] (This was 'on the last day of the unleavened bread'.) Here the fragment breaks off. I have suggested in the note at p. 183 that the next words may have been 'called as he sat at the place of toll' (cf. Mk. ii. 14, from whence 'the son of Alphaeus' is taken), that the passage then went on to say that the two Apostles entered Levi's house, and that there Jesus appeared to them, and presently perhaps to others. A few more lines of the docu-

---

[1] See the note at p. 148 after.
[2] See Burkitt *op. cit.* ii p. 142. The Syriac of the *Didascalia* was not among the early Syriac documents used by Prof. Burkitt to illustrate the Old Syriac version of the Gospels.
[3] I quote from the translation of Dr. Armitage Robinson: *The Gospel according to Peter, and the Revelation of Peter*. London (Clay), 1892.

ment would probably have settled this question; as it is we are left only to conjecture. The words quoted above from the *Didascalia* are followed by a discourse of our Lord which contains directions as to a fast six days before Easter and a weekly fast on Wednesday and Friday; and Achelis has suggested that this also, at least in substance, was drawn from *Peter*.[1] There may have been something in the apocryphon to suggest the discourse, but in my opinion it is largely our author's own composition.

The Levi text does not stand alone. On pp. 189 f. there is another passage which strongly suggests influence of the *Gospel of Peter*:

Didascalia.	*Gospel of Peter*, § 1.
For he who was a heathen and of a foreign people, Pilate the judge, did not consent to their deeds of wickedness, but took water and washed his hands, and said: I am innocent of the blood of this man. But the people answered and said: His blood be upon us, and upon our children; & Herod commanded that He should be crucified.	But of the Jews no man washed his hands, neither (did) Herod nor any one of His Judges: & whereas they would ⟨not⟩[2] wash, Pilate rose up. Then Herod the king commanded that the Lord should be taken (into their hands), saying unto them: All that I commanded you to do unto him, do ye.

In both these texts Pilate is exonerated, and it is Herod who, present at the trial before Pilate, passes the sentence.

It is difficult to believe that the foregoing coincidences with the *Gospel of Peter* can be accidental, and I do not doubt that the author of the *Didascalia* made some use of that book. Achelis regards this as evident, and infers that the author 'knew five Gospels side by side' and used them on equal terms as Scripture.[3] But this is a runaway conclusion for which there is surely insufficient warrant. Two bare allusions to *Peter* is little to set beside the abundant witness of the *Didascalia* to the canonical Gospels; and the use of apocryphal books by early writers was not incompatible with a recognition that

---

[1] *Op. cit.* p. 327.
[2] Dr. M. R. James, whose translation I quote, supplies the negative without brackets: *The Apocryphal New Testament* (Oxford, 1924), p. 90.
[3] *Op. cit.* p. 328.

they were neither authentic nor authoritative. If the argument from mere use were valid, it would have to be applied to the Old Testament as well as the New. Did our author believe that the document, or tradition, from which he drew the apocryphal details about Manasseh ranked as of equal authority with the Law and the Prophets? In a work like the *Didascalia* we must be prepared for a certain amount of make-believe, and accordingly for some latitude in the use of authorities. An author who can invent for his own purposes an entirely baseless chronology of the events of Holy Week [1] does not thereby prove his disbelief in the Gospels as Scripture; but neither is he likely to be over-scrupulous in employing written sources which he knows to be at least of doubtful authority.

We have already noted the possibility that the author owed his knowledge of the famous section on the woman taken in adultery to the Gospel according to the Hebrews. Achelis does not hold this as certain, yet he thinks it 'highly probable',[2] and is therefore inclined to believe that the author's Canon of the New Testament contained not merely five but six Gospels.[3] As to this conclusion, what has been said just above may suffice. Are there any other traces of the Gospel according to the Hebrews in the *Didascalia*? The following passages are all that seem to deserve notice:

At pp. 242–3 we read of those who 'resurgere in carne nolunt, tamquam nolentes manducare et bibere, sed demones uolunt resurgere spirituales in fantasmis' (δαιμόνια δὲ ἄσαρκα φανταζόμενοι ἐκ νεκρῶν ἀναστήσασθαι, *Apost. Const.*). This reminds us of the saying attributed to Christ by St. Ignatius (*Smyrn.* iii 2): 'Take, feel me, and see that I am not a bodiless demon' (δαιμόνιον ἀσώματον), which St. Jerome tells us was found in the Gospel according to the Hebrews. But we shall see that our author knew Ignatius, and therefore the expression δαιμόνια ἄσαρκα may be only an echo of the passage in *Smyrneans*.

Again on p. 55 we read: 'Therefore the life and manner of

---

[1] See p. xxxii. [2] *Op. cit.* p. 363, and note 6.
[3] *Ibid.*, p. 328.

conversation of the just men and patriarchs was written, that it might be known that in each one of them there was found at least some small sin.' And St. Jerome says that according to the Hebrew Gospel, after the injunction to forgive unto seventy times seven, Our Lord added: 'etenim in prophetis quoque, postquam uncti sunt Spiritu sancto, inuentus est sermo (i.e. somewhat) peccati.'[1] The coincidence may easily be accidental, but it seems worth noting, since in the *Didascalia* also the context is concerned with forgiveness.

The fact that in the *Didascalia* the deaconess is compared to the Holy Spirit (p. 88), and that in the Hebrew Gospel our Lord is made to speak of 'my mother the Holy Spirit', appears to me to be of little weight. We can only say that such ideas are of Semitic origin, 'spirit' in Hebrew and Aramaic being feminine. So the Syriac writer Aphraates speaks of God and the Holy Spirit as a man's father and mother.[2]

Though I cannot entertain the notion of Achelis, that the author of the *Didascalia* was unconscious of any distinction between canonical and apocryphal writings, yet it may be left an open question whether he did not admit as genuine a couple of spurious Pauline epistles. The apocryphal letter of the Corinthians to St. Paul, and his reply, which form part of the second-century *Acta Pauli*, came to be circulated separately in Syriac, Latin, and Armenian, and found their way into the Syrian and Armenian Bibles.[3] Thus it was that these letters were commented on by St. Ephraim († 373) with the rest of the Pauline Epistles. The use of this correspondence by the author of the *Didascalia* seems now to be recognized as a fact, and the only question is whether he knew it already as part of a Pauline collection or had read it only in the *Acta Pauli*. The points of contact are with the letter of the Corinthians to St. Paul, and are noted at pp. 200 and 202. In the first of these two passages we have Simon and a certain Cleobius set down as the first pair of heretics; and they appear together in the letter. In the

---
[1] *Dial. contra Pelagianos* iii 2.   [2] See note at p. 88.
[3] See M. R. James, *The Apocryphal New Testament* (Oxford, 1924), p. 288.

second passage we read: 'And they all had one law alike,[1] that they should not employ the Torah and the Prophets,[2] and that they should blaspheme God Almighty, and should not believe in the resurrection.' This comes very near to being a verbal quotation from the letter.

Another apocryphal work used by our author was the *Acts of Peter*, or some closely allied document, from which he drew his details about the activities of Simon Magus in Rome (pp. 200-3).

The use of other writings.

No great attempt has been made by scholars hitherto to examine the literary background of the *Didascalia* beyond noting the author's use of the Bible and certain apocryphal books. Some attention to this question seems therefore to be demanded.

In the first place we have, on p. 172, a quotation of ten lines from the Sibylline Oracles. This passage, which treats of the destruction of the world by fire, and of the resurrection, is thought to be that which is alluded to by Justin Martyr in chapter 20 of his first *Apology*.[3] So Otto *in loc.*

Then there are evident traces of several of the Apostolic Fathers. Use of the Ignatian Epistles seems manifest at p. 88. Still more clear is the borrowing from Hermas at pp. 154-6; and there are many further coincidences with the language and ideas of Hermas, some of which are pointed out in the notes and may be found by consulting the Index. I believe also that the author made use of the Epistle of Barnabas, especially in his treatment of the Sabbath at pp. 234-9. That the *Didache* was known to him is generally recognized. I have collected and discussed elsewhere the chief points of contact between the two documents,[4] and so it will be enough to point out here that one of the most striking parallels involves a

---

[1] The Syriac version has 'on earth', misreading ἐπίσης as ἐπὶ γῆς.
[2] So the Syriac, and *Ap. Const.*, νόμῳ καὶ προφήταις μὴ χρᾶσθαι, but the Latin has only 'profetas'; and the Latin version of the letter has 'non ... uatibus credi'.
[3] καὶ Σίβυλλα δὲ καὶ Ὑστάσπης γενήσεσθαι τῶν φθαρτῶν ἀνάλωσιν διὰ πυρὸς ἔφασαν.
[4] 'The use of the *Didache* in the *Didascalia*': *Journal of Theological Studies* xxix pp. 147 ff. (Jan. 1923). See also the notes in the present volume referred to in the Index.

passage of the *Didache* which is commonly (but without sufficient reason, I think) regarded as an interpolation, viz. i. 3b–ii. 1.[1] Points of connexion with the Epistle of St. Clement to the Corinthians, the so-called Second Epistle of Clement and the Epistle of St. Polycarp are slight and far less convincing. The appeal to the Phoenix as a witness to the resurrection (p. 172) may suggest knowledge of 1 Clement. But the *Didascalia* has a number of details which are not supplied by Clement and which must have been taken from another source.[2] At p. 149 it is said that the Bishop and the deacon should be 'one soul dwelling in two bodies'. This reminds us of 'second Clement' xii. 3, where the writer says, commenting on a saying attributed to our Lord: 'Now the two are one, when we speak truth among ourselves, and in two bodies there shall be one soul without dissimulation.' Polycarp reminds widows 'that they are the altar of God'; and the *Didascalia* repeatedly insists on the same idea (see p. 88, l. 6, and the note there).

To sum up, our author certainly knew Ignatius, Hermas, and the *Didache*, almost certainly 'Barnabas', and perhaps 1 and 2 Clement and Polycarp. Personally I have no difficulty in believing that he was acquainted with all these documents.

Further, I think it probable that he knew the works of Justin Martyr, and I am persuaded that he was familiar with Irenaeus.

The chief coincidences with Justin that I have noticed occur on pp. 236–7. The most striking of these is where it is said: 'But the Sabbath itself is counted even unto the Sabbath, and it becomes eight (days); thus an ogdoad is (reached), which is more (*or* better) than the Sabbath, even the first of the week.' To this Justin has a close parallel in c. 41 of the *Dialogue*. It is true that in that chapter he is not treating of the Sabbath but of the Christian worship and sacrifice; but then he goes on to speak of Sunday, the day set apart for this: it was pre-

---

[1] See p. 6, l. 16, and the note there.

[2] Nau (*La Didascalie*, first ed. p. 166) names among the 'sources' of the *Didascalia* a 'Physiologus' edited by Land in vol. iv of his *Anecdota Syriaca*, and he quotes in the note (from Land iv pp. 55 and 154) a passage on the Phoenix which must certainly be either the source of that in *Didasc.* or taken from it; but which is the earlier I have not at present the means of deciding.

figured by the command to circumcise on the eighth day, which signifies the day on which Christ rose from the dead: 'for the first of the week, while it remains the first of all the days, yet according to the number of all the days of the (weekly) cycle it is called the eighth, though it still remains the first'.[1] I have not made a systematic search through Justin for parallels, but two further points may be mentioned. On pp. 184–5 Christians are admonished that even though the Jews hate them, yet they ought to call them brethren, and then Isa. lxvi 5 is quoted: 'Call them brethren that hate and reject you, that the name of the Lord may be glorified.' Similarly Justin says (*Dial.* c. 85): 'Jesus commanded us to love our enemies', and goes on to quote the same text as far as *v.* 10. And in the *Didascalia*, a few lines on, *v.* 10 is also quoted. Again, our author refers repeatedly to the verse Deut. xxi 23 ('Cursed is every one that is hanged upon a tree') as a stumbling-block in the way of the Jews which prevented them from acknowledging Jesus as the Christ. And in the *Dialogue* c. 89 Trypho makes this verse a difficulty: the Messiah was indeed to suffer, but surely not to incur the curse attaching to crucifixion; and so Justin has to devote several chapters to meeting this objection.

Perhaps the most enlightening fact revealed by a study of the sources of the *Didascalia* is the author's acquaintance with the works of St. Irenaeus. I venture to say 'fact' because I believe that it will come to be recognized for one. The main evidence for this conclusion is derived from a comparison of Irenaeus's treatment of the Old Law (especially in *Haer.* IV xxiv–xxix) with that of the *Deuterosis* in the *Didascalia* at p. 14 and in the last chapter. There are no doubt differences of view between the two writers,[2] and Irenaeus has not the term *Deuterosis*; yet there is so much in common, both in thought and expression, that it is difficult to avoid the conviction that our author was working on the basis of Irenaeus. I have quoted some of the parallels in the notes, but the chapters indicated in Irenaeus must be read continuously if all their echoes in the *Didascalia* are to be caught. In both we

[1] Compare also *Dial.* c. 138.   [2] These are indicated at pp. lxiii f., before.

find the same sharp distinction between the Decalogue and the ceremonial legislation: the one given before the other; the one to be fulfilled, the other to be abrogated by Christ; the one a law of liberty, the other bonds (*uincula*) and servitude. Then there is the insistence that circumcision and the Sabbath were but 'signs', and the argument that if they were essential they would have been observed by the patriarchs before Abraham and Moses; and as to sacrifices, there is the reiterated assertion that God has no need of them. It is to be observed further that several of the passages quoted by Irenaeus from the Old Testament appear also in the *Didascalia*. Especially remarkable is the reappearance (p. 225) of two texts from Jeremiah (vi 2 and vii 21 f.) which occur close together in Irenaeus IV xxix 3.

But this is not all; there are other coincidences which can hardly be explained as accidental. At p. 257 I have pointed out in the note that the form of a quotation from Jeremiah, as well as its interpretation, appears to have come from Irenaeus. Again, on p. 259 we read in the Latin '.... et dormiuit, ut euangelizaret Abraham et Isac et Iacob'; and in Irenaeus (V xxxiii 1) we have 'Propter hoc autem ad passionem ueniens, ut euangelisaret Abrahae et iis qui cum eo', etc.[1] At p. 216 the words 'And I will make in the desert a way' (Isa. xliii 19) are thus explained: 'Now *deserts* the Churches formerly were'; and Irenaeus (*Demonstration of the Apostolic Preaching* c. 89), quoting 'And I will make in the wilderness a way, and in the waterless place streams', comments in the same sense, though not in exactly the same words: 'Now a *wilderness* and a *waterless place* was at first the calling of the Gentiles.' It is worth while to compare also p. 102, where the Father and the Son and the Holy Spirit are likened to the 'three witnesses' at whose mouth every testimony is established, with Irenaeus's interpretation of the 'three' spies: 'Patrem scilicet et Filium cum Spiritu sancto' (see the note *in loc.*).

[1] I have failed to record this parallel in the notes to p. 257. For 'evangelizing' the dead we must compare 1 Pet. iv 6, and also the text attributed to Jeremiah (or Isaiah) in Justin *Dial.* 72 and Irenaeus *Haer.* III xxii. Elsewhere Irenaeus has this text with other verbs than 'euangelizare', sc. 'eruere', 'erigere', 'extrahere'. In the *Gospel of Peter* c. 10 we have the question: 'Ἐκήρυξας τοῖς κοιμωμένοις;' 'Hast thou preached to them that sleep?'

Had our author any acquaintance with Hippolytus? If this question could be answered in the affirmative we should have a valuable clue to the date of the *Didascalia*. But there is little evidence on which to form a decided opinion. I have had occasion to refer to Hippolytus about a dozen times in the notes, but without intending to suggest any use of him in the *Didascalia*. The coincidence noted on p. 14 may possibly have some significance; and there is another passage, on p. 255, which deserves attention. As the parallel in Hippolytus is not indicated in the notes it may be shown here, for it is certainly worth considering:

Didasc.	*Hippol.*
et uir et mulier legibus ad nuptias conuenientes et ab alterutrum exurgentes, sine obseruatione et non loti orent, et mundi sunt.	Noli autem piger esse ad orandum: qui in nuptias conligatus est non est inquinatus; qui enim loti sunt non habent necessitatem lauandi iterum, quia mundi sunt. (*Apostolic Tradition*, Hauler p. 119.)

This is the one passage known to me which may seriously suggest acquaintance on the part of our author with writings of Hippolytus. Other points which may be noticed are the use of ἀξίως καὶ δικαίως at p. 215, and the form of doxology 'ipsi est potentia ... patri et filio' at p. 259 (see the notes in those places).

Further investigations I must leave to others. I have offered no suggestions touching Clement of Alexandria or Origen. The character of Clement's writings and the date of those of Origen hardly suggest that they would provide a fruitful field of inquiry.[1] Funk inferred from the mention of the heretic Cleobius, and his association with Simon (p. 200), that our author knew Hegesippus; but we have seen (p. lxxviii) that his source here is probably the apocryphal epistle of the Corinthians. C. Holzhey, as already noted (p. xxxvii), supposed that the *Didascalia*, in an earlier form, was known to Dionysius of Alexandria. If there were any ground for this view we might be justified in asking whether the dependence was not perhaps in the other direction; but I agree with Funk and Bardenhewer in thinking that the notion is unfounded.

---

[1] As to the *Clementine Homilies* see p. lxxxv.

Traces of the Didascalia in early writings.

Funk has brought together what traces he could find of the use of the *Didascalia* by later writers,[1] but the result is surprisingly small. Apart from the *Apostolic Constitutions* he indicates only Epiphanius, the *Opus imperfectum in Matthaeum*, a gloss to a Coptic version of a letter of St. Athanasius, the *Nomocanon* of Bar-Hebraeus and a small Syriac fragment of the *Didascalia* itself in a MS. of the British Museum.

Epiphanius is the earliest writer who makes mention of the *Didascalia*, which he cites as the $\Delta\iota\alpha\tau\acute{\alpha}\xi\epsilon\iota\varsigma$ of the Apostles. It was formerly thought that his references were to the *Apostolic Constitutions*, but some of them could not be identified as from that source, and their true origin was revealed by the publication of the *Didascalia*. They are collected by Funk, and the chief of them are indicated in the notes to the text of the present volume.

The fifth- or sixth-century *Opus imperfectum* recites practically the whole of the apocryphal account of Manasseh. This might have been drawn from the *Apostolic Constitutions*, which also have the story in full and almost verbatim as in the *Didascalia*. But the writer refers elsewhere to a *Liber Canonum* of the Apostles for a statement which is represented in the *Didascalia* but not in the *Constitutions*.[2] The passages again are collected by Funk.

Of Bar-Hebraeus (a Syriac writer of the thirteenth century) and the other two items in Funk's list it is not necessary to speak; but I must mention four other early writings in which there appear to me to be traces of the use of the *Didascalia*. These are the *Apostolic Church Order*, the *Clementine Homilies*, the *Homilies* of the early Syriac author Aphraates, and the *Canons of Hippolytus*.

I have quoted some parallels from the *Apost. Ch. Order* in the notes at pp. 30-1, 32-3, 86-7, 93 and 130. To these may be added the following:

In c. xx of the *Order* it is said of deacons: $\mu\grave{\eta}$ $\pi\rho\acute{o}\sigma\omega\pi\text{o}\nu$ $\pi\lambda\text{o}\nu\sigma\acute{\iota}\text{o}\nu$ $\lambda\alpha\mu\beta\acute{\alpha}\nu\text{o}\nu\tau\epsilon\varsigma$ $\mu\eta\delta\grave{\epsilon}$ $\pi\acute{\epsilon}\nu\eta\tau\alpha$ $\kappa\alpha\tau\alpha\delta\nu\nu\alpha\sigma\tau\epsilon\acute{\nu}\text{o}\nu\tau\epsilon\varsigma$. This

---

[1] *Didasc. et Const. Apost.* vol. ii pp. 3 ff.
[2] See p. 110 ll. 4 ff., and note; cf. also p. 143 l. 12.

is to be compared with the *Didascalia* at p. 34 ll. 11-13, where the Greek is preserved in *Apost. Const.* thus: μήτε πλούσιον ἐντρεπόμενος ἢ κολακεύων παρὰ τὸ προσῆκον, μήτε πένητα παρορῶν ἢ καταδυναστεύων (said of the bishop). We must note also, among other adjectives giving the qualifications of the various ministers, the reappearance in the *Order* of εὔσκυλτοι (c. xx: of deacons), εὐήκοος (c. xix: of the lector), and εὐμετάδοτος (cc. xviii and xx: of presbyters and deacons). In the *Didascalia* we find together εὔσκυλτοι καὶ εὐήκοοι, of deacons;[1] and εὐμετάδοτος occurs several times.[2] We have also in the *Order* (cc. xxiv, xxviii) the institution of a διακονία for women[3]; though in c. xxvi St. John is made to point out that the Master (ὁ διδάσκαλος) οὐκ ἐπέτρεψε ταύταις συστῆναι ἡμῖν. This again reminds us of the *Didascalia* at p. 133 l. 20, where the Greek in *Apost. Const.* is: εἰ γὰρ ἦν ἀναγκαῖον γυναιξὶν διδάσκειν, αὐτὸς (sc. ὁ διδάσκαλος ἡμῶν) ἂν ἐκέλευσε πρῶτος καὶ ταύταις σὺν ἡμῖν κατηχεῖν τὸν λαόν. Then we remember that the *Order* begins with a list of twelve Apostles, who are commanded to κληροῦσθαι τὰς ἐπαρχίας—to divide by lot the provinces: cf. *Didasc.* at pp. 200-202. And in c. ii the *Order* goes on: ἔδοξεν οὖν ἡμῖν πρὸς ὑπόμνησιν τῆς ἀδελφότητος καὶ νουθεσίαν ἑκάστῳ ... ἐντείλασθαι ὑμῖν, with which compare the Greek in *Apost. Const.* answering to p. 214 ll. 26 ff.: καταλιπόντες ... τήνδε τὴν καθολικὴν διδασκαλίαν ἀξίως καὶ δικαίως εἰς μνημόσυνον ἐπιστηρισμοῦ τοῖς πεπιστευκόσι. Cf. also pp. 200-201, at the top.

While I have no doubt that the *Apost. Ch. Order* is appreciably later than the *Didascalia*,[4] I think also that any one who will undertake a careful comparison of the two documents will be satisfied that there has been borrowing on one side or the other.

The *Clementine Homilies* provide a parallel to the *Didascalia*

[1] See p. 151 l. 23, 'excussior et obaudiens' Lat.; also p. 149 l. 8, where 'exercitatiores' renders εὐσκυλτότεροι. Also 'mobilis' in l. 15 on the same page probably renders εὔσκυλτος, as it does in the *Apost. Ch. O.* c. xx (the translator being the same for both documents). At p. 32 l. 30 the words 'afflicting his soul' represent εὔσκυλτος (*Apost. Const.*).
[2] Cf. Funk i 3. 2; ii 4. 1; ii. 50. 1: all *Didascalia* passages.
[3] See pp. 145 ff.
[4] I have stated one or two reasons for this belief in the *Journal of Theological Studies* vol. xxiv (Jan. 1923) pp. 155-6.

which many, I imagine, will recognize as a mark of contact between the two writings. It is quoted in the note at p. 6. But as the relative antiquity of the *Didascalia* and the *Homilies* is a matter on which all are not agreed, some may prefer to place the latter among the sources of the *Didascalia*.[1]

I have already given my reasons for thinking that Aphraates used the *Didascalia* (see p. xviii).

As to the *Canons of Hippolytus* (a document based in the main on the *Apostolic Tradition* of Hippolytus), it is my belief that this also shows marks of the influence of the *Didascalia*. Its preface appears to represent the Apostles as speaking, and to imply that they have met together to take counsel for the correction of evils, with the result that certain purveyors of false doctrines are to be 'separated' from the Church. The words to be noted are as follows :

'Hoc statuimus unanimi contra istos perditos homines qui de uerbo Dei nefaria edixerunt ... Ideo multo magis nos arcta unione in uirtute Dei coniuncti separauimus illos, quoniam non consentiunt ecclesiae in Deo, neque nobiscum sunt, qui sumus discipuli scripturarum. Ideoque separauimus illos ab ecclesia, ... nos qui iudicabimus creaturam.'[2]

The last words seem applicable only to the Apostles; the rest therefore is to be compared with the passages in the *Didascalia* beginning at pp. 211 (ll. 4 ff. and 16 ff.) and 215 ll. 4 ff. The *Canons* at the outset appear to assume a situation exactly similar to that in the *Didascalia* at the places indicated.

Then in can. xix it is said of women who are being baptized :
'Mulieres autem omnes habeant alias feminas comites, quae uestibus illas exuant.'[3] See the *Didascalia* at pp. 146-7, as to the need of a deaconess at the baptism of women.

But the most striking coincidences with the *Didascalia* are in can. xxii, as to the paschal fast :

'Hebdomas qua Iudaei pascha agunt ab omni populo summo cum studio obseruetur, caueantque imprimis ut illis diebus ieiuni maneant ab omni cupiditate, ita ut in omni sermone non loquantur cum hilaritate, sed

---
[1] Funk, *Die Apostolischen Konstitutionen* (1891) p. 72, leaves open the question of the relative dates of the *Didascalia* and the *Clementines*, but expresses the opinion that there is here no question of a 'literary dependence' on either side—a view which I cannot endorse.
[2] I quote from Achelis, *Die Canones Hippolyti*, pp. 38-9.
[3] *Ibid.* p. 94.

cum tristitia. . . . Cibus autem qui tempore πάσχα conuenit, est panis cum solo sale et aqua'.[1]

Every point emphasized here is to be found in ch. xxi of the *Didascalia*. The paschal fast is from Monday to Saturday, a week without the Sunday (p. 183). It begins in the week that the Jews celebrate the Passover (pp. 178, 192). A special feature of this season is mourning, and especially abstention from 'vain speech and words of levity and profanity' (p. 178, cf. 180). And from Monday to Thursday the food that may be taken is 'bread and salt and water only' (p. 189).

3. Place and Date.

As to the region from which the *Didascalia* comes and the date at which it was written there is now a large measure of agreement within certain limits: Syria or Palestine, and the third century, is the general verdict of scholars. We may take first the question of place.

We learn from St. Epiphanius (*Haer.* lxx 10) that the book was in favour among a sect called the Audiani, or Odiani, who appealed to it (without justification, as he points out) in support of their Quartodeciman rule for the celebration of Easter. He says also (*ib.* 1) that their founder, one Audius, hailed from Mesopotamia. He does not name any particular locality where the sect prevailed, but states that they dwelt in desert places, or on the outskirts of cities, 'or wherever they have their settlements or convents' (μονὰς ἤτοι μάνδρας). The Audiani are twice mentioned, with other heretics, by St. Ephraim in the twenty-second of his Hymns against Heretics,[2] from whence we gather that the name was of Semitic origin, for it is spelt in Syriac with initial 'ayin. With the Audiani, then, we seem to find ourselves on Syrian soil.

Further, if I am right in thinking that the Syriac version dates from the early fourth century, and also that the document was known to the early Syriac writer Aphraates, these conclusions will supply additional reasons for thinking of some part of Syria as the home of the *Didascalia*. It has also been

[1] *Ibid.* p. 115-16
[2] A good German translation of these Hymns, by Dr. Adolf Rücker, has appeared recently: *Des heiligen Ephräm des Syrers Hymnen gegen die Irrlehren*, in 'Bibliothek der Kirchenväter', Munich, 1928.

pointed out (p. xlix above) that the rite for administering baptism, as indicated in ch. xvi, is in remarkable agreement with the usage of the early Syrian churches; and the ministry of women at the baptism of women, which is put forward as a principal reason for the institution of an order of deaconesses, finds striking parallels in the third-century Syriac *Acts of Judas Thomas*. Another indication pointing to Syria may be found in the use by our author of the *Gospel of Peter*, which is first heard of at Rhossus in the neighbourhood of Antioch (Euseb. *H. E.* vi 12), and in his possible use of the Gospel according to the Hebrews.

We may now consider certain points which are suggestive merely of a Semitic environment. Amongst these may be mentioned in the first place the author's acquaintance with the apocryphal additions to the story of Manasseh, which find a parallel in the Targum on 2 Chron. xxxiii. He also shows himself familiar with Jewish Sabbath observances (p. 191), and he tells us how on the 9th of the month Ab, i. e. the anniversary of the destruction of the temple, the Jews 'come together and read the Lamentations of Jeremiah and wail and lament' (*ibid.*). He translates *raca* 'empty', showing that he was able to derive it from *rīk* (p. 9); and he tells us that 'Jew' signifies 'confession', connecting it with a verb which in Hebrew and Aramaic (including Syriac) means 'to confess' (p. 126). Possibly he connects the 'tabernacle of *witness*' (or '*testimony*') with the ordinary Syriac word for 'church' (p. 80). He likens the deaconess to the Holy Spirit, doubtless because in Semitic languages 'spirit' is feminine.[1] He makes two Old Testament quotations which are otherwise unknown: 'and that which the saints have not eaten, the Assyrians shall eat' (p. 152); and: 'Woe, woe to them that come from the spectacle', which he attributes to Isaiah (p. 128).[2]

[1] I am tempted to offer a further suggestion, though it cannot be developed here. When the case comes to be looked into, I have an idea that the use of the verb μισεῖν, instead of μὴ θέλειν, in negative forms of the Golden Rule will be found to be Semitic in origin.

[2] See also the note to this at p. 128. The quotation at p. 191 l. 16, which Achelis (*op. cit.* p. 361) suspected to be from some Jewish tract on the Sabbath, is shown by Funk to be from Isa. lviii 13 according to the LXX.

Achelis (*op. cit.* p. 364) says we shall not be far wrong if we fix on Coelesyria as the native land of the *Didascalia*, and in a note on p. 366 he refers with approval to Zahn's suggestion that its home may have been among the Nazarenes of Aleppo. Achelis, it must be observed, was largely influenced by the belief that our author's polemic against the *Deuterosis* implied the proximity of a Jewish-Christian colony. This, however, strikes me as being an insecure basis on which to settle the locality of the *Didascalia*. Judaizing tendencies were widespread; and the presence of a purely Jewish community, from which converts to Christianity might be drawn (and the *Didascalia* implies such converts in appreciable numbers), would sufficiently account for the abuses of which the author chiefly complains. We must not forget the sentence in the *Apostolic Tradition* of Hippolytus: 'Noli autem piger esse ad orandum: qui in nuptias conligatus est non est inquinatus; qui enim loti sunt non habent necessitatem lauandi iterum, quia mundi sunt.'[1] It is on other grounds therefore that I agree in the main with Achelis's conclusion, and would locate the *Didascalia*, roughly speaking, between Antioch and Edessa: yet without excluding the possibility of lower Syria, or even Palestine.

Whether the work is to be referred to the first or the second half of the third century is a question to which it is much more difficult to venture an answer. Eminent scholars have expressed themselves on this point with great diffidence, and have sometimes put forward opinions only to reverse them. Harnack, regarding chapters vi and vii as directed against the teaching of Novatian, at first declared himself in favour of the latter part of the third century; but later he preferred to think that the work as a whole was written in the first half of the century and afterwards revised in an anti-Novatianist sense. Funk began with a preference for the earlier, but ended by favouring the later date. Achelis, after balancing one consideration against another, ends with a simple *non liquet*.[2] Zahn was for the earlier period, Kattenbusch for the later.[3]

---

[1] Hauler p. 119; see also p. lxxxiii before. [2] *Op. cit.* p. 377.
[3] For a summary of opinions see Achelis *ibid.* p. 370.

So far as I am able to judge, there appears to be an entire lack of any decisive indication. One point only seems to stand out with some degree of clearness, but even this affords no definite clue: the *Didascalia* can hardly have been written during any period of official or organized persecution. The thirteenth chapter seems to imply that the Christian assemblies are free and unmolested; and this is suggested still more strongly towards the end of the last chapter, where the faithful are exhorted to come together not only in their 'assemblies' ('collectis', Lat.), but also in their cemeteries, there to offer the Eucharist for their departed (p. 252). Yet it is true that chapter xix (on martyrdom) breathes a strong atmosphere of persecution, which seems at least to imply that the writer had had experience of active persecution and was living in times that were still unsettled and far from secure. The allusion to the cemeteries, and their apparent freedom, might tempt us to think of a period after, but not far removed from, the persecutions of Decius and Valerian. Valerian, in 257, had forbidden the Christians to make use of their cemeteries or other places of worship, a prohibition which was soon after removed by Gallienus (260–268). But there is nothing to suggest that our author had heard of any edict either forbidding or restoring the use of the cemeteries, and the general tone of ch. xix is hard to reconcile with the long period of peace between Gallienus's edict of toleration and the persecution of Diocletian. On the other hand, this period would harmonize well enough with ch. xii, where we are given to understand that the existence of regular church buildings, capable of holding a good-sized congregation, was normal and widespread.

Turning to considerations of another kind, there are certain points which are apt to suggest an earlier rather than a later point in the third century. The author's literary background, so far as it can be traced with any degree of certainty, is early, not extending beyond the second century: Irenaeus is the latest writer whom he can safely be said to have made use of. Then he quotes the Book of Proverbs most frequently as 'Wisdom', which Eusebius tells us was characteristic of 'the ancients'; [1] like Justin and Irenaeus he cites individual Minor Prophets as 'the Twelve Prophets'; [2] and like Irenaeus, Clement of Alexandria and 4 Esdras he gives Malachi the title of 'the Angel'.[3] I believe also that he plays upon the ancient confusion of Χριστός and χρηστός.[4] And he makes a somewhat daring use of the *Gospel of Peter*.[5]

Perhaps we shall do best if we rest content with the safe but unsatisfying verdict of Achelis, *non liquet*. Yet my own inclination is to place the *Didascalia* earlier rather than later: or, if that is too vague, before the Decian persecution rather than after the grant of toleration by Gallienus.

From the nature of the *Didascalia* as a pseudo-apostolic work, the name of its author, as author, can hardly have been known even to his contemporaries and friends; we may, however, conjecture that he was a bishop. 'A Catholic bishop of the third century' is Achelis's confident assertion,[6] and there is much in the document to justify it, even apart from the exaltation of the episcopal office which pervades several of its chapters. Achelis makes the further interesting suggestion, that besides being a bishop the author was also a physician. He calls attention to the large number of illustrations drawn from the medical art, and goes on to cite some early examples of the exercise of the medical profession by presbyters and bishops.[7] Thus he refers to the epitaph in San Callisto, Διονυσίου ἰατροῦ πρεσβυτέρου, which, he remarks, is known to many from de Rossi's *Roma Sotterranea* (tav. XXXI 9), and to many more through the story of Fabiola by the English Cardinal Wiseman. Another interesting example is that of the presbyter and martyr Zenobius of Sidon, who is called by Eusebius 'the eminent physician', ὁ ἰατρῶν ἄριστος (*H. E.* viii 13).

With such introductory information or suggestion as has now been offered the reader must be left to form his own impressions from the varied contents of the document itself.

[1] See note at p. 16.
[2] See note at p. 36.
[3] See note at p. 216.
[4] See Additional Notes pp. 261 ff.
[5] See notes at p. 183, 189, and p. lxxv before.
[6] *Op. cit.* p. 378.
[7] *Ibid.* p. 383.

ABBREVIATIONS AND SIGNS EMPLOYED IN NOTES AND TEXT

AC: the *Apostolic Constitutions* (ed. Funk).

Achelis: *Die syrische Didaskalia*, übersetzt und erklärt von Hans Achelis und Johs. Flemming (Texte und Untersuchungen, N.F. X 2, 1904).

Flemming: as under 'Achelis' (Flemming was the translator: see p. xxiii. *ante*).

Funk: *Didascalia et Constitutiones Apostolorum*, ed. Franciscus Xaverius Funk (Paderborn, 1905).

Hauler: *Didascaliae apostolorum fragmenta Veronensia latina*, etc., ed. Edmundus Hauler (Leipzig, 1900): see pp. xviii ff. *ante*.

Irenaeus: the *Heresies* according to Harvey's edition. For the *Demonstration of the Apostolic Preaching* Dr. Armitage Robinson's translation of the Armenian is employed (S.P.C.K., 1920).

Lat.: the Latin version of the *Didascalia* (see under 'Hauler').

Pesh.: the Peshitta or Syriac version of the Bible: but here with exclusion of the Gospels, for which see '*syr. vulg.*'

Resch: *Agrapha, aussercanonische Schriftfragmente*, gesammelt und untersucht von Alfred Resch: revised edition, 1906 (Texte u. Untersuch. N.F. XV 3-4).

Ropes: *Die Sprüche Jesu die in den kanonischen Evangelien nicht überliefert sind*, James Hardy Ropes (Texte u. Untersuch. XIV 1, 1896).

Syr.: the Syriac version of the *Didascalia*. For the MSS. B (Borgian), C (Cambridge), H (Harris), S (St-Germain, Paris) see pp. xi ff. *ante*.

syr. cur.: the Curetonian MS. of the Old Syriac version of the Gospels.

syr. sin.: the Sinaitic MS. of the same.

syr. vet.: the Old Syriac version of the Gospels.

syr. vulg.: the Syriac Vulgate, or Peshitta: but here only with reference to the Gospels.

Round brackets ( ) denote that the words included are added in the English translation to help out the sense.

Square brackets [ ] denote that the words or letters included are probably to be omitted.

Pointed brackets ⟨ ⟩ denote that the words or letters included are probably to be supplied.

In the English translation references in round brackets, as (p. 10), are to the pages of Lagarde's edition of the Syriac, on which this translation is mainly based; references in square brackets, as [ii. 15], are to book and chapter of the *Didascalia* as in Funk's edition. In the Latin, references like [XX] are to the surviving pages of the Verona palimpsest as numbered consecutively in Hauler's edition.

Asterisks * ... * in the English translation signify that an evident mistranslation in the Syriac has been corrected in the text and the source of the error explained in the notes.

Daggers † ... † signify that a word or passage is thought to be corrupt; or (in the English) that the Syriac translator has probably misunderstood the original Greek.

TRANSLATION OF THE SYRIAC
WITH
THE LATIN FRAGMENTS

THE CATHOLIC DIDASCALIA
THAT IS TEACHING
OF THE TWELVE HOLY APOSTLES AND DISCIPLES OF OUR SAVIOUR

CHAPTER I
On the simple and natural Law.

GOD'S planting and the holy vineyard of His Catholic Church, the elect, who rely on the simplicity of the fear of the Lord, who by their faith inherit His everlasting kingdom, who have received the power and fellowship of His Holy Spirit, and by Him are armed and made firm in the fear of Him, who are become partakers *in the sprinkling of the* pure and precious *blood of* the Great God, *Jesus Christ*, who have received boldness to call the Almighty God Father, as joint heirs and partakers with His Son and His beloved : hear the Didascalia of God, you that hope and wait for His promises, which hath been written after the command of our Saviour and is in accord with His glorious words.

[i. 1] Give heed, children of God, and do all things so that you be obedient to God; and be you pleasing in all things to the Lord our God. For if any man run after iniquity and be contrary to the will of God, the same shall be accounted unto God as heathen and ungodly. Flee therefore and depart from all avarice and evil dealing. And you shall not desire that

---

4 Cf. 2 Cor. xiii 13.　6. 1 Pet. i 2.　7–8 Cf. 1 Pet. i 17.　8 Cf. Rom. viii 17, Eph. iii 6:

On the title see the Introduction. Three times in the course of the work it is described as 'this Catholic Didascalia' (pp. 204, 210, 214). 2 on the simplicity of the fear of the Lord] εἰς τὴν ἀπλανῆ θεοσέβειαν αὐτοῦ AC (= Lat.). Syr. has read ἁπλῆν for ἀπλανῆ. 'Fear of the Lord (*or* God)' is the Syriac equivalent of 'religion'.　3 their] Relative clauses in an address are commonly thrown into the 3rd person in Syriac; AC has a series of participles.　7 the great God, *Jesus*] om. AC (= Lat.).　10 of God] ἱερὰν AC. So elsewhere Syr. renders both ἱερός and θεῖος.

[I] DEI plantatio uineae catolica ecclesia eius et electi sunt, qui crediderunt in eam quae sine errore est uera religio, qui aeternum regnum fructuantur et per fidem regni eius uirtutem acceperunt et participationem sancti eius spiritus, armati
5 per ipsum et succincti timorem eius, *asparsionis* participes honorificandi et innocentis *sanguinis Christi*, qui fiduciam acceperunt omnipotentem Deum patrem uocare, coheredes et conparticipes dilecti pueri eius. Audite doctrinam sacram, qui promissionem eius desideratis, ex iussione saluatoris consen-
10 tienter gloriosis sonitiis eius.

Custodite, Dei fili, omnia ad oboedientiam Dei agere, et estote beneplacentes in omnibus domino Deo nostro. Si quis enim iniquitatem sectetur et ea quae contraria sunt nomini domini Dei nostri agat, ut gens iniqua aput Deum qui eiusmodi
15 est aestimabitur. Abstinete igitur ab omni auaritia et malitia,

---

1–2 Dei plantatio . . . crediderunt] φυτεία θεοῦ καὶ ἀμπελὼν ἡ καθολικὴ ἐκκλησία Epiphan. *Haer.* xlv 4 (cf. Syr.) : θεοῦ φυτεία ἡ καθολικὴ ἐκκλησία καὶ ἀμπελὼν αὐτοῦ ἐκλεκτός, οἱ πεπιστευκότες κτλ. *AC* (prob. with disturbance of the original order). Lat. might perhaps be emended 'Dei plantatio ⟨et⟩ uinea[e], catholica ecclesia eius, [et] electi [sunt]', etc. But the translator did not see that the Proem is an address in the vocative. 9–10 consentienter, etc.] ὁμοστοίχως ταῖς ἐνδόξοις φθογγαῖς αὐτοῦ *AC*. 13 nomini] τῷ θελήματι *AC* (= Syr.). Hauler and Funk alter to 'numini', but we should not expect this as a rendering of τῷ θελήματι.

---

17 as heathen and ungodly] ὡς παράνομον ἔθνος *AC*.   18 And] H : 'For' CS.

which is any man's, for it is written in the Law: *Thou shalt not desire aught of that which is thy neighbour's: neither his field, nor his wife, nor his servant, nor his maidservant, nor his ox, nor his ass, nor any thing of his possessions.* For all these desires are from the Evil One. For he that desires the wife of his companion, or his servant, or his maidservant, is already an adulterer and a thief, and is condemned of uncleanness, as they that lie with males, by our Lord and Teacher Jesus Christ: to whom (is) glory and honour for ever and ever, Amen. As also in the Gospel He renews and confirms and fulfils the Ten Words of the Law, (saying): *For it is written in the Law: Thou shalt not commit adultery: but I say unto you* this,—who in the Law spake through Moses, but now myself (p. 2) say unto you: *Whosoever shall look upon the wife of his neighbour to desire her, hath already committed adultery with her in his heart.* And thus was he who desired condemned as an adulterer. He also that desires the ox or the ass of his neighbour, it is to steal and to lead it away that he is minded. And he again that desires the field of his companion, does he not seek to straiten him in his boundary, and contrive that he may sell it to him for nothing? For this cause therefore come slayings and deaths and condemnations from God upon these persons.

But for men who obey God there is one law, simple and true and mild—without question, for Christians—this, that *what thou hatest that it should be done to thee by another, thou do not to another.* Thou wouldst not that a man should look

---

1 Ex. xx 17, Deut. v 21.   11 Mt. v 27 f.   26 Cf. Tob. iv 15.

1–4 *Thou shalt not . . . possessions*] οὐκ ἐπιθυμήσεις τὴν γυναῖκα τοῦ πλησίον σου οὐδὲ τὸν ἀγρὸν αὐτοῦ οὐδὲ τὸν παῖδα αὐτοῦ οὔτε τὴν παιδίσκην αὐτοῦ οὔτε τοῦ βοὸς αὐτοῦ οὔτε τοῦ ὑποζυγίου αὐτοῦ οὔτε ὅσα τοῦ πλησίον σου ἐστίν *AC*.   7–8 *and . . . males*] Probably a paraphrase of καὶ ὡς φθορεὺς κέκριται (cp. *Ep. Barnab.* x 7, *Didache* v 2): 'et ut corruptor iudicatus' Lat.: καὶ κέκριται (only) *AC*.   9–10 *to whom . . . Amen*] ᾧ ἡ δόξα εἰς τοὺς αἰῶνας· ἀμήν *AC*.   20–21 *does he not . . . for nothing*] οὐ πονηρεύεται ὅπως ὁρογλυφήσας ἀναγκάσῃ τὸν ἔχοντα τοῦ μηδενὸς ἀποδόσθαι αὐτῷ; *AC*.   25 *mild*] (or 'pleasant') BCS: om. H: ζῶν *AC*. The Syriac adj. *baṣṣīma* is regular as a rendering of χρηστός.   *without question, for Christians*] BCS ('question' is ζήτημα transliterated): 'that is, thou shalt not cause *zetemata* to Christians' (*sic*) H: om. *AC*. I take the words to be paren-

et nihil concupiscitis; nam et in lege scriptum est: *Non concupiscis uxorem proximi tui aut puerum aut puellam eius:* quoniam omne quod tale est desiderium de maligno est. Qui enim desiderauerit uxorem proximi aut puerum aut puellam eius, iam adulter et fur est, et ut corruptor iudicatus a domino et doctore nostro Iesu Christo, cui est gloria in saecula, Amen. Dicit enim in euangelio, recapitulans et confirmans et conplens decalogum legis, *quoniam in lege scribtum est: Non moechaberis: ego autem dico uobis*—id est, in lege per Moysen locutus sum, nunc autem ipse uobis dico: *Omnis quicumque intenderit in mulierem proximi sui ad concupiscendum eam,* ⟨*iam moechatus est eam*⟩ *in corde* [II] *suo.* †Iste iudicatus est moechus, quoniam † desiderauit. Qui autem bouem aut asinum concupiscit proximi sui, nonne furare et abducere cogitat ea? Aut hic iterum qui agrum desiderat, non id malignatur, ut terminos eius inuadens cog[it]at eum pro nihilo ei distrahere rem suam? Propter haec igitur homicidia, mortes, condemnationes a D⟨eo⟩ eos qui tales sunt subsecuntur.

Eis autem hominibus qui oboediunt Deo una lex est sinplex, uera, sine quaestione Christianis constituta, ita: *Quod tibi fieri ab alio non uis, tu alio ne feceris.* Non uis uxorem tuam ut

---

11–12 ⟨*iam* ... *eam*⟩ ... iudicatus est] ἤδη ἐμοίχευσεν αὐτὴν ἐν τῇ καρδίᾳ αὐτοῦ. οὕτως ἐκρίθη μοιχὸς κατ' ἔννοιαν ὁ ἐπιθυμήσας *AC* (cf. Syr.). In the last clause Lat. surely must have had originally 'Ita iudicatus est moechus qui desiderauit' (so Funk restores): 'iste' and 'quoniam' being readjustments occasioned by the dropping out of 'iam moechatus est eam' just before. 16 distrahere] See again p. 273, l. 4, where the form 'detraheremus' appears. 17–18 a D(eo) eos] So Funk emends: παρὰ τοῦ θεοῦ τοιούτοις *AC* (= Syr.): 'ad eos' Hauler. 20 ita] 'itaq(ue)' cod.

---

thetical; if this is right, as I believe, there appears to be a play on χρηστός (see preceding note) and Χριστιανός. 25–27 that *what* ... *another*] ὃ σὺ μισεῖς ὑφ' ἑτέρου σοὶ γενέσθαι, σὺ ἄλλῳ οὐ ποιήσεις *AC*. See again p. 145.

upon thy wife evilly to corrupt her : neither look thou upon the wife of thy companion with evil intent. Thou wouldst not that a man should take away thy garment : neither do thou take away that of another. Thou wouldst not be reviled and insulted, or beaten : neither do thou to another any one of these things. [i. 2] But if a man revile thee, do thou bless him ; for it is written in the Book of Numbers : *He that blesseth is blessed, and he that curseth is cursed.* And in the Gospel also it is written again : *Bless them that curse you.* And to them that do you evil, do not you evil ; and *do good to them that hate you*, and be patient and endure, for the Scripture saith : *Thou shalt not say: I will render to mine enemy evil, even as he hath done to me: but be patient, and the Lord will be thy helper, and will bring a recompense upon him that doeth thee evil.* And again He saith in the Gospel : *Love them that hate you, and pray for them that curse you, and ye shall have no enemy.* Let us attend then, our beloved, and understand these commandments and keep them, that we may be sons of the light.

7 Cf. Nu. xxiv 9 (comp. Gen. xxvii 29). 9 Lk. vi 28 (Mt. v 44). 10 Lk. vi 27. 12 Prov. xx 22. 15 Mt. v 44, Lk. vi 27 f. : *Didache* i 3. 18–19 Cf. Joh. xii 36, Eph. v 8, 1 Thes. v 5.

1–6 Cf. *Hom. Clem.* vii 4 ἅπερ ἕκαστος ἑαυτῷ βούλεται καλά, τὰ αὐτὰ βουλευέσθω καὶ τῷ πλησίον … οὐ θέλεις φονευθῆναι, ἕτερον μὴ φονεύσῃς· οὐ θέλεις τὴν σὴν ὑφ᾿ ἑτέρου μοιχευθῆναι γυναῖκα, τὴν ἑτέρου μὴ μοίχευε γαμετήν· οὐ θέλεις τι τῶν σῶν κλαπῆναι, ἑτέρου μὴ κλέπτε μηδέν. 10–11 and *do good . . . hate you*] om. *AC* (= Lat.). 16–17 *and ye shall have no enemy*] om. *AC* here ; but in vii 2, 2 we have φιλεῖτε τοὺς μισοῦντας ὑμᾶς, καὶ ἐχθρὸν οὐχ ἕξετε, from *Didache* i 3 which is doubtless the source of *Didasc.* in the present passage. On this and other points of contact with the *Didache* the reader is referred to an article in the *Journal of Theol. Studies* xxiv, pp. 147–157 : Jan. 1923 (' The use of the *Didache* in the *Didascalia* '). 18 sons of the light] See again pp. 93, 110.

quis attendat in malo ad corrumpendum eam : nec tu proximi
tui mulierem adtendas in malo. Non uis palleum tuum ab
alio tolli : nec tu alio tuleris. Non uis uulnerari aut iniuriam
pati aut detractari de te: nec tu alio ita facies. Sed maledi-
5 cat te quis, tu benedic illum, quoniam scribtum est in libro
Numerum : *Qui benedicit, benedicetur, et qui maledicit, maledictus erit.* Propterea similiter et in euangelio scribtum est:
Benedicite maledicentes uos. Eos qui uos nocent nolite reno-
cere, sed sustinete, quoniam dicit scribtura : *Ne dicas: Noceam
10 inimicum meum, quoniam me nocuit: sed sustine, ut dominus
tibi adiubet et uindictam faciat super eum qui te nocuit.* Nam
iterum in euangelio dicit : *Diligite odientes uos, et orate pro
maledicentibus uos, et inimicum nullum habebitis.* Intenti
igitur simus mandatis istis, dilectissimi, ut fili lucis inueniamur
15 cum ea agimus.

1 in malo] κακῶς AC.   2 in malo] κακοήθως AC: 'with evil intent
Syr.

CHAPTER II

Teaching every man that he should please his wife alone; and that he should not adorn himself and become a cause of stumbling to women; and that he should not love idleness; and that he should occupy himself with the Scriptures of life, and avoid profane writings and the bonds of the Second Legislation; and that he should not bathe in a bath with women; and that he should not give himself to the vice of harlots.

[i. 3] Bear with one another, O servants and sons of God. Let not a man despise or contemn his wife, nor be lifted up against her; but let him be merciful, and let his hand be open to give. (p. 3) And let him please his wife alone, and cherish her with honour; and let him study to be loved by her alone, and by none other. Adorn not thyself that a strange woman may see and desire thee. And if indeed thou be constrained by her and sin with her, death in fire shall come upon thee of a surety from God, even that which abides for ever, which is in sore and bitter fire; and thou shalt know and understand when thou art grievously tormented. But if thou do not this uncleanness, but put her from thee and deny her: in this only hast thou sinned, that by thy adornment thou hast caused the woman to be taken with the desire of thee; for thou hast caused her, to whom it so happened by reason of thee, to commit adultery through her desire. But not so art thou under sin, because thou didst not desire her: but there shall be mercy upon thee from the Lord, because thou didst not deliver thyself to her nor consent to her when she sent unto thee, neither

---

1 Cf. Gal. vi 2.

1-2 Bear with ... his wife] βαστάζετε οὖν, οἱ δοῦλοι καὶ υἱοὶ τοῦ θεοῦ, ἀλλήλους· ὁ μὲν ἀνὴρ τὴν γυναῖκα, μὴ ὑπερήφανος, κτλ. *AC*. The Syriac verb means to endure or put up with: βαστάζειν in this sense is rare (cf. βαστάσαι κακούς in Apoc. ii 2). 3-4 hand be open to give] A paraphrase of εὐμετάδοτος (*AC*): so again at p. 32, l. 27. 12 put her ... deny her] ἀποσεισάμενος αὐτὴν ἀρνήσῃ αὐτό (sc. 'this uncleanness'—τὸ μύσος) *AC*; but one MS. has αὐτήν, and lower down we find ἠρνήσω αὐτήν (p. 10, l. 4, Funk p. 11, l. 4). 16 But not so, etc.] ἀλλ' οὐχ οὕτως αἴτιος ὑπάρχεις *AC*.

Portate ergo sicuti serui et filii Dei inuicem, ita ut uir mulierem suam non ut superbus aut elatus . . .

in thought didst thou turn thyself to that woman who was taken with the desire of thee: but she on a sudden encountered thee, and was stricken in her thought and sent unto thee; but thou as a godfearing man didst deny her and avoid her, and didst not sin with her; but she was stricken in her heart, because thou art young and fair and comely, and didst adorn thyself and cause her to desire thee: and thou art found to be guilty of the sin of her to whom it so happened by reason of thy adornment. But entreat of the Lord God that sin be not ascribed to thee on this account. And if thou wouldst please God and not men, and lookest and hopest for the life and rest everlasting, adorn not thy natural beauty which is given thee from God, but with humility of neglect make it mean before men. In like manner also thou shalt not nourish the hair of thy head, but do thou shear it off; and thou shalt not comb and adorn it, nor anoint it, lest thou bring upon thee such women as ensnare, or are ensnared, by lust. Neither shalt thou put on fine raiment, nor be shod on thy feet with shoes which are fashioned according to the lust of folly; nor shalt thou put upon thy fingers rings of gold device: for all these things are the wiles of harlotry, and every thing that thou dost apart from nature. For to thee, a faithful man of God, it is not permitted to nourish the hair of thy head and to comb and smooth it, which is a wantonness of lust; neither shalt thou arrange and adorn it, nor adjust it so that it may be beautiful. And thou shalt not destroy the hairs of thy beard, (p. 4) nor

---

26 Cf. Lev. xix 27.

7–8 thou art found to be guilty] C : 'thou findest (? thyself) guilty' BHS (a construction which can hardly be justified): ἔνοχος εὑρίσκῃ σύ AC. 13 mean] lit. 'poor'. 18–19 nor be shod ... folly] μηδὲ ἀναξυρίδας ἢ κρηπῖδάς σου τοῖς ποσὶ κακοτέχνως ὑπορράψῃς AC. 20 rings of gold device] χρυσήλατον σφενδόνην AC. 22 apart from nature] παρὰ τὸ προσῆκον AC. Flemming accordingly vocalizes the word for 'nature' as if it were the adj. 'right', 'just', and translates 'und es ist alles (derartig), dass du (damit) wider das Rechte handelst'; but for this we should require the subst. kēnūtha, the adj. here would be untranslatable. I see no reason to alter the text, which gives a good sense. 26 And ... thy beard] ('destroy' is lit. 'corrupt'): χρὴ δὲ οὐδὲ γενείου τρίχα διαφθείρειν AC. Cf. Epiphan. Haer. lxxx 7 ἐν ταῖς διατάξεσι τῶν ἀποστόλων φάσκει ὁ θεῖος λόγος καὶ ἡ διδασκαλία μὴ φθείρειν, τουτέστι μὴ τέμνειν, τρίχας γενείου.

alter the natural form of thy face and change it to other than God created it, because that thou desirest to please men. But if thou do these things, thy soul shall be deprived of life, and thou shalt be rejected before the Lord God. As a man therefore who would please God, take heed thou do no such things; and avoid all those things which the Lord hateth.

[i. 4] And thou shalt not stray and go about idly in the streets and see the vain spectacle of those who behave themselves evilly; but be thou always attending to thy craft and thy work, and be willing to do those things that are pleasing to God; and thou shalt be meditating constantly upon the words of the Lord. [i. 5] But if thou art rich and hast no need of a craft whereby to live, thou shalt not stray and go about vacantly; but be ever constant in drawing near to the faithful and to them that are like-minded with thee, and be meditating and learning with them the living words. And if not, sit at home and read the Law, and the Book of Kings and the Prophets,

---

1 the natural form, etc.] lit. 'the form of the nature of thy face' (see below p. 26, l. 5). 14 but be ever, etc.] ἀλλ' εἴτε προσέρχῃ τοῖς πιστοῖς τε καὶ ὁμοδόξοις, συμβάλλων τὰ ζωοποιὰ προσομιλεῖ ῥήματα AC. Comp. *Didache* iv 2 ἐκζητήσεις δὲ καθ' ἡμέραν τὰ πρόσωπα τῶν ἁγίων, ἵνα ἐπαναπαῇς τοῖς λόγοις αὐτῶν.

and the Gospel the fulfilment of these. [i. 6] But avoid all books of the heathen. For what hast thou to do with strange sayings or laws or lying prophecies, which also turn away from the faith them that are young? For what is wanting to thee in the word of God, that thou shouldst cast thyself upon these fables of the heathen? If thou wouldst read historical narratives, thou hast the Book of Kings; but if wise men and philosophers, thou hast the Prophets, wherein thou shalt find wisdom and understanding more than that of the wise men and philosophers; for they are the words of the one God, the only wise. And if thou wish for songs, thou hast the Psalms of David; but if (thou wouldst read of) the beginning of the world, thou hast the Genesis of the great Moses; and if laws and commandments, thou hast *the glorious Law* of the Lord God. All strange (writings) therefore, which are contrary (to these), wholly avoid.

Yet when thou readest the Law, beware of the Second Legislation, that thou do but read it merely; but the commands and warnings that are therein much avoid, lest thou lead thyself astray and bind thyself with the bonds which may not be loosed of heavy burdens. For this cause therefore, if thou read the Second Legislation, consider this alone, that thou know and glorify God who delivered us from all these bonds. And have this set before thine eyes, that thou discern (p. 5) and know what [in the Law] is the Law, and what are the bonds that are in the Second Legislation, which after the Law were given to those who, in the Law and in the Second Legislation,

---

4 them that are young] τοὺς ἐλαφρούς *AC*. 7–8 wise men and philosophers] σοφιστικὰ κ. ποιητικά *AC*. 9 wisdom and understanding] ἀγχίνοιαν *AC*. For 'understanding' cod. H has 'erudition'. 9–10 more than ... philosophers] πάσης ποιήσεως κ. σοφιστείας πλείονα *AC*. 12–13 the beginning of the world] ἀρχαιογονίας *AC*. 13–14 of ... Moses] om. *AC* (= Lat.). 14–15 the glorious Law] We must restore this from Lat. and *AC*: Syr. has 'the Law, the Book of Exodus', misreading ἔνδοξον (*AC*) as ἔξοδον, and then supplying 'the Book of'. 15–16 which are contrary] καὶ διαβολικῶν *AC*. 17–18 of the Second Legislation] BCH, S marg.: τῶν τῆς δευτερώσεως *AC* (see note to Lat.). 19–20 lead thyself astray and] om. Lat. (*AC* differently). 25 in the Law] CS : om. H *AC* Lat.

[III] ... et euangelium, plenitudinem eorum omnium. Gentiles autem libros penitus ne tetigeris. Quid enim tibi est cum alienis uerbis uel legibus aut pseudoprofetis, quae facile leuioribus hominibus errorem praestant? Nam quid tibi deest in uerbo Dei, ut ad illas gentiles fabulas [as]pergas? Si uis storias † legere, discurre, et † habes Regnorum ; si autem sofistica et poetica, habes Profetas, in quibus totius poetiae et sofistiae maiorem †narrationem† inuenies, quoniam domini, qui solus est, sapientia et sonitus sunt. Si uero canticorum desideras, habes Psalmos ; si autem initium generationis mundi, habes Genesim ; aut si leges et praecepta, habes gloriosam domini legem. Ab omnibus igitur his tam alienis et diabolicis scribturis fortiter te abstine.

Tamen et cum legem legis, ... ab omnibus praeceptis eius et † creaturis † longe te abstine, ut non te ueteribus et qui non possunt solui laqueis conliges et [h]oneres. Nam etsi aliquando legis bis, tantum ad hoc lege, ut scias et magnifices Deum, quia de tantis et talibus nos ligaturis eripuit. Hoc autem tibi sit ante oculos, ut cognoscas quid est lex et quae post legem secunda legatio his qui per legem et per repetitam †alligationem † [eorum qui] in deserto tanta peccauerunt, et

1,-2 Gentiles ... ne tetigeris] τῶν ἐθνικῶν βιβλίων πάντων ἀπέχου *AC* (= Syr). 4 leuioribus ... praestant] παρατρέπει τῆς πίστεως τοὺς ἐλαφρούς *AC* (cf. Syr.). 5 [as]pergas] The initial *as* is prob. by dittography from the previous word: ὁρμήσῃς *AC*. 5–6 Si uis storias ... et habes] εἴτε γὰρ ἱστορικὰ θέλεις διέρχεσθαι, ἔχεις *AC*. Lat. may have had originally 'storias discurrere, habes', 'legere' being a gloss which led to the change 'discurre et'. 8 narrationem] ἀγχίνοιαν *AC* (cf. Syr.). The original word in Lat. may have been some such unfamiliar coinage as 'gnarationem'. 8–9 quoniam ... sonitus sunt] ὅτι κυρίου τοῦ μόνου σοφοῦ φθογγαί εἰσιν *AC* (= Syr.). 13 scribturis] om. *AC* (= Syr.). 14 legis] After this a clause is wanting (cf. Syr.) : *AC* reads, evidently with some alteration, πλὴν καὶ τὸν νόμον ἀναγινώσκων τῶν ἐν αὐτῷ ἐπεισάκτων ἀπόσχου, εἰ καὶ μὴ πάντων, ἀλλά τινων, τῶν τῆς δευτερώσεως. 15 creaturis] I suspect that this is a corruption of some less familiar word, but can offer no suggestion. ueteribus et] om. Syr. (*AC* omits the whole clause). 17 bis] This represents δευτέρως, adopted out of δευτέρωσιν, which the translator at first fails to understand ; cf. Syr. (*AC* has altered). 20 secunda legatio] (ἔστω δέ σοι πρὸ ὀφθαλμῶν γινώσκειν, τί νόμος φυσικός καὶ τί) τὰ τῆς δευτερώσεως *AC* (cf. Syr.). The translator is feeling after a rendering for δευτέρωσις. 20–21 et per repetitam alligationem] 'and in the Second Legislation' Syr. : 'alligationem' would seem therefore to be a corruption of 'legationem', the word used just before. *AC* has made alteration here.

committed so many sins in the wilderness. For the first Law is that which the Lord God spoke before the people had made the calf and served idols, which consists of the Ten Words and the Judgements. But after they had served idols, He justly laid upon them the bonds, as they were worthy. But do not thou therefore lay them upon thee; for our Saviour came for no other cause but to fulfil the Law, and to set us loose from the bonds of the Second Legislation. For He set loose from those bonds and thus called those who believe in Him, and said: *Come unto me, all ye that toil and are laden with heavy burdens, and I will give you rest.* Do thou therefore, without the weight of these burdens, read the simple Law, which is in accord with the Gospel; and moreover the Gospel itself, and the Prophets; and the Book of Kings likewise, that thou mayest know that as many kings as were righteous were both advanced by the Lord God in this world, and continued in God's promise of everlasting life; but those kings who turned aside from God and served idols did justly, by a summary judgement, perish miserably, and were deprived of the kingdom of God, and instead of (obtaining) rest are punished. When therefore thou readest these things, thou wilt grow the more in faith and be improved.

And afterwards rise up, go forth to the market-place and bathe in a bath of men: but not in one of women, lest, when thou hast stripped thyself and shewn the nakedness of thy bare body,

---

10–11 Mt. xi 28.

1 first] om. *AC* (= Lat.). Compare Irenaeus *Haer.* IV xxv 3 'Nam Deus primo quidem per naturalia praecepta, quae ab initio infixa dedit hominibus, admonens eos, id est per decalogum, ... nihil plus ab eis exquisiuit'; then IV xxvi 1 'At ubi conuersi sunt in uituli factionem ... aptam concupiscentiae suae acceperunt reliquam seruitutem'; and IV xxviii 'decalogi quidem uerba ipse per semetipsum omnibus similiter dominus locutus est ... Seruitutis autem praecepta separatim per Moysem praecepit populo apta illorum eruditioni siue castigationi'. Compare also the argument at pp. 218, 224, 230. 3 consists of] lit. 'is'. The 'Judgements' must be the δικαιώματα of Ex. xxi 1 ff. (see again p. 218). 8–9 For He ... called] See again p. 226, and note. 15 as many kings, etc.] Comp. Hippolytus *in Dan.* lib. iii, c. 4 (ed. Bonwetsch p. 126, l. 1) ὥστε ὅσοι βασιλεῖς εὐλαβῶς καὶ θεοφιλῶς ἀνεστράφησαν, οὗτοι καὶ παρὰ θεοῦ ἐτιμήθησαν, ὅσοι δὲ κατὰ φυσίωσιν ὑπὲρ τὸ δέον ἐπήρθησαν, οὗτοι ἀξίαν καὶ δικαίαν τὴν παρὰ τοῦ θεοῦ τιμωρίαν ἀπέλαβον (after speaking of the punishment of

DIDASCALIA APOSTOLORUM 15

quanta eis inposuit onera. Lex autem est, quae locutus est dominus Deus antequam populus uitulum faceret et ad idolatriam conuerteretur, id est decalogus et iudicia. Et ea autem quae post idolatriam eis mandauit et digne † ut legationes † in-
5 posuit, [IV] tu autem tibi uincula noli adtrahere ; nam saluator noster propter nihil aliud uenit, nisi ut legem inpleat et uincula secundationis legis infirmaret. Unde eos qui de plebe ei crediderunt soluens ab ipsis uinculis ita eos uocauit dicens: *Uenite ad me, omnes qui laboratis et [h]onerati estis*. Tu ergo, qui
10 sine [h]onere es et legis sinplicem et euuangelio consonantem legem, et ipsud euuangelium, et Prophetas, nec non et Regnorum, scire debes ex ipsis, quia quanticumque iusti fuerunt reges a domino multiplicati sunt in hoc saeculo, et repromissio perpetue uite eis in regno Dei permanet; quanticumque autem
15 reges idololatr[e]ae et praeuaricatores fuerunt a Deo, pessime in celeritate perierunt, et a regno Dei alienati sunt, et pro refrigerio poenam exceperunt. Ergo haec cum leges, ualde poteris in fide crescere et aedificari.

Et iterum cum in foro ambulas, balneas uiriles utere, ut non,
20 cum ostendis corpus tuum reuelatum in confusione, et tu in

4–5 ut legationes . . . tibi uincula] ἃ δὲ ἁμαρτήσασιν αὐτοῖς ἐπετέθη δεσμά, σὺ ἑαυτῷ μὴ ἐπισπάσῃ *AC*:. therefore 'ut legationes' is prob. for 'ut ligationes', and a rendering of δεσμά which becomes redundant through the following 'uincula'. 7 secundationis legis] The translator has at last fixed upon a rendering of δευτέρωσις, and henceforth uses either 'secundatio legis' or, perhaps more often, 'secundatio' alone. infirmaret] παύσῃ *AC*. de plebe] om. Syr.: ἡμᾶς (only) *AC*. 9 estis]+ κἀγὼ ἀναπαύσω ὑμᾶς *AC* (= Syr.). Supply 'et ego repausabo uos' (see pp. 99, 227). 14 in regno Dei] om. *AC* (= Syr.). 15–16 in celeritate] συντόμως . . . τῇ τοῦ θεοῦ δικαιοκρισίᾳ *AC* (cf. Syr.). 20 f. et tu . . . laqueari] ἢ σὺ παγιδευθῇς ἢ παγιδεύσῃς ἐπὶ σεαυτῷ *AC* (cf. Syr.).

Nebuchadnezzer and the death of Antiochus Epiphanes). 16 advanced] lit. 'known', which is also used in the above sense: ηὐξήθησαν *AC*. 16–17 and continued . . . life] καὶ ἡ ἐπαγγελία τῆς αἰωνίου ζωῆς αὐτοῖς διέμεινεν παρ' αὐτῷ *AC* (cf. Lat.). 23 and afterwards rise up] om. *AC* (= Lat.). 24 but not . . . women] om. *AC* (= Lat.). 25 the nakedness . . . body] lit. 'the nakedness of the exposure of thy body': (ἵνα μὴ διὰ) τὸ ἐπιδεικνύναι σε σῶμα ἐν ἀσχήμῳ ἀποκαλύψει *AC*.

either thou be ensnared, or thou constrain another and she slip and be ensnared by thee. Beware of these things therefore, and thou shalt live unto God.

[i. 7] Learn, then, what saith the holy word in Wisdom: *¹ My son, keep my words, and my commandments hide within thee. My son, honour the Lord, and be strengthened; and beside him thou shalt fear none other. ² Keep my commandments, and live well, and my laws as the apple of thine eye; ³ and bind them upon thy fingers, and write them on the tables of thy heart. ⁴ And say to wisdom: Thou art my sister, and make known to thy soul understanding: ⁵ that she may keep thee from a strange and adulterous woman, whose words are flattering. ⁶ For from the window of her house and from the porch she looked forth into the streets; ⁷ and whomsoever she saw of the youths that are simple and lack understanding, ⁸ that pass in the street beside the corners of the paths of her house, ⁹ and speak in the darkness, at even and in the gloom of the stillness of the night: ¹⁰ then the woman went forth and met him* (p. 6), *in the harlot's dress that fluttereth the heart of youths. ¹¹ And she is wanton and bold and dissolute: and her feet cannot be quiet in her house; ¹² but now she roameth abroad, and now she lurketh in the streets and in the corners. ¹³ And she caught him and kissed him, and made her face impudent, and said to him: ¹⁴ Sacrifices I have, even peace offerings, to-day do I pay my vows: ¹⁵ therefore am I come forth to meet thee; for I was looking to see thee, and I have found thee. ¹⁶ I have spread my couch with a coverlet, and with rugs of Egypt have I overlaid it: ¹⁷ I have sprinkled saffron upon my couch, and cinnamon in my house. ¹⁸ Come, let us take our pleasure with love until morning, and let us embrace each other with desire. ¹⁹ For my husband is not at home: he is gone a long journey, ²⁰ and hath taken a bag of money in his hand; and after many days will he come to his house. ²¹ And she beguiled him with her many words, and with the flattery of her lips she drew him unto her. ²² And he went after her like a simpleton, and as an ox that*

---

5 Prov. vii 1–27.

1 another] Perhaps only a scribe's error for 'a woman'—the words are similar in form.   3 live unto God] An expression occurring repeatedly

laqueo incidas et †facile† facias mulierem in te laqueari.
Obserua ergo ne talia agas, et uiuis Deo.

Discamus uero in Sapientia quid dicat sanctum uerbum :
¹ *Fili, custodi mea uerba, et mea mandata absconde aput te
ipsum : fili, honora Deum, et ualebis plus, et absque illo alium
ne timeas.* ² *Custodi mea mandata, et bene poteris uiuere, mea
autem uerba sicut pupillam oculi :* ³ *inpone digitis tuis et scribe ea
in latitudine cordis tui.* ⁴ *Dic sapientiam sororem tuam esse,
notam autem prudentiam fac tibi,* ⁵ *ut te custodiat a* [V] *muliere
aliena et maligna, si te uerbis gratiosis coeperit abalienare.*
⁶ *De fenestra enim domus suae in plateis prospiciens,* ⁷ *quemcumque uiderit iuuenem insipientem* ⁸ *transeuntem per angulum
itinere domus eius et loquentem* ⁹ *in tenebris uespertinis, cum
nocturna quies est,* ¹⁰ *mulier autem ei occurrit speciem habens
meretricis, quae facit iuuenum euolare corda :* ¹¹ *luxuriosa est
autem et effrenata, in domo autem non quiescunt pedes eius :*
¹² *tempore enim aliquo foris uagatur, tempus autem in plateis
per omnes angulos obsedet.* ¹³ *Et post haec adpraehendens osculata est eum, inruborato autem uultu dicit ad eum :* ¹⁴ *Sacrificium
pacificum mihi est, hodie reddo uota mea.* ¹⁵ *Propter hoc exii in
occursu tuo, desiderans faciem tuam, inueni te.* ¹⁶ *Institis extendi lectum meum, tapetis autem straui ab Aegypto :* ¹⁷ *asparsi
lectum meum de croco, domum autem meam de cinnamomo.
Ueni, et fruamur amicitias usque ad lucem, ueni, inuoluamur
in amore.* ¹⁹ *Non enim est maritus meus in domo, abiit iter*

---

1 facile] om. *AC* (= Syr.). The letters *faci* are at the end of a line, where perhaps the scribe had begun to copy 'facias'.

---

in Hermas. Elsewhere in *Didasc.* we find 'live before God', pp. 113, 163, 165.   4 Wisdom] Eusebius, *H.E.* iv 22, tells us that Hegesippus, as well as Irenaeus and ὁ πᾶς τῶν ἀρχαίων χορός, called Proverbs ἡ πανάρετος σοφία. So 1 Clem. lvii 3, while 'Wisdom' simply is found in Justin *Dial.* 129, Melito *apud* Euseb. *H.E.* iv 26, and Clem. Alex. See Lightfoot's note to 1 Clem. lvii 3.   Our author uses 'Wisdom' about ten, and 'Proverbs' about six times.   7 *other*] CH LXX : 'others' BS.   9 *tables*] So Pesh. : ἐπὶ τὸ πλάτος LXX (*AC* omits the verse 3).   12 *adulterous*] = πόρνης, for πονηρᾶς (*AC* LXX) : Pesh. has 'strange'.   *whose words are flattering*] As Pesh.   13 *and from the porch*] An addition from Pesh., which has the same Gk. word ξυστήριον.   15–16 *that pass . . . of her house*] As Pesh.

goeth to the slaughter, and as a dog to the leash, ²³ *and as a hart stricken with an arrow; and he maketh haste* [*and*] *as a bird to the snare: and he knew not that he went to the death of his soul.* ²⁴ *Now therefore, hear me, my son, and hearken to the words of my mouth.* ²⁵ *Let not thy heart incline to her ways, and draw not nigh to the door of her house, and go not astray in her paths;* ²⁶ *for many slain hath she cast down, and there is no number to them that are slain by her.* ²⁷ *The ways of her house are the ways of Sheol, which bring down to the chambers of death.* ¹ *My son, hearken to my wisdom, and to mine understanding bend thy mind:* ² *that my counsel may keep thee, and the knowledge of my lips which I command thee.* ³ *For the lips of an adulterous woman drop honey, and with her flatteries she maketh sweet thy palate:* ⁴ *but the latter end of them is more bitter than wormwood, and sharper than a two-edged sword.* ⁵ *For the feet of a foolish (woman) lead down to the chambers of Sheol them that cleave unto her: for there is no standing for her footsteps, nor treading in the land of life:* ⁶ *for her paths are error, and they are not known.* ⁷ *Now therefore, my son, hear me, and turn not aside from the words of my mouth.* ⁸ *Keep thy way far from her, and draw not nigh to the door of her house;* ⁹ *lest thou give thy life to others, and thy years to them that have no mercy;* ¹⁰ *and lest strangers be satisfied of thy strength, and thy revenues go into the houses of others:* ¹¹ *and in thine old age thy soul repent thee, when the flesh of thy body is consumed,* ¹² *and thou say: Why then did I hate correction, and my heart reject reproof;* ¹³ *and hearkened I not to the voice of my teachers, and to them that admonished me inclined not mine ears?* ¹⁴ *I am come well-nigh into every evil.*

10 Prov. v 1–14.

---

2 *with an arrow*] + εἰς τὸ ἧπαρ LXX (and so Lat.): 'into whose liver an arrow flieth' Pesh.   3–4 *and he knew not... his soul*] As Pesh.: οὐκ εἰδὼς ὅτι περὶ ψυχῆς τρέχει LXX.   6–7 *and draw not nigh... in her paths*] om. LXX (= Lat.). The second clause is from Pesh., the first is perhaps due to Prov. v 8 (below).   12 *I command thee*] + μὴ πρόσεχε φαύλῃ γυναικί AC LXX (= Lat.). The words are omitted in Syr. under influence of Pesh.   13–14 *and with her flatteries... thy palate*] ἢ πρὸς καιρὸν λιπαίνει σὸν φάρυγγα AC LXX (= Lat.): 'and her words are softer than oil' Pesh.   16 *a foolish (woman)*] H : S has (with difference of

longum ²⁰ *ligaturam pecuniae accipiens in manu sua: post dies multos ueniet in domo sua.* ²¹ *Seduxit autem illum per multam loquellam, laqueis autem labiorum adtraxit eum.* ²² *Quique secutus eam est percussus: sicut bos ad occisionem ducitur, et ut canis ad ligaturam,* ²³ *et sicut ceruus sagitta percussus in epar: festinat autem sicut auis in laqueo, nesciens quoniam* [VI] *de anima est ei certamen.* ²⁴ *Nunc igitur, fili, audi me et intende uerbis ori(s) mei:* ²⁵ *ne declinet in itinere cor tuum;* ²⁶ *multos enim plagans occidit, et sine numero sunt quos interfecit: in itinere inferorum domus eius deducens, in inferiora mortis.* ¹ *Fili, meae sapientiae intende et meo intellectu(i) offer[i] aurem tuam,* ² *ut custodias cogitationem bonam: sensus autem labiorum meorum mando tibi.* ³ *Noli intendere fallaci mulieri: mel enim destillat de lauiis mulieris meretricis, quae ad tempus quidem inpinguat fauces tuas,* ⁴ *postea uero amariorem felle inuenies illud et acutiorem magis quam gladius bis acutus.* ⁵ *Insipientiae enim pedes deducent eos qui utuntur eam cum morte in infernum: uestigia autem eius non uidentur:* ⁶ *itinera enim uitae non sequitur: fallaces autem uiae eius et non bene cognite.* ⁷ *Nunc igitur, fili, audi me, et noli infirmos facere meos sermones.* ⁸ *Longe fac ab illa tuum iter: noli adcedere ad portas domus eius,* ⁹ *ut non prodas aliis uitam tuam, et tuam conuersationem his qui sine misericordia sunt:* ¹⁰ *ut non repleantur alieni tuis uiribus et tui labores ueniant in domos alienorum,* ¹¹ *et penitearis in ultimis, cum deterentur carnes corporis tui,* ¹² *et tunc dicis: Quomodo hodio habui disciplinam et increpationes declinauit cor meum?* ¹³ *non audiebam uocem obiurgantis me nec opponebam aurem meam?* ¹⁴ *Pene factus sum in omni malo.*

---

14 *meletricis* cod.

---

one letter) 'a sinful (woman)' or 'sin': ἀφροσύνης LXX (= Lat.): om. Pesh. (simply 'and her feet'). 19 *for her paths . . . not known*] As Pesh. 23 *thy years*] As Pesh.: σὸν βίον LXX. 25 *in thine old age*] So Pesh.: ἐπ' ἐσχάτων LXX (+ σου *AC*).

And that we prolong not and extend the admonition of our teaching with many (words), (p. 7) if we have left anything, do you as wise men choose for yourselves those things that are good from the holy Scriptures and from the Gospel of God, that you may be made firm, and may put away and cast from you all evil, and be found blameless in life everlasting with God.

CHAPTER III

An instruction to women, that they should please and honour their husbands alone, caring diligently and wisely for the work of their houses with attention; and that they should not bathe with men; and that they should not adorn themselves and become a cause of stumbling to men and ensnare them; and that they should be chaste and quiet, and not quarrel with their husbands.

[i. 8] And let a woman also be subject to her husband; *because the head of the woman is the man, and the head of a man* that walks in the way of justice *is Christ*. After the Lord Almighty, our God and the Father of the worlds, of the present and of that which is to come, and the Lord of every breath and of all powers, and His living and Holy Spirit—to whom is glory and honour for evermore, Amen—woman, fear

9 Eph. v 22 f., 1 Cor. xi 3.

8-14 In punctuating this passage I have followed the guidance of *AC*, which begins a new sentence with μετὰ οὖν τὸν παντοκράτορα θεόν (l. 10). This also harmonizes with the author's manner and usage elsewhere: e. g. he says at p. 60, l. 23 that the layman should fear and love the bishop 'as father and lord, and as God after God Almighty', and at p. 93, l. 30 that the bishop is the layman's father 'after God'. For the parenthetical doxology comp. pp. 4, 156, 167. In any case I think the author intended to say that the wife should reverence her husband *after God*, not that the head of the man is Christ, after the Father *and the Holy Spirit*: though the Syriac admits of this construction, and cod. S even suggests it by placing an emphatic stop (✦) after 'Amen'. *AC* omits reference to the Holy Spirit, and it may be that 'and ... H. Sp.' is an addition due to the translator.   13-14 to whom] In plur. S: in sing. H.

Et ut non per multa extendamus correptionem, si qua praetermisimus, sicut sapientes quae . . .

thy husband and reverence him, and please him alone, and be ready to minister to him; and let thy hands be (put forth) to the wool, and thy mind be upon the spindle, as He saith in Wisdom: [10] *A valiant woman who shall find? For she is more worth than goodly stones of great price;* [11] *and the heart of her husband relieth upon her, and provision is not wanting to her.* [12] *For she is a helper to her husband in all things, and causeth that nothing be wanting to him in his living.* [13] *She made wool and linen with her ready hands.* [14] *She is become a good provider, as a merchant ship, and hath gathered all her riches from afar.* [15] *She rose up in the night and gave victuals to her household, and work to her handmaids.* [16] *She looked upon a field, and bought it; and of the fruits of her hands she planted a possession.* [17] *She girded her loins with strength, and made firm her arms,* [18] *and tasted that it is good to work: and her lamp was not put out all the night long.* [19] *Her arms she stretched forth with diligence, and her hands to the spindle.* [20] *Her hands she extended to the poor, and of her fruits she gave to the needy.* [21] *And her husband hath no anxiety for the house; for all his household have been clothed with a double raiment.* [22] *She made for her husband garments of fine linen and scarlet:* [23] *her husband is notable in the gates, when he sitteth in the seat of the elders.* [24] *She made in her house linen cloths and girdles, and sold to the Canaanites.* [25] *Strength and comeliness are her raiment: and she shall rejoice* (p. 8) *in the last day.* [26] *She opened her mouth with wisdom and with prudence, and her tongue speaketh orderly.* [27] *The ways of her house are strict: and bread she hath not eaten slothfully. She opened her mouth in wisdom, rightly:* [28] *and the law of mercy is upon her tongue. Her sons rose up and were enriched, and praised her: and she shall rejoice in them in her last days. Her husband also con-*

---

4 Prov. xxxi 10-31.

7 *to her*] H: 'to him' S.   7-8 *For she ... his living*] H: BS have 'her living': τὸν βίον *AC* LXX. The passage is quite unlike *AC* LXX Heb. Pesh.   10 *a good provider*] (or 'dispenser') om. *AC* LXX Heb. Pesh.   13 *a field*] lit. 'a cultivation' (as Pesh.): γεώργιον *AC* LXX.   30 *and were enriched, and praised her*] καὶ πλουτήσαντα (sc. τὰ τέκνα) ᾔνεσαν αὐτήν *AC*: καὶ ἐπλούτησαν (only) LXX.

gratulated her: ²⁹ *and her many daughters have gotten riches. And many great things she did, and she was exalted above all the women:* ³⁰ *for a woman that feareth God shall be blessed, and the fear of the Lord shall glorify her.* ³¹ *Give unto her of her fruits, which are worthy of her lips, and let her be praised in the gates: and in every place let her husband be praised.* And again : *A valiant woman is the crown of her husband.*

You have heard, then, how great praise a chaste woman and one that loves her husband receives of the Lord God, one that is found faithful and is minded to please God. Thou therefore, O woman, shalt not adorn thyself that thou mayest please other men; and thou shalt not be plaited with the tresses of harlotry, nor put on the dress of harlotry, nor be shod with shoes so that thou resemble them that are such; lest thou bring upon thee those who are ensnared by these things. And if thou sin not thyself in this work of uncleanness, yet in this thou wilt have sinned, that thou hast con-

7 Prov. xii 4.

---

5 *which are worthy*] om. *A C* LXX Heb. Pesh.

strained and caused that (man) to desire thee. But if thou also sin, thou hast destroyed thy life from God, and art become guilty also of the soul of that (man). And moreover, when thou hast sinned with one, thou wilt grow reckless and go also to others; as in Wisdom He said: *When the wicked is come to the depth of evil, he contemneth and groweth reckless: and there cometh upon him dishonour and reproach.* For one who is such that she is wholly stricken in her soul and taken with desire, leads captive the souls of them that lack understanding.

But let us learn concerning these also, how the holy word in Wisdom exposes them; for it saith thus: *As a ring of gold in a swine's snout, so is beauty to a woman that doeth evil.* And again: *As a worm in wood, so doth an evil woman destroy a man.* And again: ¹³ *A woman void of understanding and boastful cometh to want bread, and knoweth no shame.* ¹⁴ *For she sitteth in the street, by the door of her house, upon a high chair,* ¹⁵ *and calleth to them that pass by the way, and to them that walk in her paths, and saith:* ¹⁶ *Whoso among you is a simpleton, let him draw nigh to me; and to him that wanteth understanding I will say:* ¹⁷ *Touch lovingly the hidden bread, and stolen waters that are sweet.* ¹⁸ *And he knoweth not that valiant men perish with her, and come even to the depth of Sheol. But flee thou, and tarry not in that place; and lift not up thine eyes to look upon her.* And again: *It is better to sit upon a corner of the roof than to dwell with a prating and quarrelsome woman within the house.*

---

5 Prov. xviii 3.   12 Prov. xi 22.   14 Prov. xii 4.   15 Prov. ix 13-18.   25 Prov. xxi 9, 19.

---

2 from God] om. Lat. (*AC* omits the clause).   4 grow reckless] lit. 'let thyself go', i.e. abandon thyself: ἀπογνοῦσα *AC*.   6 *contemneth and groweth reckless*] A double trans. of καταφρονεῖ (*AC* LXX).   8-9 *wholly ... desire*] Seemingly a paraphrase of ἀφειδῶς τετρωμένη (*AC*).   11-15 But let ... *destroy a man*] CH : om. BS (by error).   12 exposes them] Or 'lays them bare': θριαμβεύει *AC*. This verb seems to have contained the idea of despoiling, cf. Col. ii 15 ἀπεκδυσάμενος τὰς ἀρχὰς ... θριαμβεύσας αὐτοὺς ἐν αὐτῷ.   15 *A woman*, etc.] The quotation is in fair agreement with LXX, but 'valiant men' (l. 23) and 'the depth of Sheol' (ll. 23-24) are due to Pesh. *AC* omits the quotation.

DIDASCALIA APOSTOLORUM 25

[VII] ... ⟨de⟩siderare t⟨e⟩. Si autem pec⟨c⟩aueris, et tu pe⟨r⟩-
d⟨idi⟩sti ⟨u⟩itam tuam, et conoxia facta es animae illius. Et
postea, si peccauerit in uno, dispiciens se iterum ad aliud
transiet, ⟨sicuti dixit in Sapientia⟩: ⟨Inpius⟩ cum uenerit in
5 profundum malorum, contempnit, et ueniet ei infamia et in-
properium. Quae ta⟨l⟩is autem est iam uulnerat et laqueat
animas insipientium.

Discamus igitur et eas, quae tales sunt, quomodo triumphat
per ipsam Sapientiam sanctum uerbum. Dicit autem ita:
10 Sicut inaures in nare porc⟨i⟩, ita mulieri maliuolae species. Et
iterum: Sicut lignum uermis exterminat, sic per[di]dit uirum
mulier malefica. Et iterum: [13] Mulier stulta et saeua indigens
panem efficitur, quae nescit ruborem. [14] In ianuis dom⟨us su⟩ae
sedet super sellam, adparens in plateis, [15] aduocans eos praeter-
15 euntes, dirigentes iter in uiis suis, et dixit: [16] Quisque ex uobis
insipiens est, declinet ad me: et eis qui sine sapientia sunt
praecipio dicens: [17] Panes absconsos in pru[i]na suauiter edetis,
et aquam furtiuam dulcem bibetis. [18] Et nesciens est quia
terrigine aput eam pereunt, et in p[l]etaurum inferorum occur-
20 rit. Sed fuge citius et nol⟨i⟩ remorari loco eius. Et iterum:
Melius est habitare in angulo obscuro quam cum muliere
linguosa et rix[i]osa.

2-4 Et postea ... transiet] εἶτα ἁμαρτήσασα ἐφ' ἑνί, ὥσπερ ἀπογνοῦσα
εἰσάπαξ, ἐφ' ἑτέρους (al. leg. ἑτέρου) ἐκτραπήσῃ 'AC. (cf. Syr). After 'transiet'
a reference to Prov. has fallen out: cf. Syr., and 'per ipsam Sapientiam'
at l. 9.   6 iam uulnerat et laqueat] ἀφειδῶς τετρωμένη παγιδεύει AC (cf.
Syr.). Prob. read 'iam uulnerata laqueat'.   10 inaures] Perhaps
'aureae' has fallen out after this: cf. AC (ἐνώτιον χρυσοῦν) and Syr.
11 Sicut ... exterminat] ὥσπερ ἐν ξύλῳ σκώληξ AC (= Syr.).   12 saeua]
θρασεῖα LXX (AC omits the quot.).   17-18 panes ... bibetis] ἄρτων κρυφίων
ἡδέως ἅψασθε, καὶ ὕδατος κλοπῆς γλυκεροῦ LXX. The 'in pru[i]na' of Lat.
is peculiar.   19 pletaurum] πέταυρον LXX.   20 remorari] 'memorari'
cod.   loco eius] + 'and lift not up thine eyes to look upon her' Syr.

Thou therefore that art a Christian, (p. 9) do not imitate such women ; but if thou wouldst be a faithful woman, please thy husband only. And when thou walkest in the street, cover thy head with thy robe, that by reason of thy veil thy great beauty may be hidden. And adorn not thy natural face; but walk with downcast looks, being veiled.

[i. 9] And take heed that thou bathe not in a bath with men. For when there is a women's bath in the city or in the village, a believing woman may not bathe in a bath with men. For if thou coverest thy face from strange men with a veil of modesty, how † then † canst thou go in with strange men to a bath? But if there is no women's bath, and thou art constrained to bathe in a bath of men and women,—which indeed is unfitting —bathe with modesty and shame, and with bashfulness and moderation: and not at all times, nor every day, and not at midday; but let there be an appointed season for thee to bathe at, (to wit) at the tenth hour. For it behoves thee, as a believing woman, by every means to fly from the vain and curious gaze of the many which is met with in a bath.

[i. 10] And thy strife with all, and especially with thy husband, check and restrain as a believing woman ; lest thy husband, if he be a heathen, be offended by reason of thee and blaspheme against God, and thou receive a Woe from God : for, *Woe to them, by reason of whom the name of God is blas-*

24 Isa. lii 5 (Rom. ii 24).

---

1 Thou, etc.] In the plural *AC* (= Lat.). 5–6 And adorn not ... veiled] μὴ καταζωγράφει σου τὸ ὑπὸ θεοῦ πεποιημένον πρόσωπον ... κάτω βλέπουσα τὴν ὁδοιπορίαν σου ποιοῦ περικαλύπτουσα ἑαυτήν *AC*. thy natural face] lit. 'the face of thy nature'; but the text has by a slight corruption 'the face of thine eyes', which is meaningless. 11 how then] πῶς γυμνὴ *AC* (= Lat.) : we should prob. restore 'how canst thou go in naked'. 13 unfitting] Equivalent to παρὰ τὸ προσῆκον. 18–19 the vain and curious gaze, etc.] lit. 'the multiplicity of vain sight of loftiness of eyes', a very clumsy paraphrase of, apparently, τὴν πολυόφθαλμον περιεργίαν (*AC*). 21 check] lit. 'cut off' : περίκοψον *AC*. 22 if he be a heathen] ἐὰν ᾖ πιστὸς (one MS. ἄπιστος) ἢ ἐθνικός *AC* (= Lat.). Syr. is logical in omitting 'a believer or', even if that be what the author wrote. 24 *Woe to*, etc.] οὐαὶ γάρ, φησίν, δι' οὗ τὸ ὄνομά μου βλασφημεῖται ἐν τοῖς ἔθνεσιν *AC*. The 'Woe' is not in Isa. or Rom. ; but comp. 2 Clem. xiii 2 λέγει γὰρ ὁ κύριος· διὰ παντὸς τὸ ὄνομά μου βλασφημεῖται ἐν πᾶσιν τοῖς ἔθνεσιν·

DIDASCALIA APOSTOLORUM

Nolite igitur eas quae tales sunt mulieres ⟨i⟩mitari, uos Christianae. Quae ergo fidelis uis esse, uiro tuo adten⟨de, ut plac⟩eas illi soli. Et cum in ⟨p⟩latea amb⟨ulaueris, e⟩t ca⟨p⟩ut tuum ⟨uel⟩a ⟨ueste, ut per⟩ uel⟨ationem magna ob⟩scuretur pul-
5 ⟨chritudo tua⟩. Et noli d⟨e⟩pin⟨gere uul⟩tum ⟨tuum a Deo p⟩er nat⟨uram tibi factu⟩m. [VIII] ⟨De⟩orsum adten⟨d⟩ens iter tu⟨u⟩m con⟨f⟩i⟨ce⟩, und⟨i⟩que ueste te[cum] cooper⟨i⟩ens.

Decl⟨i⟩na a⟨u⟩te⟨m⟩ e⟨t⟩ balneum ubi uiri labantur, quod superfluum est mulieri. Nam et si [non] fuerit in ciuitate uel
10 in regione balneum ⟨muliebre⟩, in eo balneo ubi uiri labantur mulier fidelis non labetur. Si enim uultum tuum uelas ut a⟨b⟩ alienis uiris non uidearis, quomodo nuda cum alienis uiris in balneo ingrederis? Si autem non est balneum muliebre quod utaris, et uis contra naturam cum uiris lauari, cum disciplina
15 et cum reuerentia cum mensura labare. In talibus enim ualneis non frequenter lauetur, nec diu lauetur, nec in meridie, sed et, si potest fieri, nec per ⟨sin⟩gulos dies; ⟨h⟩ora autem sit tibi superflue illius ualnei decima. Oportet enim te constitutam fidelem ab omni parte oculorum aspectum et conuentionem,
20 quae in tali balneo fit, fugire.

Ne autem sis litigios⟨a⟩ ad omnes, praeterea aduersus uirum tuum, excide hoc malum a te, quoniam fidelis es: ut uir tuus, si est fidelis aut gentilis, propter te non cogatur blasfemare in Deum, et tu uae hereditaris aput Deum: *Uae*, inquid, *per*

1–8 The restorations in these lines are those of Hauler; but for 'ueste' in l. 7, Hauler reads 'ista'.   8–9 Declina ... mulieri] περιίστασο καὶ τὴν ἐν βαλανείῳ μετὰ ἀνδρῶν γινομένην λοῦσιν *AC*.   9 Nam et si [non] fuerit... ⟨muliebre⟩] Syr. no doubt preserves the true reading. Two cases are considered: the second is (ll. 13 ff.) 'si autem *non* est balneum muliebre'; and in this case a woman may bathe in a common bath, subject to precautions. The first case, then, in which women are absolutely forbidden the common bath, must be one in which there *is* a women's bath in the locality. *AC* so alters the passage as to forbid the common bath to women altogether: ἀνδρόγυνον γυνὴ πιστὴ μὴ λουέσθω ... γυναικείου δὲ ὄντος βαλανείου, εὐτάκτως μετὰ αἰδοῦς μεμετρημένως λουέσθω.   16 non frequenter, etc.] μὴ περισσοτέραν δὲ λοῦσιν ποιείσθω, μηδὲ πολλὴν μηδὲ πολλάκις μηδὲ ἐν μέσῃ τῇ ἡμέρᾳ, ἀλλ' εἰ δύνατον μηδὲ καθ' ἡμέραν *AC*: Syr. seems to have compressed somewhat.   21 praeterea] ' =praesertim. Dig. xxxi 34, 5. L. 17. 16 pr.' Rönsch *Itala und Vulgata* p. 346. See again at p. 123, l. 23.
23 cogatur blasfemare] σκανδαλισθεὶς βλασφημήσῃ *AC* (= Syr.).

καὶ πάλιν· οὐαὶ δι' ὧν βλασφημεῖται τὸ ὄνομά μου. See also Ignatius *Trall.* viii 2 and Polycarp *Phil.* x 3 (Resch *Agrapha* p. 314).

phemed among the gentiles; or (lest) again, if thy husband be a believer, he be constrained, as one who knows the Scriptures, and say to thee the word from Wisdom: *It is better to sit upon a corner of the roof than to dwell with a prating and quarrelsome woman within the house.* For it behoves women by a veil of modesty and humility to shew (their) 'fear of God, for the conversion and the increase of faith of them that are without, (both) of men and women.

Now if we have admonished and instructed you in brief, our sisters and our daughters and our members, do you as wise women seek and choose out for yourselves those things that are good and honourable and without reproach in worldly conversation; and learn and know those things whereby you may arrive at the kingdom of our Lord, and may find rest, pleasing Him with good works.

CHAPTER IV

(p. 10)

Teaching what manner of man he is that is chosen for the Bishopric, and of what sort his conduct should be.

[ii. 1] But concerning the bishopric, hear ye. The pastor who is appointed bishop and head among the presbytery in the Church in every congregation, *it is required of him that he be blameless, in nothing reproachable*, one remote from all evil, a man not less than fifty years of age, who is now removed from the manners of youth and from the lusts of the Enemy, and from the slander and blasphemy of false brethren, which they bring against many because they understand not that word which is said in the Gospel: *Every one that shall*

---

3 Prov. xxi 9, 19.   18 1 Tim. iii 2, Tit. i 7.   20 2 Tim. ii 22.
24 Mt. xii 36 f.

5–6 a veil of] om. *AC* (= Lat.).   16 But ... hear ye] περὶ δὲ τῶν ἐπισκόπων οὕτως ἠκούσαμεν παρὰ τοῦ κυρίου ἡμῶν *AC*. In Lat. there is a blank space which once contained a rubricated heading.   18 congregation] The word is the usual equivalent of συναγωγή, but is also employed in this version

quem nomen Dei blasphematur inter gentes : si autem fidelis est
uir tuus, cogatur dicere, ut s⟨c⟩iens scribturas, quod scriptum
est in Sapientia : *Melius est habitare in deserto quam cum
muliere linguosa et litigios⟨a⟩*. Mulieres igitur per confusio-
5 ⟨ne⟩m et m⟨a⟩ns⟨uet⟩udinem reli⟨gi⟩onem ostendite ad c⟨onuer⟩-
sionem ⟨et fid⟩e⟨i⟩ auctum de eth⟨nicis quantis⟩cunque, ⟨si⟩u⟨e
uir⟩i ⟨sun⟩t siue mulieres.

⟨Et si pau⟩cis ⟨ipsi admonuimu⟩s et co⟨rreximus uo⟩s, sorores [IX] et filiae et membra nostra, tamen sicut sapientes et
10 uos quae bona sunt et sine repraehensione quaerite uitae istius
documenta, ut sciatis per quae possitis regno Dei nostri propin-
quare et bene placentes repausare.

Pastor qui constituitur in uisitatione praesbyterii et in eccle-
siis omnibus et parrociis, *oportet eum sine quaerella esse, in-*
15 *reprehensibilem.* alienum ab omni iniquitate, uirum non minus
annorum cinquaginta. quoniam per quandam rationem iuuve-
nilis luxurias et diabolica uitia aufugisse iam uidetur, et ab
eis quae a falsis fratribus in multos iactantur blasfemiis, qui
ignorant uerbum Dei quod in euuangelio est : *Quoniam*, inquid,

---

3 *in deserto*] From Prov. xxi 19.   5–8 The restorations are those
of Hauler.   13 in uisitatione] Probably for εἰς ἐπισκοπήν (cf. p. 31 l. 10).
AC has here τὸν ποιμένα τὸν καθιστάμενον ἐπίσκοπον εἰς τὰς ἐκκλησίας ἐν πάσῃ
παροικίᾳ δεῖ ὑπάρχειν κτλ.

---

for παροικία.   18–19 *it is required ... reproachable*] δεῖ ὑπάρχειν ἀνέγκλητον,
ἀνεπίληπτον *AC*.   20–21 who is now ... youth] ὅτι τρόπῳ τινὶ τὰς νεωτερικὰς
ἀταξίας ... ἐκπεφευγὼς ὑπάρχει *AC*, which shows that 2 Tim. ii 22 is in
mind (τὰς δὲ νεωτερικὰς ἐπιθυμίας φεῦγε).

say an idle word, shall give an answer concerning it to the Lord in the day of judgement: *for from thy words thou shalt be justified, and from thy words thou shalt be condemned.* But if it be possible, let him be instructed and apt to teach; but if he know not letters, let him be versed and skilled in the word, and let him be advanced in years.

But if the congregation be a small one, and there be not found a man advanced in years of whom they give testimony that he is wise and suitable to stand in the bishopric: but there be found there one who is young, of whom they that are with him give testimony that he is worthy to stand in the bishopric, and who, though he is young, yet by meekness and quietness of conduct shows maturity: let him be proved whether all give testimony concerning him, and so let him sit in peace. For Solomon also at the age of twelve years reigned over Israel; and Josiah at the age of eight years reigned with righteousness; and Joash likewise reigned when seven years old. Wherefore, even though he be young, yet let him be meek and fearful and quiet; for the Lord God said in Isaiah: *On whom shall I look and take pleasure (in him), but on the quiet and meek, that trembleth at my words?* And in the Gospel also He spoke thus: *Blessed are the meek, for they shall inherit the earth.* And let him be merciful; for He said again in the Gospel thus: *Blessed are the merciful, for upon them there shall be mercy.* And again let him be a peacemaker; for He saith: *Blessed are the peacemakers, for they shall be called the sons of God.* And let him be clear of all

---

20 Isa. lxvi 2 (cf. *Didache* iii 8).   22 Mt. v 5 (cf. *Didache* iii 7).
24 Mt. v 7.   26 Mt. v 9.

---

4 instructed and apt to teach] Apparently a double rendering of πεπαιδευμένος (*AC*).   4–6 but if . . . the word] See the note to l. 18. 7 But if, etc.] εἰ δὲ καὶ ἐν παροικίᾳ μικρᾷ ὑπαρχούσῃ που προβεβηκὼς τῷ χρόνῳ μὴ εὑρίσκηται μεμαρτυρημένος καὶ σοφὸς εἰς ἐπισκοπὴν καταστᾰθῆναι *AC*. 10 one] BH: S, by a small error, reads 'a brother'.   13–14 let him be, etc.] δοκιμασθεὶς, εἰ ὑπὸ τῶν πάντων οὕτως μαρτυρεῖται, καθιστάσθω ἐν εἰρήνῃ *AC*. 18 Wherefore, even though . . . yet, etc.] *AC* has the same unexpected sequence, ὥστε εἰ καὶ νέος, ἀλλὰ πρᾷος ὑπαρχέτω. Comp. with this passage *Apost. Ch. Order* xvii 2 δυνάμενος τὰς γραφὰς ἑρμηνεύειν, εἰ δὲ ἀγράμματος,

*qui dixerit uerbum otiosum, reddet rationem pro eo domino in
die iudicii. De uerbis enim tuis,* ait, *iustificaueris, et de uerbis
tuis condemnaueris.* Sit igitur, si possibile est, ad omnia eru-
ditus; et si sine litteris est, sed notitiam habens uerbi diuini
5 et stabilis aetate.

Si autem in parocia modica ordinandus est episcopus, et
non inuenitur qui tempora aetatis iam transisse uideatur et
testimonium habere et sapiens : est autem iuuenis, et testimonium habet ab his qui cum eodem sunt quia dignus est ad
10 episcopatum, et per iuuenilem aetatem per mansuetudinem
et bonam conuersationem senectutem ostendit: probetur et,
si ab omnibus tale testimonium habet, constituatur episcopus
in pace. Nam Sa⟨lomon⟩ duodecim annorum constit⟨utus
regnauit⟩ [X] in Istrahel, et Iosias in iustitia octo annorum
15 constitutus regnauit, similiter et Io[si]as, cum esset septem
annorum, regnauit. Unde, etiamsi iuuenis est, tamen ut
mansuetus sit, timidus et quietus, quoniam dicit per Eseiam
dominus Deus: *Super quem respiciam, nisi super mansuetum
et quietum et trementem uerba mea semper?* Similiter et in
20 euangelio dicit ita: *Beati mansueti, quia ipsi hereditabunt
terram.* Sit autem et misericors, quoniam dicit: *Beati misericordes, quia ipsis miserebitur Deus.* Similiter et pacificus,
quoniam iterum dicit: *Beati pacifici, quoniam filii Dei uoca-
buntur.* Sit autem et sine malitia et inquitate et malignitate,

---

2–3 *iustificaueris . . . condemnaueris*] With *u* for *b*.   3 ad omnia]
om. *AC* (= Syr.).   12 episcopus] om. *AC* (= Syr.).   16 ut] Should
we read 'et'?   19 *semper*] διαπαντός *AC* (though two MSS. omit): om.
Syr. The word in *AC* is undoubtedly original, for whereas it is absent
from the Heb. and from all versions of Isa. lxvi 2, it is found in *Didache*
iii 8, which our author has here in mind. See *J. T. S.* xxiv p. 150 (Jan.
1923).   22 pacificos cod.

πραῢς ὑπάρχων. With this again cf. l. 4 above, where *AC* reads ἔστω
οὖν, εἰ δυνατόν, πεπαιδευμένος· εἰ δὲ καὶ ἀγράμματος, ἀλλ' οὖν ἔμπειρος τοῦ
λόγου. It is to be observed further that *Apost. Ch. O.*, in discussing the
election of the bishop, considers the case of a diocese in which there is
ὀλιγανδρία (xvi 1): cf. l. 7 above. This and other passages leave little
doubt in my mind that there has been contact between the *Apost. Ch. O.*
and the *Didascalia*, and I have as little doubt that the borrowing was on
the part of the first-mentioned.   21 *my words*] + διαπαντός *AC* (= Lat.):
see note to Lat.

evil and wrong and iniquity; for He saith again: *Blessed are the pure in heart, for they shall see God.* [ii. 2] And let him be *watchful and chaste and staid* and orderly; and let him not be turbulent, *and let him not be one that exceeds in wine; and let him not be a backbiter; but let him be quiet, and not be quarrelsome; and let him not* (p. 11) *be money-loving.* And let him not be youthful in mind, lest he be lifted up and fall into the judgement of Satan: *for every one that exalteth himself shall be humbled.* But it is required that the bishop be thus: *a man that hath taken one wife, that hath governed his house well.* And thus let him be proved when he receives the imposition of hands to sit in the office of the bishopric: whether he be chaste, and whether his wife also be a believer and chaste; and whether he has brought up his children in the fear of God, and admonished and taught them; and whether his household fear and reverence him, and all of them obey him. For if his household in the flesh withstand him and obey him not, how shall they that are without his house become his, and be subject to him?

[ii. 3] And let him be proved whether he be without blemish in the things of the world, and likewise in his body; for it is written: *See that there be no blemish in him that standeth up to be priest.* But let him be also without anger; for the Lord saith: *Anger destroyeth even the wise.* And let him be merciful and gracious and full of love; for the Lord saith: *Love covereth a multitude of sins.* [ii. 4] And let his hand be open to give; and let him love the orphans with the widows, and be a lover of the poor and of strangers. And let him be alert in his ministry, and constant in ministration; and let him be afflicting his soul, and not be one that is put to confusion. And let him know who is the more

1 Mt. v 8.   3 1 Tim. iii 2 f.   6 1 Tim. iii 6.   8 Lk. xiv 11, xviii 14.   10 1 Tim. iii 2, 4.   14 Cf. 1 Tim. iii 4 f.   22 cf. Lev. xxi 17.   24 Prov. xv 1.   26 Cf. 1 Pet. iv 8 (comp. Prov. x 12).

3 *watchful . . . staid*] νηφάλιος, σώφρων, κόσμιος *AC*.   orderly] εὐσταθής *AC*: om. Lat.   5 *a backbiter*] BCHS: πλήκτης *AC* (= 1 Tim. iii 3). This word has given trouble to the translator, or else his rendering

DIDASCALIA APOSTOLORUM

quoniam dicit iterum: *Beati mundo corde, quia ipsi uidebunt Deum.* Sit ergo *sobrius, castus, ornatus,* non turbulentus, *non uino multo deditus, non percussor, sed innocens, non litigiosus, non auarus, non neofitus, ut non infletur et in iudicium in-*
5 *cidat*: quoniam *omnis qui se exaltat humiliabitur*. Talem decet esse episcopum, *unius uxoris uirum, curam domus suae bene agentem*. Ita ergo probetur, cum manus inpositionis accipit, et sic ordinetur in episcopatum, si est castus, si uxorem castam aut fidelem habuit aut habet, si filios caste
10 edocauit ⟨et⟩ erudiens produxit, si hii qui intra domum eius sunt reuerentur eum et honorant eum, et omnes subditi illi sunt. Si enim qui secundum carnem illius proprii sunt s⟨editio⟩nem faciunt aduersum eum et ⟨non pare⟩nt ei, quomodo hii qui foris domum ...

---

2 non turbulentus] ἀτάραχος *AC.* Comp. *Reg. S. Benedicti* c. xxxi (as to the cellarer) 'sapiens, maturus moribus, sobrius, non multum edax, non elatus, non turbulentus, non iniuriosus'. 4–5 *incedat* cod.: + τοῦ διαβόλου *AC* (cf. Syr.). 7 manus inpositionis] τὴν χειροτονίαν *AC* (cf. Syr.). Prob. read 'm. inpositionem'. 9 habet] 'auet' cod. caste] θεοσεβῶς *AC*: 'in the fear of God' Syr. (= *AC*). 11 honurant cod.

has troubled the scribes. Here all the MSS. have ܡܘܼܢ; but at p. 76, l. 27 CH have ܡܘܼܢ, 'tyrannical', while BS have (with transposition of the first two letters) ܘܡܢ, 'murmurers': 'tyrannical' is read again at p. 119 l. 9 by BHS (C is wanting). 7 *youthful in mind*] A paraphrase of νεόφυτος (*AC*). 13–14 and whether ... chaste] εἰ γυναῖκα σεμνὴν καὶ πιστὴν ἔχει ἢ ἔσχηκεν *AC* (cf. Lat.). 18 how shall they, etc.] πῶς οἱ ἔξω τῆς οἰκίας αὐτοῦ ἴδιοι γενόμενοι αὐτῷ ὑποταγήσονται; *AC.* 21 in the things ... body] περὶ τὰς βιωτικὰς χρείας *AC.* 23–24 But let ... *the wise*] ὑπαρχέτω οὖν καὶ ἀόργητος, ὅτι λέγει ἡ Σοφία· ὀργὴ καὶ φρονίμους ἀπόλλυσιν *AC.* Cf. *Apost. Ch. Order* xx (as to deacons) μὴ ὀργίλοι, ὀργὴ γὰρ ἀπόλλυσι ἄνδρα φρόνιμον. 25–26 for the Lord saith, etc.] ὅτι λέγει κύριος *AC*, then substituting Joh. xiii 35. Comp. 1 Clem. xlix 5, 2 Clem. xvi 4, Clem. Alex. *Paed.* iii 12. 91, etc. (see Resch p. 311). It is certain that our author knew 1 Pet., but here the saying is ascribed to 'the Lord' with the same formula just used (in Syr.) to introduce a quotation from Prov. 30–31 and let him ... confusion] A paraphrase of εὔκυλος, ἀνεπαίσχυντος (*AC*).

worthy to receive; for if there be a widow who has (somewhat), or is able to nourish herself with that which she needs for her bodily sustenance; and there be another who, though she is not a widow, is in want, whether by reason of sickness, or of the rearing of children, or of bodily infirmity: to this (latter) rather let him stretch out his hand. But if there be any man who is dissolute, or drunken, or idle, and he be in straits for bodily nourishment, the same is not worthy of an alms, neither of the Church.

[ii. 5] And let the bishop be also without respect of persons, and let him not defer to the rich nor favour them unduly; and let him not disregard or neglect the poor, nor be lifted up against them. And let him be scant and poor in his food and drink, that he may be able to be watchful in admonishing and correcting those who are undisciplined. And let him not be crafty and extravagant, nor luxurious, nor pleasure-loving, nor fond of dainty meats. And let him not be resentful, but let him be patient in his admonition; and let him be assiduous in his teaching, (p. 12) and constant in reading the divine Scriptures with diligence, that he may interpret and expound the Scriptures fittingly. And let him compare the Law and the Prophets with the Gospel, so that the sayings of the Law and the Prophets may be in accord with the Gospel. But before all let him be a good discriminator between the Law and the Second Legislation, that he may distinguish and show what is the Law of the faithful, and what are the bonds of them that believe not; lest any one of those under thy authority take the bonds for the Law, and lay upon himself heavy burdens, and become a son of perdition. Be diligent

---

3 sustenance] H: 'old age' S (with change of one letter). 16–17 crafty . . . meats] ἔστω μὴ δάπανος, μὴ τρυφητής, μὴ ἡδύβιος, μὴ χρηστοφάγος AC. The combination 'crafty and extravagant' in Syr. is odd, unless the former word should mean *recherché*, as Nau translates it (it is not represented in AC). The second word (*nappīk*) is rendered 'worldly-wise', *weltgewandt*, by Flemming, since the root means primarily 'go out'; but other formations have the meanings 'spend', 'expenses', and here the word appears to translate δάπανος (see also p. 78, l. 2). 17 not be resentful] ἀνεξίκακος AC.

therefore and attentive to the word, O bishop, so that, if thou canst, thou explain every saying: that with much doctrine thou mayest abundantly nourish and give drink to thy people; for it is written in Wisdom: *Be careful of the herb of the field,* 5 *that thou mayest shear thy flock: and gather the grass of summer, that thou mayest have sheep for thy clothing: give attention and care to thy pasture, that thou mayest have lambs.*

[ii. 6] Let not the bishop therefore be *a lover of filthy lucre,* and especially from the heathen. Let him be suffering a 10 wrong, and not doing a wrong; and let him not love riches. And let him not think ill of any man, nor bear false witness; and let him not be wrathful, nor quarrelsome; and let him not love the presidency; and let him not be double-minded nor double-tongued, nor given to incline his ear to words of 15 slander and murmuring; and let him be no respecter of persons. And let him not love the festivals of the heathen, nor occupy himself with vain error. And let him not be lustful, nor money-loving: for all these things are of the agency of demons.

20 Now all these things let the bishop command and enjoin upon all the people. And let him be wise and lowly; and let him be admonishing and teaching with the doctrine and discipline of God. And let him be of a noble mind, and aloof from all the evil artifices of this world, and from all 25 the evil lust of the heathen. And let his mind be keen to discern, that he may know beforehand them that are evil: and do you keep yourselves from them. But let him be the friend of all, being a righteous judge. And whatever of good

---

4 Prov. xxvii 25 f.   8 1 Tim. iii 8.   13 Cf. *Didache* ii 4.

---

11 not think ill of any man] μὴ κατάλαλος *AC*.   13–14 not be double-minded nor double-tongued] μὴ δίγνωμος, μὴ δίγλωσσος *AC* (and in lib. vii c. 4 οὐκ ἔσῃ δίγνωμος οὐδὲ δίγλωσσος). Cf. *Didache* ii 4 οὐκ ἔσῃ διγνώμων οὐδὲ δίγλωσσος (= *Ep. Barnab.* xix 7). The preceding words in *Didache* (not in *Barnab.*) are οὐ ψευδομαρτυρήσεις, οὐ κακολογήσεις, οὐ μνησικακήσεις, and in *Didasc.* also we have just before μὴ κατάλαλος, μὴ ψευδομάρτυς, according to *AC*; hence *Didache* and not *Barnab.* appears to be the source here. 23 of a noble mind] lit. 'well-minded', rendering καλογνώμων (*AC*). 26 discern] lit. 'compare', i.e. infer from observation.

there be that is found in men, let the same be in the bishop. For when the pastor shall be remote from all evil, he will be able to constrain his disciples also and encourage them by his good manners to be imitators of his good works; as (p. 13) the Lord has said in the Twelve Prophets: *The people shall be even as the priest.* For it behoves you to be an example to the people, for you also have Christ for an example. Be you therefore also a good example to your people, for the Lord said in Ezekiel: *¹And the word of the Lord came unto me, saying: ²Son of man, speak to the sons of thy people, and say unto them: When I bring the sword upon a land, let the people of that land take one man from among them and make him their watchman: ³and he shall see the sword coming upon the land, and shall blow the trumpet and warn the people; ⁴and every one that heareth the sound of the trumpet shall give ear. And if he take not warning, and the sword come and take him away, his blood shall be upon his head. ⁵Because he heard the sound of the trumpet, and took not warning, his blood shall be upon his head. But he that took warning hath delivered his soul. ⁶But if the watchman see the sword coming, and blow not the trumpet, and the people be not warned, and the sword come and take away a soul from them: he hath been taken away in his sins, and his blood will I require at the hands of the watchman.* Now the sword is the judgement, and the trumpet is the Gospel, but the watchman is the bishop who is set over the Church.

5 Hos. iv 9. 9 Ez. xxxiii 1–6.

5 the Twelve Prophets] So again at pp. 170, 254. This collective form of reference is found in Irenaeus *Apost. Preaching* c. 77 (cf. c. 93), *Haer.* IV xxix 5, and several times in Justin. 9–24 *And the word of the Lord*, etc.] *AC* has shortened and adapted this quotation: for 'sword' and 'trumpet' it reads μάχαιρα and κερατίνη, while LXX have ῥομφαία and σάλπιγξ.

CHAPTER V

A teaching on judgement.

It behoves thee therefore, O bishop, when thou preachest, to testify and affirm concerning the judgement according as it is (found) in the Gospel. For to thee also has the Lord said: *And thee, son of man, I have set as a watchman to the house of Israel; that thou mayest hear a word from my mouth, and give warning and preach it as from me. And when I say to the ungodly: The ungodly shall surely die, and thou preach not and say that the ungodly should depart from his iniquity: the ungodly shall die in his iniquity, and at thy hands will I require his blood. But if thou warn the ungodly from his way, and he take not warning: the ungodly shall die in his iniquity, and thou shalt deliver thy soul.* Wherefore you also, since to your account is laid the blame of them that sin in ignorance, do you preach and testify; and those who behave themselves without discipline admonish and rebuke openly.

Now whereas we speak and repeat these things often, we are not blameworthy; for through much teaching and hearing it happens that a man is put to shame, and does good and avoids evil. For the Lord also said in the Law: *Hear, O Israel*; and unto (p. 14) this day they have not heard. And in the Gospel likewise He often proclaims and says: *Every one that hath ears to hear, let him hear.* But not even they have heard who thought that they heard; for they cast them-

---

4 Ez. xxxiii 7–9.   19 Deut. vi 4.   21 Mt. xi 15, xiii 9, etc.

1 It behoves, etc.] In *AC* this forms part of the sentence begun in ch. iv: (σκοπὸς δὲ ὁ κατασταθεὶς τῇ ἐκκλησίᾳ ἐπίσκοπος,) ὃν δεῖ κηρύσσοντα διαμαρτύρεσθαι καὶ διαβεβαιοῦσθαι περὶ τῆς κρίσεως. The division into chapters is later than the Syriac translation, for we shall find that in one instance a Syriac sentence has been cut in two (see p. 167).   4 *And thee, son of man,* etc.] These verses are given in full in *AC*, and in a text which differs notably from LXX. In his extensive quotations from Ezekiel our author used a text, other than LXX, which frequently agrees with hexaplaric readings quoted by Field.   6 *and give warning . . . as from me*] καὶ διαφυλάξεις καὶ διαγγελεῖς αὐτὸν παρ' ἐμοῦ *AC*: 'and warn them from me' Heb.: om. LXX.   21 often proclaims] πολλάκις μιμνήσκεται *AC*. The Syriac verb also means 'to commemorate' or 'mention'.

selves swiftly into the dire destruction of heresy : †upon whom the word of sentence is about to go forth.† [ii. 7] For we believe not, brethren, that when a man has (once) gone down into the water he will do again the abominable and filthy works of the ungodly heathen. For this is manifest and known to all, that whosoever does evil after baptism, the same is already condemned to the Gehenna of fire.

[ii. 8] And we think indeed that the heathen also will blaspheme on this account, that we do not mix with them nor hold communication with them. But through the falsehood of the heathen our brethren have the rather attained to the truth ; for in the Gospel He saith thus : *Blessed are ye when they shall revile you, and persecute you, and speak against you every evil word for my sake, falsely. But do ye rejoice and be glad, for your reward is great in heaven: for so did their fathers persecute the prophets.* If therefore they shall blaspheme against any man falsely, blessed is he, even because that he is tempted ; for the Scripture has said : *A man that is not tempted, neither is he approved.* But if a man be convicted of doing the works of iniquity, he is no Christian but a liar, and he holds the fear of the Lord in hypocrisy. Wherefore these persons, when they have been exposed and convicted by the truth openly, let the bishop who is without offence and without hypocrisy avoid.

[ii. 9] But if the bishop himself is not of a clean conscience, and accepts persons for the sake of filthy lucre, or for the sake of the presents which he receives, and spares one who impiously sins, and suffers him to remain in the Church : [ii. 10] such a bishop has polluted his congregation with God ; yea, and with men also, and with many of the receivers who are young in their minds, or with the hearers ; and youths and maidens

---

8 Cf. 1 Pet. iv 4.   12 Mt. v 11 f., Lk. vi 23.   16 Cf. 1 Pet. iii 14.
18 ? (cf. Ja. i. 12, Ecclus. xxxiv 10).

1-2 upon whom ... go forth] περὶ ὧν αὖθις ἐροῦμεν *AC* (see Lat.) : a strange mistranslation in Syr.   9 on this account] lit. 'on account of these things': so H and S marg.: 'on account of these' (masc.) CS.   15 *their fathers*] BS : 'your fathers' CH. The latter is the reading (in Mt.) of *syr. sin.* and *syr. cur.*: om. *syr. vulg.*   18-19 *A man ... approved*] ἀνὴρ ἀδόκιμος ἀπείραστος παρὰ τῷ θεῷ *AC*. Cf. Tertull. *de Bapt.* 20

DIDASCALIA APOSTOLORUM

[XI] ... ⟨? horren⟩das heresis cito deuenerunt, de quibus continuo dicetur. Non enim credimus, fratres, lotum quemquam adhuc agere gentilium execrandas iniquitates; quoniam notum est omnibus quod, si quis peccauerit iniquum aliquid post baptismum, hic in gehenna condemnatur.

Suspicamur autem et blasfemari nos a gentilibus, eo quod iam non eis miscemur nec cumpopulamur cum eis. Et per falsitatem gentilium ueritatem fratres nostri adsecuti sunt, de quibus dictum est in euuangelio : *Beati eritis, cum inproperauerint uobis et dixerint omne malum contra uos mentientes. Gaudete et laetamini, quoniam merces uestra magna est in caelis : sic enim persecuti sunt profetas.* Si quis ergo blasfimatur per mendacium, beatus est, quoniam temptatur ; dicit enim scriptura : *Uir qui non est temptatus, non est probatus a Deo.* Si qui autem conuictus fuerit quia egit aliquit iniquum, qui talis est non est Christianus, magis autem per hypocrisim domino mentitus est. Unde ab his qui tales sunt, cum conuicti fuerint uerius, cum fiducia se abstineat episcopus qui sine offensione est et non accipi[a]t personam.

Si autem et ipse non est bonae conscientiae, et personam acceperit propter quoddam turpe lucrum, et pepercerit ei qui inique peccat et permittit eum in ecclesia manere, hic co⟨i⟩nquinauit ecclesiam suam ad Deum et ad homines, et multos neofitos et caticuminos et iuuenes et iuniores puellas perdet cum eo.

'nam et praecesserat dictum : Neminem intentatum regna caelestia consecuturum'. See Resch p. 130, Ropes 124.   21–22 when they have been, etc.] ἐλεγχθέντας ἀληθῶς παραιτήσεται μετὰ παρρησίας ὁ ἐπίσκοπος *AC*. The above is the natural way of taking the Syriac, but it admits absolutely of being translated 'convicted in truth, openly let the bishop ... avoid' (as *AC*).   25–26 for the sake of ... receives] διά τινα αἰσχροκερδῆ δωροληψίαν *AC*.   28 has polluted his congregation] ἐβεβήλωσεν ... τὴν τοῦ θεοῦ ἐκκλησίαν *AC*.   29–30 receivers ... minds] νεοφωτίστοις *AC*, but 'neofitos' Lat. 'Receivers' means, according to Syriac usage, communicants, and the whole expression denotes those who have recently been baptized.   30 hearers] i.e. catechumens.

beside he destroys with him. For by reason of the lewdness of an ungodly man, when they have seen such a one in their midst they too will doubt in their soul, and will imitate him, and themselves also will stumble and be taken with the same malady, and will perish with him. But if he who sins sees that the bishop and the deacons are clear of reproach, and the whole (p. 15) flock pure: first of all he will not dare to enter the congregation, because he is reproved by his conscience; but if it should happen that he is bold, and comes to the Church in his arrogance, and he is reproved and rebuked by the bishop, and looking upon all (present) finds no offence in any of them, neither in the bishop nor in those who are with him: he will then be put to confusion, and will go forth quietly, in great shame, weeping and in remorse of soul; and so shall the flock remain pure. Moreover, when he is gone out he will repent of his sin and weep and sigh before God, and there shall be hope for him. And the whole flock itself also, when it sees the weeping and tears of that man, will fear, knowing and understanding that every one who sins perishes.

[ii. 11] Wherefore, O bishop, strive to be pure in thy works. And know thy place, that thou art set in the likeness of God Almighty, and holdest the place of God Almighty; and so sit in the Church and teach as having authority to judge them that sin in the room of God Almighty. For to you bishops it is said in the Gospel: *That which ye shall bind on earth, shall be bound in heaven.*

CHAPTER VI

Concerning transgressors, and concerning those who repent.

[ii. 12] Judge therefore, O bishop, strictly as God Almighty; and those who repent receive with mercy as God Almighty. And rebuke and exhort and teach; for the Lord God also

25 Mt. xviii 18.

---

1 him] Or 'himself': but cf. Lat.   For ... ungodly man] διὰ γὰρ τὴν τῆς ἀκρισίας ἀνομίαν *AC*, which may be the true reading: Lat. and Syr. imply ἀκρασίας: with a different vocalization 'ungodly man' would become 'ungodliness' or 'iniquity'.   27 strictly] Or 'with decision': μετὰ ἐξουσίας *AC* (and ἀπ' ἐξουσίας at p. 42, l. 25).

Per intemperantiam ⟨enim⟩ suam sine sensu effecti, uidentes eum qui talis [XII] est inter se, incipient discernere aput se et imitari eum : et ipsi scandalizabu⟨n⟩tur, et participes effecti infirmitatis eius peribunt cum eo. Si autem uiderit hic, qui peccat, episcopum et diaconos innocentes et alienos a crimine et gregem mundum constitutum, primum quidem non usurpat contemnere et ingredi in synagogam, per conscientiam suam semet ipsum repraehendens. ⟨Si⟩ autem inuentus fuerit inerubidus et non confundatur, et ingressus fuerit ecclesiam, arguitur et corripitur ab episcopo, circumspiciens singulos et in nullo offendiculum inueniens, tam episcopum quam eos qui cum eo sunt : confusus cum grandi reuerentia et fletu egredietur pacifice stupens; et manet mundatus grex, et ille egrediens fleuit ad Deum et penetebitur de his quae egit, et habebit spem; et tota grex, cum uiderit lacrimas illius, correptionem aput se sentit, quoniam qui peccat perit.

Propterea igitur, o episcope, festina ut mundus sis ex operibus, et agnosce[re] locum tuum, quoniam in omnipotentis uirtute positus es, obseruans similitudinem Dei omnipotentis. Et ita in ecclesia sede uerbum faciens, quasi potestatem habens iudicare pro Deo eos qui peccauerunt : quoniam uobis episcopis dictum est per euuangelium : *Quodcumque legaueritis super terram, erit legatum et in caelo.*

Iudica, episcope, cum fiducia ut Deus: sed paenitentes ...

1 ⟨enim⟩] γάρ *AC* (= Syr.).   2 eum] 'enim' cod.   incipient discernere] διακριθήσονται *AC*, i. e. 'will doubt' (cf. Syr.).   3 effecti] 'esse et' (*sic*) Hauler; but 'effecti' was suggested to him and later verified by Hauler (see Funk *Didasc. et Const. Apost.* vol. i, p. xi note). 9-12 et ingressus ... confusus] The construction would be eased by the omission of 'fuerit' after 'ingressus' and the addition of 'et' before 'circumspiciens'.   15-16 correptionem ... perit] This represents νουθεσίαν ἕξει, ὅτι ὁ ἁμαρτὼν ... ἀπόλλυται *AC* (where however διὰ μετάνοιαν οὐκ has been inserted).

with an oath promised forgiveness to them that have sinned, as He said in Ezekiel: *And thou, son of man, say to the house of Israel: Ye have said thus: Our crimes and our sins are upon us, and in them we are wasted away: how then can we live? Say unto them: As I live, saith the Lord Adonai, I desire not the death of the sinner, but that the wicked return from his evil way and live. Return, therefore, and be converted from your evil ways, and ye shall not die, O house of Israel.* Here, then, He gave hope to them that sin, when they shall have repented, that they may have salvation by their repentance, and may not despair of themselves and continue in their sins and further add to them, but may repent and sigh and weep for their sins, and be converted with all their heart.

[ii. 13] But let them that have not (p. 16) sinned continue without sin, lest they also come to have need of weeping and sighs and sorrow, and of forgiveness. For whence knowest thou, O man that sinnest, how many are the days of thy life in this world, that thou mayest repent? For thou knowest not thy exit from the world, whether haply thou die in thy sins and there be no more repentance for thee; as it is said in David: *In Sheol who shall confess to thee?* Wherefore he remains without danger, whosoever spares his soul and remains without sin: so that the righteousness also which was done by him in time past may be preserved to him.

Do thou therefore, O bishop, thus judge: first of all strictly; and afterwards receive (the sinner) with mercy and compas-

---

2 Ez. xxxiii 10 f.   11–12 Cf. Hermas *Mand.* xii 6–2.   22 Ps. vi 6.

2–5 *And thou . . . we live?*] om. *AC*. In the next verse *AC* presents a different text from that of LXX.   7 *evil way*] H *AC*: om. 'evil' CS. 11–12 and may not despair . . . add to them] μή ποτε ὡς ἀπηλγηκότες ἑαυτοὺς ἐκδῶσιν ταῖς παρανομίαις *AC*, which however can hardly be the whole of the Gk. lying behind Syr. With the latter comp. Hermas *Mand.* xii 6. 2 οἱ διὰ τὰς ἁμαρτίας ὑμῶν ἀπεγνωκότες τὴν ζωὴν ὑμῶν καὶ προστιθέντες ἁμαρτίαις. For 'add to sins' see further *Mand.* iv 3. 7, *Sim.* vi 1. 4, viii 11. 3.   23 spares his soul] ὁ φειδόμενος τῆς ἑαυτοῦ ζωῆς *AC*. See again p. 54, l. 5.   25 strictly] ἀπ' ἐξουσίας *AC* (see p. 40, l. 27 and note).

sion, when he promises to repent. And rebuke and afflict him, and (afterwards) be entreated of him, [ii. 14] because of the word which is spoken in David thus: *Deliver not up the soul that confesseth to thee.* And in Jeremiah again He speaks thus concerning the repentance of them that sin: *Shall he that is fallen not rise up? or he that is turned away not return? Wherefore are my people turned away with a shameless perversion, and are held fast in their own devices, and have refused to repent and to return?* For this cause, then, receive him that repents without hesitating ever so little; and be not hindered by those who are without mercy, who say: 'It is not fitting that we should be defiled with these.' For the Lord God has said: *The fathers shall not die for the sons, nor the sons for the fathers.* And again in Ezekiel He speaketh thus: *And the word of the Lord came unto me saying: Son of man, if a land sin against me, and do iniquity before me, I will stretch forth my hand against her, and will destroy out of her the staff of bread, and will send a famine upon her, and will destroy out of her men and beasts. But if there be in her these three men, Noah and Daniel and Job, they by their righteousness shall deliver their souls, saith the Lord Adonai.* The Scripture, then, has shown clearly that if there be found a righteous man with an ungodly, he shall not perish with him, but every man shall be saved by his righteousness: and if he is hindered, it is by his own sins that he is hindered. And again in Wisdom He saith: *Every man is tied with the cord of his sins.* Each one therefore of the laity is to render an account of his own sins; and a man is not hurt by reason of

---

3 Ps. lxxiii (lxxiv) 19.   5 Jer. viii 4 f.   13 Deut. xxiv 16.   15 Ez. xiv 12–14.   26 Prov. v 22.

---

1 afflict] στύφων AC. Elsewhere the verb renders ὑποπιέζειν, cf. p. 54, l. 19: here it is explained in the margin of S by another verb which means 'to pound'.   3 *Deliver not up*] CHS: B and S marg. add 'to breaking' (from Pesh.): AC adds τοῖς θηρίοις, as LXX. 15 Syr. in this quotation is much influenced by Pesh.: AC again differs notably from LXX.

the sins of others. For neither did Judas harm us at all when he was praying with us, but he alone perished. And in the ark, Noah and his two sons who were saved alive, they were blessed; but Ham, his other son, was not (p. 17) blessed, but his seed was cursed; and the animals that went in, animals they came forth.

It behoves you not therefore to hearken to those who desire (to put to) death, and hate their brethren and love accusations, and are ready to slay on any pretext: ⟨for one shall not die for another⟩. But do you help them that are sore sick and exposed to danger and are sinning, that you may deliver them from death; and (do) not according to the hardness of heart and the word and thought of men, ⟨but according to the will and command of the Lord our God⟩. For it behoves thee not, O bishop, that being the head thou shouldst obey the tail, that is a layman, a contentious man who desires the destruction of another; but do thou regard only the word of the Lord God. And concerning this, that (men) are not to suppose that they perish or are defiled by the sins of others, He again cut off their evil thought, and by Ezekiel also the Lord our God spoke thus: [1] *And the word of the Lord came unto me, saying:* [2] *Son of man, why use ye this proverb in the land of Israel, and say: The fathers do eat sour grapes, and their sons' teeth are on edge?* [3] *As I live, saith the Lord Adonai, there shall no more be any that useth this proverb in Israel.* [4] *For all the souls are mine: as the soul of the father is mine, so also the soul of the son is mine. The soul that sinneth, the same shall die.* [5] *And a man, if he be righteous, and do judgement and righteousness,* [6] *and eat not upon the*

---

4 Cf. Gen. ix 25.   21 Ez. xviii 1–32.

2–6 And in the ark, etc.] καὶ ἐν τῇ κιβωτῷ Νῶε καὶ οἱ υἱοὶ αὐτοῦ ὑπῆρχον, ἀλλὰ πονηρὸς ὁ Χὰμ εὑρεθεὶς μόνος εἷς τῶν υἱῶν ἐδέξατο τιμωρίαν *AC*. The author of *AC* has removed the apparent suggestion that only two of Noah's sons were 'saved' (from the flood), and has introduced some other modifications. Lat. omits 'other' before 'son'. Cf. Irenaeus *Apost. Preaching* c. 20 (ed. J. A. Robinson): he quotes 'Cursed be Ham the child; a servant shall he be unto his brethren', following the reading of some LXX codd. ἐπικατάρατος Χάμ· παῖς οἰκέτης ἔσται κτλ. (see Dr. Robinson's note). The

[XIII] ... ⟨alieno de⟩licto. Neque enim Iudas nos nocuit cum nobiscum oraret, sed solus periit. Nam et in arca Noe ⟨et⟩ duo filii eius saluati et benedicti sunt, Cham autem filius eius, non, sed semen eius maledictum est: bestiae etiam, quae ingresse sunt, exierunt.

Non ergo oportet his, qui parati sunt ad mortem et odiunt fratres et diligunt crimina et cum occa[n]sionibus mortem quaerunt, uos adtendere: alius enim pro alio non morietur. Sed uos iuuate infirmis et periclitantibus et errantibus, et liberate eos de morte: non secundum duritiam cordis et uoluntatem hominum, sed secundum domini Dei nostri uoluntatem et praeceptum. Non enim oportet te, o episcope, cum sis caput, caude adtendere, id est laico uel seditioso homini, qui facile ducitur ad alterius perditionem, sed solum intendere uerbo domini Dei †de his†. Quod enim non potest quis perire pro alterius peccatis aut coinquinari [manifestum est], ut extollatur et abscidatur haec suspicio et malignorum hominum mens, per Ezechiel sic dicit dominus Deus noster: *¹Et factum est uerbum domini ad me dicens: ²Quare dicitis uos parabolam hanc in terra Istrahel: Patres manducauerunt uuam aceruam, et dentes filiorum indurati sunt? ³Uiuo ego, dicit Adonai dominus, si amplius dicetur parabola haec in Istrahel. ⁴Quoniam omnes anime meae sunt: quemadmodum anima patris, ita et anima fili, meae sunt: et anima quae peccat, ipsa morietur. ⁵Homo autem qui erit iustus, qui facit*

---

3 ⟨et⟩] καὶ AC (= Syr.).   8 alius] 'alios' cod.   15 de his] Perhaps read 'debes' (?).   quod enim non potest, etc.] περὶ γὰρ τοῦ μὴ δοκεῖν... συμμολύνεσθαι ἢ κοινωνεῖν ταῖς αὐτῶν ἁμαρτίαις ὁ Ἰεζεκιὴλ ἐκκόπτων τὴν τῶν κακοήθων ὑπόνοιαν λέγει AC (cf. Syr.).   16-17 manifestum est] Apparently an insertion by the translator, who has got into difficulties with the construction.   21 indurati sunt] ἐγομφίασαν LXX, but ἡμωδίασαν AC.

---

author of *Didasc.* may similarly have written ὁ δὲ Χὰμ παῖς.   5 animals 2°] om. Lat. (AC has not the clause). The word, even if added in Syr., appears to bring out the sense intended.   9-10 ⟨for ... another⟩] Supplied from Lat. AC.   13-14 ⟨but ... our God⟩] Supplied from Lat.: cf. AC οὐ γὰρ τὴν τῶν σκληροκαρδίων ἀνθρώπων βούλησιν ἰστᾶν χρή, ἀλλὰ τὴν τοῦ θεοῦ.   21 And the word, etc.] The text in Syr. is considerably influenced by Pesh., but the original Gk. also differed in many points from LXX, as appears from readings in the verses preserved by AC.

mountains, and lift not up his eyes to the idols of the house of Israel, and defile not the wife of his neighbour, and come not near to a woman in her menstruation, ⁷ *and treat no man with violence, and restore the pledge of his debtor which he hath taken, and clothe the naked with a garment,* ⁸ *and give not out his money on usury, and receive not (back) with overcharge, and turn away his hand from iniquity, and judge right judgement betwixt a man and his neighbour,* ⁹ *and walk in my laws, and keep my judgements and do them: this man is righteous, he shall surely live, saith the Lord Adonai.* ¹⁰ *And if he beget an evil son, that sheddeth blood and doeth iniquity,* ¹¹ *and walketh not in the way of his righteous father, and eateth upon the mountains, and defileth his neighbour's wife,* ¹² *and evil entreateth the poor and needy, and committeth robbery, and restoreth not the pledge which he hath taken, and lifteth up his eyes to idols, and doeth iniquity,* ¹³ *and giveth out his money on usury, and receiveth (back) with overcharge: this man shall not live: because he hath done all this iniquity, he shall surely die, and his blood shall be upon him.* ¹⁴ *But if he beget a son, and he see those sins which his father did, and fear and do not the like of them* (p. 18), ¹⁵ *and eat not upon the mountains, and lift not up his eyes to the idols of the house of Israel, and defile not his neighbour's wife,* ¹⁶ *and evil entreat no man, and take not a pledge, and commit not robbery, and give his bread to the hungry, and clothe the naked with a garment,* ¹⁷ *and turn away his hand from iniquity, and receive not usury and overcharge, and do righteousness and walk in my laws: this man shall not die for the iniquity of his father, but he shall surely live.* ¹⁸ *But his father, because he indeed committed oppression and robbery, and did not good to my people, shall die for his iniquity.* ¹⁹ *And ye say: Wherefore is not the son requited for the iniquity of his father? Because the son did righteousness and mercy, and kept all my commandments and did them, he shall surely live:* ²⁰ *the soul that sinneth, the same shall die. A son shall not be requited for the sins of his father; and a father*

---

1 *idols*] As Pesh. : 'desideria' Lat. = ἐνθυμήματα (and again in *v.* 15).
4–5 *which he hath taken*] From Pesh. (and again in *v.* 12) : after this a couple of clauses are wanting.

iudicium et iustitiam, ⁶ *in montibus non manducauit, et oculos*
[XIV] *suos non extollit ad desideria domus Istrahel, et uxorem
proximi sui non contaminauit, et ad mulierem menstruatam
non accedet,* ⁷ *et hominem inopem non deprimet, et pignus de-*
5 *bentis reddet, et rapinam non rapiet, et panem suum esurienti
dabit, et nudum operiet tunicam,* ⁸ *et pecuniam suam in usuram
non dabit, et superabundantiam non accipiet, et ab iniustitia
auertet manum suam, iudicium iustum faciet inter uirum et
inter proximum eius,* ⁹ *et in praeceptis meis ambulauit, iustifi-*
10 *cationes meas custodiuit ut faceret eas: iustus est hic, uita
uiuit, dicit Adonai dominus.* ¹⁰ *Et si genuerit filium pestem,
effundentem sanguinem et facientem peccata:* ¹¹ *in uia patris
sui iusti non ambulauit, sed in montibus manducauit, et uxorem
proximi sui contaminauit,* ¹² *et mendicum et pauperem depres-*
15 *sit, et rapinam rapiuit, et pignus non reddidit, et in simulacra
adposuit oculos suos, inquitatem fecit,* ¹³ *cum usura dedit, et
superabundantiam accepit: hic uita non uiuet: omnes has
iniquitates fecit, morte moriatur: sanguis eius super ipsum
erit.* ¹⁴ *Si autem genuerit filium, et uiderit omnia peccata*
20 *patris sui quae fecit, et timuerit et non fecerit secundum ista:*
¹⁵ *in montibus non manducauit, et oculos suos non posuit ad
desideria domus Istrahel, et uxorem proximi sui non contaminauit,* ¹⁶ *et hominem inopem non depressit, et pignus non pigne-
rauit, et rapinam non rapuit, panem suum* [XV] *esurienti dedit,*
25 *et nudum operuit uestimento,* ¹⁷ *et ab iniquitate auertit manum
suam, usuram et superabundantiam non accepit, iustitiam fecit
et in praeceptis meis ambulauit: non morietur in patris sui
iniquitatibus, uita uiuet.* ¹⁸ *Pater autem eius, si tribulationem
tribulauerit et rapuerit rapinam: contraria fecit in medio*
30 *populo meo, et morietur in sua iniquitate.* ¹⁹ *Et dicitis: Quid
est quod ⟨non⟩ recepit iniquitatem patris filius? Quia filius
iustitiam et misericordiam fecit, omnia legitima mea conseruabit et fecit ea, uita uiuet.* ²⁰ *Anima autem que peccat, ipsa
morietur; filius uero non accipiet ⟨in⟩iustitiam patris sui, neque*

4 *inopem* om. LXX (and again in *v.* 16).   11 *pestem*] λοιμόν *AC*
LXX.   18 *moriatur*] For 'morietur'.   32-33 *conseruabit*] For 'conseruauit'.

shall not be requited for the sins of his son. The righteousness of the righteous shall be upon him; and the iniquity of the ungodly shall be upon him. ²¹ *And if the ungodly shall turn away from all his iniquity which he did, and keep all my commandments, and do judgement and righteousness, he shall surely live and not die;* ²² *and all the iniquity which he did shall not be remembered unto him: for the righteousness which he did, for the same he shall live.* ²³ *For I desire not the death of the sinner, saith the Lord Adonai: but every one that shall turn from his evil way shall live.* ²⁴ *And if the righteous turn away from his righteousness, and do iniquity according to all the iniquity which the ungodly did: all his righteousness which he did shall not be remembered unto him, but for the iniquity which he did, and for the sins which he sinned, for the same he shall die.* ²⁵ *And they have said: The way of the Lord is not well. Hear ye, house of Israel: my way is well, but your own ways are not well.* ²⁶ *And if the righteous shall turn away from his righteousness and do iniquity: for the iniquity which he hath done he shall die.* ²⁷ *And if the ungodly shall turn away from his iniquity which he did, and shall do judgement and righteousness: this man hath delivered his soul.* ²⁸ *Because he turned away from all the iniquity which he did, he shall surely live and not die.* ²⁹ *And the house of Israel say: The way of the Lord is not well. My way is well, O house of Israel, but your own ways are not well.* ³⁰ *Therefore will I judge every man of you according to his ways, saith the Lord Adonai. Return and be converted from all your iniquity and your wickedness, lest these things be unto you for an evil torment.* ³¹ *And cast away and put from you all the wickedness which ye have done, and make to yourselves a new heart and a new spirit, and ye shall not die, O house of Israel:* ³² *for I desire not the death of the sinner, saith the Lord* (p. 19) *Adonai: but do ye return and live.*

[ii. 15] You see, beloved and dear children, how abundant are the mercies of the Lord our God and His goodness and loving-kindness towards us, and (how) He exhorts them that

---

34 ff. Cf. Hermas *Sim.* viii 6. 1, 5.

pater accipiet iniustitiam fili sui: iustitia iusti super ipsum erit, et iniquitas iniqui (super ipsum erit. ²¹ *Et iniquus,) si conuertat se ab omnibus iniustitiis suis quas fecit, et custodiat omnia mandata mea, et faciat iustitiam et misericordiam, uita uiuet et non morietur.* ²² *Omnia delicta eius quaecumque fecit non erunt in memoriam: in sua iustitia quam fecit uita uiuet.* ²³ *Numquid uoluntate uolo mortem iniusti, dicit dominus Deus, quam ut auertat se a uia sua mala et uiuet?* ²⁴ *Cum se autem auerterit iustus a sua iustitia et fecerit iniquitatem secundum omnes iniquitates quas fecit iniquus, omnes iustitiae eius quas fecit non erunt in memoria: in delicto suo quo excidit, et in peccatis suis quibus peccauit, in ipsis morietur.* ²⁵ *Et dixistis: Non dirigit uia domini. Audite nunc, omnes domus Istrahel: numquid uia mea non dirigit?* ²⁶ *Cum conuertet* [XVI] *se iustus a sua iustitia et faciet delictum, et morietur: in delicto quo fecit, in ipso morietur.* ²⁷ *Et in conuertendo se iniquus ab iniquitate sua quam fecit, et faciet iudicium et iustitiam: hic animam suam custodiuit.* ²⁸ *Et odit et auertet se ab omnibus iniquitatibus suis quas fecit: uita uiuet et non morietur.* ²⁹ *Et dicent domus Istrahel: Non corrigit uia*[m] *domini. Numquid uia mea non corrigit, domus Istrahel? Nonne uia uestra non corrigit?* ³⁰ *Ideoque unumquemque secundum uiam ipsius iudicabo, domus Istrahel, dicit Adonai dominus. Conuertimini et auertite uos ab omnibus inpietatibus uestris, et non erunt uobis in poenam (iniquitatis.* ³¹ *Proicite a uobis) omnes inpietates uestras quas inpie fecistis in me, et facite uobis cor nouum et spiritum nouum: et ut quid moriemini, domus Istrahel?* ³² *Quoniam nolo mortem morientis, dicit Adonai dominus: sed conuertimini ut uiuatis.*

Uidete, filioli, †dilectionem nostram, et† quomodo misericors est dominus Deus noster et in nos bonus et amabilis, et con-

8 *uiuet*] For 'uiuat'.   11 *excidit*] παρέπεσεν LXX: 'excedit' cod.
30 dilectionem nostram, et] (τέκνα) ἡμῶν ἠγαπημένα AC (cf. Syr.).   31 consulatur cod.

have sinned to repent. And in many places He speaks of these things; and He gives no place to the thought of those who are hard of heart and wish to judge strictly and without mercy, and to cast away altogether them that have sinned as though there were no repentance for them. But God (is) not so, but even sinners He calls to repentance and gives them hope; and those who have not sinned He teaches, and tells them that they should not suppose that we bear or partake in the sins of others. Simply, then, receive them that repent, rejoicing. For He spoke again in the same prophet concerning repentance thus: [12] *And thou, son of man, say to the sons of thy people: The righteousness of the righteous shall not deliver him in the day that he doeth wickedly; and the iniquity of the ungodly shall not hurt him in the day that he returneth from his iniquity: and the righteous cannot live in the day that he sinneth.* [13] *And when I shall say to the righteous that he shall surely live, and he rely upon his righteousness and do iniquity: all his righteousness shall not be remembered unto him, but for the iniquity which he hath done, for the same he shall die.* [14] *And when I shall say to the ungodly: Thou shalt surely die; and he turn from his sin and do judgement and righteousness,* [15] *and return the pledge which he hath taken, and restore that which he hath robbed, and walk in the judgements and commandments of life so that he do no iniquity: he shall surely live and not die,* [16] *and all his sins which he sinned shall not be remembered unto him: he hath done judgement and righteousness, he shall surely live.* [17] *And the sons of thy people say: The way of the Lord Adonai is not well. Say unto them: It is your own ways are not well:* [18] *for if the righteous shall turn away from his righteousness and do iniquity, he shall surely die for his iniquity;* [19] *and if the ungodly shall turn away from his iniquity and do judgement and righteousness, for the same he shall live.*

It behoves you then, O bishops, to judge according to the

11 Ez. xxxiii 12-19.

3-4 strictly and without mercy] ἀπηνῶς *AC*. (= Lat.). 11 *AC* omits this quotation. 9 simply] ἀσμένως *AC*

DIDASCALIA APOSTOLORUM 51

solatur peccatores ut conuertantur; et quotiens de ipsis repetens dicit, non reli⟨n⟩quens locum suspicionis his qui duro corde et sine misericordia uolunt iudicare et aperte expellere eos qui peccauerunt, tamquam non relinquatur illis penitentia.
5 Sed Deus non sic, sed et eos qui peccauerunt uocans ad paenitentiam bonam spem habere fecit; et qui non peccauerunt, non eos suspicari tamquam participes portare aliorum peccata, gratanter autem paenitentes suscipi et gratulari iubet. Similiter autem per eundem profetam de paeni⟨tentia⟩ . . .

3 aperte] .τέλεον AC (= Syr.).   4-5 tamquam . . . qui peccauerunt] Omitted by homoeoteleuton, but restored by a corrector's hand in the lower margin. Hauler, following the indication of the corrector, inserts the words after 'suspicari' (l. 7).   8 gratanter . . . iubet] ἀσμένως δὲ τοὺς μετανοοῦντας προσδέχεσθε, χαίροντες ἐπ' αὐτοῖς AC (cf. Syr.).

Scriptures those who sin, with gentleness and with mercy. For if, when a man is walking by the brink of a river and is ready to slip, thou by suffering him (to slip) hast thrust (and) cast him into the river, thou hast also committed murder. But if a man were to slip on the brink of a river and be near to perish, thou wouldst quickly reach out a hand to him and draw him out, lest he perish altogether. So do therefore (with the sinner); that both thy people may learn and understand, and he also that sins may not utterly perish.

[ii. 16] But when thou hast seen one who has sinned, be stern (p. 20) with him, and command that they put him forth; and when he is gone forth let them be stern with him, and take him to task, and keep him without the Church; and then let them come in and plead for him. For our Saviour Himself also was pleading with His Father for sinners, as it is written in the Gospel: *My Father, they know not what they do, neither what they speak: but if it be possible, do Thou forgive them.* And then do thou, O bishop, command him to come in, and examine him whether he be repentant. And if he is worthy to be received into the Church, appoint him days of fasting according to his offence, two or three weeks, or five, or seven; and so dismiss him that he may depart, saying to him whatever is right for admonition and instruction; and rebuke him, and say to him that he be by himself in

16 ? (Cf. Lk. xxiii 34, Mt. xxvi 39, 1 Tim. i 7).

2–4 For if ... committed murder] I am not sure that my rendering of this difficult passage is correct. *AC* reads (I bracket out some evident interpolations) ἐὰν γὰρ τὸν παρὰ ποταμὸν βαδίζοντα καὶ μέλλοντα ὀλισθαίνειν κεραίαις ὥσας εἰς τὸν ποταμὸν ἐμβάλῃς [ἀντὶ τοῦ χεῖρα μᾶλλον ὀρέξαι], ἐφόνευσάς [σου τὸν ἀδελφόν]. But here the words 'by suffering him', which seem important to the sense, do not appear. Perhaps there has been some confusion between ὥσας and ἐάσας: Syr. appears to represent both verbs. 13 take him to task] lit. 'judge with him', an expression which has the meaning to argue or wrangle with: ἐπιζητοῦντες *AC*. 16 *My Father, they know not*, etc.] CH: 'My brethren know not' (or, 'My brethren, they know not') BS. This strange quotation occurs again at p. 212, where Lat. is extant, and where BS read, with Lat., 'My Father' (CH are there wanting). In the present passage *AC* alters into agreement with Lk. xxiii 34, in the later place it omits. The text is not noticed by Resch or Ropes, yet the question whether it is not from some uncanonical source seems to deserve consideration.

humiliation, and that he beg and beseech during the days of his fast that he may be found worthy of the forgiveness of sins: as it is written in Genesis: *Hast thou sinned? be silent: thy repentance shall be with thee, and thou shalt have power over it.* To Mary the sister of Moses also, when she had spoken against Moses, and afterwards repented and was held worthy of forgiveness, it was said of the Lord: *If her father had but spit in her face, it were right for her to be ashamed, and to be separate seven days without the camp, and then to come in.* So it behoves you also to do: to put forth from the Church those who promise to repent of their sins (for a space) proportionate to their offences: and afterwards do you receive them as merciful fathers.

[ii. 17] But if the bishop be in himself a (cause of) offence, how can he stand up and make inquisition of any man's misdeeds, or rebuke him and give sentence upon him? For by reason of partiality, or of the presents which they receive—either he or the deacons, whose conscience is not pure—they (the deacons) cannot exert themselves to help the bishop; for they are afraid lest they should hear (from the sinner), as from an insolent man, that word which is written in the Gospel: *Why seest thou the mote that is in thy brother's eye, and perceivest not the beam that is in thine own eye? Thou hypocrite, cast out first the beam from thine eye; and then shalt thou perceive to cast the mote out of thy brother's eye.* The reason, then, that the bishop, with his deacons, is afraid, (is) lest they should hear from the sinner, as from an insolent man, that

---

3 Gen. iv 7.   7 Nu. xii 14.   22 Mt. vii 3, 5, Lk. vi 41 f.

---

3 *Hast thou sinned?* etc.] ἥμαρτες; ἡσύχασον· πρὸς σὲ ἡ ἀποστροφὴ αὐτοῦ, καὶ σὺ ἄρξεις αὐτοῦ LXX. If Syr. has rendered correctly, the author must have written ἡ ἀποστροφή σου, and this the context appears to imply. *AC* keeps only the first two words, evidently finding a difficulty in the rest. 16 give sentence upon him] This appears to be the meaning of ܘܡܦܣܩ ܚܠܛܝܗܘ, though I cannot find any other example of the expression. 25 The reason, etc.] lit. 'because, then, the bishop . . . is afraid, (it is) lest', etc. (HS). I take the construction to be one of the type in Nöldeke *Gram.* § 358 B, and I am not inclined with Flemming to emend into agreement with *AC* (εὐλαβείσθω οὖν . . . ἀκοῦσαι): it is the author's complaint that the bishop and deacons *are* afraid.

word of the Lord. For he knows not that it is a perilous thing for a man to speak against the bishop, and that he (the bishop) may be made an offence throughout the (p. 21) whole of that district. For one who has been sinning lacks understanding, and no more spares his soul. Hence, for whatever cause it be that the bishop is afraid, he feigns not to have knowledge of him who sins, and passes him over and rebukes and corrects him not. And hence Satan, when he has found him an occasion by means of one, gets power over others also—which God forbid that it should come about—and so it happens that the flock becomes such that it can no longer be set right. For when there are found many that sin, evil waxes strong; and whereas they that sin are not corrected and reproved that they should repent, this becomes to all an inducement to sin: and that which is said is fulfilled: *My house is called a house of prayer; but ye have made it a den of thieves.* But if the bishop keeps not silent from them that sin, but rebukes and reproves and corrects and admonishes and afflicts him that sins, he casts dread and fear upon others also. For it behoves the bishop to be by his doctrine a restrainer of sins and an example and encourager of righteousness, and by the admonition of his teaching a director of good works, and one who lauds and magnifies the good things which are to come and are promised by God in the place of life everlasting: a proclaimer also of the wrath to come in the judgement of God, with threatening of the grievous fire which is unquenchable and intolerable. And let him know the meaning of God's will, that he despise no man; because our Saviour has said: *See that ye despise not any of these little ones that believe in me.*

[ii. 18] Let the bishop therefore be careful of all, both of

---

15 Mt. xxi 13, Lk. xix 46.   29 Mt. xviii 10 (cf. *v.* 6).

5 spares his soul] Cf. p. 42, l. 23.   19 afflicts] ὑποπιέζειν *AC* (and again at p. 56, l. 13).   27 meaning] lit. 'working' or 'effect'. Flemming takes the expression to mean the working of God's good pleasure, and so 'the course of action that is pleasing to God'.   29 *any*] lit. 'anyone', after which is added 'one' (the numeral), prob. as a gloss.   *that believe in me*] om. *AC*. The addition (from Mt. xviii 6) is found here in *syr. cur.* and Aphraates, but not in *syr. sin.* or *syr. vulg.* (see Burkitt *in loc.*).

them that have not sinned, that they may continue as they are without sin, and of them that have sinned, that they may repent, and that he may grant them forgiveness of sins, as it is written in Isaiah that the Lord saith: *Loose every bond of iniquity, and sever all bands of violence and extortion.*

CHAPTER VII

To Bishops.

Do thou therefore, O bishop, teach and rebuke, and loose by forgiveness. And know thy place, that it is that of God Almighty, and that thou hast received authority to forgive sins. For to you bishops it was said: *All that ye shall bind on earth, it shall be bound in heaven; and all that ye shall loose, it shall be loosed.* As therefore thou hast authority to loose, know thyself and thy manners and thy conversation (p. 22) in this life, that they be worthy of thy place. But without sin there is none among men, for it is written: *There is no man pure of defilement, not even though his life in the world be but one day.* Therefore the life and manner of conversation of the just men and patriarchs was written, that it might be known that in each one of them there was found at least some small sin; that it might be understood that the Lord God alone is without sin, as He said in David: *That thou mayest be justified in thy words, and prevail in thy judgements.* For the little defilement of the just is to us a solace and an encouragement, and a (source of) trust that we also, if we sin but a little, have a hope of obtaining forgiveness.

4 Isa. lviii 6.   9 Mt. xviii 18.   13 Cf. 3 Reg. viii 46, 2 Paral. vi. 36.   14 Job xiv 4 f. (LXX).   20 Ps. l (li) 6.

---

24 but a little] lit. 'provided that (it be) a little': ܐܢ ܩܠܝܠ. For ܐܢ in this sense see again p. 178, l. 11: a man's sins are forgiven by baptism, 'but after baptism also, *provided that* he has *not* (ܠܐ ܐܢ) sinned a deadly sin'. The word ordinarily means 'even if', 'although', sometimes 'at least', answering in meaning and formation to Gk. κἄν; but the present examples seem to show that it was capable of an almost opposite sense. The words might possibly be taken with what follows: 'if we sin, have *at least a little* hope', but I do not think this is intended.

There is no man, then, without sin. But do thou strive according to thy power to be *in nothing reproachable*. And have a care of all, that none may stumble and perish by reason of thee. For a layman has the care of himself alone, but thou carriest the burden of all. And very great is the load that thou bearest; *for to whom the Lord hath given much, much also will he require at his hand.* As therefore thou carriest the burden of all, be watchful; for it is written: *The Lord said unto Moses: Thou and Aaron shall take upon you the sins of the priesthood.* For as thou art to render an account for many, so be careful of all; for those that are sound thou shalt preserve, but those that have sinned do thou admonish and rebuke and afflict; and (afterwards) ease them with forgiveness. And when he that sinned has repented and wept, receive him; and while the whole people prays over him, lay hand upon him, and suffer him henceforth to be in the Church. But those who are drowsy and slack do thou bring back and stir up and make firm, and exhort them and make them sound: for thou knowest what reward thou hast if thou do thus; but if thou neglect it, danger shall come upon thee; for the Lord spoke thus in Ezekiel concerning those bishops who neglect their people: [1] *And the word of the Lord came unto me, saying:* [2] *Son of man, prophesy against the shepherds of Israel, and say to them: Thus saith the Lord, Adonai: Woe unto the shepherds of Israel, who feed themselves; and my sheep the shepherds have not fed.* [3] *The milk*

---

2 1 Tim. iii 2.   6 Lk. xii 48.   9 Nu. xviii 1.   22 Ez. xxxiv 1–31.

2 *in nothing reproachable*] ἀνεπίληπτος *AC*.   14 And when, etc.] καὶ προσκλαύσαντα εἰσδέχου πάσης τῆς ἐκκλησίας ὑπὲρ αὐτοῦ δεομένης, καὶ χειροθετήσας αὐτὸν ἔα λοιπὸν εἶναι ἐν τῷ ποιμνίῳ *AC*.   22 ff. Of this quotation *AC* has kept only vv. 2–5, 8, 10, 17–19, 30–31, but a few of the intervening verses appear in the subsequent commentary. The passage well illustrates what has already been noted, that the author of *Didasc.* used a text of Ezek. which had the character of a revision of the LXX. Lat. is extant from v. 12; but it is to be observed that Lat. has been assimilated in part to the LXX under influence of some pre-Vulgate Latin text. Only a selection of the variants from LXX can be considered in these notes. 25 *Woe*, etc.] οὐαὶ τοῖς ποιμέσι τοῦ Ἰσραήλ, οἳ ἐποίμαινον ἑαυτούς· οὐ τὰ πρόβατα ποιμαίνουσιν οἱ ποιμένες, ἀλλ' ἑαυτούς *AC*: ὦ ποιμένες Ἰσραήλ, μὴ βόσκουσιν ποιμένες ἑαυτούς; οὐ τὰ πρόβατα βόσκουσιν οἱ ποιμένες; LXX.

ye eat, and with the wool ye are clothed, and that which is fat ye kill; and the sheep ye feed not. ⁴ That which was sick ye healed not, and that which was weak ye strengthened not, and that which was broken ye bound not up, and that which was gone astray (p. 23) ye brought not back, and that which was lost ye sought not out; but with force and with derision ye have subdued them. ⁵ And my sheep were scattered for lack of a shepherd, and became meat for every beast of the field. ⁶ And my sheep were scattered and gone astray on all the high mountains and on all the high hills, and on all the face of the land were my sheep scattered, and there was none to require and seek. ⁷ Wherefore, ye shepherds, hear the word of the Lord Adonai. ⁸ Forasmuch as my sheep are become a spoil and meat to every beast of the field for lack of a shepherd, and the shepherds have not sought my sheep, but the shepherds have fed themselves, and my sheep the shepherds have not fed: ⁹ therefore, ye shepherds, hear the word of the Lord. ¹⁰ Thus saith the Lord Adonai: Behold, I am against the shepherds, and I will seek my sheep at their hands; and I will cause them to cease, that henceforth they feed not my sheep: and the shepherds shall no more feed themselves; but I will deliver my sheep out of their hands, and they shall no more be to them for meat. ¹¹ For thus saith the Lord Adonai: Therefore, behold, I will seek my sheep and visit them: ¹² as a shepherd visiteth his sheep in the day of tempest, when he is in their midst, so will I visit my sheep.

6–7 *but with force ... subdued them*] CH; BS omit 'and with derision' here, but read the words later in the commentary: καὶ ἐν κράτει ἐπαιδεύσατε αὐτὰ μετὰ ἐμπαιγμοῦ AC (and cf. Lat. at p. 64, l. 16): καὶ τὸ ἰσχυρὸν κατειργάσασθε μόχθῳ LXX. The reading of AC is found approximately in a group of hexaplaric MSS. which frequently support Syr. and AC against LXX (see Field *in loc.*). 19 *and I will cause them to cease*] As Pesh.: but also καὶ καταπαύσω αὐτούς AC: καὶ ἀποστρέψω αὐτούς LXX.

And I will gather them together from all places wherein they were scattered in the day of cloud and thick darkness; ¹³ and I will bring them forth from the peoples, and gather them from the lands, and bring them into their land; and I will feed them in the mountains of Israel, and in all the waste places of the land. ¹⁴ And in a good and fat pasture will I feed them, and in the mountains of the Most High of Israel shall be the glory of their beauty. There shall they be encamped in a good encampment, and in a fat pasture shall they be fed in the mountains of Israel. ¹⁵ I will feed my sheep, and I will stablish them, saith the Lord Adonai: ¹⁶ that which is lost will I seek, and that which is gone astray will I bring back, and that which is broken will I bind up, and that which is sick will I strengthen, and that which is fat and sound will I keep: and I will feed them in judgement. ¹⁷ And ye, my sheep, the sheep of my flock, thus saith the Lord Adonai: Behold, I will judge between ewe and ewe, and between ram and ram. ¹⁸ Is this a small thing to you, that ye devour a good and fat pasture, and the residue of your pasture ye trample upon with your feet, ¹⁹ and my sheep did drink that which was trodden with your feet? ²⁰ Wherefore thus saith the Lord Adonai: Behold, I will judge between ewe and ewe, and between them that are sick: ²¹ because that ye were thrusting them with your sides and with your shoulders, and with your horns ye were butting all the sick ones, until ye had scattered them abroad. ²² And I will deliver my sheep, and they shall no more be for a spoil: (p. 24) and I will judge between ewe and ewe. ²³ And I will set over them one shepherd, and he shall feed them, and he shall be their shepherd; ²⁴ and David my servant shall be their ruler in their midst: I the Lord have spoken it. ²⁵ And I will make for them a covenant of peace, and will cause evil beasts to cease from the land; and they shall dwell in the wilderness securely, and sleep in the

---

5 *waste places*] κατοικίᾳ LXX (= Lat.). Syr. omits the preceding clause καὶ ἐν ταῖς φάραγξιν. 6–7 *in the mountains of the Most High*] ἐν τῷ ὄρει τῷ ὑψηλῷ LXX. 7–8 *shall be the glory of their beauty*] Apparently from ἔσται εὐπρέπεια αὐτῶν, found in hexaplaric MSS. 15 *the sheep of my flock*] om. Heb. Pesh. LXX : prob. due to influence of *v*. 31. 18–20 *that ye ... your feet*] AC shows a similar shortening of *vv*. 18–19, μὴ μικρὸν (ἱκανόν LXX) ἦν ὑμῖν ὅτι τὴν νομὴν τὴν καλὴν ἐνέμεσθε, καὶ τὰ κατάλοιπα τῆς

DIDASCALIA APOSTOLORUM

[XVII] ... [12] *et congregabo illas ab omni loco in quo disperse erant illic in die nubis et globi.* [13] *Et educam illos de nationibus, et congregabo eas de regionibus omnibus, et inducam illos in terram ipsorum, et pascam illos in montibus Istrahel et in conuallibus et in omni habitatione terrae.* [14] *In pascua bona pascam illas, in monte alto Istrahel: et erunt cubilia eorum illic, et dormient et illic* [*et*] ⟨*re*⟩*quiescent in diliciis optimis, in pascua pinguia pascentur in montibus Istrahel.* [15] *Ego pascam oues meas, et ego reficiam eas, et scient quod ego sum dominus.* *Haec dicit dominus:* [16] *Quod periit requiram, et quod errat conuertam, et adtritum alligabo, et quod defecit confortabo, et quod est forte custodiam: et pascam illas cum iudicio.* [17] *Et uos, oues, haec dicit dominus Deus: Ecce ego discernam inter ouem et ouem, arietem et hircum.* [18] *Et non est* ⟨*satis*⟩ *uobis quod bona pascua pascebatis et residua pascua pedibus uestris conculcabatis, et decolatam aquam bibebatis et residuam pedibus uestris turbabatis?* [19] *et oues meae conculcationem pedum uestrorum pascebantur, et aquam turbatam pedibus uestris bibebant?* [20] *Propterea haec dicit dominus Deus: Ecce discerno inter medium ouis firmae et inter medium ouis infirmae.* [21] *Lateribus et umeris uestris inpellebatis, et omne quod deficiebat uexabatis.* [22] *Et liberabo oues meas, et amplius non erint in direptionem, et iudicabo inter medium arietis et arietem.* [23] *Et suscitabo illis pastorem unum, et reget eos* [XVIII] *seruus meus Dauid, et erit eorum pastor:* [24] *et ego dominus ero illis in Deum, et Dauid in medio eorum princeps: ego dominus locutus sum.* [25] *Et disponam cum Dauid testamentum pacis, et exterminabo bestias malas de terra, et habitabunt in deserto et*

14 *arietem et hircum*] = κριοῦ κ. τράγου LXX (A): κριὸν πρὸς κριόν AC (= Syr.). *Et non est* ⟨*satis*⟩ *uobis*] Possibly 'parum' should be supplied: μὴ μικρὸν ἦν ὑμῖν AC (= Syr.): καὶ οὐχ ἱκανὸν ὑμῖν LXX. 21 *inpellebatis*] After this καὶ τοῖς κέρασιν ὑμῶν ἐκερατίζετε is not represented.

νομῆς κατεπατεῖτε τοῖς ποσὶν ὑμῶν, καὶ τὰ πρόβατα τὰ πατήματα τῶν ποδῶν ὑμῶν ἤσθιον (where also two MSS. read ἔπινεν for the last verb). 24–25 *until ... abroad*] om. LXX: ἕως οὗ ἐξώσατε (ἐξεθλίψατε) αὐτὰ ἔξω codd. hexàpl. 27 *ewe and ewe*] As Pesh. *shepherd*] After this the words 'even my servant David' have perhaps fallen out. 28 *shepherd*] After this the words 'and I the Lord will be their God' are wanting. 30 *for them*] As Pesh. 32 *securely*] om. LXX: 'in quiet' Pesh.: πεποιθότες Aq. Theod.

woods. ²⁶ *And I will give to them round about my mountain a blessing; and I will send down rain in its season, and it shall be rain of blessing.* ²⁷ *And the trees of the field shall give their fruits, and the land shall give its increase. And they shall dwell in their land securely: and they shall know that I am the Lord, when I shall cut the thongs of their yoke. And I will deliver them from the hand of them that subdued them,* ²⁸ *and they shall no more be for a prey to the peoples, and the beasts of the field shall no more devour them; but they shall lie down securely, and there shall be none to make them afraid.* ²⁹ *And I will establish for them a plantation for renown; and they shall no more be few and forsaken in the land, and they shall no more bear the shame of the peoples.* ³⁰ *And they shall know that I am the Lord their God with them, and they are my people of the house of Israel, saith the Lord Adonai.* ³¹ *And ye my sheep, the sheep of my flock, are men, and I am your God, saith the Lord Adonai.*

[ii. 19.] Hear, then, ye bishops, and hear, ye laymen, how the Lord saith: *I will judge between ram and ram, and between ewe and ewe*; that is, between bishop and bishop, and between layman and layman: whether layman loves layman, [ii. 20] and whether again the layman loves the bishop and honours and fears him as father and lord, and (as) God after God Almighty; for to the bishop it was said through the apostles: *Every one that heareth you, heareth me; and every one that rejecteth you rejecteth me, and him that sent me*: and again, whether the bishop loves the laity as his children, and cherishes and keeps them warm with loving care, as eggs from which

---

19 Ez. xxxiv 17 (cf. 22).   25 Lk. x 16.

2 *a blessing*] om. LXX: εὐλογίαν codd. hexapl.   *in its season*] As Pesh. (= Heb.).   5 *securely*] As Heb.: ἐν ἐλπίδι εἰρήνης LXX: 'in hope' Pesh.   10 *securely*] As Heb.: ἐν ἐλπίδι LXX (= Pesh.)   11 *for renown*] lit. 'for name' (= לְשֵׁם of the Mass. Text): εἰρήνης (= שָׁלוֹם) LXX (= Pesh.): εἰς ὄνομα codd. hexapl.   12 *few . . . in the land*] ἀπολλύμενοι λιμῷ ἐπὶ τῆς γῆς LXX: 'vexed with famine in the land' Pesh.: ὀλίγοι ἀριθμῷ ἐν τῇ γῇ codd. hexapl.   14 *with them*] μετ' αὐτῶν Aq. Theod.: om. LXX Pesh.   15 *And ye*, etc.] Nearly as Pesh.: *AC* has (for *vv*. 30, 31) καὶ γνώσεσθε ὅτι ἐγὼ κύριος· καὶ ὑμεῖς, πρόβατα τῆς νομῆς μου, ἄνθρωποί μου ἐστέ, και ἐγὼ θεὸς ὑμῶν, λέγει Ἀδωναῒ κύριος: LXX omit (but codd. hexapl. read) ἄνθρωποί (μου) ἐστέ.   20 *that is*, etc.] τοῦτ' ἔστιν

dormient in saltibus. [26] *Et dabo eis percircuitum montis mei, et dabo uobis pluuiam benedictionis.* [27] *Et ligna quae in campo sunt dabunt fructum suum, et terra dabit uires suas: et habitabunt in terra sua in spe pacis, et scient quod ego sum dominus, dum contero iugum ipsorum. Et eripiam eos de manu ipsorum qui illos in seruitutem redigerunt,* [28] *et amplius non erunt in direptionem nationibus, et bestiae terrae amplius non manducabunt eos: et habitabunt in spe, nec erit qui exterreat eos.* [29] *Et suscitabo eis plantationem pacis, et ultra non erunt fame pereuntes super terram, et non fient amplius obprobrium nationum.* [30] *Et scient quod ego sum dominus Deus ipsorum, et ipsi populus meus domus Istrahel, dicit dominus:* [31] *et uos (oues) gregis mei estis, et ego dominus Deus uester, dicit dominus Deus.*

Audite, episcopi, et audite, laici, quomodo dicit dominus: *Et iudicabo arietem contra arietem et ouem contra ouem,* id est episcopum contra episcopum et laicum contra laicum, et laicum contra episcopum. Diligite ergo et honorate episcopum, et timete sicut patrem et dominum et secundum Deum. Episcopis ergo dictum est per apostolos: *Qui uos audit, me audit: et qui uos spernit, me spernit, et eum qui me misit.* Similiter episcopus . . .

7 *besteis* cod.   12 ⟨*oues*⟩] Probably several words are missing, cf. *A* and Syr.: LXX have πρόβατά μου καὶ πρόβατα ποιμνίου μού ἐστε.   16-17 et laicum contra episcopum] Not represented in *AC*, but possibly paraphrased in Syr.   18 secundum Deum] 'after God' Syr. (see note to p. 20, l. 8 f.).   Perh. supply 'Deum' before this (cf. Syr.).

ἐπίσκοπον πρὸς ἐπίσκοπον κρινῶ καὶ λαϊκὸν πρὸς λαϊκόν . . . τὸν μέντοι ποιμένα [τὸν ἀγαθὸν] ὁ λαϊκὸς τιμάτω, ἀγαπάτω, φοβείσθω ὡς πατέρα, ὡς κύριον, ὡς δεσπότην . . . *AC*. The words 'whether layman loves layman' are not represented in Lat. or *AC*.   25-26 *and every one . . . sent me*] Lat. also omits the equivalent of καὶ ὁ ἐμὲ ἀθετῶν ἀθετεῖ after 'me spernet, et': *AC* supplies those words. The same form of text appears in Syr. again at p. 93, l. 7, where *AC* omits the quotation: *syr. sin*, reads (but with a different verb) 'and he that rejecteth you rejecteth him that sent me'.   26-27 and again, whether, etc.] ὁμοίως ὁ ἐπίσκοπος ὡς τέκνα τοὺς λαϊκοὺς ἀγαπάτω, θέλγων καὶ θερμαίνων τῇ σπουδῇ τῆς ἀγάπης ὡς ᾠὰ εἰς περιποίησιν νοσσίων ἢ ὡς νοσσία ἀγκαλιζόμενος εἰς περιποίησιν ὀρνίθων *AC*. cherishes] lit. 'rears' in the sense of developing.

young birds are to come; or broods over them and cherishes them as young birds, for the rearing up of winged fowl. Teach, then, and admonish all; and them that deserve rebuke, rebuke and afflict: but unto conversion and not unto destruction; and admonish unto repentance and correct them, so that thou make 5 their ways straight and fair, and order well the conduct of their life in the world.

That which is whole preserve: that is, him that is established in the faith guard watchfully; and shepherd the whole people in peace. (p. 25) *And that which is weak strengthen*: that is, 10 him that is tempted confirm with admonition. *And that which is sick heal*: that is, him that is sick with doubting of his faith, heal with doctrine. *And that which is broken bind up*: that is, him that is stricken or buffeted or broken by his sins, and halts from the right way, bind up; that is, with the exhorta- 15 tion of admonition cure him, and lighten him of his transgressions, and comfort him and show him that there is hope for him; and bind him up and heal him and bring him into the Church. *And that which is gone astray bring back*: that is, him that was left in sins and was put forth for reproof, 20 leave not without, but teach and admonish him, and bring him back and receive him into thy flock, that is, into the people of the Church. *And that which is lost seek out*: that is, him who by reason of the multitude of his transgressions has despaired and abandoned himself to destruction, suffer 25 not to perish altogether, lest through utter neglect and indifference he fall asleep, and under the weight of his sleep forget his life, and hold aloof and depart from his flock, that is from the Church, and come to perdition. For when he shall be without the fold and removed from the flock, wolves 30

---

8 Ez. xxxiv 16.   10 *Ibid.* 4.   11 *Ibid.* 4.   13 *Ibid.* 4, 16.
19 *Ibid.* 4, 16.   23 *Ibid.* 4, 16.

13 with doctrine] διὰ τῆς διδασκαλίας *AC* (not transliterated in Syr.).
14 stricken] τὸ πεπλανημένον *AC*. Syr. represents τὸ πεπληγμένον, which here must be right. See p. 64, l. 10 for the same variant with the authorities reversed.   19 bring back] ἐπίστρεφε *AC*. Here Syr. (BCHS) reads 'persuade' or 'entreat', but we must correct ܐܦܝܣ to ܐܗܦܟ, as in the continuous text above, and at l. 21 below.   20 left] γενόμενον *AC*.

will devour him while he is astray, and he will perish utterly. But do thou seek him out, and admonish and teach him, and bring him back; and visit him, and encourage him to be wakeful, and let him know that there is hope for him. And cut away this from men's thought, that they should say or imagine that which has already been rehearsed: *Our crimes and our sins are upon us, and in them we are wasted away: how then can we live?* For they ought not to say or to imagine these things; and they are not to think that their hope is cut off by reason of the multitude of their sins; but they are to know that the mercies of God are many, for that with an oath and with gracious intent He has promised forgiveness to them that sin.

But if a man sin and know not the Scriptures, and is not aware of the patience and mercy of God, and knows not the limit of forgiveness and repentance: by this very thing, that he is ignorant, he perishes. Do thou therefore as a compassionate shepherd, full of love and mercy and careful of his flock, visit and count thy flock, and seek that which is gone astray; as said the Lord God, Jesus Christ our good Teacher and Saviour: (p. 26) 'Leave the ninety and nine upon the mountains, and go seek that one which is gone astray. And when thou hast found it, bear it upon thy shoulders, rejoicing because thou hast found that which was gone astray; and bring it and let it mix with the flock.' So be thou also obedient, O bishop, and search out him that is lost, and seek him that is gone astray, and bring back him that is holding

---

6 Ez. xxxiii 10.   21 Cf. Mt. xviii 12 ff., Lk. xv 4 ff.   26 Cf. Ez. xxxiv 16.

---

20 ff. as said ... Christ] ὡς κύριος ὁ θεὸς ὁ ἀγαθὸς πατὴρ ἡμῶν, ἀποστείλας τὸν ἑαυτοῦ υἱὸν ποιμένα καλὸν καὶ σωτῆρα τὸν διδάσκαλον ἡμῶν Ἰησοῦν, ἐπιτρέψας αὐτῷ ἐάσαι τὰ ἐνενήκοντα ἐννέα ἐπὶ τὰ ὄρη κτλ. *AC*. Here no doubt there is much alteration, and it might seem that the compiler of *AC* took exception to the words κύριος ὁ θεός as applied to our Lord. But the following words in Syr. also ('so be thou also obedient' = οὕτως οὖν ὑπήκοος γίνου καὶ σύ *AC*) imply that an example of obedience has been set the bishop by Christ. Perhaps then we should read 'to (*or* through) Jesus Christ our good Teacher'. As regards the Gospel reference, *AC* probably gives it in the correct form, while Syr. by using the direct speech has made it look as if the author intended a verbal quotation.

aloof. For thou hast authority *to forgive sins to him that offendeth*; for thou hast put on the person of Christ. Wherefore our Saviour also said to him that had sinned: *Thy sins are forgiven thee: thy faith hath saved thee alive: go in peace.* Now 'peace' is the Church of tranquillity and rest, into which He restored those whom He loosed from sins, sound (and) without blemish, having a good hope and earnest in exercises of labours and afflictions. For as a wise and compassionate physician He was healing all, and especially those who were †gone astray† in their sins; for *they that are whole have no need of a physician, but they that are sick.* And thou also, O bishop, art made the physician of the Church: do not therefore withhold the cure whereby thou mayest heal them that are sick with sins, but by all means cure and heal, and restore them sound to the Church. And be not reproached with this word which the Lord spoke: *With force and with derision ye were subduing them.* [ii. 21.] Do not then use force, and be not violent, and pass not sentence sharply, and be not unmerciful; and deride not the people that is under thy charge, nor hide from them the word of repentance. For this is that, *With force and with derision ye were subduing them,* if thou deal harshly with thy lay folk, and correct them *with force,* and thrust and drive out and receive not (back) them that sin, but harshly and without mercy hide away repentance from them, and become a helper for the †return of evil,† and for the scattering of the flock *for meat to the beasts of the field,* that is, to evil men of this world: nay, not to men in truth, but to beasts, to the heathen and to heretics. For to him who goes forth from the Church they presently join themselves, and like evil beasts devour him as meat. And by reason of thy harshness, he who goes forth from the Church

---

1 Lk. iv 18, Isa. lviii 6 (cf. *AC* and Lat.). 3 Mt. ix 2 (etc.). 4 Mk. x 52, Lk. xvii 19: Mk. v 34, Lk. vii 50, viii 48. 10 Mt. ix 12 (etc.). 16 Ez. xxxiv 4 (see p. 57 and note). 26 Ez. xxxiv 5.

---

1 *to forgive,* etc.] ἀποστέλλειν τεθραυσμένους ἐν ἀφέσει *AC* (Lk. iv 18, Isa. lviii 6). Syr. has obscured the quotation. 5 into which] Referring to εἰς εἰρήνην of the Gospel text. 6 He restored, etc.] λύων ... ἀποκαθίστα *AC* (=Lat.). 7–8 earnest ... afflictions] σπουδαίους, ἐργοπόνους *AC*. 10 gone

[XIX] . . . *dimittere in remissione quod quassatum est*, Christi uultum portans. Per te saluator dicit his qui peccauerunt: *Remittuntur tibi peccata tua. Fidis tua saluum te fecit, uade in pace.* Pax uero est tranquilla ecclesia, in qua
5 soluens eos qui peccauerunt restitue sanos, inmaculatos, bonam spem gerentes, efficaces, in opere dolentes, sicut peritus et condolens medicus omnes sanans qui per peccata plagati sunt: *non enim opus habent hii qui sani sunt medicum, sed qui male habent.* Ut medicus ergo super ecclesiam constitutus, noli
10 cessare offerendo medicinam his qui in peccatis egrotant, sed omni modo cura eos et sana, et integros redde ecclesiae, ut non incurras in hunc uerbum quem dicit dominus: *Et in potentia erudiebatis illa cum inlusione.* Non potens nec austerus nec durus nec abscisus nec sine misericordia: noli
15 inludere populo qui sub te ligatus est, abscondens ab eo paenitentiae locum. Hoc enim est quod dicit: *Et in potentia erudiebatis ea cum inlusione,* si [ergo] durius agas cum laicis et fortiter corripias eos, ita ut abicias eos et proicias et non suscipias qui peccauerunt, sed absque miseratione abscondas
20 ab eis paenitentiam et conuersionem, et cum non fueris cooperans eis, disseminas oues *ad escam bistearum agri,* id est maligni⟨s⟩ saeculi huius hominibus, magis autem non hominibus, sed besteis, hoc est gentilibus et hereticis. Ei enim qui expulsus est de ecclesia mox se adiungunt, et sicut [XX]
25 agnum besteae, ita eum illi comidere existimant: et per tuam

---

2 uultum] Prob. for πρόσωπον, 'person' (= Syr.): *AC* omits the phrase.
6 in opere dolentes] = ἐργοπόνους *AC*.   14 abscisus] ἀπότομος *AC*.
17 ergo] To be omitted, with Syr.   23 Ei enim qui] Cf. Syr.: 'etenim qui' cod.

---

astray] πεπληγμένους *AC* (= Lat.): Syr. has mistaken this for πεπλανημένους, or actually read the latter word. See p. 62, l. 14 for the same variant with the authorities reversed.   16 *With force,* etc.] See on this reading p. 57, l. 6.   22 thy lay folk] lit. 'the sons of thy people'; but elsewhere in this version 'son of the people' is used for layman, and Lat. has here 'laicis'.   25 and become, etc.] Cf. Lat.: Syr. appears to have paraphrased in a very curious way, unless there is some corruption. The word rendered 'return' more naturally means 'overturning'; I am inclined therefore to correct: 'and become a helper for the overthrow [of evil] and scattering of the flock', omitting 'of evil'.   30 and . . . as meat] ὡς ἄρνα βορὰν (*al. leg.* ἀρνοβόρα) ἡγοῦνται *AC* (cf. Lat.).

will either depart and enter among the heathen, or will be sunk in the heresies; and he will become an alien altogether, and will depart (p. 27) from the Church and from the hope of God. And of the perdition of that (man) thou wilt be guilty, because thou art ready to drive out and cast away them that sin, and when they have repented and been converted thou wilt not receive them again. And thou hast fallen under the condemnation of that word of the Lord which He spoke: *Their feet are swift to evil, and they hasten to shed blood. Affliction and misery are in their ways; and the way of peace they have not known.* Now *the way of peace* is our Saviour Himself, as He said: *Forgive ye the sins of them that sin, that to you also your sins may be forgiven: give, and it shall be given unto you*; which means: *Give* forgiveness of sins, that you also may receive forgiveness. And again He taught us that we should be constantly praying at all times and saying: *Forgive us our debts, as we also have forgiven our debtors.* But if thou forgive not them that sin, how shalt thou receive forgiveness? Lo, is not thine own mouth against thee, and dost not thou condemn thyself in that thou hast said, 'I have forgiven', when thou hast not forgiven, but in sooth hast slain? For he who drives a man out of the Church without mercy, what does he else but cruelly slay and shed blood without pity? For if by any a righteous man is unjustly slain with the sword, with God he shall be received into rest; but he who drives a man out of the Church and receives him not again, has committed everlasting murder, evilly and bitterly, and [God] gives for food to the grievous fire eternal him that is driven out from the Church, and regards not the mercy of God, and remembers not His goodness towards penitents,

---

9 Isa. lix 7 f.   12 Lk. vi. 37 f.   16 Mt. vi 12   24 Wisd. iv 7.

1 among the heathen] εἰς ἔθνη *AC*: Flemming treats the prep. *bēth*, 'among', as if it were the subst. 'house', and translates 'to the temple of the heathen'.   be sunk] συμποδισθήσεται *AC*: see again p. 194, l. 12.   12–14 *Forgive* . . . *given unto you*] ἄφετε, καὶ ἀφεθήσεται ὑμῖν· δίδοτε, καὶ δοθήσεται ὑμῖν *AC*, then continuing τοῦτ' ἔστιν, δίδοτε ἄφεσιν ἁμαρτιῶν. Thus Lat. is clearly wrong in omitting the second clause of the text, 'give . . . given unto you'. Moreover, it is possible

DIDASCALIA APOSTOLORUM 67

abscisionem is qui expulsus est ad gentiles reuertitur, et omni modo ab ecclesia et ea quae in Deo est spes alienabitur; et perditionis eius tu eris reus. Et cum paratissimus es eos qui peccant expellere, et iam non reuersantes suscipis eos, in-
5 curras in uerbum domini, ubi dicit: *Pedes illorum currunt ad malignitatem, ueloces ad effundendum sanguinem : contri[fi]tio et infelicitas in uiis eorum, et uiam pacis non cognouerunt.* Uia autem pacis est saluator noster, qui et dicit nobis : *Dimittite, et dimittitur uobis*, hoc est: Date remissionem peccato-
10 rum, et recipietis. Nam et docuit nos incessanter orantes dicere : *Remitte nobis debita nostra, sicut et nos remisimus debitoribus nostris.* Si ergo non remiseris his qui peccauerunt, quomodo recipies? Nonne econtra per tuum ipsius os te conlegas, dicens remisisse, et non remisisti, sed inter-
15 fecisti? Qui enim de ecclesia pellit eum qui conuertitur, interfecit eum pessim[a]e et sanguinem eius effundit sine misericordia. Si autem iustus iniuste a quoquam gladio interfectus fuerit, aput Deum in requie est in refrigerium ; qui autem pellit de ecclesia et iam non suscipit, in aeternum pessime et amare
20 interficit eum, et perpetuo et pessimo igni in escam tradit eum qui expulsus est, non adtendens ad misericordiam domini et reminiscens eam quae super paenitentes est [XXI] bonitatem

---

1. reuertitur] + ἢ εἰς αἱρέσεις συμποδισθήσεται *AC* (cf. Syr.). 4 reuersantes] 'reuersanset' cod. 9 *uobis*] + δίδοτε, καὶ δοθήσεται ὑμῖν *AC* (= Syr.). The words are required by the following comment, 'hoc est: Date', etc.

that the explanatory words in the first clause in Syr., 'the sins of them that sin' and 'your sins' are original, and have been omitted in *AC* and Lat. as not belonging to the Gospel text. 19–21 Lo, ... not forgiven] οὐχὶ τοὐναντίον (ἑαυτὸν δεσμεύεις, λέγων ἀφιέναι καὶ μὴ ἀφιῶν;—two MSS omit these words) τῷ ἑαυτῶν στόματι ἐναντιωθήσεσθε, λέγοντες ἀφιέναι καὶ μὴ ἀφιέντες *AC*—a very curious conflate reading, of which the first part is nearer to Lat., the second nearer to Syr. For the comment, comp. Aphraates Hom. ii 15 'lest when a man pray : *Forgive us our debts, and we also will forgive our debtors*, he be caught by his own mouth, and it be said to him ... Thou forgivest not thy debtor, and how shall they forgive thee?' 24–25 For if ... rest] δίκαιος γὰρ ἀδίκως φονευθεὶς ὑπό τινος παρὰ θεῷ ἐν ἀναπαύσει ἔσται *AC* (cf. Wisd. iv 7). 29 driven out] *mappak*, not *mappek* ('drives out'): but a scribe has read it as active, and then supplied as subject 'God'.

and takes not the example of Christ, nor considers those who repented of their many transgressions and received of Him forgiveness.

[ii. 22] It behoves thee then, O bishop, to have before thine eyes those things which happened of old time, that from them thou mayest learn by comparison the healing of souls, and the admonition and reproof and exhortation of them that repent and have need of exhortation. And when thou judgest any persons, do thou with diligence and much investigation compare and follow out God's will: and as He did, so ought you also to do in your judgements. Hear then, O bishops, in regard to these things an apt and helpful example. It is written in the fourth Book of Kingdoms, and likewise in the second Book of Chronicles, thus: ¹*In those days reigned Manasseh*, (p. 28) *being twelve years old; and fifty years he reigned in Jerusalem: and the name of his mother was Hephzibah.* ² *And he did that which was evil before the Lord, after the uncleanness of those peoples which the Lord destroyed from before the children of Israel.* ³ *And he turned again and built the shrines which Hezekiah his father had thrown down; and he set up pillars to Baal, and made abominations, as Ahab king of Israel had done. And he made altars for all the service of heaven, and worshipped all the hosts of heaven.* ⁴ *And he built altars to demons in the house of the Lord, whereof the Lord had said: In the house of the Lord in Jerusalem, there*

---

14 4 Reg. xxi 1–17 (2 Paral. xxxiii 1–13).

1 and takes not, etc.] οὐδὲ λαμβάνων σκοποὺς τῶν τοιούτων τοὺς ἐκ πλήθους παραπτωμάτων ἐν μετανοίᾳ εἰληφότας ἄφεσιν *AC*. 5 that from them, etc.] καὶ ἐμπείρως αὐτοῖς κεχρῆσθαι πρὸς νουθεσίαν τῶν στυπτικῶν ἢ παρακλητικῶν δεομένων λόγων· ἔτι καὶ ἐν τῷ κρίνειν σε δίκαιον τῷ τοῦ θεοῦ ἐξακολουθεῖν θελήματι, καὶ ᾗ θεὸς δικάζει ... παραπλησίως καὶ σὲ κρίνειν *AC*. 14 of Chronicles] lit. 'of the Words (Acts) of the Days'. The Greek of the whole story, canonical and uncanonical alike, is preserved in *AC*, but only the more interesting variants can be noticed here. The apocryphal portions (without the Prayer of Manasseh) are quoted also in the *Opus imperf. in Matth.* Hom. i (see Funk vol. ii, p. 10). *In those days*] See note to Lat. 17 *Hephzibah*] 'Aphība Syr. 20 *shrines*] Or 'altars', but used chiefly of heathen altars: τὰ ὑψηλά *AC* LXX. 21 *and ... pillars to Baal*] From 2 Paral. xxxiii 3: +καὶ ἀνέστησεν θυσιαστήριον τῇ Βάαλ *AC* (= Lat.). *abominations*] In the sense of idols (and again

eius, nec oblect⟨a⟩ns eos qui tales sunt et in multitudine peccatorum in penitentia acciperunt remissionem a Deo.

Oportet autem te, o episcope, ante oculos habere et ea quae praecesserunt, simul ad scientiam sanitatis ad eos qui corri-
5 piendi sunt et obtrectandi, adhuc et ad iudicandu⟨m⟩, ad conparationem causae, per multam doctrinam exquirere Dei uoluntatem; ⟨et⟩ sicut ipse fecit, ita et nos oportet facere in iudiciis. DE MANASSE. Audite, o episcopi, ad[huc] haec quae talia sunt iuuamentum similitudinis. Scriptum est in
10 quarto libro Regnorum et in secundo Paralipomenum, quod est praetermissarum, sic : ¹ *In diebus filius erat duodecim annorum Manasses cum regnasset, et inperauit quinquaginta annos in Hierusalem : et nomen matris eius Epsiba.* ² *Et fecit malignum coram domino abominationibus gentilium, quos disperdidit*
15 *dominus a facie filiorum Istrahel.* ³ *Et conuersus est et aedificauit excelsa, quae distruxit Ezecias pater ipsius, et constituit sculptilia Bahalim, et eregit altarem Bahal, et fecit condensa, sicut fecit Achab rex Istrahel, et fecit altaria omni militiae caeli, et adorauit omnem uirtutem caeli.* ⁴ *Et aedificauit altarem*
20 *in domo domini, in qua dixit dominus : In domo Hierusalem*

---

1 oblectans eos qui tales sunt] λαμβάνων σκοποὺς τῶν τοιούτων τοὺς κτλ. *A C* (see note to Syr.). Hauler and Funk are perhaps right in reading 'obiectans'. 4 simul . . . ad eos] Hauler conjectures 'simul ad scientiam sanitatis adhibere ad eos': but the whole clause is obscure. Possibly supply 'et ad admonitionem' after 'sanitatis' (cf. Syr.). 7 ⟨et⟩] Cf. Syr. and *AC*. nos] 'you' Syr. : σέ *AC*: therefore prob. read 'uos'. 11 *In diebus*] 'in those days' Syr., which is apt to suggest a lectionary prefix. But *AC* has καὶ ἐν τῇ δευτέρᾳ τῶν παραλειπομένων, τῇ τῶν ἡμερῶν, οὕτως· υἱὸς Μανασσῆς ἐν τῷ βασιλεύειν αὐτὸν δωδεκαετής. For the origin of τῇ τῶν ἡμερῶν we must go to the Hebrew title of Chronicles, 'The Words (Acts) of the Days'. The indication by the author of this alternative title has troubled the translators : Syr. already knows, and uses, the Heb. title, but fails to recognize it again in the form τῇ τῶν ἡμερῶν : Lat. provides a translation of ' Paralipomenon', and then makes τῇ τῶν ἡμερῶν part of the quotation (unless Lat. had originally ' praetermissarum in diebus, sic :'). 17 *condensa*] ἄλση *AC* LXX.

in *v*. 7) : ἄλση *AC* LXX, for *Asherah, Asheroth* of Heb. 24 *to demons*] 'to idols' Pesh.: om. Lat. *AC* LXX Heb. 24-25 *the Lord had said*] +πρὸς Δαυὶδ καὶ πρὸς Σολομῶνα τὸν υἱὸν αὐτοῦ *A C* (cf. *v*. 7).

will I set my name. And Manasseh served the shrines, and said: My name shall endure for ever. ⁵ *And he built altars for all the service of heaven in the two courts of the house of the Lord;* ⁶ *and he made his sons to pass through the fire in the valley of Bar-Hinnom. And he practised augury and used magic; and he made soothsayers and enchanters and diviners, and did much evil before the eyes of the Lord to provoke him to anger.* ⁷ *And he set the molten and graven image of abomination, which he had made, in the house of the Lord, whereof the Lord had said to David and to Solomon his son: In this house and in Jerusalem, which I have chosen out of all the tribes of Israel, will I set my name for ever;* ⁸ *and I will no more withhold my feet from the land of Israel, which I gave to their fathers: yet only if they will keep all that I have commanded them, according to all the commandments which my servant Moses commanded them.* ⁹ *And they hearkened not: and Manasseh seduced them to do that which was evil before the eyes of the Lord, after the works of those peoples which the Lord destroyed from before the children of Israel.* ¹⁰ *And the Lord spake against Manasseh and against his people by the hand of his servants the prophets, and said:* ¹¹ *Because Manasseh king of Judah hath done these evil abominations, as did the Amorites which were before him, and hath made Judah also to sin with his idols:* ¹² *therefore, thus saith the Lord the God of Israel: Behold, I bring such evils upon Jerusalem and upon Judah that every one that heareth of them, both his ears shall tingle.* ¹³ *And I will stretch over Jerusalem the measuring line of Samaria and the plummet of the house of Ahab; and I will wipe Jerusalem as a water-pot is wiped, when it is overturned and falleth upon its face.* ¹⁴ *And I will give the residue of mine inheritance to the sword, and will deliver them into the hand of their enemies; and they shall be for a prey and a spoil to all them that hate them,* ¹⁵ *because they have done evil before mine eyes: for they are a provoking (people), from the day that*

4-5 *in...Bar-Hinnom*] From 2 Paral. xxxiii 6. 6 *diviners*] + καὶ θεραφεὶν AC. 9–12 *whereof...for ever*] ἐν ᾧ ἐξελέξατο κύριος θέσθαι τὸ ὄνομα αὐτοῦ ἐκεῖ ἐν Ἰερουσαλὴμ τῇ ἁγίᾳ πόλει εἰς τὸν αἰῶνα, καὶ εἶπεν AC. 13 *my feet... land of Israel*] τὸν πόδα μου (σαλεῦσαι) ἀπὸ τῆς γῆς τοῦ

ponam nom⟨e⟩n meum. Et seruiit altaribus Manasses et dixit : Sit nomen meum in aeternum. ⁵ ⟨*E*⟩*t aedificauit altaria omni militiae caeli in utrisque atriis domus* [XXII] *domini.* ⁶ *Et ipse t⟨r⟩ansponebat filios suos per ignem in Gae-Uanaemon, et augu-*
5 *riabatur et maleficia faciebat, et fecit sibi pitones et procantatores et praescios, et multiplicauit facere malignum in oculis domini, ut inritaret eum.* ⁷ *Et posuit sculptilem et fusilem condensi imaginem, quam fecit, in domo domini, quibus* (sic) *dixit dominus ad Dauid et ad Solomonem filium eius* : *In domo hac*
10 *in Hierusalem,* ⟨*quam*⟩ *elegi ex omnibus tribus Istrahel,* [*et*] *ponam nomen meum in aeternum,* ⁸ *et non adponam mouere pedem meum a terra Istrahel, quam dedi patribus ipsorum : ita tamen, si custodierint omnia quaecumque mandaui eis, secundum omne praeceptum quod mandauit eis seruus meus Moyses.* ⁹ *Et*
15 *non audierunt eum : et seduxit eos Manasses ut facerent malignum in oculis domini super gentes quas abstulit dominus a facie filiorum Istrahel.* ¹⁰ *Et locutus est dominus super Manassem et super populum eius in manus seruorum suorum profetarum dicens :* ¹¹ *Propter abominationes iniquas quas fecit*
20 *Manasses rex Iuda ex omnibus quibus fecit Amorreus coram ipso, et peccare fecit Iudam in simulacris eius,* ¹² *haec dicit dominus Deus Istrahel : Ecce ego inducam mala super locum istum, ita ut omnium audientium resonent utreque aures :* ¹³ *et extendam mala super Hierusalem, mensuram Samariae et pon-*
25 *derationem domus Achab : et deleam Hierusalem sicut deletur alabastrus unguenti*[*s*], †*euertitur et euertitur*† *in faciem* ⟨*s*⟩*uam :* ¹⁴ *et retribuam reliquias hereditatis meae . . .*

5–6 *pitones . . . praescios*] ἐγγαστριμύθους καὶ ἐπαοιδοὺς καὶ γνώστας καὶ θεραφεῖν *AC*. 7 *sculptilem et fusilem*] τὸν χωνευτὸν καὶ τὸν γλυπτόν *AC* (= Syr.). 20–21 *coram ipso*] ἔμπροσθεν αὐτοῦ (temporal) *AC* 22–23 *super locum istum*] ἐπὶ Ἱερουσαλὴμ καὶ Ἰούδαν *AC* (= Syr.). 26 *alabastrus unguentis*] ὁ ἀλάβαστρος LXX : τὸ πυξίον *AC*, which is also found in hexaplaric codd. In Lat. 'unguenti' has prob. come in from Mt. xxvi 7, and parallels. 26 *euertitur et euertitur*] ἀπαλειφόμενος, καὶ καταστρέφεται LXX 4 Reg. xxi 13 : ἀπαλειφόμενον (sc. πυξίον), καὶ κιταστρέψω *AC*. Perhaps read '⟨cum⟩ euerritur et euertitur'. 27 *retribuam*] ἀποδώσομαι (τὸ ὑπόλειμμα τῆς κληρονομίας μου) *AC*: ἀπεώσομαι κτλ. LXX.

Ἰσραὴλ *AC*: τὸν πόδα Ἰσραὴλ ἀπὸ τῆς γῆς LXX. 29 *wipe*] The word means usually to wipe out, *delere*: ἀπαλείψω *AC* LXX. 31 *to the sword*] om. *AC* LXX.

I brought out their fathers from (p. 29) *Egypt even unto this day.* [16] *Moreover Manasseh shed much innocent blood, till he had filled Jerusalem from one end to the other with slain: by reason of the sins which he sinned, and caused Judah also to sin, in doing that which was evil before the Lord. And the Lord brought against them the chieftains of Assyria; and they took Manasseh and fettered him and cast ropes about him, and led him away to Babylon, and shut him up in prison all bound and fettered with iron. And there was given him bran-bread by weight, and water mingled with gall in small measure, that he might be alive and be sore afflicted and vexed. And when he was afflicted exceeding much, he entreated the face of the Lord his God, and humbled himself exceedingly before the God of his fathers; and he prayed before the Lord God and said:*

THE PRAYER OF MANASSEH. [1] *O Lord God of my fathers, the God of Abraham and of Isaac and of Jacob and of their righteous seed,* [2] *who madest the heaven and the earth with all the adornment thereof;* [3] *who didst bind the sea and fix it by the commandment of thy word; who didst shut up the abyss and seal it with thy fearful and glorious name;* [4] *before whose power all things fear and tremble:* [5] *for unsupportable is the exceeding beauty of thy glory, and none can endure to stand before thine anger and thy wrath against sinners:* [6] *without*

5-8 2 Paral. xxxiii 11   8-11?   11 2 Paral. xxxiii 12 f.   14 Cf.
2 Paral. xxxiii 13, 18.   15 *Oratio Manassis.*

6-7 *and they took ... about him*] καὶ κατέλαβον (κατελάβοντο *AC*) τὸν Μανασσὴ ἐν δεσμοῖς καὶ ἔδησαν αὐτὸν ἐν πέδαις (+ χαλκαῖς *AC*) LXX *AC*. 8-11 *and shut ... vexed*] καὶ ἦν δεδεμένος καὶ κατασεσιδηρωμένος ὅλος ἐν οἴκῳ φυλακῆς, καὶ ἐδίδοτο αὐτῷ ἐκ πιτύρων ἄρτος ἐν σταθμῷ βραχὺς καὶ ὕδωρ σὺν ὄξει ὀλίγον ἐν μέτρῳ, ὥστε ζῆν αὐτόν, καὶ ἦν συνεχόμενος καὶ ὀδυρώμενος σφόδρα *AC*: 'Et erat ligatus et catenatus in domo carceris, et dabatur ei panis hordeaceus ad mensuram modicus et aqua cum aceto modica ad mensuram, ut uiueret tantum, et erat constrictus in doloribus ualde' *Op. imperf. in Matth.* After 'Babylon' (l. 8) cod. H adds 'in a ζῴδιον of brass', which must have some connexion with the story in the late Targum on 2 Chron. xxxiii, to the effect that Manasseh was inclosed in 'a mule of brass' (see Additional Notes). 19-20 *who didst shut up the abyss and seal it*] Comp. Apoc. xx 2, 3. 20-21 *before ... tremble*] This clause is introduced into the liturgy in *AC* viii 7. 5.

DIDASCALIA APOSTOLORUM 73

bound and without measure are the mercies of thy promises; ⁷*for thou art a Lord long-suffering and merciful and very gracious, and dost repent thee of the evil of men.* ⁸*And thou, O Lord, according to the gentleness of thy goodness hast promised forgiveness to them that repent of their sins, and in the multitude of thy mercies hast appointed repentance for the salvation of sinners. If then, O Lord God of the righteous, thou didst not appoint repentance to the righteous, to Abraham and to Isaac and to Jacob: for neither did they sin against thee: yet hast thou appointed repentance to me a sinner.* ⁹*For more than the sands of the sea are my sins multiplied, and I have no respite to lift up my head for the multitude of mine iniquities. And now, O Lord, behold, I am justly afflicted; and as I am worthy, (so) am I vexed.* ¹⁰*For lo, I am bound and bowed down with (these) many bands of iron, so that I may not lift up my head: for neither am I worthy to lift up mine eyes and behold and see the height of heaven, by reason of the exceeding malice of my wickedness. For I have done evil before thee, and provoked thy wrath, and have set up idols and multiplied abominations.* ¹¹*And now, behold, I bend the knees of my heart* (p. 30) *before thee, and beseech thy kindness:* ¹²*I have sinned, O Lord, I have sinned; and because that I know my sins,* ¹³*I make supplication before thee. Forgive me, O Lord, and destroy me not with mine offences, and be not angry with me for ever, nor keep against me mine evil (deeds), neither condemn and cast me into the nether parts of the earth. For thou art the God of penitents:* ¹⁴*wherefore in me also, O Lord, show thy*

8, 10 *appoint repentance*] ἔθου μετάνοιαν *AC*. Comp. Hermas *Mand.* iv 3. 4 τοῖς οὖν κληθεῖσι πρὸ τούτων τῶν ἡμερῶν ἔθηκεν ὁ κύριος μετάνοιαν. 10–18 *For more ... my wickedness*] There is considerable variation here between the texts of Syr., *AC*, and codd. AT (in Swete iii 825, *vv.* 9, 10ᵃ).

goodness, that whereas I am unworthy, thou deliverest me after the multitude of thy mercies. ¹⁵ *And for this will I praise thee ever and all the days of my life: for thee do all the hosts of heaven praise, and unto thee do they sing for evermore.*

And the Lord hearkened to the voice of Manasseh, and had mercy on him. And there was made over him a flame of fire, and all the iron (bands) that were upon him were melted and dissolved. And the Lord delivered Manasseh from his afflictions, and caused him to return to Jerusalem over his kingdom. And Manasseh knew the Lord, and said: He is the Lord God alone. And he served the Lord only, with all his heart and with all his soul, all the days of his life: and he was accounted righteous. And he slept with his fathers; and Amon his son reigned after him.

[ii. 23] You have heard, beloved children, how Manasseh served idols evilly and bitterly, and slew righteous men; yet when he repented God forgave him, albeit there is no sin worse than idolatry. Wherefore, there is granted a place for repentance. But concerning one who says: *I shall have good (success) when I shall walk in the perverse desire of my heart*, thus saith the Lord: *I will stretch out my hand against him, and he shall be for a byword and a parable.* For Amon also

---

5 2 Paral. xxxiii 13   5–8?   8–9 Cf. 2 Paral. xxxiii 13.   10–13?
13 4 Reg. xxi 18, 2 Paral. xxxiii 20.   19 Deut. xxix 19 (18).   21 Cf. Ez. xiv 9: Jer. xxiv 9, Deut. xxviii 37.

5–14 *and had mercy*, etc.] καὶ ᾠκτείρησεν αὐτόν· καὶ ἐγένετο περὶ αὐτὸν φλὸξ πυρός, καὶ ἐτάκησαν πάντα τὰ περὶ αὐτὸν σίδηρα, καὶ ἰάσατο τὸν Μανασσῆν ἐκ τῆς θλίψεως αὐτοῦ καὶ ἐπέστρεψεν αὐτὸν εἰς Ἱερουσαλὴμ ἐπὶ τὴν βασιλείαν αὐτοῦ. καὶ ἔγνω Μανασσῆς ὅτι κύριος αὐτός ἐστιν θεὸς μόνος, καὶ ἐλάτρευσεν μόνῳ κυρίῳ τῷ θεῷ ἐν ὅλῃ τῇ καρδίᾳ αὐτοῦ καὶ ἐν ὅλῃ τῇ ψυχῇ αὐτοῦ πάσας τὰς ἡμέρας τῆς ζωῆς αὐτοῦ, καὶ ἐλογίσθη δίκαιος *AC* (for the *Op. imperf.* see under Lat.).   7–8 *and all the iron ... dissolved*] Comp. the *Odes of Solomon* xvii 9 'And I cut through the bars of iron; but my own iron (sing.) melted and was dissolved before me'.   13 slept]+ἐν εἰρήνῃ *AC* (= Lat.).   *Amon*] CH *AC* Lat.: BS omit.   19 But ... says] Syr. appears to have omitted a clause (cf. Lat.). *AC* reads, with some expansion, ἐὰν δέ τις ἐκ παρατάξεως ἁμαρτάνῃ, ... ὁ τοιοῦτος ἄφεσιν οὐχ ἕξει, κἂν λέγῃ παρ' ἑαυτῷ κτλ.   *I shall have*, etc.] lit. 'Good things shall be to me': 'I shall have peace' Heb. Pesh.: ὅσιά μοι γένοιτο, (ὅτι ἐν τῇ ἀποπλανήσει τῆς καρδίας μου πορεύσομαι) LXX: ὅσ. μ. γ. (ὅτι πορεύσομαι ἐν τῇ ἀναστροφῇ τ. κ. μ.) *AC*, omitting the next quotation.

[XXIII] ... *indignum me saluum facies secundum misericordiam tuam,* [15] *et glorificabo te semper in omni uita mea: quoniam te laudant omnes uirtutes caelorum et glorificant in aeternum. Amen.*

5 *Et exaudiuit vocem eius dominus et miseritus est eum. Et facta est circa eum flamma ignis, et liquauit omne quod circa eum erat ferrum. Et sanauit Manassem de tribulatione eius, et reuertit illum in Hierusalem super regnum suum. Et cognouit Manasses dominum dicens: Ipse solus est dominus; et* 10 *seruiit domino Deo soli in toto corde suo et in tota anima sua omnes dies uitae suae, et inputatus est iustus. Et dormiit in pace cum patribus suis: et regnauit Amor filius eius pro ipso.*

Audistis, filioli dilectissimi nobis, quomodo dominus pessime ei qui idolatra fuit et innocentes interfecit, et penituit, re-
15 misit, id est Manasseti: praesertim cum peiore peccatum non sit aliut idolatriae. Sed locus paenitentiae concessus est. Si quis autem ex apparatione peccat, remissionem non habet, sicut scriptum est: *Si autem dixeris in corde tuo: Sancta mihi erunt, quia ambulabo in reuersione cordis mei: et extendam*
20 *manum meum super ipsum et disperdam eum in signum et in similitudinem, dicit dominus.* Nam et Amor cogitauit cogi-

5-11 *Et exaudiuit ... iustus*] 'Et exaudiuit dominus uocem eius et misertus est ei. Et facta est circa eum flamma ignis et liquefacta sunt omnia uincula eius... Et cognouit dominum Manasses dicens: Ipse est Deus solus. Et seruiit soli domino Deo in toto corde suo et in tota anima sua omnibus diebus uitae suae, et reputatus iustus ...' *Op. imperf. in Matth.*
17 ex apparatione] ἐκ παρατάξεως *AC.* 18 *in reuersione*] ἐν τῇ ἀναστροφῇ *AC.* 21 ff. 'Fuit enim (Amos) ualde iniquus, ut extant opera eius maligna, quibus imitatus fuerat Manassen, ut etiam Deum posse se fallere aestimaret, dicens: Pater meus multa ex iuuentute sua iniqua fecit, et in senectute sua paenituit: et ego nunc ambulabo secundum quod desiderat anima mea, et postmodum conuertar ad dominum ... et exterminauit eum dominus Deus uelociter. Attendite ergo, laici, ne quis ex uobis cogitationem Amos in corde suo ponat' *Op. imperf. in Matth.*

22 ff. τοιοῦτος γὰρ ἐγένετο καὶ Ἀμὼς ὁ τοῦ Μανασσῆ υἱός. φησὶν γὰρ ἡ γραφή· καὶ παρελογίσατο Ἀμὼς λογισμὸν παραβάσεως κακὸν καὶ εἶπεν· ὁ πατήρ μου ἐκ νεότητος πολλὰ παρηνόμησεν καὶ ἐν γήρᾳ μετέγνω· καὶ νῦν ἐγὼ πορεύσομαι καθὰ ἐπιθυμεῖ ἡ ψυχή μου, καὶ ὕστερον ἐπιστρέψω πρὸς κύριον *AC.*

the son of Manasseh, when he conceived a design that he should transgress the Law, and said: '*My father from his youth did exceeding wickedly, and in his old age he repented: I also will walk in all the desires of my soul, and in the end will return to the Lord*', *and did that which was evil before the Lord: he reigned but two years, because the Lord God quickly destroyed him from ⟨his⟩ good land.* [ii. 24] Beware therefore, †you that are without faith†, lest any man of you establish in his heart the thought of Amon, and perish suddenly and swiftly.

Wherefore, O bishop, so far as thou canst, keep those that have not sinned, that they may continue without sinning; and those that repent of (their) sins heal and receive. But if thou receive not him who repents, because thou art without mercy, thou shalt sin against the Lord God; (p. 31) for thou obeyest not our Saviour and our God, to do as He also did with her that had sinned, whom the elders set before Him, and leaving the judgement in His hands, departed. But He, the Searcher of hearts, asked her and said to her: *Have the elders condemned thee, my daughter? She saith to him: Nay, Lord. And he said unto her: Go thy way: neither do I condemn thee.* In Him therefore, our Saviour and King and God, be your pattern, O bishops, and do you imitate Him, that you may be quiet and meek, and merciful and compassionate, and peacemakers, and without anger, and teachers and correctors and receivers and exhorters; and that you be *not wrathful, nor tyrannical;* and that you be not insolent, nor haughty, nor boastful.

2–7? (Cf. 4 Reg. xxi 19 f.)   17 ff. Cf. Joh. viii 3–11.   26 Tit. i 7, cf. 1 Tim. iii 3.

6–7 καὶ ἐξωλόθρευσεν αὐτὸν κύριος ὁ θεὸς ἐν τάχει ἐκ τῆς γῆς τῆς ἀγαθῆς αὐτοῦ ... (4 Reg. xxi 23), καὶ ἐβασίλευσεν ἔτη δύο μόνα AC. I have treated the whole passage as a quotation, though some of it may be only comment. 8 you that are without faith] οἱ λαϊκοί AC (= Lat. and *Op. imperf. in Matth.*): Syr. strangely mistranslates. 16–18 to her that had sinned, etc.] ἑτέραν δέ τινα ἡμαρτηκυῖαν ἔστησαν οἱ πρεσβύτεροι ἔμπροσθεν αὐτοῦ, καὶ ἐπ' αὐτῷ θέμενοι τὴν κρίσιν ἐξῆλθον AC.   18 But He, etc.] ὁ δὲ καρδιογνώστης κύριος πυθόμενος αὐτῆς εἰ κατέκριναν αὐτὴν οἱ πρεσβύτεροι, καὶ εἰπούσης ὅτι οὔ, ἔφη πρὸς αὐτήν· ὕπαγε οὖν, οὐδὲ ἐγώ σε κατακρίνω AC (cf. Lat.). Syr.,

tationem preuaricationis malam, et dixit: *Pater meus in
iuuentute multas iniquitates fecit, et in senectute penituit: et
ego nunc ambulabo sicut desiderat anima mea,* [XXIV] *et in
nouissimo conuertar ad dominum. Et fecit malignum coram*
5 *domino, et regnauit annos duodecim solos, et exterminauit illum
dominus Deus in celeritate de terra bona sua.* Adtendite
igitur, laici, ne quis ex uobis cogitationem Amor in cor suum
confirmet, et uelociter pereat.

Similiter, o episcope, conserua quantum potes eos qui non
10 peccauerunt, ut sine peccato maneant, et eos qui a peccatis
conuertuntur sanans suscipe. Si autem penitentem, cum sis
sine misericordia, non susciperis, peccauis in dominum Deum;
quoniam non es[t] persuasus nec credidisti saluatori Deo
nostro, ut faceres sicut ille fecit in ea muliere quae peccauerat,
15 quam statuerunt praesbyteri ante eum, et in eo ponentes
iudicium exierunt. Scrutator autem cordis interrogabat eam,
si condemnassent illam praesbyteri. Cum autem dixisset,
('Non', dixit) ad eam: *Uade, nec ego te condemno.* Hunc
saluatorem, regem et dominum nostrum, o episcopi, pro-
20 spectorem uobis habere oportet et eius imitatores esse, mansu-
etos, quietos, uiscera habentes, misericordes, pacificos, sine
ira, docibiles, exhortatores, susceptores, obsecratores, *non ira-
cundos, non percussores,* non contumeliosos, non elatos, *non
superbos,*

5 *annos duodecim solos*] ('solus' cod.) ἔτη δύο μόνα *AC* (= Syr.).
19 dominum] θεόν *AC* (= Syr.). 19 episcope cod. 19-20 prospectorem
... oportet] σκοπὸν ὑμᾶς ἔχειν δεῖ *AC* (cf. Syr.).

by throwing the first part into the direct speech, has given the passage a
more unfamiliar look. 27 *tyrannical*] CH: 'murmurers' S. On these
renderings of πλήκτης see note to p. 32 l. 5. In *AC* the next three adjs.
are ὑβριστάς, ἀλαζόνας, ὑπεροπτικούς.

CHAPTER VIII

Warnings to Bishops, how they ought to conduct themselves.

You shall *not be lovers of wine*, nor drunken; and you shall not be extravagant, nor luxurious, nor spending money improperly. You shall make use of the gifts of God not ⟨as alien (funds), but⟩ as your own, *as* being appointed *good stewards* of God, who is ready to require at your hands an account of the discharge of the stewardship entrusted to you. [ii. 25] Let that suffice you therefore which is enough for you, food and clothing and whatsoever is necessary. And you shall not make use of the revenues (of the Church) improperly, as alien (funds), but with moderation; and you shall not procure pleasure and luxury from the revenues of the Church: *for sufficient for the labourer is his clothing and his food*. As good stewards of God, therefore, dispense well, according to the command, those things that are given and accrue to the Church, to orphans and widows and to those who are in distress and to strangers, as knowing that you have God who will require an account at your hands, who delivered this stewardship unto you. Divide and give therefore to all who are in want.

But be you also nourished and live from the revenues of the Church; yet do not devour them by yourselves, but let them that are in want be partakers with you, and you shall be without offence with God. For God upbraids those bishops who greedily and by themselves make use (p. 32) of the revenues of the Church, and make not the poor to be partakers with them, saying thus: *The milk ye eat, and with the wool ye are clothed.* For the bishops ought to be nourished from the revenues of the Church, but not to devour them; for

---

1 1 Tim. iii 2, Tit. i 7.   4 Cf. 1 Pet. iv 10.   12 Cf. Mt. x 10, Lk. x 7, 1 Tim. v 18.   13 Cf. 1 Pet. iv 10.   26 Ez. xxxiv 3.

2–3 extravagant ... improperly] μὴ εἰκαιοδαπάνους, μὴ τρυφητάς, μὴ πολυδαπάνους *AC*. In Syr. the first and third of these adjs. seem to have changed places. In rendering 'extravagant' I have corrected the text from ܦܠܘܣ

non uino multo deditos, non ebriosos, non in uano expendentes non ut alienis sed sicut propriis his quae a Deo dantur utentes, moderatores *sicut bonos despensatores* Dei, qui incipiet rationem ab ea quae in uobis est dispensatione exigere. . . .

1 expendentes] + μὴ τρυφητάς, μὴ πολυδαπάνους *AC* (cf. Syr.). 3 moderatores *sicut*] ὡς καθεστῶτας *AC* (= Syr.).

ܡܣܒ, 'much puffed up', to ܡܣܒ ܣܓܝ (see note to p. 34 l. 16). 3-4 not (as alien (funds), but)] μὴ ὡς ἀλλοτρίοις, ἀλλ' (ὡς ἰδίοις) *AC* (=Lat.). Syr. reads 'As not your own you shall make use of the gifts of God', but see l. 9 f. below. For ἀλλοτρίοις comp. Lk. xvi 12. 4-5 *as . . . of God*] ὡς καθεστῶτας ἀγαθοὺς οἰκονόμους *AC*. 9 the revenues] τοῖς κυριακοῖς *AC*. 12 *for sufficient*, etc.] Cf. Epiphanius *Haer*. lxxx 5 ἄξιος γὰρ ὁ ἐργάτης τοῦ μισθοῦ αὐτοῦ, καὶ ἀρκετὸν τῷ ἐργαζομένῳ ἡ τροφὴ αὐτοῦ. See Resch p. 147, and Ropes p. 93 : neither makes reference to this passage of *Didasc.*, though possibly it suggested Epiphanius' second clause. *AC* conforms the saying to Lk. x 7. 14 according to the command] Cf. *Didache* i 5 : *AC* has here τὰ διδόμενα κατ' ἐντολὴν θεοῦ τῶν δεκατῶν καὶ τῶν ἀπαρχῶν ὡς θεοῦ ἄνθρωπος ἀναλισκέτω. 21 yet do not devour, etc.] ἀλλὰ μὴ κατεσθίοντες αὐτὰ μόνοι, κοινωνοῦντες δὲ τοῖς χρῄζουσιν *AC*. Cf. Hermas *Vis.* iii 9. 2 καὶ μὴ μόνοι τὰ κτίσματα τοῦ θεοῦ μεταλαμβάνετε ἐκ καταχύματος, ἀλλὰ μεταδίδοτε καὶ τοῖς ὑστερουμένοις.

it is written: *Thou shalt not muzzle the ox that treadeth out (the corn)*. As then the ox which works unmuzzled in the threshing floor eats, indeed, but does not consume the whole, so do you also, who work in the threshing floor which is the Church of God, be nourished from the Church, after the manner of the Levites who ministered in the tabernacle of witness, which in all things was a type of the Church: for even by its name it declares (this), for the tabernacle 'of witness' foreshowed the Church. Now the Levites who ministered therein were nourished from those things which were given as offerings to God by all the people—gifts, and part-offerings, and firstfruits, and tithes, and sacrifices, and offerings, and holocausts—without restraint, they and their wives and their sons and their daughters; because their work was the ministry of the tabernacle alone; and therefore they received no inheritance of land among the children of Israel, because the inheritance of Levi and his tribe was the produce of the people.

You also then to-day, O bishops, are priests to your people, and the Levites who minister to the tabernacle of God, the holy Catholic Church, who stand continually before the Lord God. You then are to your people priests and prophets, and princes and leaders and kings, and mediators between God and His faithful, and receivers of the word, and preachers and proclaimers thereof, and knowers of the Scriptures and of the utterances of God, and witnesses of His will, who bear the sins of all, and are to give an answer for all. You are they

---

1 Deut. xxv 4 (1 Cor. ix 9, 1 Tim. v 18).

7-8 for even by its name, etc.] προσέτι δὲ καὶ ἐκ τοῦ ὀνόματος μαρτύριον τῆς ἐκκλησίας ἡ σκηνὴ προωρίζετο *AC*. Our author may only be playing on the Gk. word μαρτύριον; but it has been suggested that he is connecting the Heb. word עֵדוּת, 'testimony', with the regular Syriac word for 'church' (עדתא): so Nestle in *Zeitschrift für neutestam. Wissenschaft*, 1901, p. 263.   11-12 part-offerings] I adopt this as a rendering of the word *purshāne*, which here translates ἀφαιρεμάτων (*AC*), and in the following passage from Num. xviii (see p. 82) represents both ἀφαιρέματα and ἐπιθέματα. The word signifies separation, distinction, and then something set apart as a gift or sacrifice. 'Part-offering', therefore, is to be understood in the sense of an offering set apart.   20-21 to the... Catholic Church] τῇ ἱερᾷ σκηνῇ, τῇ ἁγίᾳ καθολικῇ ἐκκλησίᾳ *AC*.

who have heard how the word sternly threatens you if you neglect and preach not God's will, who are in sore peril of destruction if you neglect your people. You again are they to whom is promised from God the great reward which is not falsified nor withheld, and grace unspeakable in great glory, when you shall minister well to the tabernacle of God, His Catholic Church. As then you have undertaken the burden of all, so also ought you to receive from all your people the ministration of food (p. 33) and clothing, and of other things needful. And so again, from these same gifts that are given you by the people which is under your charge, do you nourish the deacons and widows and orphans, and those who are in want, and strangers. For it behoves thee, O bishop, as a faithful steward to care for all; for as thou bearest the sins of all those under thy charge, so shalt thou beyond all men receive more abundant glory of God. For thou art an imitator of Christ: and as He took upon Him the sins of us all, so it behoves thee also to bear the sins of all those under thy charge; for it is written in Isaiah concerning our Saviour thus: *We saw him having no splendour nor beauty, but as one whose aspect was marred and dejected beyond that of men; and as a man that suffereth, and knoweth to bear infirmities. For his face was changed: he was despised, and was nothing accounted in our eyes. But he endured our sins, and for our sake did sigh. But we accounted him as one smitten and plagued and brought low. Yet for our sins was he smitten, and was made sick for our iniquities: and by his stripes all we are healed.* And again He saith: *He bare the sins of many, and for their iniquity was delivered up.* And in David and in all the prophets, and in the Gospel also, our Saviour makes intercession for our sins, whereas He is without sin. Therefore, as you have Christ for a pattern, so be you also a pattern to the people under your charge; and as He took upon Him (our) sins, so do you also take upon you the sins of the people. For you are not to think that the burden of the bishopric is light or easy.

Wherefore, as you have taken up the burden of all, so the

17 Cf. 1 Pet. ii 24   19 Isa. liii 2-5.   28 Isa. liii 12.

fruits also which you receive from all the people shall be yours, for all things of which you have need. And do you nourish well them that are in want, as being to render an account to Him who will require it, who can make no mistake nor be evaded. For as you administer the office of the bishopric, so from the same office of the bishopric ought you to be nourished, as the priests and Levites and ministers who serve before God, according as it is written in the Book of Numbers: ¹ *The Lord spake with Aaron and said: Thou and thy sons and thy father's house* (p. 34) *shall take upon you the sins of the sanctuary; and thou and thy sons shall take upon you the sins of your priesthood.* ² *And thy brethren the sons of thy father, the tribe of Levi, bring nigh unto thee, and let them be added to thee and minister unto thee.* ³ *And thou and thy sons with thee shall minister before this tabernacle of witness. Howbeit the sons of Levi shall not come nigh unto the vessels of the sanctuary and unto the altar, lest they die, they and you;* ⁴ *but let them be added unto thee, and let them keep the charges of the tabernacle of witness, according to all the ministry of the tabernacle: and a stranger shall not come nigh unto thee.* ⁵ *And ye shall keep the charges of the sanctuary and the charges of the altar: and there shall be no wrath against the children of Israel.* ⁶ *And I, behold, I have taken your brethren the sons of Levi from among the children of Israel: as a gift they are given unto the Lord, that they may perform the ministry of the tabernacle of witness.* ⁷ *And do thou and thy sons with thee keep your priesthood, according to all the ministry of the altar and of that which is within the veil; and perform your ministry as that which is given to your priesthood. But the stranger that cometh near shall die the death.* ⁸ *And the Lord spake with Aaron and said: Behold, I have given to you the charges of the firstfruits, of every thing which is hallowed unto me by the children of Israel: to thee have I given them for a ministry, and to thy children after thee: (it is) an everlasting ordinance.*

9 Nu. xviii 1-32.

---

9 This quotation is in fair agreement with LXX. *AC* has kept only *vv.* 1, 8-10, and a few words from 21-22.

⁹ *And this shall be yours, of every holy thing which is hallowed of their fruits and of their offerings, and of all their sacrifices, and of all their trespass offerings, and of all their sin offerings: all that they shall offer to me of things hallowed shall be for thee and for thy sons.* ¹⁰ *In the holy place ye shall eat thereof: every male of you shall eat thereof, thou and thy sons: it shall be for thee a holy thing.* ¹¹ *And these shall be for thee the firstfruits of their gifts, of all the part-offerings of the children of Israel: to thee have I given them, and to thy sons and thy daughters with thee: (it is) an everlasting ordinance: every one that is clean in thy house shall eat thereof.* ¹² *All the firstfruits of oil, and all the firstfruits of wine, and the firstfruits of corn, even all things that they shall give to the Lord, shall be thine:* ¹³ *every one that is clean in thy house shall eat thereof.* ¹⁴ *And every devoted thing of the children of Israel shall be thine;* ¹⁵ *and all that openeth the womb of all flesh, even all which they offer to the Lord, from men even unto beasts, shall be thine. Howbeit the firstborn of men and the firstlings of unclean beasts which shall be offered, shall be redeemed.* ¹⁶ *And the redemption of them (shall be on this wise): from a month old and upward thou shalt redeem with a price, five shekels according to the shekel of the sanctuary, which are twenty shekels of silver.* (p. 35) ¹⁷ *But the firstlings of oxen, and the firstlings of sheep and of goats, thou shalt not redeem: they are holy: their blood thou shalt pour out before the altar, and the fat of them thou shalt offer up for an offering of a sweet savour unto the Lord;* ¹⁸ *and their flesh shall be clean to thee. And the top of the breast of the part-offering, and the right shoulder shall be thine.* ¹⁹ *All part-offerings of the sanctuary, which the children of Israel shall set apart unto the Lord, to thee have I given them and to thy sons and to thy daughters with thee: an ordinance for ever and an everlasting covenant is it before the Lord unto thee and unto thy seed after thee.* ²⁰ *And the Lord spake with Aaron and said: In their land thou shalt receive no inheritance, and thou shalt have no portion among them; for I am thy portion and thine inheritance among the children of*

13–14 *shall be thine*] Here the first part of v. 13 is wanting.

Israel. ²¹ *And to the sons of Levi, behold, I have given all the tithes of the children of Israel for an inheritance, in return for their ministry which they minister in the tabernacle of witness.* ²² *And the children of Israel shall no more come nigh to the tabernacle of witness, lest they contract a sin of death;* ²³ *but the Levites shall perform the ministry of the tabernacle of witness, and they shall take upon them their sins: it is an everlasting ordinance unto their generations. And among the children of Israel they shall receive no inheritance;* ²⁴ *because the tithes of the children of Israel, even all that they shall set apart as part-offerings to the Lord, I have given to the Levites for an inheritance. For which cause I said unto them: Among the children of Israel they shall receive no inheritance.* ²⁵ *And the Lord spake with Moses and said unto him:* ²⁶ *Speak to the Levites and say to them: When ye receive of the children of Israel the tithes which I have given you from them for an inheritance, set by thereof, ye also, a part-offering unto the Lord, a tithe of the tithes:* ²⁷ *and your part-offering shall be accounted unto you as the corn from the threshing floor, and as the part-offering of the winepress.* ²⁸ *So shall ye set apart, ye also, a part-offering unto the Lord of all your tithes which ye receive from all the children of Israel; and ye shall give thereof a part-offering for the Lord unto Aaron the priest.* ²⁹ *Of all your gifts ye shall set by a part-offering unto the Lord, even of the firstfruits, (part) whereof he halloweth unto himself.* ³⁰ *And say thou unto them: When ye have set apart his firstfruits therefrom, it shall be reckoned unto the Levites as the produce of the threshing floor and as the produce of the winepress:* ³¹ *and do ye eat thereof in every place, ye and your households, because it is your reward in return for your ministry in the tabernacle of witness:* ³² *and ye shall contract no sin by reason thereof, when ye shall set apart the firstfruits thereof. And the holy things of the children of Israel ye shall not profane, lest ye die.*

CHAPTER IX
(p. 36)

An admonition to the People, that they should honour the Bishop.

[ii. 26] Hear these things then, ye laymen also, the elect Church of God. For the former People also was called a

---

1–2 the elect Church of God] ἡ ἐκλεκτὴ ἐκκλησία τοῦ θεοῦ *AC*. Compare the opening address at p. 2.   2 f. a church] *AC* substitutes θεοῦ λαὸς καὶ ἔθνος ἅγιον (cf. Ex. xix 5).

church; but you are the Catholic Church, the holy and perfect, *a royal priesthood, a holy multitude, a people for inheritance*, the great Church, the bride adorned for the Lord God. Those things then which were said beforetime, hear thou also now. Set by part-offerings and tithes and firstfruits to Christ, the true High Priest, and to His ministers, even tithes of salvation (to Him) the beginning of whose name is the Decade. Hear, thou Catholic Church of God, that wast delivered from the ten plagues, and didst receive the Ten Words, and didst learn the Law, and hold the faith, ⟨and know the Decade,⟩ and believe in the Yod in the beginning of the Name, and art established in the perfection of His glory: instead of the sacrifices which then were, offer now prayers and petitions and thanksgivings. Then were firstfruits and tithes and part-offerings and gifts; but to-day the oblations which are offered through the bishops to the Lord God. For they are your high priests; but the priests and Levites now are the presbyters and deacons, and the orphans and widows: but the Levite and high priest is the bishop. He is minister of the word and mediator; but to you a teacher, and your father after God, who begot you through the water. This is your chief and your leader, and he is your mighty king. He rules in the place of the Almighty: but let him be honoured by you as

---

1 Pet. ii 9 (cf. Ex. xix 5 f.).   2 Cf. Apoc. xxi 2, Isa. lxi 10.   15 Cf. *Didache* xiii 3.

---

2 *multitude*] So Lat.: ἔθνος *AC* (= 1 Pet. and Ex.), but the author of *Didasc.* must have written πλῆθος.   3 the bride adorned, etc.] νύμφη κεκαλλωπισμένη κυρίῳ τῷ θεῷ *AC*. Cf. Apoc. xxi 2 ὡς νύμφην κεκοσμημένην τῷ ἀνδρὶ αὐτῆς (κατεκόσμησέν με Isa. lxi. 10). Use of Apoc. here is possible, but very doubtful.   5 Set by] Supplied by the translator, as Lat. supplies 'sunt': *AC* has no verb, ἀφαιρέματα ... τῷ ἀρχιερεῖ Χριστῷ. 6-7 tithes of salvation, etc.] δεκάται σωτηρίου, ἀρχὴ ὀνόματος Ἰησοῦ *AC* (continuing the verbless construction just noticed). Lat. and Syr. show that *AC* has substituted 'of Jesus' for (probably) δεκάς. On *iota* as a mystical link between the Decalogue and Jesus, see again p. 216.   8 of God] ἱερά *AC*.   10 ⟨and know the Decade⟩] Supplied from Lat. and *AC* (καὶ τὴν δεκάδα ἐγνωκυῖα).   13-14 prayers ... thanksgivings] εὐχαὶ καὶ δεήσεις καὶ εὐχαριστίαι *AC*.   16 For ... high priests] οὗτοι γάρ εἰσιν ὑμῶν οἱ ἀρχιερεῖς *AC*. The phrase is probably taken from *Didache* xiii 3 (see *J. T. S.* xxiv 152: Jan. 1923).   17-18 but the priests ... the bishop] οἱ δὲ

[XXV] ... ⟨ca⟩tholica sacrosancta ecclesia, *regale sacerdotium, multitudo sancta, plebs adoptata,* ecclesia magna, sponsa exornata domino Deo. Quae primum dicta sunt, tu nunc audi: delibationes ⟨et⟩ decumae ⟨et⟩ primitiua sunt principi
5 sacerdotum Christo et ministri⟨s⟩ eius, decumae salutaris, initium nominis decuma. Audite, sacra et catholica ecclesia, quae decem plagas aufugisti, et decem uerba accepisti, et legem didicisti et fidem tenuisti, quae decimam cognouisti et in iota credidisti in initio nominis, et in finem in gloriam
10 eius confirmata es. Quae tunc erant sacrificia, modo sunt orationes et praecationes et gratiarum actiones: quae tunc fuerunt primitiuae et decumae et delibationes et dona, nunc sunt prosforae quae per episcopos offeruntur domino Deo in remissione peccatorum. Isti enim primi sacerdotes uestri.
15 Qui tunc erant Leuitae, modo sunt diacones, praesbyteri, uiduae et orfani. Primus uero sacerdos uobis est Leuita, episcopus. Hic est qui uerbum uobis ministrat et mediator uester est: hic est rex uester potens: hic est magister et post Deum, per aquam regenerans, pater uester. Hic locum Dei
20 sequens sicuti Deus honoretur a uobis, quoniam episcopus in

6 nominis] 'omnis' cod. 8–9 et in iota] 'et initio . ita' cod. (so says Hauler's note): καὶ ἐπὶ τὸ ἰῶτα *AC* (= Syr.). 9 et in finem in gloriam] καὶ ἐπὶ τῇ τελειώσει τῆς δόξης *AC* (= Syr.). 13–14 in remissione peccatorum] om. *AC* (= Syr.): perhaps an insertion by the Latin translator. 17–19 Hic est qui ... pater uester] οὗτος λόγου διάκονος, [γνώσεως φύλαξ,] μεσίτης θεοῦ καὶ ὑμῶν ... οὗτος διδάσκαλος [εὐσεβείας], οὗτος μετὰ θεὸν πατὴρ ὑμῶν, δι' ὕδατος [καὶ πνεύματος] ἀναγεννήσας ὑμᾶς [εἰς υἱοθεσίαν·] οὗτος ἄρχων καὶ ἡγούμενος ὑμῶν, οὗτος ὑμῶν βασιλεὺς καὶ δυνάστης, οὗτος ὑμῶν ἐπίγειος θεὸς μετὰ θεόν *AC* (cf. Syr.). Lat. has apparently misplaced the clause 'hic est rex uester potens' (which should come after 'pater uester'), and has omitted immediately before it some such words as 'hic princeps et dux uester'.

ἱερεῖς ὑμῶν οἱ πρεσβύτεροι, καὶ οἱ λευῖται ὑμῶν οἱ νῦν διάκονοι ... καὶ αἱ χῆραι καὶ αἱ παρθένοι καὶ οἱ ὀρφανοὶ ὑμῶν. ὁ δὲ ... ἀρχιερεύς ἐστιν ὁ ἐπίσκοπος *AC* (evidently with much 'correction' of the original). 19 He is minister, etc.] Comp. *Apost. Ch. Order* xii 1 τὸν λαλοῦντά σοι τὸν λόγον τοῦ θεοῦ, καὶ παραίτιόν σοι γινόμενον τῆς ζωῆς, καὶ δόντα σοι τὴν ἐν κυρίῳ σφραγῖδα ... τιμήσεις αὐτὸν ὡς τὸν κύριον (see again p. 93, l. 22).

88 DIDASCALIA APOSTOLORUM

God, for the bishop sits for you in the place of God Almighty. But the deacon stands in the place of Christ; and do you love him. And the deaconess shall be honoured by you in the place of the Holy Spirit; and the presbyters shall be to you in the likeness of the Apostles; and the orphans and widows shall be reckoned by you in the likeness of the altar. [ii. 27] And as it was not lawful for a stranger, that is for one who was not a Levite, to draw near to the altar or to offer aught without the high priest, so you also shall do nothing without the bishop. But if any man do aught without the bishop, he does it in vain, for it shall not be accounted to him for a work; for it is not (p. 37) fitting that any man should do aught apart from the high priest.

Do you therefore present your offerings to the bishop, either you yourselves, or through the deacons; and when he has received he will distribute them justly. For the bishop is well acquainted of those who are in distress, and dispenses and gives to each one as is fitting for him; so that one may not receive often in the same day or in the same week, and another receive not even a little. For whom the priest and steward of God knows to be the more in distress, him he succours according as he requires.

[ii. 28] And to those who invite widows to suppers let him send frequently her whom he knows to be in the more distress. [And again, if any one gives bounties to widows, let him send

---

1-6 in the place of God, etc.] See also p. 40. These analogies, so far as bishop, presbyters, and deacons are concerned, show dependence on the Ignatian Epistles: cf. especially *Magn*. vi προκαθημένου τοῦ ἐπισκόπου εἰς τύπον θεοῦ, καὶ τῶν πρεσβυτέρων εἰς τύπον συνεδρίου τῶν ἀποστόλων, καὶ τῶν διακόνων ... πεπιστευμένων διακονίαν Ἰησοῦ Χριστοῦ. Compare also *Eph*. vi, *Trall*. ii, iii, *Smyrn*. viii. *AC* reads here ὁ γὰρ ἐπίσκοπος προκαθεζέσθω ὑμῶν ὡς θεοῦ ἀξίᾳ τετιμημένος ... ὁ δὲ διάκονος τούτῳ παριστάσθω ὡς ὁ Χριστὸς τῷ πατρί ... ἡ δὲ διάκονος εἰς τύπον τοῦ ἁγίου πνεύματος τετιμήσθω ὑμῖν ... οἵ τε πρεσβύτεροι εἰς τύπον ἡμῶν τῶν ἀποστόλων ὑμῖν νενομίσθωσαν ... αἵ τε χῆραι καὶ οἱ ὀρφανοὶ εἰς τύπον τοῦ θυσιαστηρίου λελογίσθωσαν ὑμῖν· [αἵ τε παρθένοι εἰς τύπον τοῦ θυμιατηρίου τετιμήσθωσαν καὶ τοῦ θυμιάματος]. 3-4 deaconess ... Holy Spirit] Cf. *Gosp. acc. to the Hebrews* 'the Holy Spirit my mother'; and Aphraates Hom. xviii 10 (explaining Gen. ii 24) 'a man who is yet unmarried loves and honours God his father and the Holy Spirit his mother'. The origin of such expressions is doubtless to be sought in the Semitic languages: in Hebrew and Aramaic (including Syriac) 'spirit' is feminine. 5-6 the widows ... the altar] See again

typum Dei praesedet uobis. Diaconus autem in typum Christi adstat: ergo diligatur a uobis. Diaconissa uero in typum sancti spiritus honoretur a uobis. Praesbyteri etiam in typum apostolorum sperentur a uobis: uiduae et orfani in typum [XXVI] altaris putentur autem a uobis. Sicuti ergo non licebat eum qui non erat Leuita offerre aliquid aut accedere ad altarem sine sacerdote, ita et uos sine episcopo nolite aliquid facere. Si quis autem sine episcopo facit aliquid, in uano illud facit: non enim illi inputabitur in opus, quia non decet absque sacerdotem aliquid facere.

Prosforas ergo uestras sacerdoti offerite, siue per uos ipsos siue per diacones; quique suscipiet et, ut decet, diuidet unicuique: episcopus enim optime nouit eos qui tribulantur, et unicuique dat secundum dispensationem, ut non unus aut frequenter et in ipso die aut in ipsa ebdomada accipiat, alius autem nec semel. Horum aliquem ⟨quem⟩ tribulari cognoscit sacerdos magis, sicut dispensator Dei facit et cum ipso sicut decet.

His iterum qui agapam desiderant facere, et petunt aniculas, hanc quam scit tribulari frequenter etiam mittat. Et haec

---

4 sperentur] νενομίσθωσαν *AC*. Hauler corrects to 'spectentur', but without necessity, for 'sperare' is used several times in this version for 'putare': cf. pp. 243, 249, 257. 5–6 sicuti ... Leuita] ὡς οὖν οὐκ ἦν ἐξὸν ἀλλογενῆ, μὴ ὄντα λευίτην *AC* (cf. Syr.). 16 nec semel] μηδὲ ὅλως *AC*. 17 dispensatur Deus cod. 19 etiam] The reading is far from certain; perhaps it should be 'ipsam' (αὐτὴν πλειστάκις πεμπέτωσαν *AC*, and Syr. has the same construction).

---

pp. 133, 134, 143, 156, 159. Similarly Polycarp *Phil*. iv, comp. Tertullian *ad Uxor*. i 7. 9–10 do nothing without the bishop] Comp. Ignatius *Magn*. vii, *Trall*. ii, *Phil*. vii, *Smyrn*. viii. 23–24 And to those ... distress] τοῖς εἰς ἀγάπην [ἤτοι δοχήν] . . . προαιρουμένοις καλεῖν πρεσβυτέρας, ἣν ἐπίστανται [οἱ διάκονοι] θλιβομένην, αὐτὴν πλειστάκις πεμπέτωσαν *AC*. A charity supper for widows is found in the *Apost. Trad*. of Hippolytus (Hauler p. 115). The Syriac word here rendered 'suppers' was used especially of funeral feasts. 25 etc. And ... in want] om. *AC* (= Lat.). The words are a gloss, and possibly represent later practice or ideas. 25 bounties] lit. 'gifts', and so again at p. 90, l. 3.

her the rather who is in want.] But let the portion of the pastor be separated and set apart for him according to rule at the suppers or the bounties, even though he be not present, in honour of Almighty God. But how much (soever) is given to one of the widows, let the double be given to each of the deacons in honour of Christ, (but) twice twofold to the leader for the glory of the Almighty. But if any one wish to honour the presbyters also, let him give them a double (portion), as to the deacons; for they ought to be honoured as the Apostles, and as the counsellors of the bishop, and as the crown of the Church; for they are the moderators and councillors of the Church. But if there be also a lector, let him too receive with the presbyters. To every order, therefore, let every one of the laity pay the honour which is befitting him, with gifts and presents and with the respect due to his worldly condition.

But let them have very free access to the deacons, and let them not be troubling the head at all times, but making known what they require through the ministers, that is through the deacons. For neither can any man approach the Lord God Almighty except through Christ. All things therefore that they desire to do, let them make known to the bishop through the deacons, and then do them. For neither formerly in the temple of the sanctuary was anything offered or done without the priest. And moreover, even the idol-temples of the impure and abhorred and reprobate heathen to this day imitate the sanctuary. Far indeed in comparison be the house of abomination from the sanctuary: nevertheless, even in (p. 38) their absurd rites they neither offer nor do anything without their unclean priest; but so they imagine, that the unclean priest is the mouthpiece of the stones; and they wait for what he will command them to do. And in all that they purpose to do they consult their unclean priest, and without him do nothing, And because they imagine that

---

1-12 But let the portion ... councillors of the Church] ἀφοριζέσθω δὲ ἐν τῇ δοχῇ τὸ τῷ ποιμένι ἔθιμον, ... κἂν μὴ παρῇ τῇ δοχῇ, εἰς τιμὴν θεοῦ ... ὡσεὶ δὲ ἑκάστῃ τῶν πρεσβυτίδων δίδοται, διπλοῦν διδόσθω τοῖς διακόνοις εἰς γέρας Χριστοῦ. τοῖς δὲ πρεσβυτέροις ... διπλῇ καὶ αὐτοῖς

DIDASCALIA APOSTOLORUM

pars quae ex consuetudine sacerdoti debetur, separetur, etiamsi non est praesens in agapis et erogationibus, in honorem omnipotentis Dei. Sicut ergo unicuique praesbyterorum datur, duplum dabitur singulis diaconibus in sacerdotio Christi, 5 quadruplum autem ei qui praeest, tamquam in omnipotentis gloria. Si quis autem et praesbyteros uoluerit honorare, duplum sicuti diaconibus dabit illis: nam et ipsi tamquam apostoli et consiliarii honorentur episcopi, et corona ecclesiae: sunt enim consilium et curia ecclesia⟨e⟩. Si autem . . .

---

1 sacerdoti] τῷ ποιμένι AC (= Syr.).   3 presbyterorum] cod.: πρεσβυτίδων AC (cf. Syr.).   4 in sacerdotio] εἰς γέρας AC (cf. Syr.).

ἀφοριζέσθω ἡ μοῖρα εἰς χάριν τῶν τοῦ κυρίου ἀποστόλων, . . . ὡς σύμβουλοι τοῦ ἐπισκόπου καὶ τῆς ἐκκλησίας στέφανος· εἰσὶν γὰρ συνέδριον καὶ βουλὴ τῆς ἐκκλησίας AC (with insertions). As to presbyters as 'counsellors', compare Ignatius *Magn.* vi, *Trall.* iii, and Hippolytus *Apost. Trad.* (in the ordination prayer for a presbyter) 'et inpartire spiritum gratiae et consilii presbyterii'; and contrasting deacon with presbyter he says 'non est enim particeps consilii in clero' (Hauler pp. 108, 109).   12–16 εἰ δὲ καὶ ἀναγνώστης ἔστιν, λαμβανέτω καὶ αὐτὸς μοῖραν μίαν εἰς τιμὴν τῶν προφητῶν· [ὡσαύτως καὶ ψαλτῳδὸς καὶ πυλωρός]. ἑκάστῳ οὖν ἀξιώματι οἱ λαϊκοὶ τὴν προσήκουσαν τιμὴν νεμέτωσαν ἐν τοῖς δόμασι καὶ τῇ κατὰ τὸν βίον ἐντροπῇ AC.   15–16 due . . . condition] lit. 'of the world'.   24 in the temple . . . offered] ἐν τῷ ἱερῷ ἁγίασμά τι προσεφέρετο AC.   27 sanctuary] τὰ ἅγια AC, and again p. 92, l. 6.   30 unclean priest] τοῦ μιερέως AC (and in following lines).

what they do is acceptable, they honour him and worship him, as it were for the honour of the dumb stones that are fixed in the walls, and for the service of the foul and evil and cruel demons. If then those who are vain, and their customs false, and who have no hope, but are deceived by an empty hope, study and desire to imitate the sanctuary, and bestow all honour upon those who stand before their absurd idols: you who manifestly and openly believe in the truth, and hold fast to the hope that is not belied, and wait for the glorious promise which shall never pass away nor be made void—why should not you rather honour the Lord God through those who preside over you?

Do you therefore esteem the bishop as the mouth of God. [ii. 29] For if Aaron, because he interpreted to Pharaoh the words which were given through Moses, was called a prophet, as the Lord said to Moses: *Behold, I have given thee as a god to Pharaoh; and Aaron thy brother shall be to thee a prophet*: why then should not you also reckon them as prophets who are for you the mediators of the word, and worship them as God? [ii. 30] But for us now, Aaron is the deacon, and Moses is the bishop. Now if Moses was called a god by the Lord, let the bishop also be honoured by you as God, and the deacon as a prophet. [ii. 31] Wherefore, for the honour of the bishop, make known to him all things that you do, and let them be performed through him. And if thou know of one who is in much distress, and the bishop know not of him, do thou inform him; and without him do not, to his discredit, anything, lest thou bring a reproach upon him as one who neglects the poor. For he who sets abroad an evil report against the bishop, whether by word or by deed, sins against God Almighty. And again, if any man speaks (p. 39) evil of a deacon, whether by word or deed, he offends against Christ. Wherefore in the Law also it is written: *Thou shalt not revile*

---

16 Ex. vii 1.   33 Ex. xxii 28.

---

4 and their customs false] The text (HS) has 'and are false customs': I have translated from a conjectural reading.   10 promise] ἐπαγγελίαν AC. Vocalize *melka*, not *malka* ('king'), or else read *mulkāna*.

thy gods; and thou shalt not speak evil of a prince of thy people. Now let no man think that the Lord speaks (here) of idols of stone; but he calls 'gods' those who preside over you. [ii. 32] Moses also saith in the Book of Numbers, when
5 the people had murmured against him and against Aaron: *Not against us do ye murmur, but against the Lord God*. And our Saviour likewise said: *Every one that rejecteth you, rejecteth me, and him that sent me*. For what hope at all is there for him who speaks evil of the bishop, or of the deacon? For
10 if one call a layman *fool*, or *raca, he is liable to the assembly*, as one of those who rise up against Christ: because that he calls 'empty' his brother in whom Christ dwells, who is not empty but fulfilled; or (calls) him 'fool' in whom dwells the Holy Spirit of God, fulfilled with all wisdom: as though he
15 should become a fool by the very Spirit that dwells in him! If then one who should say any of these things to a layman is found to fall under so great condemnation, how much more if he should dare to say aught against the deacon, or against the bishop, through whom the Lord gave you the
20 Holy Spirit, and through whom you have learned the word and have known God, and through whom you have been known of God, and through whom you were sealed, and through whom you became sons of the light, and through whom the Lord in baptism, by the imposition of hand of the
25 bishop, bore witness to each one of you and uttered His holy voice, saying: *Thou art my son: I this day have begotten thee*.

[ii. 33] Wherefore, O man, know thy bishops, through whom thou wast made a son of God, and the right hand, thy mother;
30 and love him who is become, after God, thy father and thy

6 Ex. xvi 8 (cf. Nu. xiv 2).   7 Lk. x 16.   10 Mt. v 22.   21 Cf. Gal. iv 9. Cf. Joh. xii 36, 1 Thes. v. 5.   26 Ps. ii 7 (Lk. iii 22).

---

7 *Every one*, etc.] On the reading see p. 60, l. 25.   12 empty] Our author knows the derivation of '*raca*' from *rîk*.   22 were sealed] ἐσφραγίσθητε *AC*: comp. *Apost. Ch. Order* xii 1 καὶ δόντα σοι τὴν ἐν κυρίῳ σφραγίδα (cf. p. 86 above).   26 *Thou art*, etc.] Implying the 'Western' reading at Lk. iii 22, on which see Otto's note to Justin *Dial*. 88.   29 the right hand, etc.] τὴν δεξιάν, τὴν μητέρα σου *AC*.

mother: for *whosoever shall revile his father or his mother, shall die the death.* But do you honour the bishops, who have loosed you from sins, who by the water regenerated you, who filled you with the Holy Spirit, who reared you with the word as with milk, who bred you up with doctrine, who confirmed you with admonition, and made you to partake of the holy Eucharist of God, and made you partakers and joint heirs of the promise of God. These reverence, (p. 40) and honour them with all honour; for they have received from God the authority of life and death: not as judging those who sin and condemning them to death in fire everlasting, by cutting off and casting away those who are judged, which God forbid, but that they may receive and save alive those who return and repent.

[ii. 34] Let them be your rulers therefore, and let them be accounted of by you as kings; and do you offer them tribute in service as to kings; for by you they ought to be sustained, and those who are with them: for thus is it written in the first Book of Kingdoms: ¹⁰ *Samuel spake all the words of the Lord unto the people, which had asked of him a king,* ¹¹ *and said to them: This is the law of the king that shall reign over you: your sons he will take, and will set them upon his chariots; and he will make of them runners before him,* ¹² *and will make him captains of thousands and captains of hundreds. And they shall reap his harvest, and gather his vintage, and fashion the instruments of his chariots.* ¹³ *And your daughters he will take to be weavers, and to be the ministers of his house.* ¹⁴ *And your fields, and your vineyards, and your oliveyards, even the best (of them), he will take away and give to his servants.* ¹⁵ *And he will take the tenth of your seed and of your vineyards, and give to his servants and to his eunuchs.* ¹⁶ *And your servants and your handmaids, and the best of your cattle, and your asses, he will take and tithe for the service of his work;* ¹⁷ *and he will take the tenth of your sheep: and ye also shall be*

---

1 Ex. xxi 17, Mt. xv 4.   19 1 Reg. viii 10–17.

6 and made you to partake, etc.] καὶ τῆς ἁγίας καὶ ἱερᾶς εὐχαριστίας μετόχους ποιήσαντας *A C*.   16–17 tribute in service] lit. 'presents in works': *A C* has simply δασμούς.   25 *and fashion*] The equivalent of σκεύη πολεμικὰ

[XXVII] . . . ¹² *uasa bellica eius et facere uasa in curribus eius:* ¹³ *et filias uestras accipiet in unguentarias et frarias et pensarias:* ¹⁴ *et agros uestros et uineas uestras et oliueta uestra bona sumet et dabit seruis suis:* ¹⁵ *et semina uestra et uineas uestras decumabit et dabit eunuchis suis et seruis suis:* ¹⁶ *et seruos uestros et ancillas uestras et armenta bona uestra et asinos uestros sumet et decumauit in operibus suis,* ¹⁷ *et greges uestras decumauit: et uos eritis serui illius.* Ipsam rationem

2 *frarias*] The Latin Vulg. has 'focarias', '*et sic fort. scrib.*', says Hauler.   3 *pensarias*] Apparently from 'pinsor', a baker.

αὐτοῦ καί is wanting after this (cf. Lat.).   27 *weavers*] As Pesh.: μυρεψούς LXX (= Lat.).   *the ministers of his house*] εἰς μαγειρίσσας καὶ εἰς πεσσούσας LXX: 'millers and bakers' Pesh.

his servants. Now in like case is also the bishop. For if the king who reigned over so numerous a people—as it is written in Hosea: *The people of the children of Israel was numerous as the sand which is upon the seashore, which may not be measured nor numbered*—took also from the people the ministrations which he required according to the multitude of that people: so now does the bishop also take for himself from the people those whom he accounts and knows to be worthy of him and of his office, and appoints him presbyters as counsellors and assessors, and deacons and subdeacons, as many as he has need of in proportion to the ministry of the house. And what can we say more? For the king who wears the diadem reigns over the body alone, and binds and looses it but on earth; but the bishop reigns over soul and body, to bind and to loose on earth with heavenly power. For great power, heavenly, almighty, is given (p. 41) to him. Therefore love the bishop as a father, and fear him as a king, and honour him as God. Your fruits and the works of your hands present to him, that you may be blessed; your firstfruits and your tithes and your vows and your part-offerings give to him; for he has need of them that he may be sustained, and that he may dispense also to those who are in want, to each as is just for him. And so shall thine offering be acceptable to the Lord thy God for a sweet savour, in the heights of heaven before the Lord thy God; and He will bless thee and multiply for thee the good things of His promise. For it is written in Wisdom: *Every simple soul shall be blessed: and a blessing shall be upon the head of him that giveth.*

Wherefore be constantly doing work, and be labouring and

---

3 Hos. i 10.   15 Mt. xvi 19, xviii 18.   27 Prov. xi 25 f.

1 in like case is also the bishop] lit. 'the same likeness does the bishop also hold' (cf. Lat.). Flemming renders 'In diesem Typus ist auch der Bischof mit einbegriffen'. This is possible; but the participle '*aḥīdh* is more often active in sense ('holds'), and may be followed by the prep. *b* ('in', or 'by'). 1–2 For if... a people] εἰ γὰρ ἐκεῖ πλῆθος τηλικούτου βασιλέως ἀναλόγως τὰς ὑπηρεσίας ἐδίδου *AC* (but cf. Lat.). 9 office] lit. 'place'.   9–16 presbyters, etc.] Altered in *AC*. The word for 'subdeacons' is ὑποδιάκονοι transliterated. Achelis (p. 265) considers the

DIDASCALIA APOSTOLORUM

optinet et episcopus: si enim ibi, cum tante multitudini ⟨rex⟩ regnaret—sicuti et in Osee scriptum est: *Et erat multitudo filiorum Istrahel sicut harena quae est secus mare, quae non potest numerari nec mensurari*—secundum [ergo] ratam et multitudinem plebis suae et ministeria accipiebat: et modo episcopus de populo accipie⟨n⟩s ⟨s⟩ibi quoscumque loci dignos esse existimauerit, praesbyteros constituet et consiliarios sibi et contractatores, diaconos et subdiaconos intra domum ministrare eis. Nam quid plus est dicere? Ille quidem qui diademam portat rex, corporis solius regnat, super terram solum soluens aut ligans. Episcopus autem et animae et corporis regnat, ligans et soluens super terram caelesti potestate: magna enim et caelestis et deifica data est ei potestas. Episcopum ergo diligite ut patrem, timete sicuti regem, honorate ut Deum. Fructum et operam manuum uestrarum ad benedictionem uestram [XXVIII] offerte, decimas uestras et primitiuas et delibationes et dona dantes ei: et ipse utetur ea, et eis qui indigent dabit omnibus, unicuique sicuti dignus est. Et erit oblatio tua suscepta domino Deo tuo in odorem suauitatis in latitudinem caelorum in conspectu domini Dei tui: et benedictus eris, et multiplicabit super bona promissionis suae, quoniam scriptum est in Sapientia: *Anima benedicta omnis sinplex. Benedictio autem super caput porrigentis.*

Incumbe in labore, adsiduus esto in operandum, et offer:

6 accipiens sibi] 'accipies ibi' cod. Hauler and Funk correct to 'accipiens', but leave 'ibi': 'take for himself' Syr. 17 diliuationes cod. 19 oderem cod.

subdeacon here a later insertion, but he appears also in Lat. 19 that ... blessed] εἰς εὐλογίαν ὑμῶν *AC* (= Lat.). 21–22 has need ... sustained] 'utetur ea' Lat. Did Syr. take χρήσεται as from χρῄζειν? *AC* has not the clause. 23 And so, etc.] Cf. the Syriac Liturgy of St. James (Brightman *L. E. W.* i 91–92) 'Thou receiving their sacrifices upon the breadth of thy heaven'. 25 heights] 'latitudinem' Lat.: om. *AC*.

offering an oblation. For the Lord has lightened the weight from you, and has loosed from you the collar-bands, and lifted from you the yoke of burden; and He has put away from you the Second Legislation after the abundance of His mercy; as it is written in Isaiah: *Say to them that are in bonds, Go forth*; and again: *To bring forth the prisoners from bonds.* And in David he said: *His prisoners he hath not despised.* And likewise in the Gospel He said: *Come unto me, all ye that toil and are laden with heavy burdens, and I will give you rest. Take my yoke upon you, and learn of me; for I am gentle and lowly in heart: and ye shall find rest unto your souls. For my yoke is pleasant, and my burden is light.*

[ii. 35] If then the Lord, by the gift of His grace, has set you loose and given you rest, *and brought you out into refreshment*, that you should no more be bound with sacrifices and oblations, and with sin offerings, and purifications, and vows, and gifts, and holocausts, and burnt offerings, and (Sabbath) idlings, and shewbread, and the observing of purifications; nor yet with tithes and firstfruits, and part-offerings, and gifts and oblations,—for it was laid upon them to give all these things as of necessity, but you are not bound by these things,—it behoves you to know the word of the Lord, who said: *Except your righteousness abound more than that of the scribes and Pharisees, ye shall not enter into the kingdom of heaven.* Now thus shall your righteousness abound more than their tithes and firstfruits and part-offerings, when you shall do as it is written: *Sell all thou hast, and give to the poor.* So do, therefore, and keep the command through (him who is) bishop and priest and thy mediator with the Lord (p. 42) God. For thou art commanded to give, but he to dispense. And thou shalt require no account of the bishop, nor observe him, how he dispenses

---

5 Isa. xlix. 9   6 Isa. xlii 7.   7 Ps. lxviii (lxix) 34.
8 Mt. xi. 28–30.   14 Ps. lxv (lxvi) 12.   22 Mt. v 20.
27 Mt. xix 21 (cf. Lk. xii 33).

30 And thou shalt require, etc.] Cf. *Didache* xi 11 οὐ κριθήσεται (sc. the prophet) ἐφ' ὑμῶν· μετὰ θεοῦ γὰρ ἔχει τὴν κρίσιν, and xi 12 ἐὰν δὲ περὶ ἄλλων ὑστερούντων εἴπῃ δοῦναι, μηδεὶς αὐτὸν κρινέτω. See again p. 100 l. 30 'thou shalt not judge thy bishop nor thy fellow layman'.

DIDASCALIA APOSTOLORUM

quoniam dominus adleuauit uos de uinculis et sustulit a uobis collarem constrictionis et euacuauit a uobis iugum graue, tollens a uobis secundam dationem legis secundum bonitatem suam, sicuti scribtum est in Esaia: *Dicente eis qui in uinculis erant,* 5 *Exite.* Et iterum : *Educere de uinculis legatos.* Et in Dauid dicit: *Et in conpedibus conligatos eius non spreuit.* Similiter et in euangelio dicit: *Uenite ad me, omnes qui laboratis et onerati estis, et ego repausabo uos. Tollite iugum meum super uos et discite a me, quoniam mansuetus sum et humilis corde, et* 10 *inuenietis requiem animabus uestris: iugum enim meum suaue est, et onus meum leue est.*

Si ergo secundum donationem gratiae soluens repausauit uos et *eduxit in refrigerium,* iam non ligans sacrificiis et †orationibus† et pro peccatis et purificationibus et donis et oblationibus 15 et olocaustis et combustionibus et en⟨caeniis(?)⟩ . . .

---

2 constructionis cod. (*uid.*). 3 secundam] 'secundum' cod. Only here does 'secunda datio' appear for the *deuterosis*, and perh. we should read 'secundationem'. 4 *Dicente*] λέγοντα LXX: therefore perh. read 'dicentem'. 13-14 orationibus] Prob. read 'oblationibus', with Syr.: though this comes again in the same line, presumably it does not stand for the same Gk. word in both places. 15 et combustionibus] Hauler says this is written over 'et olocaustis', '*explicandi causa ut uid.*'; but 'holocaustis' would not need explanation, and Syr. has 'holocausts and burnt offerings'.

and discharges his stewardship, or when he gives, or to whom, or where, or whether well or ill, or whether he gives fairly; for he has One who will require, even the Lord God, who delivered this stewardship into his hands and held him worthy of the priesthood of so great an office. Wherefore, that thou observe not the bishop, nor require an account of him, nor speak ill of him and oppose God, nor offend the Lord, [ii. 36] let that be set before thine eyes which is said to thee in Jeremiah (*sic*): *Shall the clay say to the potter: Thou workest not, and hast not hands? as one who should say to his father or his mother: Why bearest thou me?* But do thou work and labour simply in the house of God; and let that saving word of the renewing of the Law be ever written and laid up in thy heart, and remember it, as the Lord said: *Thou shalt love the Lord thy God with all thy soul, and with all thy strength.* Now *thy strength* is thy worldly substance. And not with the lips only shall you love the Lord, as did that People, to whom upbraiding them He saith: *This people honoureth me with their lips, but their heart is very far from me;* but do thou love and honour the Lord *with all thy strength*, and offer His oblations ever at all times.

And hold not aloof from the Church; but when thou hast received the Eucharist of the oblation, that which comes into thy hands cast (in), that thou mayest share it with strangers: for this is collected (and brought) to the bishop for the entertainment of all strangers. Wherefore lay up and set by as much as thou canst, for the Lord has said in the Law: *Thou shalt not appear before me empty.* Be doing good works therefore, and *laying up to thyself treasure* everlasting *in heaven, where the moth corrupteth not, neither do thieves steal.* And in so doing thou shalt not judge thy bishop nor thy fellow layman;

---

9 Isa. xlv 9 f.   14 Mk. xii 30, Lk. x 27 (Deut. vi 5).   18 Isa. xxix. 13, Mt. xv 8.   26 Ex. xxiii 15.   28 Mt. vi 20, Lk. xii 33.

4-5 and held him worthy ... office] καὶ καταξιώσαντα αὐτὸν τῆς ἱερωσύνης τοῦ τηλικούτου τόπου *AC.*   22-23 comes into thy hands] Cf. *Didache* iv 6.   23 cast (in)] There is an allusion to Mk. xii 41 ff., a passage quoted later (p. 138).   24 for this is collected, etc.] Cf. Justin *Apol.* i 67 καὶ τὸ συλλεγόμενον παρὰ τῷ προεστῶτι ἀποτίθεται, καὶ αὐτὸς ἐπικουρεῖ ὀρφανοῖς τε καὶ χήραις καὶ τοῖς διὰ νόσον ἢ δι' ἄλλην αἰτίαν λειπομένοις.   30 thou shalt not judge] See note to p. 98 l. 30.

for to you laymen it is said: *Judge not, that ye be not judged.* For if thou judge thy brother and condemn him, thou hast reckoned thy brother guilty: that is, thou hast condemned thyself; for thou shalt be judged with them that are guilty. [ii. 37] For it is lawful for the bishops to judge, because to them it is said: *Be ye approved money-changers*: so that it behoves (p. 43) the bishop, as one who proves money, to separate the bad from the good, and to reject and cast away those that are altogether bad, and to leave in the melting-pot those that are hard, and for whatever reason faulty, like faulty (coins). But to the layman it is not permitted to judge his neighbour, nor to lay upon himself a burden that is not his. For the weight of this burden is not for laymen, but for the bishop. Wherefore, being a layman, thou shalt not lay snares for thyself; but leave judgement in the hand of those who will have to render an account, and do thou study to work peace with all men; and love thy members, thy fellow laymen, for the Lord saith: *Love thy neighbour as thyself.*

CHAPTER X

Of False Brethren

But if there be false brethren who, through envy or jealousy of the Enemy and Satan, who works in them, bring an accusation against any of the brethren falsely, or even truly, let them know that every one who searches out such things for the purpose of accusing or slandering any man, is a son of

---

1 Mt. vii 1, Lk. vi 37.   6 Agraphon.   18 Mt. xix 19 (Lev. xix 18).

6 *Be ye approved money-changers*] γίνεσθε τραπεζῖται δόκιμοι *A C*. On this extremely popular 'agraphon' Resch p. 112 may be consulted: it first appears in Clem. Alex. *Strom.* i 28. 177. The Syriac word rendered 'money-changers' means one who separates, discerns, explains; the technical sense here is inferred from the Greek.

wrath: and where wrath is, God is not; for wrath is of Satan, and through these false brethren he never suffers peace to be in the Church. Wherefore, when you have known those who are thus void of understanding, first of all believe them not; and secondly, do you the bishops and deacons be wary of them; and when you hear them saying anything against one of the brethren, [ii. 38] take knowledge of him against whom they bring the accusation, and make inquiry prudently, and weigh his conduct; and if he is found blameworthy, do according to the teaching of our Lord which is written in the Gospel: *Reprove him between thyself and him; and save him when he repenteth and returneth.* But if he be not persuaded, *reprove him among two or three;* that that may be fulfilled which is said: *At the mouth of two or three witnesses every word shall be established.* Now why, brethren, is it required that a testimony be established at the mouth of two or three witnesses? Because the Father and the Son and the Holy Spirit bear witness to the works of men. For where there is the admonition of doctrine, there also is correction and conversion of them that err. (p. 44) Wherefore, *at the mouth of two or three witnesses every word shall be established. But if he obey not, reprove him before the whole church. But if he obey not even the church, let him be accounted by thee as the heathen and as the publican.* For the Lord has commanded you, O bishops, that you should not henceforth receive such a one into the Church as a Christian, nor communicate with him. For

---

11 Mt. xviii 15 f. (cf. Lk. xvii 3); Deut. xix 15.   20 Mt. xviii 16, 17

---

1 and where ... God is not] ὅπου δὲ ὀργή, ἐκεῖ κύριος οὐκ ἔστιν *AC*. Comp. Ignatius *Phil.* viii 1 οὗ δὲ μερισμός ἐστιν καὶ ὀργή, θεὸς οὐ κατοικεῖ. 6 saying anything] lit. 'blaspheming'. 11 *and him*] Without 'alone', as *syr. sin.* and Aphraates (Hom. xiv 44). *and save*, etc.] Cf. Lk. xvii 3. Aphraates similarly adds 'and if he has repented, forgive him', from Lk. 17 Because the Father, etc.] Cf. Irenaeus *Haer.* IV xxxiv 12 'suscepit autem (sc. Rahab) tres speculatores, qui speculabantur uniuersam terram, et apud se abscondit, Patrem scilicet et Filium cum Spiritu sancto'. Funk refers to the 'comma Ioanneum' (1 Joh. v 7), but adds that he does not suggest knowledge of it on the part of our author. 23 *let him be accounted*] So *syr. cur.* and (with a different construction) *syr. sin.*: Aphraates (*loc. cit.*) has 'then let him be accounted'.

neither dost thou receive the evil heathen or publicans into the Church and communicate with them except they first repent, professing that they believe and henceforth will do no more evil works: for to this end did our Lord and Saviour grant a place for repentance to those who have sinned. [ii. 39] For I Matthew also, who am one of the twelve Apostles who speak to you in this Didascalia, was formerly a publican; but now, because that I believed, I have obtained mercy, and have repented of my former deeds, and have been counted worthy also to be an apostle and preacher of the word. And the prophet John likewise preached in the Gospel to publicans; and he deprived them not of hope, but taught them how they should order themselves; and when they asked him for advice, he said to them: *Exact no more than that which is commanded and appointed you.* And Zacchaeus, too, the Lord received unto repentance when he besought Him. Nor do we withhold life even from the heathen, if they will repent and put away and reject their error.

As a heathen, then, *and as a publican let him be accounted by you* who has been convicted of evil deeds and falsehood; and afterwards, if he promise to repent—even as when the heathen desire and promise to repent, and say 'We believe', we receive them into the congregation that they may hear the word, but do not communicate with them until they receive the seal and are fully initiated: so neither do we communicate with these until they show the fruits of repentance. But let them by all means come in, if they desire to hear the word, that they may not wholly perish; but let them not communicate in prayer, but go forth without. For they also, when they have seen that they do not communicate with the Church, will submit themselves, and repent of their former works, and strive to be

---

14 Lk. iii 13.   15 Lk. xix 1 ff.   19 Mt. xviii 17.

6-7 in this Didascalia] ἐν τῇδε τῇ διδασκαλίᾳ *AC*.   13 advice] lit. 'a word' or 'answer'.   24-25 until ... initiated] μέχρις οὗ τὴν σφαγίδα λαβόντες τελειωθῶσιν *AC*.   28 but let them not, etc.] An allusion to the dismissal of penitents and catechumens from the church after the Scripture lessons and homily and before the 'prayers of the faithful'.

received into the Church for prayer; and they likewise who see and hear them go forth like the heathen and publicans, will fear and take warning to themselves not to sin, (p. 45) lest it so happen to them also, and being convicted of sin or falsehood they be put forth from the Church.

[ii. 40] But thou shalt by no means forbid them to enter the Church and hear the word, O bishop; for neither did our Lord and Saviour utterly thrust away and reject publicans and sinners, but did even eat with them. And for this cause the Pharisees murmured against Him, and said: *He eateth with publicans and sinners.* Then did our Saviour make answer against their thoughts and their murmuring, and say: *They that are whole have no need of a physician, but they that are sick.* Do you therefore consort with those who have been convicted of sins and are sick, and attach them to you, and be careful of them, and speak to them and comfort them, and keep hold of them and convert them. [ii. 41] And afterwards, as each one of them repents and shows the fruits of repentance, receive him to prayer after the manner of a heathen. And as thou baptizest a heathen and then receivest him, so also lay hand upon this man, whilst all pray for him, and then bring him in and let him communicate with the Church. For the imposition of hand shall be to him in the place of baptism: for whether by the imposition of hand, or by baptism, they receive the communication of the Holy Spirit.

Wherefore, as a compassionate physician, heal all those who sin; and go about with all skill, and bring healing to bear for the succour of their lives. And thou shalt not be ready to cut off the members of the Church; but employ the bandages of the word, and the fomentations of admonition, and the

---

10 Mk. ii 16 f., Mt. ix 11 f., Lk. v 30 f.

14 Do you therefore consort, etc.] συναναστρέφεσθε καὶ συναυλίζεσθε, ἐπιμελούμενοι, παρακαλοῦντες, ὑποστηρίζοντες *AC*. 23 For the imposition of hand, etc.] καὶ ἔσται αὐτῷ ἀντὶ τοῦ λούσματος ἡ χειροθεσία· καὶ γὰρ διὰ τῆς ἐπιθέσεως τῶν [ἡμετέρων] χειρῶν ἐδίδοτο τὸ πνεῦμα τὸ ἅγιον [τοῖς πιστεύουσιν] *AC*, with some modification.

compress of exhortation. But if the sore be sunken and lack flesh, nourish it and level it up with healing drugs; and if there be dirt in it, cleanse it with a pungent drug, that is with the word of rebuke. But if the flesh be over swollen, wear it
5 down and level it with a violent drug, that is with the threat of judgement. But if gangrene should set in, cauterize it with burnings, that is, with incisions of much fasting cut away and clear out the rottenness of the sore. But if the gangrene assert itself and prevail even over the burnings, give judge-
10 ment: and then, whichever member it be that is putrified, with advice and much consultation with other physicians, cut off that putrefied member, that it may not corrupt the whole body. Yet be not ready to amputate straightway, and be not in haste to have recourse at once to the saw (p. 46) of many
15 teeth; but use first the knife and cut the sore, that it may be clearly seen, and that it may be known what is the cause of the disease that is hidden within; so that the whole body may be kept uninjured. But if thou see that a man will not repent, but has altogether abandoned himself, then with grief and
20 sorrow cut him off and cast him out of the Church.

[ii. 42] But if it be found that the hostile charge is false, and you the pastors, with the deacons, accept the falsehood as truth—whether through respect of persons, or by reason of the presents which you receive—and pervert judgement
25 because you desire to do the will of the Evil One, and expel and cast out from the Church him that is accused, whereas he is innocent of this charge: you shall render an account in the day of the Lord; for it is written: *Thou shalt not respect persons in judgement*; and again the Scripture saith: *A bribe*

28 Deut. i 17.   29 Ex. xxiii 8 (cf. Deut. xvi 19).

---

1 But if the sore, etc.] ἐὰν δὲ κοῖλον ᾖ τὸ τραῦμα, θρέψον αὐτὸ δι' ἐμπλάστρων, ἵνα γεμισθὲν ἴσον τῷ ἀρτίῳ ἀποτελεσθῇ· ἐὰν δὲ ῥυπανθῇ, τότε κάθαρον ξηρίῳ, τοῦτ' ἔστιν λόγῳ ἐπιτιμητικῷ· ἐὰν δὲ ὑπέρογκον γένηται, δριμεῖ κολλυρίῳ ἐξομάλισον αὐτό, ἀπειλῇ κρίσεως· κἂν νομὴ γένηται, καυτηρίασον αὐτὸ καὶ τὴν σηπεδόνα ἔκκοψον, στιβώσας νηστείαις *AC*.   7 incisions] The word may also mean 'decrees', and so impositions.   14-15 to the saw of many teeth] ἐπὶ τὸν μυριόδοντα πρίονα (ὅρμα) *AC*.   21 the hostile charge] lit. 'the charge of accusation (*or* slander)': ἡ κατηγορία τῆς διαβολῆς *AC*.

blindeth the eyes of them that see, and perverteth right words; and again it hath said: *Deliver ye the oppressed, and judge the fatherless, and acquit the widows*; and: *Judge right judgement in the gates.*

Give heed therefore that you be not respecters of persons and incur the judgement of the Lord's word, which He spoke thus: *Woe to them that make bitter sweet, and sweet bitter; and call light darkness, and darkness light; and acquit the wicked for his bribe, and turn away the innocency of the innocent.* But beware that you condemn not a man wrongfully, nor abet them that are evil; for when you judge others, you judge your own selves, as the Lord said: *With the judgement that ye judge, ye shall be judged; and as ye condemn, ye shall be condemned.* Wherefore, remember and have ready by you this saying: *Forgive, and it shall be forgiven you; and condemn not, that ye may not be condemned.*

But if your judgement be without respect of persons, O bishops, observe him that accuses his brother, whether he be not a false brother, and has brought the accusation out of envy or jealousy, that he may disturb the Church of God and slay him who is accused by him through his expulsion from the Church and his delivery over to the sword of fire. Judge him therefore, thou, sternly, because he has brought evil upon his brother. For as regards his own intent, if he had been able to catch beforehand the judge's ear, he would have slain his brother in fire. It is written: *Whoso sheddeth man's blood, his own blood shall be shed for the blood which he hath shed.* (p. 47) [ii. 43] If then he is found to be such,

---

2 Isa. i 17. 3 Zech. viii 16. 7 Isa. v 20, 23. 12 Mt. vii 2: cf. Lk. vi 37. 15 Lk. vi 37 (cf. Mt. vi 14 f.). 26 Gen. ix 6.

---

15 *Forgive ... forgiven you*] This reading is found in Aphraates, followed by 'remit, and ye shall be remitted'; i.e. ἀπολύετε, καὶ ἀπολυθήσεσθε (see Burkitt's note to Lk. vi 37): *syr. vulg.* and *syr. sin. (cur.* is wanting) have only 'remit ... remitted'. Compare 1 Clem. xiii 2 ἀφίετε ἵνα ἀφεθῇ ὑμῖν ... ὡς κρίνετε, οὕτως κριθήσεσθε (cf. l. 13) 24 For as regards, etc.] ὅσον γὰρ τὸ ἐπ' αὐτῷ ἐφόνευσεν τὸν ἀδελφόν, προλαβὼν τὰ ὦτα τοῦ κριτοῦ *AC*. 26 *Whoso sheddeth,* etc.] ὁ ἐκχέων αἷμα ἀνθρώπου ἀντὶ τοῦ αἵματος αὐτοῦ ἐκχυθήσεται *AC* LXX: cf. Iren. *Haer.* V xiv 1 'Qui effundet sanguinem hominis, pro sanguine eius effundetur'. Syr. is perh. a paraphrase *ad sensum*.

expel him from the Church with great denunciation as a murderer; and after a time, if he promise to repent, warn him and correct him sternly; and then lay hand upon him and receive him into the Church. And be wary and guard such a one; that he no more disturb any other. But if, after he is come in, you see that he is still contentious and minded to accuse others also, and mischievous and designing, and making false complaints against many: drive him out, that he may no further disturb and trouble the Church. For such a one, though he be within, yet because he is unseemly to the Church, he is superfluous to her, and there is no profit in him. For we see that there are some men born with superfluous members to their bodies, as fingers or other excessive flesh; but these, though they pertain to the body, are a reproach and a disgrace both to the body and to the man, because they are superfluous to him. Yet when they are removed by the surgeon, that man recovers the comeliness and beauty of his body; and he suffers no defect by the removal from it of that which was superfluous, but is even the more conspicuous in his beauty.

In like manner then do you also act, O pastors. For since the Church is a body, and the members are we who believe in God and abide in love in the fear of the Lord, even as we have received command to be perfect; therefore, one who contrives evil against the Church, and troubles her members, and loves the complaints and fault-findings of the Enemy, to wit, disturbances, quarrels, slanders, murmurings, contentions, controversies, accusations, charges, vexations: he that loves and does these things—rather it is the Enemy that works in him—and remains within the Church, the same is alien to the Church and a domestic of the Enemy; for to him he ministers that he may be working through him and may thwart and harass the Church. Such a one therefore, if he remain within,

---

23 abide] lit. 'are'. 24 command to be perfect] lit. 'the command of perfection' (cf. Mt. v 48). With a different pointing the second noun would mean 'tradition', and the sense would then be 'the commandment delivered (to us)'. 27 disturbances, etc.] στάσει καὶ μάχῃ καὶ καταλαλιᾷ . . . ψόγους, πράγματα, μώμους, καταλαλιάς, ἐγκλήματα, ἀκαταστασίας *A C* (differently introduced).

is a disgrace to the Church by reason of his blasphemies and his manifold disorder; for through him the Church of God comes in danger of being scattered. Deal with him therefore as it is written in Wisdom: *Put forth an evil man from the assembly, and his contention will go out with him; and make an end of strife and ignominy: lest, if* (p. 48) *he sit in the assembly, he dishonour you all.* For when he has gone forth twice from the Church, he is justly cut off; and the Church is the more beautiful in her proper form, forasmuch as peace has been restored to her, which (before) was wanting to her: for from that hour the Church remains free from blasphemy and disorder.

But if your mind be not pure—whether it be through respect of persons, or the gifts of filthy lucre which you receive—and you endure that an evil person should remain among you; or again, (if) you thrust away and expel from the Church them that are of good conversation, and foster among you many that are evil, contentious persons and scatterers (of the flock) and riotous: you will bring blasphemy upon the assembly of the Church, and will run the risk of scattering her through these persons; and you will have put yourselves in deadly peril of forfeiting eternal life—because you have pleased men, and have turned back from the truth of God, through respect of persons and the habit of receiving empty gifts: and you will have scattered the Catholic Church, the beloved daughter of the Lord God.

---

4 Prov. xxii 10.

5–6 *and ... ignominy*] From Pesh., and so too the following words. 22 of forfeiting ... life] lit. 'that you have been deprived of eternal life', i.e. 'of having been deprived', etc. 24 the habit of receiving] lit. 'the frequent receiving'.

CHAPTER XI

An Exhortation to Bishops and Deacons

[ii. 44] Strive therefore, O bishops, together with the deacons, to be right with the Lord; for the Lord has said: *If ye will be right with me, I also will be right with you; and if ye will walk perversely with me, I also will walk perversely with you, saith the Lord of Hosts.* Be *right* therefore, that you may deserve to receive praise of the Lord, and not blame (from him who is) of the contrary part.

Let the bishops and the deacons, then, be of one mind; and do you shepherd the people diligently with one accord. For you ought both to be one body, father and son; for you are in the likeness of the Lordship. And let the deacon make known all things to the bishop, even as Christ to His Father. But what things he can, let the deacon order, and all the rest let the bishop judge. Yet let the deacon be the hearing of the bishop, and his mouth and his heart and his soul; for when you are both of one mind, through your agreement there will be peace also in the Church.

[ii. 45] Now for a Christian this is becoming praise, that he have no evil word with any man. But if by the agency of the Enemy some temptation befall (p. 49) a man, and he have a lawsuit, let him strive to be quit of it, even though he be to suffer some loss: and at all events let him not go to the tribunals of the heathen. And you shall not admit a testi-

---

3 ? (Cf. Ps. xvii 26 f., Lev. xxvi 23-24, 27-28).

---

3 *If ye will*, etc.] The second part of this text would be satisfied by the references given to Lev. xxvi, but the first part is not from any scriptural source. Funk points out that the whole is found in some later writers, of whom Macarius Chrysocephalus (*s.* xiv) refers it to Clem. Alex. in the form ἐὰν ὀρθοὶ πρός με ἥκητε, κἀγὼ ὀρθὸς πρὸς ὑμᾶς· ἐὰν πλάγιοι πορευήσθε, κἀγὼ πλάγιος, λέγει κύριος τῶν δυνάμεων. *AC* has only the second clause, thus, ἐὰν πλάγιοι πορεύησθε, κἀγὼ πρὸς ὑμᾶς πλαγίως πορεύσομαι, and then adds Ps. xvii (xviii) 26 f.   10 one body] Cf. p. 148 l. 25, and note.   10-11 for you ... the Lordship] A peculiar expression: cf. *Didache* iv 1 ὅθεν γὰρ ἡ κυριότης λαλεῖται, ἐκεῖ κύριός ἐστιν. See again p. 129 l. 4, and note.

mony from the heathen against any of our own people; for through the heathen the Enemy contrives against the servants of God. Wherefore, because the heathen are to stand on the left, He called them 'the left hand'; for our Saviour spoke thus to us: *Let not your left hand know what your right hand doeth.* [ii. 46] For the heathen are not to know of your lawsuits, and you shall not admit a testimony from them against yourselves, nor go to law before them: as also in the Gospel He saith: *Give what is Caesar's to Caesar, and what is God's to God.* Be thou willing therefore to suffer a loss, and striving rather to make peace. For when thou shalt suffer any worldly loss for the sake of peace, with God it shall be gain to thee, because that thou fearest God and doest according to His commandment.

But if there be brethren who have a quarrel one with another—which God forbid—you the leaders should know forthwith that it is no work of brotherhood in the Lord that they perform who have dared so to do. But if one of them be found to be of the sons of God, being meek and yielding, he is a son of the light. But one who is hard and froward, and overreaching and blasphemous, is a hypocrite, and the Enemy works in him. Reprove him therefore, and rebuke and upbraid him, and put him forth for correction; and afterwards, as we have already said, receive him, that he may not utterly perish. For when such are corrected and reproved, you will not have many lawsuits. But if they know not the word which was spoken by our Lord in the Gospel, which saith: *How many times, if my brother offend against me, shall*

---

3 Cf. Mt. xxv 33.   5 Mt. vi 3.   8 Cf. 1 Cor. vi 1.   9 Mt. xxii 21, Lk. xx 25.   20 Cf. Joh. xii 36.   28 Mt. xviii 21.

4 the left hand] See again p. 143, l. 12. The author of the *Op. imperf. in Matth.*, Hom. xiii, refers to a *Liber Canonum* of the Apostles for the following: 'Dextera est populus christianus, qui est ad dexteram Christi; sinistra autem omnis populus, qui est ad sinistram. Hoc ergo dicit: ne christianum facientem eleemosynam, qui est dextera, infidelis aspiciat, qui est sinistra' (see Funk vol. ii p. 8). *AC* has substituted other words for the passage in *Didasc.*, and therefore cannot be the source of this reference. 20 son of the light] See pp. 6, 63.   25 For when such, etc.] καὶ οὕτω σωφρονιζόμενοι ἐπικουφίσουσιν ὑμῖν τὰ κριτήρια *AC*.

I forgive him? but are angry one with another and become
enemies, teach them, you, and reprove them, and make peace
between them; for the Lord has said: *Blessed are the peacemakers*. And know that it behoves the bishop and the presbyters to judge warily: as our Saviour said when we asked
Him, *How many times, if my brother offend against me, shall
I forgive him? unto seven times?* But our Lord taught us
and said to us: *Not seven times, I say, only, but even unto
seventyfold seven*. For so (p. 50) the Lord desires, that they
who are His in truth should never have anything at all
against any man, and should not be angry with any man:
how much less does He desire that men should have lawsuits
one with another? [ii. 47] But if aught should happen to
come about through the agency of the Enemy, so let them
be judged before you as you also are surely to be judged.

First, then, let your judgements be held on the second day
of the week, that if perchance any one should contest the
sentence of your words, you may have space until the Sabbath
to compose the matter, and may make peace between them
that are at odds and reconcile them on the Sunday. Now let
the presbyters and the deacons be ever present in all judgements with the bishops. Judge without respect of persons.

When therefore the two parties who have the suit or
quarrel one with another shall come and stand together in
the judgement, as the Scripture saith, after you have heard
them, pass sentence righteously. And give diligence to keep
them in friendship before the sentence is pronounced upon
them, lest there go forth from you against one of them, being
a brother, a condemnation of earthly judgement. And so
judge as you also are surely to be judged, even as you have
Christ for partner and assessor and counsellor and spectator

3 Mt. v 9.   6 Mt. xviii 21.   8 Mt. xviii 22.   23 ff. Cf.
Deut. xix. 17.

17 that if perchance, etc.] ὅπως, ἐὰν ἀντιλογία τῇ ἀποφάσει ὑμῶν γένηται, ἕως
σαββάτου ἔχοντες ἄδειαν δυνηθείητε εὐθῦναι τὴν ἀντιλογίαν κτλ. *AC*.   20 are
at odds] lit. 'are held (*or* holding) one against the other': τοὺς διαφερο-
μένους πρὸς ἀλλήλους *AC*.   on the Sunday] εἰς τὴν κυριακήν *AC*.
23 parties] lit. 'persons' (πρόσωπα): προσώπων *AC*. See also p. 112, l. 25.

with you in the same cause. But if there be any who are accused by some one, it being charged against them that they conduct themselves not well in the way of the Lord: again, hearing both parties, make diligent inquiry, as being to give sentence in a matter of everlasting life or cruel and bitter death. For if a man is truly convicted, and he be condemned and go forth from the Church, he has been cast out from life and glory everlasting, and is become reprobate among men and guilty before God. [ii. 48] Judge therefore, according to the magnitude of the charge, whatever it be, with much mercy; and incline rather to save alive without respect of persons than to destroy, by condemning, those who are judged.

But if there be one who is innocent, and he be condemned by the judges through respect of persons, the judgement of unjust judges shall do him no hurt with God, but shall rather profit him; for but for a little while is he unjustly judged by men, but afterwards, in the day (p. 51) of judgement, because he has been unjustly condemned, he shall be the judge of (his) unjust judges. For you have been the arbiters of an unjust judgement, and therefore shall be requited by God accordingly, and cast out of the Catholic Church of God. And that shall be fulfilled in your case: *With what judgement ye judge, ye shall be judged.*

[ii. 49] Wherefore, when you sit to judge, let both parties— for we do not call them brothers until peace has been made between them—come and stand together; and do you make prudent and diligent inquiry as between those who have the suit and quarrel one with another. And learn first concerning him who makes the accusation, whether there be any accusation against him also, or whether perchance he has brought charges against others as well; and again, whether he has brought his accusation out of any former enmity or quarrel, or out of envy; and (inquire) also of what manner his con-

---

23 Mt. vii 2.

---

11 rather] lit. 'a little', or 'somewhat'. 20 arbiters] lit. 'mediators' μεσίται AC.   25 parties] lit. 'persons'. Cf. p. 111, l. 23.

versation is—whether he is meek, and without anger, and not given to slander, and whether he loves the widows and the poor and strangers, and is *not greedy of filthy lucre*; and whether he is quiet, and friendly to all and a lover of all; whether he is merciful and open-handed to give, and not a glutton and greedy, nor grasping, nor drunken, nor intemperate, nor slothful: for *the perverse heart contriveth evil, and the same disturbeth cities at all times*; and whether no such evil has been committed by him as is (done) in the world. And if he that makes the accusation is free from all these things, it is already evident and manifest that he is trustworthy, and that his accusation is true. But if he is known to be perverse and contentious, and his conduct not right, this (also) is evident, that he brings false witness against your brother. When therefore he is found and known to be an injurious person, rebuke him and put him forth for a time, until he repent and be converted and weep: lest perchance he again blaspheme against some other of our brethren who is of good conversation; or lest, while he sits in your congregation, some other like him, seeing him unreproved, should himself dare to do in like manner to one of our brethren, and should perish before God. But if he who has sinned is rebuked and corrected and put forth for a season, he also who was ready to imitate him and to do as he did, having seen him put forth, will fear lest it happen to him in like manner, and will submit himself: and he shall live before God, (p. 52) and in no wise be put to shame among men.

[ii. 50] And concerning him again who is judged take counsel and thought among you in like manner: and observe his manners and conduct in the world, whether perchance you have heard many charges against him, or whether he has committed many crimes. For if he is found to have committed crimes, it is likely that this charge also which they prefer against him is true. But again, it may happen that he had formerly com-

---

3 1 Tim. iii 8.   7 Prov. vi 14.

5 open-handed to give] So εὐμετάδοτος is rendered at p. 8, l. 3.
26 live before God] Cf. p. 16, l. 3 and note.

mitted some sin, but is innocent of this present charge. Wherefore, make diligent investigation of these things, that you may give sentence with great caution and surety; and do you judge rightfully concerning him who is found to be guilty, and pass judgement upon him. But let any one of them who will not abide by your judgement be reproved and put forth from the congregation until he repent and make entreaty of the bishop or of the Church, and confess that he has sinned, and is penitent. And thus shall advantage accrue to many: lest at any time some other, seeing him sit in the Church unrebuked and uncorrected, should himself dare to do as he did, thinking him alive among men, whereas with God he is lost.

[ii. 51] But if you hear one party alone, while the other is not present to make his defence to the charge which they bring against him, and you pass sentence hastily, without counsel and without inquiry, and, in accordance with the falsehoods which you have believed, condemn him while he is not present to defend himself: you shall be partners before God of him that brought the false witness, and with him you shall be punished by God. For the Lord has said in Proverbs: *He that meddleth in a quarrel that is not his own, is as he that taketh hold of a dog's tail*; and again in another place He has said: *Judge right judgement*; and again He has said: *Judge the fatherless, and justify the widows*; and again He saith: *Deliver the oppressed, and sever every bond of iniquity*. But if you resemble those elders who were in Babylon, who bore false witness against Susanna and wickedly condemned her to

---

20 Prov. xxvi 17.   23 Cf. Deut. i 16, Zech. viii 16 (cp. Joh. vii 24).
25 Isa. i 17: lviii 6.   26 Dan. xiii (Susanna).

---

13 But if, etc.] Comp. Hermas *Mand.* ii 2 πρῶτον μὲν μηδενὸς καταλάλει, μηδὲ ἡδέως ἄκουε καταλαλοῦντος· εἰ δὲ μή, καὶ σὺ ὁ ἀκούων ἔνοχος ἔσῃ τῆς ἁμαρτίας τοῦ καταλαλοῦντος, ἐὰν πιστεύσῃς τῇ καταλαλιᾷ.   party] lit. 'person'.   20 Proverbs] This title appears here for the first time in *Didasc.* (see note on p. 17). *AC* introduces the quotation differently, and without naming the source.   25 *bond*] Here a written bond (*shĕṭāra*): twice elsewhere the text is quoted with the reading *keṭra*, 'knot' or 'band', which is the word in Pesh. answering to σύνδεσμον. The word used here corresponds to συγγραφήν in the second half of the verse.

death, you also shall be partners of their judgement and of their condemnation; for the Lord by Daniel saved Susanna from the hand of the ungodly, and those elders who were guilty of her blood He condemned to fire.

[ii. 52] Now very far apart do we set (p. 53) the things of the sanctuary from those of the world; nevertheless (this) we say: You see, brethren, how, when murderers are brought before the (civil) authority, the judges question diligently those who bring them, and learn from them what they have done. And then again they ask the criminal whether these things are so; and though he himself confess and say, 'Yea', they do not send him straightway to death, but question him again for many days, and drawing the curtain take thought and counsel much together. And then at length they pass upon him the sentence of death, and lifting up their hands to heaven protest that they are innocent of the man's blood. And these things they do though they are heathens and know not God nor the requital they receive from God for those whom they judge and condemn unjustly. And do you, who know who is our God and what His judgements, dare to give sentence upon one who is not guilty? We counsel you therefore that you make inquiry with diligence and much caution. For the word of sentence which you decree ascends straightway to God; and if you have justly judged, you shall receive of God the reward of justice, both now and hereafter; but if you have judged unjustly, again you shall receive of God a recompense accordingly. Strive thererefore, brethren, that you be worthy to receive praise from God, and not blame; for praise from God is everlasting life to men, but blame from God is eternal death to men.

[ii. 53] Have a care therefore, O bishops, that you be not in haste to sit in judgement forthwith, lest you be constrained to condemn a man; but before they come and stand in the judgement, admonish them and make peace between them. And admonish those who have the suit and quarrel one with another, and teach them in the first place that it is not right for any

---

16 the man's] 'men's' text: τοῦ ἀνθρώπου *AC*.

man to be angry, because the Lord has said: *Every one that is angry with his brother is liable to the judgement*; and secondly, that if it should happen through the agency of the Enemy that some anger arise, they ought at once, that very day, to be reconciled and appeased, and to be at peace with one another. For it is written: *Let not the sun go down upon thine anger* against thy brother; and in David also He saith: (p. 54) *Be angry, and sin not*; that is, be speedily reconciled, lest, if anger continue, malice arise and beget sin. He saith in Proverbs: *The soul that keepeth malice shall die*. And our Lord and Saviour also said: *If thou offer thy gift upon the altar, and there remember that thy brother keepeth any malice against thee, leave thy gift before the altar, and go, first be reconciled with thy brother: and then come, offer thy gift*. Now the gift of God is our prayer and our Eucharist. If then thou keep any malice against thy brother, or he against thee, thy prayer is not heard and thy Eucharist is not accepted; and thou shalt be found void (both) of prayer and Eucharist by reason of the anger which thou keepest. A man ought to pray diligently at all times; but those who bear anger and malice towards their brethren God does not hear; and though thou pray three times in one hour, thou shalt gain nothing, for thou art not heard by reason of thine enmity against thy brother. Wherefore, if thou carest and strivest to be a Christian, follow the saying of the Lord which saith: *Loose all ties of iniquity; and sever the bands of violence and oppression*. For upon thee has our Saviour laid this power, that thou shouldst forgive thy brother who has offended

---

1 Mt. v 22. 6 Eph. iv 26. 8 Ps. iv 5, Eph. iv 26. 9 Cf. Hermas *Vis.* ii 3. 1. 10 Prov. xii 28. 11 Mt. v 23 f. 26 Isa. lviii 6.

---

9 lest ... beget sin] ὅπως μὴ ἡ ἐπίμονος ὀργὴ μνησικακία γένηται καὶ ἁμαρτίαν ἀπεργάσηται *AC*. Cf. Hermas *Vis.* ii 3. 1 μνησικακία θάνατον κατεργάζεται. The word which I translate 'malice' here and in the following lines denotes animosity or resentment: here it renders μνησικακία, and in the text from Prov. μνησίκακος. 10 *The soul*, etc.] ψυχαὶ γὰρ μνησικάκων εἰς θάνατον *AC*: ὁδοὶ δὲ κτλ. LXX. 12 *malice*] this insertion appears in *syr. cur.*, *sin.* and *vulg.*, and also in Aphraates (see Burkitt *in loc.*).

against thee *unto seventyfold seven times*, that is, four hundred and ninety. How many times then hast thou forgiven thy brother, that thou wilt no more forgive him, but keepest malice and maintainest enmity, and desirest to go to law? Therefore is thy prayer hindered. But even if thou hast forgiven the full four hundred and ninety times, add still more for thine own sake, and of thy bounty, without anger, forgive thy brother. And if thou do it not for thy brother's sake, bethink thee and do it at least for thine own; and forgive thy neighbour, that thou mayest be heard when thou prayest, and mayest offer an acceptable oblation to the Lord.

[ii. 54] Wherefore, O bishops, that your oblations and your prayers may be acceptable, when you stand in the Church to pray let the deacon say with a loud voice: 'Is there any man that keepeth aught against his fellow?', that if there be found any who have a lawsuit or quarrel one with another, thou mayest entreat them and make peace between them. They who enter a house and say, *Peace be in this house*, (p. 55) both are proclaimers of peace and do bring peace. If then thou preach peace to others, still more does it behove thee to have peace with thy brethren. As a son of light and peace therefore, be thou light and peace to all men; and contend with no man, but be in quiet and peace with all men. And be a helper with God that (the number of) those who are saved may be increased; for this is the will of the Lord God. But they who love enmity and quarrels, and contentions and lawsuits, are enemies of God. [ii. 55] For the Lord from the beginning, through the prophets and righteous men, called all generations to repentance and salvation; and we, moreover, the Apostles, who have been accounted worthy to be the witnesses of His

---

1 Mt. xviii 22.   18 Mt. x 12, Lk. x 5.

1-2 four hundred and ninety] Comp. Aphraates Hom. ii 13 (after quoting Mt. xviii 22) 'Even, saith He, if he offend against thee 490 times, forgive him in one day' (see also Hom. xiv 44 *ad fin.*).   14-15 'Is there ... his fellow] μή τις κατά τινος· [μή τις ἐν ὑποκρίσει] AC (and again in the liturgy of bk. viii 12). The Syriac can only be read as a question. This is the earliest example of a form of words to be spoken by the deacon during the service.

manifestation and preachers of His divine word, have heard from the mouth of the Lord Jesus Christ, and do know of a surety and say what is His will, and the will of His Father, *that no man should perish, but that all men should* believe and *be saved.* [ii. 56] For this is that which He taught us to say when we pray: *Thy will be done in earth, as in heaven;* that as the angels of heaven and the hosts and all (His) ministers praise God, so too on earth all men should praise God. It is His will, then, to save all; and this is His pleasure, that they who are saved should be many.

He who is contentious, or makes himself an enemy to his neighbour, diminishes the people of God. For either he drives out of the Church him whom he accuses, and diminishes her and deprives God of the soul of a man which was being saved, or by his contention he expels and ejects himself from the Church, and so again he sins against God. For God our Saviour spoke thus: *Every one that is not with me, is against me; and every one that gathereth not with me, scattereth.* Wherefore thou art no helper with God for the gathering together of the people, because thou art a disturber and a scatterer of the flock, and an adversary and enemy of God. Be not therefore for ever embroiled in contentions and quarrels, or wrangling, or enmity, or lawsuits, lest thou scatter some one from the Church. For we by the power of the Lord God have gathered (men) from all peoples and from all tongues, and have brought them to the Church with much labour and toil and in daily peril, that we might do the will of God and *fill the house with guests,* that is His holy Catholic Church, that they might

---

4 Cf. 2 Pet. iii 9: 1 Tim. ii 4. 6 Mt. vi 10. 17 Mt. xii 30.
27 Mt. xxii 10.

---

1 manifestation] παρουσίας *AC.* 4 *that no man,* etc.] ἵνα μηδεὶς ἀπόληται, ἀλλὰ πάντες ἄνθρωποι [συμφώνως] πιστεύσαντες [αὐτῷ αἶνον σύμφωνον ἀναπέμψαντες αὐτῷ] ζήσωσιν [αἰωνίως] *AC.* The second part of the text above appears to be from 1 Tim. ii 4; the first words may imply acquaintance with 2 Pet. (iii 9) μὴ βουλόμενός τινας ἀπολέσθαι, ἀλλὰ πάντας εἰς μετάνοιαν χωρῆσαι. Funk and Flemming refer only to Joh. iii 16, which hardly seems to be in view here. 28 His holy Catholic Church] τὴν ἱερὰν καὶ καθολικὴν ἐκκλησίαν *AC.*

be glad and rejoicing, and be praising (p. 56) and glorifying God who called them to life.

Be you then, O laymen, peaceable one with another, and strive like wise doves to fill the Church, and to convert and tame those that are wild and bring them into her midst. And (for) this is the great reward that is promised by God: if you deliver them from fire, and present them to the Church firmly established and faithful.

CHAPTER XII

To Bishops: that they should be peaceable.

[ii. 57] And you the bishops, be not hard, nor tyrannical, nor wrathful, and be not rough with the people of God which is delivered into your hands. And destroy not the Lord's house nor scatter His people; but convert all, that you may be helpers with God; and gather the faithful with much meekness and long-suffering and patience, and without anger, and with doctrine and exhortation, as ministers of the kingdom everlasting.

And in your congregations in the holy churches hold your assemblies with all decent order, and appoint the places for the brethren with care and gravity. And for the presbyters let there be assigned a place in the eastern part of the house; and let the bishop's throne be set in their midst, and let the presbyters sit with him. And again, let the lay men sit in another part of the house toward the east. For so it should be, that in the eastern part of the house the presbyters sit with the bishops, and next the lay men, and then the women; that when you stand up to pray, the rulers may stand first, and after them the lay men, and then the women also. For it is required that you pray toward the east, as knowing

---

5-6 And (for) this, etc.] Compare for the construction, and in part for the sense, 2 Clem. iii 3 οὗτος οὖν ἐστὶν ὁ μισθὸς ἡμῶν, ἐὰν οὖν ὁμολογήσωμεν δι' οὗ ἐσώθημεν.   9 nor tyrannical] μὴ πλήκτης *A C*. See note to p. 32, l. 5.
20 part] lit. 'side', and so in ll. 23, 24.   25 bishops] (plur.) HS.

that which is written: *Give ye glory to God, who rideth upon the heaven of heavens toward the east.*

But of the deacons let one stand always by the oblations of the Eucharist; and let another stand without by the door and observe them that come in; and afterwards, when you offer, let them minister together in the Church. And if any one be found sitting out of his place, let the deacon who is within reprove him and make him to rise up and sit in a place that is meet for him. For our Lord likened the Church to a fold; for as we see the dumb animals, oxen and sheep (p. 57) and goats, lie down and rise up, and feed and chew the cud, according to their families, and none of them separate itself from its kind; and (see) the wild beasts also severally range with their like upon the mountains: so likewise in the Church ought those who are young to sit apart, if there be room, and if not to stand up; and those who are advanced in years to sit apart. And let the children stand on one side, or let their fathers and mothers take them to them; and let them stand up. And let the young girls also sit apart; but if there be no room, let them stand up behind the women. And let the young women who are married and have children stand apart, and the aged women and widows sit apart. And let the deacon see that each of them on entering goes to his place, that no one may sit out of his place. And let the deacon also see that no one whispers, or falls asleep, or laughs, or makes signs. For so it should be, that with decency and decorum they watch in the Church, with ears attentive to the word of the Lord.

[ii. 58] But if any brother or sister come from another congregation, let the deacon question her and learn whether she is married, or again whether she is a widow (who is) a believer; and whether she is a daughter of the Church, or belongs perchance to one of the heresies; and then let him conduct her and set her in a place that is suitable for her. But if a

---

1 Ps. lxvii (lxviii) 34.   9 Cf. Joh. x 1, 16.

---

16 stand up] lit. 'stand upon their feet'; and so in the following lines.
17 And let the children, etc.] τὰ δὲ παιδία ἑστῶτα προσλαμβανέσθωσαν αὐτῶν οἱ πατέρες καὶ αἱ μητέρες *AC*. This has been worked into the liturgy

[XXIX] ... cum disciplina et sobrietate uigilare et intentam aurem habere ad uerbum domini.

Si quis autem de parrocia frater aut soror uenerit, diaconus requirat ab ea si adhuc uirum habet, si uidua est aut fidelis, et
5 si de ecclesia est et non de heresi.   Et sic iam perducens eam faciat in decreto loco sedere.   Si autem praesbyter de ecclesia

6 de ecclesia parrociae] ἀπὸ παροικίας *AC*.

---

of *AC* viii 12, in the form τὰ παιδία προσλαμβάνεσθε, αἱ μητέρες.   28-29 from another congregation] ἀπὸ παροικίας *AC*.   29 her] So Lat., 'ab ea', neglecting the 'brother': plur. *AC*.

presbyter should come from another congregation, do you the presbyters receive him with fellowship into your place. And if it be a bishop, let him sit with the bishop; and let him accord him the honour of his rank, even as himself. And do thou, O bishop, invite him to discourse to thy people; for the exhortation and admonition of strangers is very profitable, especially as it is written: *There is no prophet that is acceptable in his own place.* And when you offer the oblation, let him speak. But if he is wise and gives the honour to thee, and is unwilling to offer, at least let him speak over the cup.

But if, as you are sitting, some one else should come, whether a man or a woman, who has some worldly honour, either of the same district or of another congregation: thou, O bishop, if thou art speaking the word of God, or hearing, or reading, shalt not respect (p. 58) persons and leave the ministry of thy word and appoint them a place; but do thou remain still as thou art and not interrupt thy word, and let the brethren themselves receive them. And if there be no place, let one of the brethren who is full of charity and loves his brethren, and is one fitted to do an honour, rise and give them place, and himself stand up. But if, while younger men or women sit, an older man or woman should rise and give up their place, do thou, O deacon, scan those who sit, and see which man or woman of them is younger than the rest, and make them stand up, and cause him to sit who had risen and given up his place; and him whom thou hast caused to stand up, lead away and make him to stand behind his neighbours: that others also may be trained and learn to give place to those more honourable than themselves. But if a poor man or woman should come, ⟨whether of the same district⟩

---

7 Lk. iv 24.   29 ff. Cf. Ja. ii 2.

4 accord . . . as himself] τῆς αὐτῆς ἀξιούμενος ὑπ' αὐτοῦ τιμῆς *AC*.
8 And when you offer, etc.] ἐπιτρέψεις δὲ αὐτῷ καὶ τὴν εὐχαριστίαν ἀνοῖσαι· ἐὰν δὲ δι' εὐλάβειαν ὡς σοφὸς τὴν τιμήν σοι τηρῶν μὴ θελήσῃ ἀνενέγκαι, κἂν τὴν εἰς τὸν λαὸν εὐλογίαν αὐτὸν ποιήσασθαι καταναγκάσεις *AC*, avoiding the reference to the cup. I take it that the visiting bishop is offered the honour of celebrating the Eucharist; but this he declines. It would appear therefore that the cup mentioned as an alternative was not the eucharistic

parrociae uenerit, suscipite eum, praesbyteri, communiter in loco uestro. Et si episcopus aduenerit, cum episcopo sedeat, eundem honorem ab eo recipiens. Et petes eum tu, episcope, ut adloquatur plebem tuam, quoniam peregrinus, cum adlo- 5 quium dat, deiubat populum; scriptum est enim : *Nullus profeta susceptus est in patria sua.* Et in gratia agenda ipse dicat. Si autem, cum sit prudens et honorem tibi reseruans, non uelit, super calicem dicat.

Si autem, cum sedis, alius quis aut alia superuenerit honora- 10 bilior secundum saeculum, aut ⟨peregrinus aut⟩ de ipso loco, tu, o episcope, cum dicis uerbum Dei aut audis aut legis, noli propter personarum acceptionem relinquere ministerium uerbi tui et disponere eis sessoria, sed permane [in]quietus et noli mediare uerbum : fratres autem eos suscipient. Sin uero locus 15 non fuerit, qui dilectionem fraternam habet et caritatem et honorabilis est, surgens concedet ei⟨s⟩ locum, et ipse stabit. Si autem, iuuenioribus sedentibus, senior aut anicula surgens concesserint locum, tu, diaconus, circuminspice de iuuenioribus [XXX] qui magis iunior est aut iuuencula, et exsurgere facies 20 eam, et sedere eam quae locum concessit : eam uero, quae non cessit exsurgens, facies posteriorem omnibus stare, ut discant et ceteri concedere maioribus aetate. Si autem egenus aut egena, siue de loco siue peregrinus, superuenerit, et praeterea

---

10 aut ⟨peregrinus aut⟩ de ipso loco] See l. 23 below : ἢ ξένος ἢ ἐγχώριος *AC* (cf. Syr.).   11 tu, o episcope] σὺ ὁ ἐπίσκοπος *AC* (cf. Syr.). Hauler prints 'loco tuo, episcope'.   22 maioribus aetate] τοῖς ἐντι- μοτέροις *AC* (= Syr.)   23 praeterea] = 'praesertim': see note to p. 27 l. 21.

---

cup : more probably it was that offered later at the Agape (cf. Hippolytus *Apost. Trad.*, and Cyprian Ep. lxiii 16). A partition of the eucharistic prayer is hardly to be thought of. With the first part of the passage compare the story told by Irenaeus of Anicetus and Polycarp : καὶ ἐν τῇ ἐκκλησίᾳ παρεχώρησεν ὁ Ἀνίκητος τὴν εὐχαριστίαν τῷ Πολυκάρπῳ, κατ' ἐντροπὴν δηλονότι (Euseb. *H. E.* v 24).   10 to offer] Cf. *AC* : om. Lat.   20 and is one fitted to do an honour] The adj. *mĕyakkĕrānā* naturally has an active sense ; and so Flemming takes it.   30 (whether . . . district)] ἢ ἐγχώριος ἢ ξένος *AC* (= Lat.) : and see l. 13 above.

or of another congregation, and especially if they are stricken in years, and there be no place for such, do thou, O bishop, with all thy heart provide a place for them, even if thou have to sit upon the ground; that thou be not as one who respects the persons of men, but that thy ministry may be acceptable with God.

CHAPTER XIII

An Instruction to the People to be constant in assembling in the Church.

[ii. 59] Now when thou teachest, command and warn the people to be constant in assembling in the Church, and not to withdraw themselves but always to assemble, lest any man diminish the Church by not assembling, and cause the body of Christ to be short of a member. For let not a man take thought of others only, but of himself as well, hearkening to that which our Lord said: *Every one that gathereth not with me, scattereth.* Since therefore you are the members of Christ, do not scatter yourselves from the Church by not assembling. Seeing that you have Christ for your head, as He promised— †for you are partakers with us†—be not then neglectful of yourselves, and deprive not our Saviour of His members, and do not rend and scatter His body. And make not your worldly affairs of more account than the word of God; but on the Lord's day leave every thing and run eagerly to your Church; for she is (p. 59) your glory. Otherwise, what excuse have they before God who do not assemble on the Lord's day to hear the word of life and be nourished with the divine food which abides for ever? [ii. 60] For you are

---

13 Mt. xii 30.

---

17 for ... with us] συνόντα καὶ κοινωνοῦντα ὑμῖν *AC* (= Lat.).   22 for she is your glory] om. Lat.: *AC* has altered.   23-24 on the Lord's day] ἐν τῇδε τῇ ἡμέρᾳ *AC* (= Lat.).

senior aetate, et locus non fuerit, tu, episcope, talibus locum ex toto corde fac, etiamsi tu ipse super humum sederis, ut non fiat aput homines a te personarum acceptio, sed aput Deum ministerium tuum placeat.

5 QUONIAM EXPEDIT NUMQUAM DEESSE AB ECCLESIA. Docens autem iube et hortare populum in ecclesia frequentare, et penitus numquam deesse sed conuenire semper, et ecclesiam non angustare, cum se subtrahunt, et minus membrum facere corpus Christi. Unusquisque autem non 10 de alio hoc cogitet, sed de seipso, quoniam dictum est: *Qui non colligit mecum, spargit.* Nolite ergo ⟨uos⟩met ipsos, cum sitis membra Christi, spargere ab ecclesia, cum non coadunamini. Christum enim caput habentes secundum promissionem ipsius praesentem et conmunicantem uobis, nolite ipsi 15 uos neclegere, nec alienare saluatorem a membris suis, nec scindere nec spargere corpus eius, nec praeponere a uerbo necessitates temporarie uitae uestrae, sed die dominica omnia seponentes concurrite ad ecclesiam. Nam qualem excusationem daturus est Deo, qui non conuenit in eodem die audire 20 salutare uerbum et nutriri ab . . .

---

5 QUONIAM, etc.] For another such headline see p. 149. 11 ⟨uos⟩ met] For omission of the pronoun before 'met ipse'. see again p. 251, l. 20. 16 nec . . . a uerbo] μηδὲ προκρίνετε τοῦ θείου λόγου (τὰς βιωτικὰς χρείας) *AC* (cf. Syr.). Perhaps 'diuino' should be supplied.

eager to receive temporal things and those that are but for a day and an hour, (but) those that are eternal you neglect; and you are anxious about baths, and to be fed with the meat and drink of the belly, and about other things, but for the things eternal you have no care, but neglect your soul and have no zeal for the Church, to hear and receive the word of God.

And in comparison of them that err what excuse have you? For the heathen, when they daily rise from their sleep, go in the morning to worship and minister to their idols; and before all their works and undertakings they go first and worship their idols. Neither at their festivals and their fairs are they wanting, but are constant in assembling: not only they who are of the district, but even those who come from afar; and all likewise assemble and come to the spectacle of their theatre. And so in like manner they who are vainly called Jews, they remain idle one day after six, and assemble in their synagogue; and never do they withdraw themselves or neglect their synagogue, nor disregard their (days of) idleness—even they who by reason of their unbelief are made void of the power of the word, and of the very name by which they call themselves, Jews; for 'Jew' is interpreted 'confession', but these are no confessors, since they do not confess the passion of Christ, which by transgression of the Law they caused, that they should repent and be saved. If then they who are not saved bestow care at all times on things wherein there is no profit and which avail them nothing, what excuse has he before the Lord God who withdraws himself from the assembly of the Church, and does not even imitate the gentiles, but by reason of his non-attendance grows indifferent and careless, and stands aloof and does evil? to whom the Lord said by Jeremiah (*sic*): *My laws ye have not kept: but neither have ye conversed after*

---

32 Ez. v 7.

3 baths] lit. 'washing' (sing.): λουτρῶν *AC*. 12 fairs] πανηγύρεσιν *AC*. 17 one day after six] lit. 'one day to six': καθ' ἐξ ἡμέρας *AC*. 22 Jews; for 'Jew', etc.] 'Ιούδα· 'Ιούδας γὰρ ἐξομολόγησις ἑρμηνεύεται *AC*. 23 the passion] lit. 'the slaying': τὸ πάθημα *AC*. 31 Jeremiah] So also *AC*.

the laws of the gentiles; and ye have well nigh surpassed them in evildoing; and: *Do the gentiles exchange their gods, which yet be no gods? But my people have exchanged their honour for that which is without profit.* How then shall he excuse himself who is indifferent (p. 60) and has no zeal for the assembly of the Church? But if there be any one who takes occasion of worldly business to withdraw himself, let him know this, that the trades of the faithful are called works of superfluity; for their true work is religion. Pursue your trades therefore as a work of superfluity, for your sustenance, but let your true work be religion.

[ii. 61] Have a care therefore that you never withdraw yourselves from the assembly of the Church. But if any man leave the assembly of the Church of God and go to the assembly of the gentiles, what shall he say, and what excuse can he make to God in the day of judgement? seeing that he has left the holy Church, and the words of the living God, which are living and lifegiving and able to redeem and to deliver from fire and to save alive, and has gone to the assembly of the gentiles, because he has lusted after the spectacle of the theatre. Therefore shall he be accounted as one of them that go in thither; because he has lusted to hear and receive their fables, which are those of dead men and are from the spirit of Satan: for they are dead and deadly, and turn away from the faith and bring to everlasting fire. Nay, but the things of the world are your care, and you attend to the affairs of this life and scorn to betake yourselves to the Catholic Church, the beloved daughter of the Lord God Most High, that you may receive the teaching of God which endures for ever and is able to save them that receive the word of life.

Be constant therefore in coming together with the faithful who are being saved in your mother the Church, the living and lifegiving.

1 Ez. xvi 47.   2 Jer. ii 11.

8–9 are called works of superfluity] ἐπέργιά εἰσιν *AC*.   10 as a work of superfluity] ὡς ἐν παρέργῳ *AC*.

[ii. 62] And beware of assembling with them that are perishing in the theatre, which is the assembly of the heathen, of error and of destruction. For he who enters an assembly of the gentiles shall be accounted as one of them, and shall receive the Woe. For to such the Lord God said by Isaiah: *Woe, woe to them that come from the spectacle.* And again He saith: *Ye women that come from the spectacle, come: for it is a people without understanding.* 'Women', then, He called the Churches, which He called and redeemed and brought forth from the spectacle of the theatre, and took and received; and He taught us from henceforth to go thither no more. For He saith in Jeremiah: *Ye shall not learn according to the ways of the gentiles.* And He saith again in the Gospel: *In the way of the gentiles ye shall not go; (and into the cities of the Samaritans ye shall not enter.)* Here then He commands and warns us wholly to avoid all heresies, (p. 61) which are *the cities of the Samaritans*; and furthermore, that we should keep far away from the assemblies of the gentiles, and not enter strange congregations; and that we should utterly avoid the theatre, and their fairs which are held for the sake of idols. A believer must not even come near to a fair, except to buy him nourishment for body †and soul†. Therefore, avoid all vain shows of the idols, and the festivals of their fairs.

[ii. 63] And let those who are young in the Church be ministering diligently, without sloth, in all things that are needful, with much reverence and modesty. Do you the

---

6 Cf. Targum on Deut. xxviii 19.   7 Isa. xxvii 11 (LXX)   12 Jer. x. 2.   13 Mt. x. 5.

---

6 *Woe*, etc.] Funk cites the late Targum of Ps.-Jonathan on Deut. xxviii 9 'Cursed are ye when ye enter your theatre-houses and the places of your shows, to make void the precepts of the Law; and cursed are ye when ye come forth to your business.'   8 'Women', then, etc.] Flemming and Funk have here misunderstood the text, rendering in this sense: 'Women therefore he calls to the Church, even those (women) whom', etc.   14–15 ⟨*and into* ... *enter*⟩] The words are presupposed in the comment here, and are quoted with a similar comment at p. 212. 21 A believer, etc.] πιστὸν γὰρ ἐν πανηγύρει οὐ χρὴ παραβάλλειν πλεῖον τοῦ σωμάτιον πρίασθαι καὶ ψυχὴν περιποιήσασθαι *AC.* Perh. therefore emend 'to buy nourishment for the body and *to gain* a soul'.

faithful therefore, all of you, daily and hourly, whenever you are not in the Church, devote yourselves to your work; so that in all the conduct of your life you may either be occupied in the things of the Lord or engaged upon your work, and may never be idle. For the Lord has said: ⁶*Imitate the ant, O sluggard, and emulate her ways, and be wiser than she.* ⁷*For she hath no husbandry, nor any to compel her, nor is she under authority:* ⁸*yet she gathereth her bread in summer, and storeth up for her much food in the harvest.* And again He saith: ⁸ᵃ*Go to the bee, and learn how she worketh. For her work she performeth in wisdom:* ⁸ᵇ*and there is brought of her labour to be food for rich and poor. Beloved and praiseworthy is she:* ⁸ᶜ*and albeit she is little in strength, she honoureth wisdom, and is commended (thereby).* ⁹*How long wilt thou sleep, thou sluggard? When wilt thou arise from thy sleep?* ¹⁰*Thou shalt slumber a little, and sleep a little, and sit a little, and lay thy hand upon thy bosom a little:* ¹¹*and poverty shall overtake thee as a runner, and want as a lusty man.* ¹¹ᵃ*But if thou wilt not be slothful, thine increase shall abound and overflow as a fountain; and poverty as a feeble runner shall depart from thee.* Therefore, be always working, for idleness is a blot for which there is no cure. *But if any man among you will not work, let him not eat*: for the Lord God also hateth sluggards; for it is not possible for a sluggard to be a believer.

5 Prov. vi 6-8.   10 Prov. vi 8ᵃ⁻ᶜ, 9–11ᵃ (cf. Ecclus. xi 3).   22 2 Thes. iii 10.

---

4 in the things of the Lord] lit. 'in the (things) of the Lordship' BS : 'in discipline', or 'correction' CH (i. e. ܠܡܪܕܘܬܐ for ܠܡܪܘܬܐ), which gives no good sense. I see no reason to suspect the text of BS, which may be a rendering of τοῖς κυριακοῖς: 'Lordship' has already occurred at p. 109, l. 11. 10 *Go to the bee*, etc.] *vv.* 8ᵃ⁻ᶜ and 11ᵃ do not occur in the Hebrew. The transl. in Syr. is influenced by Pesh.   21 for idleness, etc.] ἀθεράπευτος γάρ ἐστιν ἀργοῦ μῶμος *A C.*

CHAPTER XIV

On the time for the appointment of Widows.

[iii. 1] *Appoint as a widow one that is not under fifty years old*, who in some sort, by reason of her years, shall be remote from the suspicion of taking a second husband. But if you appoint one who is young to the widows' order, (p. 62) and she endure not widowhood because of her youth, and marry, she will bring a reproach upon the glory of widowhood; and she shall render an account to God, first, because she has married a second husband; and again, because she promised to be a widow unto God, and was receiving (alms) as a widow, but did not continue in widowhood. But if there be one who is young, who has been a short time with her husband, and her husband die, or for any other cause there be a separation, and she continue by herself alone, having the honour of widowhood: she shall be blessed of God; for she is likened to the widow of Sarepta of Sidon with whom rested the holy angel, the prophet of God. Or again, she shall be like Anna, who hailed the coming of Christ and received a (good) testimony; and she shall be honoured for her virtue, winning honour on earth from men, and praise from God in heaven.

[iii. 2] But let not young widows be appointed to the widows' order: yet let them be taken care of and helped, lest by reason of their being in want they be minded to marry

---

1 1 Tim. v 9.

---

1 *a widow*] 'widows' HS; but the construction goes on in the singular: χήρας δὲ καθιστᾶτε μὴ ἔλαττον ἐτῶν ἑξήκοντα, ἵνα τρόπῳ τινὶ τὸ τῆς διγαμίας αὐτῶν ἀνύποπτον βέβαιον ὑμῖν διὰ τῆς ἡλικίας ὑπάρχῃ AC. We may compare what is said as to presbyters in *Apost. Ch. Order* xviii 3 δεῖ οὖν εἶναι τοὺς πρεσβυτέρους ἤδη κεχρονικότας ἐπὶ τῷ κόσμῳ, τρόπῳ τινὶ ἀπεχομένους τῆς πρὸς γυναῖκας συνελεύσεως. 13 honour] In the sense of honorarium, as often: δῶρον AC. 16 angel] Cf. Mal. iii 1, iv 4, and compare Irenaeus *Apost. Preaching* c. 94 (trans. J. A. Robinson) 'because no longer Moses (as) mediator nor Elijah (as) messenger, but the Lord himself has redeemed us', referring to Isa. lxiii 9 οὐ πρέσβυς οὐδὲ ἄγγελος, ἀλλ' αὐτὸς ἔσωσεν αὐτούς. 18 virtue] lit. 'grace'. Is this possibly a play upon the name Anna? AC omits the word.

DIDASCALIA APOSTOLORUM

a second time, and some harmful matter ensue. For this you know, that she who marries one husband may lawfully marry also a second; but she who goes beyond this is a harlot. [iii. 3] Wherefore, assist those who are young, that they may persevere in chastity unto God. And do thou accordingly, O bishop, bestow care upon these. And be mindful also of the poor, and assist and support them, [iii. 4] even though there be among them those who are not widowers or widows, yet are in need of help through want or sickness or the rearing of children, and are in distress.

It behoves thee to be careful of all and heedful of all. And hence it is that they who give gifts do not themselves with their own hands give them to the widows, but bring them to thee; that thou who art well acquainted of those who are in distress mayest, like a good steward, make distribution to them of those things which are given to thee: for God knows who it is that gives, even though he does not chance to be present. And when thou makest distribution, tell them the name of him who gave, that they may pray for him by name. For in all the Scriptures the Lord makes mention of the poor, and gives command concerning them; ... and even if they be married persons. And he adds further by Isaiah and says thus: *Break* (p. 63) *thy bread to the hungry: and the poor*

---

1 Cf. 1 Cor. vii 39, Rom. vii 2 f.   23 Isa. lviii 7.

---

2 marries one husband, etc.] Or possibly 'marries one husband according to law, may also marry a second'. Cf. Hermas *Mand.* iv 4. 1-2, as well as St. Paul.   3 but she, etc.] τριγαμία δὲ ἀκρασίας σημεῖον *AC*.   4 assist] lit. 'take by the hand', and again l. 7, where *AC* has αὐτοῖς χεῖρα ὀρέγων.   22 married persons] The word means 'those who communicate', but admits of the sense 'consorts'. Something has fallen out at the point indicated, and the context implies that it contained at least one Scripture quotation. Probably *AC* has preserved the general drift of the missing passage: χρὴ γὰρ εὖ ποιεῖν πάντας ἀνθρώπους, μὴ φιλοκρινοῦντα τοῦτον ὅστις ἢ ἢ ἐκεῖνον· ὁ γὰρ κύριός φησι· παντὶ τῷ αἰτοῦντί σε δίδου· (Lk. vi 30; cf. *Didache* i 5, Herm. *Mand.* ii 4-6) δῆλον δὲ ὡς τῷ χρῄζοντι κατὰ ἀλήθειαν, κἂν φίλος ᾖ κἂν ἐχθρός, κἂν συγγενὴς κἂν ἀλλότριος, κἂν ἄγαμος κἂν γεγαμηκὼς ὑπάρχῃ. It is on the strength of these last words that I have ventured to translate 'married persons' above: the preceding 'and even if' appears to represent κἂν of *AC*, and to belong to a series.

man, that hath no roof, bring into thine house; and when thou seest the naked, cover him: and thou shalt not despise one that is of thine own flesh. By all means therefore be careful of the poor.

CHAPTER XV

How Widows ought to deport themselves.

[iii. 5] Every widow therefore ought to be meek and quiet and gentle. And let her also be without malice and without anger; and let her not be talkative or clamorous, or forward in tongue, or quarrelsome. And when she sees anything unseemly done, or hears it, let her be as though she saw and heard it not. For a widow should have no other care save to be praying for those who give, and for the whole Church. And when she is asked a question by any one, let her not straightway give an answer, except only concerning righteousness and faith in God; but let her send them that desire to be instructed to the rulers. And to those who question them let them (the widows) make answer only in refutation of idols and concerning the unity of God. But concerning punishment and reward, and the kingdom of the name of Christ, and His dispensation, neither a widow nor a layman ought to speak; for when they speak without the knowledge of doctrine, they will bring blasphemy upon the word. For our Lord likened the word of His tidings to mustard; but mustard, unless it be skilfully tempered, is bitter and sharp to

---

7-8 forward in tongue] lit. 'long of tongue': πρόγλωσσος *AC* (cf. *Ep. Barnab.* xix 8).　　15 the rulers] H: sing. S: τοῖς ἡγουμένοις *AC*. 16 make answer only] Here Flemming and Funk place a full stop (indicated in cod. S), and connect what follows with the next sentence as part of what the widow is *not* to teach. I follow the general indications of the passage and the evidence of *AC*: μόνα δὲ ἀποκρινέσθω τὰ περὶ ἀνατροπῆς πολυθέου πλάνης, ἀποδεικνύουσα τὸν περὶ μοναρχίας θεοῦ λόγον· περὶ δὲ τῶν ἑξῆς προπετῶς τι μὴ ἀποκρινέσθω. What the widow is especially forbidden to speak of is the economy of the Incarnation: it has just been said that she *may* give an answer 'concerning righteousness and faith in God'. 18 reward] lit. 'rest', but prob. rendering κατάπαυσις—rest in the promised land, or in the future life.

those who use it. Wherefore our Lord said in the Gospel, to widows and to all the laity: *Cast not your pearls before swine, lest they trample upon them and turn against you and rend you.* For when the Gentiles who are being instructed hear the word of God not fittingly spoken, as it ought to be, unto edification of eternal life—and all the more in that it is spoken to them by a woman—how that our Lord clothed Himself in a body, and concerning the passion of Christ: they will mock and scoff, instead of applauding the word of doctrine; and she shall incur a heavy judgement for sin.

[iii. 6] It is neither right nor necessary therefore that women should be teachers, and especially concerning the name of Christ and the redemption of His passion. For you have not been appointed to this, (p. 64) O women, and especially widows, that you should teach, but that you should pray and entreat the Lord God. For He the Lord God, Jesus Christ our Teacher, sent us the Twelve to instruct the People and the Gentiles; and there were with us women disciples, Mary Magdalene and Mary the daughter of James and the other Mary; but He did not send them to instruct the people with us. For if it were required that women should teach, our Master Himself would have commanded these to give instruction with us. But let a widow know that she is the altar of God; and let her sit ever at home, and not stray or run about among the houses of the faithful to receive. For the altar of God never strays or runs about anywhere, but is fixed in one place.

A widow must not therefore stray or run about among the

2 Mt. vii 6.

---

3 *against you*] The Greek fragment published by Dr. Bartlet (*J. T. S.* xviii 303 ff.) begins here, and ends at the words 'unworthy of Him who called them', p. 134, l. 7. It is so mutilated that little help can be got from it for the criticism of the text.   10 incur . . . sin] lit. 'be guilty of a great judgement of sin'. After this Fragm. (p. 304) adds a quotation from Prov. x 19.   19 daughter of James] This is merely the *syr. vet.* rendering of ἡ τοῦ Ἰακώβου: see again pp. 148, 183.   and the other Mary] καὶ ⟨τὴν Σαλώ⟩μην Fragm. p. 305.   22 Master] lit. 'Teacher', i. e. διδάσκαλος.

houses. For those who are gadabouts and without shame cannot be still even in their houses; for they are no widows, but *wallets*, and they care for nothing else but to be making ready to receive. And because they are gossips and chatterers and murmurers, they stir up quarrels; and they are bold and shameless. Now they that are such are unworthy of Him who called them; for neither in the common assembly of rest of the Sunday, when they have come, are such women or men watchful, but they either fall asleep or prate about some other matter: so that through them others also are taken captive by the enemy Satan, who suffers not such persons to be watchful unto the Lord. And they who are such, coming in empty to the Church, go out more empty still, since they hearken not to that which is spoken or read to receive it with the ears of their hearts. Such persons, then, are like those of whom Isaiah said: *Hearing ye shall hear, and shall not understand; and seeing ye shall see, and shall not see. For the heart of this people is waxed gross, and with their ears they hear heavily, and their eyes they have shut: lest at any time they should see with their eyes, aud hear with their ears.* [iii. 7] So in like manner the ears of such widows' hearts are stopped, because they will not sit beneath the roof of their houses and pray and entreat the Lord, but are impatient (p. 65) to be running after gain; and by their chattering they execute the desires of the Enemy. Now such a widow does not conform to the altar of Christ; for it is written in the Gospel: *If two shall agree together, and shall ask concerning any thing whatsoever, it shall be given them. And if they shall say to a mountain that it be removed and fall into the sea, it shall so be done.*

---

1 Cf. Prov. vii 11.   16 Isa. vi 9 f. (Mt. xiii 14 f., Acts xxviii 26 f.). 26 Mt. xviii 19: xvii 20, xxi 21, etc.

---

1 gadabouts] ῥεμβοί AC.   2 be still] H reads 'assemble': but οὐχ ἡσυχάζουσιν AC. There is an allusion to Prov. vii 11.   3 wallets] 'blind' Syr.: διὰ τὸ μὴ χήρας, ἀλλὰ πήρας αὐτὰς ὑπάρχειν AC. The translator took πήρας for πηράς, as Funk observes.   4-5 gossips ... quarrels] φλυάρους, καταλάλους, μαχοσυμβούλους AC.   7-9 for neither ... watchful] οὐ γὰρ ἐπὶ τὸ κοινὸν τῆς συναγωγῆς ἀνάπαυμα ἐν τῇ κυριακῇ καταντῶσιν ὡς οἱ ἐγρηγορότες AC.   9 prate] lit. 'split talk', which

[XXXI] ... ⟨detrac⟩tatrices, litium commissatrices, inpudoratae, inpudicae: quaeque, si tales fuerint, non iudicabuntur dignae eius qui eas uocauit. Non enim ad communem synagogae refrigerium in dominica die conueniunt ut uigilent, quae tales sunt aut qui tales sunt, sed aut dormitant aut uerbosantur suauia quaedam, ut et alii captiui ducantur per ipsos ab aduersario maligno, qui non permittit sobrios esse in domino qui tale[n]s sunt. Et ingrediuntur eiusmodi uacui in ecclesia, et euacuat⟨i⟩ores iterum egrediuntur, quoniam non audiunt uerbum ab eis qui docent uel legent, et suscipere illud in auribus cordis sui non possunt. Similes ergo inueniuntur, qui eiusmodi sunt, his qui ab Esaia significantur, sicuti dicit: *Auditu audietis, et non intelligitis, et uidentes uidebitis, et non uidebitis: inpinguatum est enim cor populi huius, et auribus grauiter audierunt, et oculos suos curbauerunt, ut non uideant oculis et auribus audiant.* Simili ratione et earum uiduarum, que tales sunt, cl⟨a⟩usi sunt oculi cordis, ut non sedentes intus in domos suas adloquantur dominum, sed discurrunt ad exinuentionem lucri, et per uerbositates quae aduersarii sunt desideria agunt. Quae talis ergo est uidua non est conlegata altario Christi, quoniam scriptum est in euangelio: *Duo si conuenerint in unum et dixerint monti huic: Tolle et mitte te in mari, fiet.*

---

1 ⟨detrac⟩tatrices] Cf. 'contractatores' p. 97, l. 7.   7–8 in domino ... sunt. Et] 'in domino. Qui tales sunt et' Hauler and Funk; but this leaves no room for 'eiusmodi' which follows.   15 *curbauerunt*] i.e. 'curuauerunt': as if reading ἔκαμψαν for ἐκάμμυσαν, or confusing the meanings.   17 oculi] τὰ ὦτα *AC* (= Syr.).

---

perh. means 'exchange gossip'; but the verb is said also to denote 'speak while yawning', and 'speak abruptly'.   9–10 about some other matter] 'suauia quaedam' Lat.: *AC* alters to ἢ αἰτοῦσιν.   11 who suffers not] 'and he suffers not' text: I have made a slight correction. 25 does not conform to] i.e. tally with her description as 'the altar of Christ': οὐ προσήρτηται *AC* (cf. Lat.).   27–28 shall ask ... And if] om. Lat.: *AC* omits the whole text.

Now we see that there are widows who esteem the matter as one of traffic, and receive greedily; and instead of doing good (works) and giving to the bishop for the entertainment of strangers and the refreshment of those in distress, they lend out on bitter usury; and they care only for Mammon, *whose god is their purse* and *their belly: for where their treasure is, there is also their heart.* For she who is in the habit of roaming abroad and running about to receive takes no thought for good works, but serves Mammon and ministers to filthy lucre. And she cannot please God, nor is she obedient to His ministry, so as to be constantly praying and making intercession, because her mind is quite taken captive by the greed of avarice. And when she stands up to pray, she remembers whither she may go to receive somewhat; or else that she has forgotten to tell some matter to her friends. And when she stands (in prayer), her mind is not upon her prayer, but upon that thought which has occurred to her mind. Now the prayer of such a one is not heard in regard to any thing. But she soon interrupts her prayer by reason of the distraction of her mind; for she does not offer prayer to God with all her heart, but goes off with the thought suggested by the Enemy, and talks with her friends about some unprofitable matter. For she knows not †how she has believed†, or of what order she has been accounted worthy.

But a widow who wishes to please God sits at home and meditates upon the Lord day and night, and without ceasing at all times offers intercession and prays with purity before the Lord. And she receives whatever she asks, because her whole mind is set upon this. For her mind is not greedy to receive,

---

5 Phil. iii 19: Mt. vi 21.   26 Cf. 1 Cor. vii 32, 34 (see Lat.).

1–2 Now ... traffic] εἰσὶ γὰρ ἔνιαι χῆραι ἐργασίαν ἡγούμεναι τὸ πρᾶγμα *AC*.
6 and *their belly*] om. *AC* (= Lat.).   22–23 how she has believed] Lat. shows that the verb must have been passive; so that the meaning should be 'with what she has been entrusted'.   23 order] lit. 'place'.
25–28 But ... the Lord] ἡ δὲ θεῷ βουλομένη προσανέχειν καθημένη ἔνδον φρονεῖ τὰ τοῦ κυρίου, νυκτὸς καὶ ἡμέρας ἀκαταπαύστῳ στόματι δέησιν προσφέρουσα εἰλικρινῆ *AC*.   28 ff. And ... expenses] καὶ εἰσακούσεται αὐτῆς διὰ τὸ τὴν διάνοιαν αὐτῆς πρὸς μόνῳ τούτῳ ἠρτῆσθαι καὶ μήτε πρὸς ἀπληστίαν μήτε πρὸς

DIDASCALIA APOSTOLORUM

Videmus ergo aliquantas uiduas [XXXII] non conuenire, quia non inpetrant cum petant. Quae tales itaque fuerint tamquam operationem rem ipsam existimant, [et] ex eo quod abare accipiunt; et pro ⟨eo⟩, ut deberent fructuare sibi, aut dare episcopo ad
5 susceptionem peregrinorum aut tribulantium repausationem, ad amarissimas usuras commodant, et de solo mammona cogitant: *quorum deus est saculus : ubi est thensaurus eorum, ibi et mens eorum est.* Illa enim quae ad circumeundum iam instituta est, ad opus spiritale non recte sentit, seruit autem mammonae, id
10 est lucro; Deo uero placere non potest nec ministeriis eius adbunde obaudire poterit, quoniam uoluntas eius circum multa occupatur et ad lucrum magis festinat. Tamen etsi adstat interpellare, et rememorata fuerit ubi debeat ire propter accipiendum lucrum, aut quia amice suae oblita est uerbum aliquod
15 dicere; et cum stat, iam non orationi intendit, sed ei quae circumuenit eam cogitationi. Quae talis ergo fuerit non exauditur citius, quia dereli⟨n⟩quid praecem, et mens eius uentilatur, et non ex toto corde offeret Deo praecem, et pergit magis ad inspirationes maligni, quae non possunt saluare eam,
20 et amice suae exponit eas : quoniam nescit qui ei locus creditus est uel cuius gradus digna effecta est.

Quae autem Deo placere uult uidua sedens intra tectum suum quae domini sunt sapit, noctu et die incessabili ore sincer-[t]am praecem offerens : et inpetrat pro [XXXIII] his quibus
25 petit, cum sinceram praecem fundit, quoniam mens eius ad hoc solum uacat. Nec enim uoluntas eius abara est ad accipiendum,

---

1-2 non conuenire ... fuerint] om. *AC* (= Syr.) : yet the reading of Lat. is prob. original, giving point to the next phrase.   9-12 seruit autem ... magis festinat] λατρεύει τῷ μαμωνᾷ, τοῦτ' ἔστιν δουλεύει τῷ κέρδει, τῷ δὲ θεῷ εὐάρεστος εἶναι οὐ δύναται οὐδὲ ταῖς λατρείαις αὐτοῦ ὑπήκοος, συνεχῶς οὐ δυναμένη ἐντυγχάνειν αὐτῷ, ἐπὶ τὸ ἀργυρολογεῖν τὸν νοῦν καὶ τὴν διάθεσιν ἔχουσα *AC* (cf. Syr.).   17 citius, quia] Syr. would suggest 'quia citius': *AC* has compressed the passage.   25 cum ... fundit] om. *AC* (= Syr.).

ἐπιθυμίαν πολυδάπανον ἐκκεῖσθαι *AC*.   29 greedy] H : S has a defective and ungrammatical form.

nor has she much desire to make large expenses; nor does her eye wander, that she should see aught and desire it, and her mind be withdrawn; nor does she hear evil words to give heed to them, because she does not go forth and run about abroad. Therefore her prayer suffers no hindrance from any thing; and thus her quietness (p. 66) and tranquillity and modesty are acceptable before God, and whatsoever she asks of God, she presently receives her request. For such a widow, not loving money or filthy lucre, and not avaricious nor greedy, but constant in prayer, and meek and unperturbed, and modest and reverent, sits at home and works at (her) wool, that she may provide somewhat for those who are in distress, or that she may make a return to others, so that she receive nothing from them. For she bethinks her of that widow of whom our Lord gave testimony in the Gospel, who *came and cast into the treasury two mites, which is one dinar*: whom when our Lord and Teacher, the trier of hearts, saw, He said to us: O my disciples, *this poor widow hath cast in more alms than any one; for every one hath cast in of that which was superfluous to him: but this, of all that she possessed she hath laid her up treasure.*

[iii. 8] Widows ought then to be modest, and obedient to the bishops and the deacons, and to reverence and respect and fear the bishop as God. And let them not act after their own will, nor desire to do any thing apart from that which is commanded them, or without counsel to speak with any one by way of making answer, or to go to any one to eat or drink, or to fast with any one, or to receive aught of any one, or to lay hand on and pray over any one without the command of the bishop or the deacon. But if she do aught that is not commanded her, let her be rebuked for having acted without discipline. For whence knowest thou, O woman, from whom

---

15 ff. Mk. xii 41-44.   20 Cf. Mt. vi 20.

1-14 nor does her eye, etc.] There is much divergence here between Syr. and Lat. which *AC* does not help to explain. Syr. is probably paraphrastic, while Lat. appears in places to be corrupt.   13-14 so that ... from them] So literally: the sense may be 'rather than that she should receive any thing from them': (ἑτέροις μᾶλλον ἐπιχορηγείτω) ἤπερ αὐτή τινος δεέσθω *AC* (cf. Lat.).   25-26 to speak ... answer, or] om. *AC* (= Lat.).   27-28 lay hand on] *AC* omits this and the following references to laying on of hand.

DIDASCALIA APOSTOLORUM

nec desiderium eius est ut multum expendat ad expensa sua; nec oculis aliquid potest desiderare, quia nec uidit aliquid tale, nec insedit menti eius, †nec quae cum audit, in uerba malorum† adcommodauit aurem suam aut ipsa ministrauit, quoniam nec curam habuit. De his ergo nihil poterit inpediri orationi eius. Sic igitur castitas eius et inturbulentia cum sit Deo manifesta, mox cum ceperit petere aliquit a Deo, praeueniet praecem eius. Quoniam quae talis est uidua, non diligens pecuniam neque turpilucrum amans nec abara nec gluterix, sed magis mansueta, sine turbulentia agens omnia, religiosa et uerecunda, [et] sedens in domo sua [et] lanam deforis accipit, ut magis praebeat tribulantibus quam ipsa alicui sit molesta ut accipiat ab eis: rememorans eius uiduae cui in euangelio testimonium fertur a domino, quae *ueniens misit in gazofylacio denarios minutos duos, quod est quadrantes;* quam cum uidisset magister et dominus noster cordis scientiam habens, dixit nobis: O discipuli mei, *ista uidua pauperrima ab omnibus plus misit elemosynam: quoniam omne populum de abundantia sua misit, haec autem omnem uitam suam uel substantiam, quam habebat, in caelo sibi thensaurizauit.*

Sinceras ergo oportet esse uiduas, subditas [XXXIV] episcopis et diaconibus, et metuentes sicut Deum et reuerentes et trementes episcopum, non habentes potestatem in aliquo nec absque dispositionem aliquid facientes et citra consilium aut imperium episcopi: et ne uellint ad aliquem pergere ad manducandum aut bibendum, aut ieiunari cum aliquo, aut accipere ab aliquo quicquam, aut manus alicui inponere et orare, ut superius diximus, absque consilio episcopi uel diaconis. Si quid autem non iussa fecerit, corripiatur illa quae sine disciplina est. Quid enim scis, o mulier, a quo accipias,

3 nec quae cum] Hauler prints 'nec q(uae) cu(m)'. - Perhaps read 'neque, cum'. uerba malorum] So Hauler prints; but the first word was originally 'uerborum', and its correction to 'uerba' seems uncertain. 4 ministrauit] This again is difficult, but I can offer no suggestion. 5 habuit. De his ergo] So Hauler and Funk punctuate: 'habuit de his. Ergo' would be easier. 6 cum sit Deo manifesta] εὐάρεστος ἔσται τῷ θεῷ *AC* (cf. Syr.). 9 gluterix] λίχνος *AC*. 11 deforis accipit] ἐκλαμβάνουσα *AC*. 12 tribulantibus] ἑτέροις *AC* (= Syr.). 19 *in caelo*] om. Syr.: *AC* omits also the next two words. 23 non ... in aliquo] μὴ κατεξουσιαζούσας *AC* (cf. Syr.). 28 ut superius diximus] om. Syr. 29 fecerit] 'fuerit' cod.

thou receivest, or from what ministry thou art nourished, or for whom thou fastest, or upon whom thou layest hand? For knowest thou not that concerning every one of these thou shalt render an account to the Lord in the day of judgement, seeing that thou communicatest in their works?

But thou, O widow who art without discipline, seest thy fellow widows or thy brethren in sickness, and hast no care to fast and pray over thy members, and to lay hand upon them and to visit them, but feignest thyself to be not in health, or not at leisure; but to others, who are (p. 67) in sins or are gone forth from the Church, because they give much, thou art ready and glad to go and to visit them. You then who are such ought to be ashamed; for you wish to be wiser and to know better, not only than the men, but even than the presbyters and the bishops. Know then, sisters, that whatsoever the pastors with the deacons command you, and you obey them, you obey God; and with whomsoever you communicate by the command of the bishop, you are without blame before God; and so is every brother of the laity who obeys the bishop and submits to him: for they (the bishops) are to render an account for all. But if you obey not the mind of the bishops and deacons, they indeed will be quit of your offences, but you shall render an account of all that you do of your own will, whether men or women.

Now whosoever prays or communicates with one that is expelled from the Church, must rightly be reckoned with him; for these things lead to the undoing and destruction of souls. For if one communicate and pray with him who is expelled from the Church, and obey not the bishop, he obeys not God; and he is defiled with him (that is expelled). And moreover he suffers not that man to repent. For if no one communicate with him, he will feel compunction and weep, and will ask and beseech to be received (again); and he will repent of what he has done, and will be saved.

---

3 these] fem., with neuter sense of 'these things': 'eorum' Lat., rightly. 10 in sins] The word would naturally represent ἐν παραπτώμασι. 14 know better] lit. 'be more understanding'. 24 of your own will, whether men or women] lit. 'of your (*masc.*) will and of your (*fem.*) will'.

aut de cuius diaconia edes, aut pro quo ieiunaris, aut cui manum commodasti? Nescis quia rationem reddere habes domino pro unoquoque eorum in die iudicii, quoniam communicas operibus eorum?

5 Tu quidem, o uidua indisciplinata, uides conuiduas tuas aut fratres infirmitatibus positos: ad membra tua non festinas, ut facias super eos ieiunium et orationem adhuc et manus inpositionem. Dicis autem non uacare tibi, et fingis te male ualere. Aput aliquantos uero, qui sunt in peccatis aut extra synagogam, 10 quoniam multa donant, paratissime celeritatem tuam praestas illis. Confundemini, quae tales estis, quia non solum amplius a uiris, set et a praesbyteris et ab episcopis uultis sapere. Scitote igitur, o sorores, quod pastores uestri si quid uobis disposuerunt una cum diaconibus suis, et audieritis eos, Deo uos 15 obaudisse; et secundum iussionem episcopi si cuiquam communi⟨caueritis⟩ . . .

9 extra synagogam] ἀποσυναγώγου *AC*; cf. Joh. ix 22, xii 42, xvi 2 (see again p. 160, l. 3).

[iii. 9] That a woman should baptize, or that one should be baptized by a woman, we do not counsel, for it is a transgression of the commandment, and a great peril to her who baptizes and to him who is baptized. For if it were lawful to be baptized by a woman, our Lord and Teacher Himself would have been baptized by Mary His mother, whereas He was baptized by John, like others of the people. Do not therefore imperil yourselves, brethren and sisters, by acting beside the law of the Gospel.

[iii. 10] But concerning envy or jealousy, or slander and fault-finding, or contention and ill-will, and carping or rivalry, we have already told you that these things ought not to be found in a Christian; but among widows it is not fitting that any one of them should so much as be named. Yet because the author of evil (p. 68) has many wiles and devices, he enters into those who are no widows and boasts himself in them. For there are some indeed who profess themselves widows, but do not works worthy of their name. For not for the name of widowhood are they found worthy to enter into the kingdom, but for faith and works. For if one practise good works, she shall be praised and accepted; but if she practise evil works and do the works of the Evil One, she shall be blamed and cast out of the kingdom everlasting: because she has left the things eternal and desired and loved those that are temporal.

Now we see and hear that there are widows in whom there is envy one towards another. For when thy fellow aged woman has been clothed, or has received somewhat from some one, thou oughtest, O widow, on seeing thy sister refreshed—if thou be a widow of God—to say: 'Blessed be God, who hath refreshed my fellow aged woman,' and to praise God; and afterwards (to praise) him that ministered, and say: 'May his work be acceptable in truth,' and: 'Remember him, Lord, for good in the day of Thy recompense, and my bishop who hath ministered well before Thee and hath dis-

---

10 But concerning, etc.] περὶ δὲ φθόνου ἢ ζήλου ἢ καταλαλιᾶς ἢ ἔριδος ἢ φιλονεικίας *AC*: The last three terms have duplicate renderings in Syr.
15–17 he enters ... in them] εἰς τὰς μὴ χήρας ἐμπομπεύει *AC*.

pensed the alms fairly; for my fellow aged woman was naked, and hath been provided: and add unto him glory, and give him also a crown of glory in the day of the manifestation of Thy coming.' And likewise also the widow who has received
5 an alms of the Lord, let her pray for him that provided this ministration, suppressing his name like a wise woman, that his righteousness may be with God and not with men,—as He said in the Gospel: *When thou doest an alms, let not thy left hand know what thy right hand doeth*—lest, when thou pro-
10 nounce and reveal his name in praying for him that gave, his name be disclosed and come to the ears of a heathen, and the heathen, being a man of the left hand, know it. Or it may even chance that one of the faithful, hearing thee, will go out and talk: and it is not expedient that those things which are
15 done or spoken in the Church should come abroad and be revealed; for he that divulges and speaks of them disobeys God, and becomes a betrayer of the Church. But do thou in praying for him suppress his name; and so shalt thou fulfil that which is written, thou and the widows who are such
20 (as thou): for you are the holy altar of God, (even of) Jesus Christ.

But now we hear that there are widows who do not behave according to the commandment, (p. 69) but care only for this, that they may stray and run about asking questions. And
25 moreover she who has received an alms of the Lord—being without sense, in that she discloses (the matter) to her that asks her—has revealed and declared the name of the giver; and the other, hearing it, murmurs and finds fault with the bishop who has dispensed, or with the deacon, or with him

---

7 Cf. Mt. vi 1.   8 Mt. vi 3.

---

12 a man of the left hand] See p. 110.   20 altar of God] See p. 88, l. 6 and note: ἅγιον θυσιαστήριον θεοῦ ὑπάρχουσα *AC*, omitting 'Jesus Christ'.   24 that they ... asking questions] lit. 'that they may ask (questions) and stray and run about'. In conjunction with the last two verbs 'ask' might seem to mean 'beg' (so Flemming and Funk take it); but the form used here (the *pa'el*) hardly admits of that sense, and *AC* (otherwise changing and compressing) has φροντίζουσιν πολυπευστεῖν, which leads on naturally to the next sentence.

who has made some gift, saying: 'Knewest thou not that I was nearer to thee and in more distress than she?' And she knows not that it was not by man's will that this was done, but by the command of God. For if thou protest and say to him: 'I was nearer to thee, and thou knewest that I was more naked than she': it behoved thee to know who it was that commanded, and to be silent and not find fault with him that ministered, but to go into thy house and fall upon thy face and give thanks to God for thy fellow widow; and to pray likewise for him that gave and for him that ministered, and to beseech the Lord that He would open to thee also the door of His favour. And the Lord would presently have heard thy prayer bountifully, and have sent thee more favour than thy fellow widow, from whence thou never thoughtest to receive a ministry; and (such) proof of thy patience would have been praiseworthy. Or know you not that it is written in the Gospel: *When thou doest an alms, sound not the trumpet before men to be seen of them, as the hypocrites do. For verily I say unto you, they have received their reward.*

Now if God has commanded that a ministry be ministered in secret, and he that ministered did so minister: why then dost thou, who hast received in secret, proclaim it openly? Or thou, again (who hast not received), why dost thou question it? For thou not only findest fault and murmurest, as one who is no widow, but even utterest a curse like the heathen. Or hast thou not heard what the Scripture saith: *Every one that blesseth, is blessed; and every one that curseth, is cursed?* And again in the Gospel He saith: *Bless them that curse you;* and again: *When ye enter into a house, say: Peace be in this*

17 Mt. vi 2, cf. *v*. 1. 26 Cf. Nu. xxiv 9, Gen. xxvii 29. 28 Lk. vi 28 (cf. Mt. v 44). 29 Mt. x 12 f.

12-13 thy prayer bountifully] Or 'thy prayer (made) without envy'; but 'without envy' is used to render ἀφθόνως.   18 *before men to be seen of them*] From the previous verse, Mt. vi 1.   23 Or thou, again] Clearly the other widow is meant, who grumbled and asked questions (see above) because she did not receive. Flemming and Funk miss the point in rendering 'Or again, why dost thou ask?' (i. e. beg): the pronoun after 'Or' is expressed, and is emphatic.

house. And if that house be worthy of peace, your peace shall come upon it; but if it be not worthy, your peace shall return unto you. [iii. 11] (p. 70) If then peace returns to them that send it, much more will a curse return upon those who utter it idly: because that he upon whom it was sent does not merit to receive a curse. For every one who curses a man idly, curses himself, since it is written in Proverbs: *As birds and fowl fly, so do idle curses return.* And again He saith: *They that utter curses are void of understanding.* For we are set forth in a parable by the example of the bee, as the Lord saith: *Go to the bee, and learn how she worketh. For her work she performeth in wisdom; and there is brought of her labour to be food for rich and poor. Beloved and praiseworthy is she, albeit she is little in strength.* As then the bee is *little in strength*, and when she has stung a man she loses her sting, and becomes barren and presently dies; so also we the faithful in like manner: whatever evil we do to another, we do it to ourselves; for, *Whatsoever thou hatest that it should be done to thee, thou shalt not do to another.* Wherefore, *every one that blesseth is blessed.*

Do you therefore admonish and rebuke those (widows) who are undisciplined and likewise exhort and encourage and help forward those who conduct themselves rightly. And let widows keep themselves from cursing, for they have been appointed to bless. Wherefore, let not the bishop, nor a presbyter, nor a deacon, nor a widow utter a curse out of their mouth, *that they may* not *inherit* a curse but *a blessing.* And let this also be thy care, O bishop, that not even one of the laity utter from his mouth a curse: for thou hast the care of all.

---

7 Prov. xxvi 2. 9 Prov. x 18. 11 Prov. vi 8 (LXX) 18 Cf. Tob. iv 15. 19 Cf. Nu. xxiv 9. 27 1 Pet. iii 9.

---

18 *Whatsoever thou hatest,* etc.] See p. 4, l. 26.

CHAPTER XVI

On the appointment of Deacons and Deaconesses.

[iii. 12] Wherefore, O bishop, appoint thee workers of righteousness as helpers who may co-operate with thee unto salvation. Those that please thee out of all the people thou shalt choose and appoint as deacons: a man for the performance of the most things that are required, but a woman for the ministry of women. For there are houses whither thou canst not send a deacon to the women, on account of the heathen, but mayest send a deaconess. Also, because in many other matters the office of a woman deacon is required. In the first place, when women go down into the water, those who go down into the water ought (p. 71) to be anointed by a deaconess with the oil of anointing; and where there is no woman at hand, and especially no deaconess, he who baptizes must of necessity anoint her who is being baptized. But where there is a woman, and especially a deaconess, it is not fitting that women should be seen by men: but with the imposition of hand do thou anoint the head only. As of old the priests and kings were anointed in Israel, do thou in like manner, with the imposition of hand, anoint the head of those who receive baptism, whether of men or of women; and afterwards—whether thou thyself baptize, or thou command the

---

1-2 workers of righteousness] τῆς δικαιοσύνης ἐργάτας *AC*. Flemming's rendering, 'workers in the matter of *almsgiving*', confuses *zaddīkūtha* with *zedhkĕtha*.   2-3 who may ... salvation] 'populum tuum ad uitam adiuuantes' Funk, mistaking the prep. *'ammākh*, 'with thee', for the subst. 'thy people'.   8 a deaconess] H : plur. S.   20-21 and afterwards] i. e., no doubt, after the bishop has anointed the head, not after the baptism itself : *AC*, though otherwise altering, makes this clear—καὶ πρῶτον μὲν ἐν τῷ φωτίζεσθαι γυναῖκας ὁ διάκονος χρίσει μὲν μόνον τὸ μέτωπον αὐτῶν τῷ ἁγίῳ ἐλαίῳ, καὶ μετ' αὐτὸν ἡ διάκονος ἀλείψει αὐτάς. The baptismal rite of *Didasc.*, so far as here described, is thus in agreement with that of the early Syrian churches, which had a double anointing before, and no anointing after, the baptism (see *Liturgical Homilies of Narsai*, 'Texts and Studies' viii 1, pp. xlii ff.). For examples of the baptism of women, and their anointing by women, see *Acts of Thomas*, Syriac in Wright's trans. pp. 258, 289, Greek in Bonnet, pp. 231, 267.

deacons or presbyters to baptize—let a woman deacon, as we have already said, anoint the women. But let a man pronounce over them the invocation of the divine Names in the water.

5 And when she who is being baptized has come up from the water, let the deaconess receive her, and teach and instruct her how the seal of baptism ought to be (kept) unbroken in purity and holiness. For this cause we say that the ministry of a woman deacon is especially needful and important. For
10 our Lord and Saviour also was ministered unto by women

---

3 The invocation of the divine Names] lit. 'the names of invocation of the Divinity': τὴν ἱερὰν ἐπ' αὐτοῖς εἰπὼν καὶ ἐπονομάσας ἐπίκλησιν [πατρὸς καὶ υἱοῦ καὶ ἁγίου πνεύματος] *AC*. On ἐπίκλησις and its special connexion with *names*, and particularly with the divine Names of the baptismal formula, the reader may be referred to *J. T. S.* xxv 337 ff. (July 1924).   7-8 how the seal . . . holiness] Comp. 2 Clem. vi 9, vii 6, viii 6.

ministers, *Mary Magdalene, and Mary the daughter of James and mother of Jose, and the mother of the sons of Zebedee*, with other women beside. And thou also hast need of the ministry of a deaconess for many things; for a deaconess is required to go into the houses of the heathen where there are believing women, and to visit those who are sick, and to minister to them in that of which they have need, and to bathe those who have begun to recover from sickness.

[iii. 13] And let the deacons imitate the bishops in their conversation: nay, let them even be labouring more than he. And let them *not love filthy lucre*; but let them be diligent in the ministry. And in proportion to the number of the congregation of the people of the Church, so let the deacons be, that they may be able to take knowledge (of each) severally and refresh all; so that for the aged women who are infirm, and for brethren and sisters who are in sickness—for every one they may provide the ministry which is proper for him.

But let a woman rather be devoted to the ministry of women, and a male deacon to the ministry of men. And let him be ready to obey (p. 72) and to submit himself to the command of the bishop. And let him labour and toil in every place whither he is sent to minister or to speak of some matter to any one. For it behoves each one to know his office and to be diligent in executing it. And be you (bishop and deacon) of one counsel and of one purpose, and one soul dwelling in two bodies. And know what the ministry is, according as our Lord and Saviour said in the Gospel: *Whoso among you desireth to be chief, let him be your servant: even as the Son of Man came not to be ministered unto, but to minister, and to give his life a*

1 Mt. xxvii 56.   11 1 Tim. iii 8.   27 Mt. xx 26-28.

---

1 *daughter of James*] See also pp. 133, 183. 'Daughter of James' for ἡ (τοῦ) Ἰακώβου is found in *syr. sin.* here and at Mk. xv 40 (*syr. cur.* is wanting in both places), and in *syr. sin.* and *cur.* at Lk. xxiv 10.   10 nay, ... than he] μόνον δὲ εὐσκυλτότεροι *AC*.   12 And in proportion, etc.] ἀνάλογοι πρὸς τὸ πλῆθος τῆς ἐκκλησίας *AC*.   19–22 And let him ... to any one] om. Lat.; but the clause appears to be genuine.   23 office] lit. 'place': τόπον *AC*.   25 one soul dwelling in two bodies] Cf. 2 Clem. xii 3   τὰ δύο δὲ ἕν ἐστιν, ὅταν λαλῶμεν ἑαυτοῖς ἀλήθειαν, καὶ ἐν δυσὶ σώμασιν ἀνυποκρίτως εἴη μία ψυχή.

[XXXV] ... *et Maria Iacobi et Ioseph mater et mater filiorum Zebedei.* Tu ergo in aliis rebus diaconissam necessariam habebis, et ut eas gentilium domos ingredia[n]tur, ubi uos accedere non potestis, propter fideles mulieres, et ut eis quae infirmantur ministret quae necessantur, et in balneis iterum eas quae meliorant ut labe[n]t.

QUALIS DEBET ESSE DIACONUS. Diacones sint in actibus similes episcopis suis, sed exercitatiores, et *non malum adpetentes lucrum*, ut bene ministrent. Secundum multitudinem ecclesiae sufficientes erunt; ut et senioribus mulieribus quae iam non possunt, fratribus et sororibus quae in infirmitate ditinentur, possint placere, in celeritate ministeria sua conplentes.

Et mulier circa mulieres festinabit, diaconus uero, quoniam uir est, [et] circa uiros: et ad peregrinationem et ministerium et seruitium ad iussionem episcopi paratissimus et mobilis sit. Ita ergo unusquisque proprium agnoscat locum, ⟨et⟩ in festinatione inpleto; et unum sentiendo, unum spirantes et duo corpora in una anima portantes, cognoscite quantum sit ministerium diaconiae, sicuti dicit dominus Deus in euangelio: *Qui uult esse inter uos maior, sit uester diaconus; et qui uult esse inter uos primus, sit uester seruus: sicut filius hominis non uenit ministrari, sed ministrare, et dare animam*

---

6 meliorant ut] Or should we read 'meliorantur'? (cf. *Reg. S. Bened.* xxxvi). 10–11 quae iam non possunt] τοῖς ἀδυνάτοις *AC* (without reference to women). 15 mobilis] 'mobiles' renders εὔκυλτοι in *Apost. Ch. Order* (Hauler lxv 23). *AC* has not the present context. 17 duo] 'dño' cod. 17–18 duo corpora ... portantes] 'one soul dwelling in two bodies' Syr., which seems more probable. *AC* omits the phrase.

ransom for many. So ought you the deacons also to do, if it fall to you to lay down your life for your brethren in the ministry which is due to them. For neither did our Lord and Saviour Himself disdain (to be) ministering to us, as it is written in Isaiah: *To justify the righteous, who hath per-* *formed well a service for many.* If then the Lord of heaven and earth *performed a service* for us, and bore and endured everything for us, how much more ought we to do the like for our brethren, that we may imitate Him. For we are imitators of Him, and hold the place of Christ. And again in the Gospel you find it written how our Lord *girded a linen cloth about his loins and cast water into a wash-basin*, while we reclined (at supper), and drew nigh *and washed the feet of* us all *and wiped them with the cloth.* Now this He did that He might show us (an example of) charity and brotherly love, that we also should do in like manner one to another. If then our Lord did thus, will you, O deacons, hesitate to do the like for them that are sick and infirm, you who are workmen of the truth, and bear the likeness of Christ? Do you therefore minister with love, and neither murmur nor hesitate; otherwise you will have ministered as it were for men's sake and not for the sake of God, and you will receive your reward according to your ministry in the day of judgement. It is required of you deacons therefore that you visit all who are in need, and inform the bishop of those who are in distress; and you shall be his soul and his mind; and in all things you shall be taking trouble and be obedient to him.

---

5 Isa. liii 11.   11 Joh. xiii 4 f.   16 Cf. Joh. xiii 14 f.

1–3 if... due to them] Cf. Lat. *AC*, which suggest 'and if... due to them, do not hesitate'.   4 disdain (to be) ministering] lit. 'disdain while ministering': *AC* has ἐδίστασεν, otherwise altering (cf. Lat.).   6–7 Lord of heaven and earth] ὁ κύριος τοῦ οὐρανοῦ καὶ τῆς γῆς *AC*.   12 *wash-basin*] The word in *syr. sin.* and Aphraates.   19 workmen of the truth] ἐργάται ὄντες ἀληθείας *AC*.   26–28 and... obedient to him] εὔσκυλτοι καὶ εὐήκοοι εἰς πάντα ὄντες αὐτῷ *AC*.

suam redemptionem pro multis. Ita ergo et uos diaconos oportet facere, [XXXVI] ut si necessitas uos exegerit et animam pro fratre ponere per ministerium uestrum, ponatis. Nolite dubitare: nec enim dominus et saluator noster haesitabat seruiens nobis, sicuti et per Eseiam mandatum est: *Iustificare iustum bene seruientem multis.* Si ergo dominus caeli et terrae nobis seruiit et omnia passus est propter nos et sustinuit, quomodo non magis nos oportet hoc facere pro fratribus, quia discipuli eius sumus et locum Christi sortiti? Nam et in euangelio inuenietis scriptum, quomodo dominus noster *succingens se linteum et accipiens in pelue aquam* recumbentibus omnibus nobis ueniens *lauit pedes* nostros *et detersit de linteo.* Hoc autem faciens ostendebat fraternam caritatem, ut et nos inuicem hoc faciamus. Si ergo dominus hoc fecit, uos, diacones, nolite dubitare ut super inpotentes et infirmos hoc faciatis, quia operarii ueritatis estis, Christi exemplo succincti. Ministrate igitur cum dilectione, non murmurantes nec dubitantes: nam si ita agitis, secundum hominem facitis ea et non secundum Deum, et mercedem uestram similem diaconiae uestrae accipie[n]tis in die uisitationis. Oportet ergo uos diacones uisitare omnes qui egent: et de his qui tribulantur renuntiate episcopo. Et debes anima eius esse, et eri[ti]s ad omnia excussior et obaudiens ei.

2–4 ut si . . . Nolite dubitare] Hauler punctuates 'ponere, per ministerium uestrum ponatis nolite dubitare'. *AC* reads κἂν δέῃ ψυχὴν ὑπὲρ ἀδελφοῦ ἀποθέσθαι, μὴ διστάσωσιν· οὐδὲ γάρ κτλ. This suggests that we should read 'et si necessitas . . . ponere per ministerium uestrum, nolite dubitare: nec enim', etc., and regard 'ponatis' as a duplicate rendering of ἀποθέσθαι.   9 discipuli] 'imitators' Syr.: cf. μιμηταὶ ὀφείλοντες αὐτοῦ εἶναι *AC*.   15–16 super inpotentes et infirmos] 'superinponentes et infirmis' cod.   23 excussior] εὔσκυλτοι *AC* (all in plur., as Syr.).

CHAPTER XVII
On the upbringing of Orphan Children

[iv. 1] Now if any one of the children of Christians be an orphan, whether boy or (p. 73) girl, it is well that, if there be one of the brethren who has no children, he should adopt the child in the place of children. And whoever has a son, let him adopt a girl; and when her time is come, let him give her to him to wife, that his work may be completed in the ministry of God. But if there be any who are unwilling to do thus because they would please men, and by reason of their riches are ashamed of orphan members: they who are such shall arrive at †this very pass, and therein† shall spend what they have spared; *and that which the saints have not eaten, the Assyrians shall eat: and their land strangers shall devour before their eyes.*

[iv. 2] Do you therefore, O bishops, take pains over their upbringing, so that nothing may be wanting to them. And when a virgin's time is come, give her in marriage to one of the brethren. But when a boy is being brought up, let him learn a craft; and when he is become a man, let him receive the wage that is worthy of his craft, and let him fashion for himself the implements required for his craft, and not henceforth be a burden upon the love of the brethren, which was shown him without guile and without partiality.

---

6 Cf. Ecclus. vii 25.   11 ?   12 Isa. i 7.

---

6 that his work, etc.] i.e. the father's: there appears to be an allusion to Ecclus. vii 25 ἔκδου θυγατέρα, καὶ ἔσῃ τετελεκὼς ἔργον μέγα. This has not escaped the author of *AC*, who supplies the adj. 'great': τοῦτο γὰρ οἱ ποιοῦντες ἔργον μέγα ἐπιτελοῦσιν.   10 at this very pass] lit. 'to these very-things'. But Syr. has misunderstood the Gk., for *AC* has αὐτῷ δὲ ἐμπεσεῖται τοιοῦτος, ὅστις αὐτοῦ δαπανήσει τὴν φειδώ (cf. Lat.)   11-12 *and ... shall eat*] From an unknown source (see Resch p. 314): (τὸ εἰρημένον)· ἃ οὐκ ἔφαγον ἅγιοι, ταῦτα φάγονται Ἀσσύριοι *AC*.   14-15 over their upbringing] lit. 'how they may be brought up' (H): 'how they may behave' S: περὶ τῆς ἀνατροφῆς αὐτῶν *AC*.   18 and ... a man] om. Lat.: ἵνα ὅταν

Si quis autem orfanus fuerit de Christianis, puer uel uirgo, bonum quidem est si quis fratrum, non habens filium, puerum habuerit in locum filii. Uirginem uero [XXXVII] accipiat qui habet puerum, id est filium, qui tempore nuptiarum possit
5 eam accipere : et sic opera eius consummata est ad ministerium Dei. Si qui[s] autem non sunt tales, sed ambulant ut hominibus placeant, confusionem habentes propter diuitias suas, et contemnunt membra orfanitatis : ipsi in talibus incident qui abundantiam eorum consumant : *Quae enim non manducarunt*
10 *sancti, manducarunt Assyrii : et regionem uestram in conspectu uestro alienigine consummabunt eam.*

Uos ergo, episcopi, solliciti estote de educatione eorum, ut nihil eis desit. Et uirginem, quamdiu uellit nubi, date fratri. Puer[um] autem accipiens substantiam, artem discat, ut merce-
15 dem dignam accipiat per artem, ut possit construere sibi et ea quae ad artem necessaria sunt instrumenta, et iam non grauet eam quae ⟨a⟩ fratribus in eum facta est sine dolo caritas.

---

4 puerum, id est filium] υἱόν *AC*: but *Didasc.* would seem to have had παῖδα or τέκνον.   10 *manducarunt*] Perhaps an error for 'manducabunt' (cf. Syr. and *AC*).

δεξιῶς τὴν τεχνὴν κατορθώσῃ *AC*.   20–22 and not henceforth, etc.] ὅπως μηκέτι βαρύνῃ τὴν τῶν ἀδελφῶν ἀνυπόκριτον εἰς αὐτὸν ἀγάπην *AC*. I have made a slight correction in Syr., which has 'with whom he was' for 'which was shown him'.

[iv. 3] And truly blessed is every one that is able to help himself, and shall not straiten the place of the orphan and the widow and the stranger. For woe from God to them that have, and receive in falsehood, ⟨or are able to help themselves and (yet) receive;⟩ for every one of those who receive shall give an account to the Lord God in the day of judgement, how he received. If a man has received on account of a fatherless childhood, or on account of indigence in old age, or on account of infirmity and sickness, or on account of the rearing of children, he shall even be praised: for he is esteemed as the altar of God, therefore shall he be honoured of God. For he did not receive idly; because he was praying diligently (and) unremittingly at all times for those who give; for his prayer, †which is his strength†, he offered as his payment. Those then who are such shall be declared blessed by God in the life everlasting.

[iv. 4] But those who have, and receive under pretence, or else are slothful, and instead of working and helping others rather themselves receive, shall be held to account for that which they receive, because they have straitened the place of the faithful poor. For every one who has some possession, and neither gives to others nor (p. 74) uses it himself, lays up for himself a perishable treasure on earth; and he has inherited the place of the snake lying upon the treasure, and will come in danger of being reckoned with him. For whoever has, and receives in falsehood, puts his faith not in God but in the Mammon of iniquity; and for the gain of avarice he holds the word in

---

1-7 Hermas *Mand.* ii 5-6, *Didache* i 5.   17 Hermas *Mand.* ii 5.
22 Mt. vi 19.   26 Lk. xvi 9.

1-7 This passage is discussed in *J. T. S.* xxiv 148 ff. (Jan. 1923). The main source is certainly Hermas, but the *Didache* also has contributed certain features, notably the 'Woe' to those who receive.   1 truly blessed] Cf. *Didache* i 5 μακάριος ὁ διδοὺς κατὰ τὴν ἐντολήν.   3 For woe, etc.] Cf. *Didache* (*ibid.*) οὐαὶ τῷ λαμβάνοντι: οὐαὶ τοῖς ἔχουσιν καὶ ἐν ὑποκρίσει λαμβάνουσιν *AC*.   4-5 ⟨or ... receive⟩] Supplied from Lat.: ἢ δυναμένοις βοηθεῖν ἑαυτοῖς καὶ λαμβάνειν παρ' ἑτέρων βουλομένοις *AC* (but in place of the last five words Lat. has only 'et accipiunt' = καὶ λαμβάνουσιν, i. e. the participle).   5-7 for ... how he received] ἑκάτερος γὰρ ἀποδώσει λόγον κυρίῳ τῷ θεῷ ἐν ἡμέρᾳ κρίσεως *AC*: cf. Herm. *Mand.* ii 5 οἱ οὖν λαμβάνοντες ἀποδώσουσιν λόγον τῷ θεῷ, διατί ἔλαβον καὶ εἰς τί.   7 If a man has

DIDASCALIA APOSTOLORUM

Nam uere beatus est qui potest iubare se, ut non tribulet locum orfani, peregrini et uiduae: haec autem gratia a Deo est. Uae autem his qui habent, et cum dolo accipiunt, aut qui possunt sibi iubare, et accipiunt. Unusquisque uero de acci-
5 pientibus dabit rationem domino Deo in die iudicii, quare acceperit. Si enim in orfanitate constitutus [est] aut in paupertate, aut per senectutis defectionem aut propter egritudinis infirmitatem aut propter filiorum, quia multi sunt, nutrimenta, accipit: qui talis, inquit, est et laudabitur; altaris enim
10 Dei deputatus [XXXVIII] est a Deo, et honorabitur, quoniam sine dubitatione pro his qui dant illi frequenter orat, et non otiose accipiebat, sed pro eo quod dabatur illi, merces, quantum uirtus illius admittebat, ⟨dabat per orationem suam⟩. Hii igitur in aeterna uita a Deo beatificabuntur.

15 Qui habent autem et in hypocrisi accipiunt, aut iterum cum sunt pigri, et cum debeant operari et iuuare sibi et aliis, ipsi accipientes praestabunt rationem, quoniam pauperorum fidelium grauarent locum. Qui enim habet pecunias et non erogat eas aliis neque ipse utitur, sed thensaurizat thensaurum
20 sibi qui perit, consimilabitur serpenti super thensaurum dormienti, et periclitatur per momenta ut cum thensauro suo deputetur. Qui autem habet, ⟨et accipit⟩ in hypocrisi[m], non credidit Deo sed iniquo mammonae: lucri causa uerbum in

---

12 eo] 'id' cod. merces] 'mercis' cod.: τὸν μισθόν *AC*. 13 ⟨dabat... suam⟩] διδοὺς διὰ τῆς προσευχῆς *AC* (cf. Syr.). 16 sibi] om. *AC* Syr. 17-18 quoniam... grauarent] *AC* substitutes ὅτι πενήτων ἥρπασε ψωμόν (cf. Job xxii 7): 'grauarent' should prob. be 'grauarunt'. 20 consimilabitur serpenti] τόπον ὄφεως κεκλήρωται *AC* (= Syr.). 20-21 durmienti cod. 21 per momenta ut cum thensauro suo] 'with him' Syr.: *AC* has not the clause. 22 See Syr. and l. 15 above.

---

received, etc.] Cf. *Didache* εἰ μὲν γὰρ χρείαν ἔχων λαμβάνει κτλ. 14 which is his strength] ὅση δύναμις *AC* (= Lat.), which Syr. has strangely mistranslated. 14-15 Those then, etc.] ὁ τοιοῦτος οὖν ἐν τῇ αἰωνίῳ ζωῇ ὑπὸ θεοῦ μακαρισθήσεται *AC*. 17-20 But those ... they receive] ὁ δὲ ἔχων καὶ ἐν ὑποκρίσει λαμβάνων ἢ δι' ἀργίαν, ἀντὶ τοῦ ἐργαζόμενον βοηθεῖν καὶ ἑτέροις, δίκην ὀφλήσει τῷ θεῷ *AC*: cf. Herm. *Mand*. ii 5 οἱ δὲ ἐν ὑποκρίσει λαμβάνοντες τίσουσιν δίκην. 17 under pretence] S (but meaning here doubtful): 'by craft' H: 'by imposture' BC, S marg.

hypocrisy, and he is fulfilled in unbelief. Now such a one will come in danger of being reckoned with the unbelievers. But he who gives simply to every man, does well in giving, and he is innocent. He also who receives on account of distress, and uses sparingly those things which he has received, has received well; and he shall be praised by God in the life and rest everlasting.

CHAPTER XVIII

That it is not right to receive gifts of alms from reprehensible persons.

[iv. 5] Do you the bishops and the deacons be constant therefore in the ministry of the altar of Christ,—we mean the widows and the orphans,—so that with all care and with all diligence you make it your endeavour to search out concerning the things that are given, (and to learn) of what manner is the conversation of him, or of her, who gives for the nourishment—we say again—of 'the altar'. For when widows are nourished from (the fruits of) righteous labour, they will offer a holy and acceptable ministry before Almighty God through His beloved Son and His holy Spirit: to whom be glory and honour for evermore.

Make it your care and endeavour therefore to minister to widows out of the ministry of a clean conscience, that what they ask and request may be granted them at once upon their praying for it. But if there be bishops who are careless and give no heed to these matters, through respect of persons, or for the sake of filthy lucre, or because they neglect to make

---

2-4 Cf. Hermas *Mand.* ii 4-6, *Didache* i 5.

2-4 But he ... is innocent] Cf. Herm. *Mand.* ii 6 ὁ οὖν διδοὺς ἀθῷός ἐστιν : and *Didache* i 5 μακάριος ὁ διδοὺς ... ἀθῷος γάρ ἐστιν.   6 praised] Or 'glorified' (cf. Lat.).   8 bishops] CH : sing. S.   13-14 nourishment ... 'the altar'] Flemming places a full stop after 'nourishment'; but this, though it does not alter the general sense, interferes with the con-

DIDASCALIA APOSTOLORUM 157

hypocrisi porta[n]t, et est repletus incredulitate. Qui talis ergo fuerit, periclitabitur et deputabitur cum infidelibus in condemnatione. Qui ergo dat simpliciter omnibus, bene dat, sicut est illi, et est innocens. Qui autem propter tribulationem
5 accipit, †se pascet scitus et† bene accipit, et a Deo in uita aeterna constitutus glorificabitur.

Episcopi ergo et diacones, obseruate altario Christi, id est uiduis et orfanis, cum omni diligentia, curam facientes de his quae accipiuntur cum scrupulositate, qualis est ille qui dat, aut
10 illa quae dat, ut adescentur. Iterum adque iterum dicimus, quoniam altare de laboribus iustitiae accipere debet . . .

2–3 in condemnatione] om. Syr.   3–4 sicut est illi] om. Syr.   5 se pascet scitus] ' uses sparingly ' Syr., which would suggest ' si parce utitur, bene ' etc.   8 curam facientes] After this some verb like 'exquirere' seems to be wanted.   10 adescentur] sc. the widows and orphans, if the plural be right. The verb 'adescare', according to Du Cange, answers to ψωμίζω, to feed by putting small bits into the mouth.   Iterum, etc.] Syr. would suggest that the Latin translator has failed to understand his text at this point, or that Lat. itself is corrupt. Substantial agreement with Syr. would be reached if we might correct: ' ut adescetur, iterum adque iterum dicimus, ⟨altare⟩, quoniam altare ', etc.

struction. The writer insists on his identification of widows and orphans with the altar, and so explains how it is that he can speak of the 'nourishment' of the altar.   16–18 through, etc.] διὰ τοῦ ἠγαπημένου υἱοῦ αὐτοῦ Ἰησοῦ Χριστοῦ τοῦ κυρίου ἡμῶν, δι' οὗ ἡ δόξα τῷ θεῷ ἐν πνεύματι καὶ ἀληθείᾳ εἰς τοὺς αἰῶνας· ἀμήν AC.   17 to whom] In the singular.

inquiry; they shall render no ordinary account. [iv. 6] For they receive, forsooth, to administer for the nourishment of orphans and widows, from rich persons who keep men shut up in prison, or ill-treat their slaves, or behave with cruelty in their cities, or oppress the poor; or from the lewd, and those who abuse their bodies; or from evildoers; or from forgers; or from dishonest advocates, or (p. 75) false accusers; or from hypocritical lawyers; or from painters of pictures; or from makers of idols; or from workers of gold and silver and bronze (who are) thieves; or from dishonest tax-gatherers; or from spectators of shows; or from those who alter weights or measure deceitfully; or from inn-keepers who mingle water (with their wine); or from soldiers who act lawlessly; or from murderers; or from spies who procure condemnations; or from any Roman officials, who are defiled with wars and have shed innocent blood without trial: perverters of judgement who, in order to rob them, deal unjustly and deceitfully with the peasantry and with all the poor; and from idolaters; or from the unclean; or from those who practise usury, and extortioners. Now they who nourish widows from these (sources) shall be found guilty in judgement in the day of the Lord; for the Scripture has said: *Better is a supper of herbs with love and amity than the slaughter of fatted oxen with hatred.* For if a widow be nourished with bread only from the labour of righteousness, it shall even be abundant for her; but if much be given her from (the proceeds) of iniquity it shall be insufficient for her. But again, if she be nourished from (the proceeds) of iniquity, she cannot offer her ministry and her intercession

---

22 Prov. xv 17.

1 ff. To the references supplied by Funk (p. 224) in illustration of this passage may be added the *Syntagma doctrinae*, ascribed to St. Athanasius, c. 8. The author knew the *Didache*, and shows acquaintance also with the *Didascalia*, but whether in its original form or in the *AC* recension, I cannot determine.   6 forgers] lit. 'those who subtract and add', i. e. perhaps those who falsify accounts or other documents: $ῥᾳδιουργούς$ *AC*. 11–12 alter ... deceitfully] $ζυγοκρούστας καὶ δολομέτρας$ *AC*.   14 spies ... condemnations] lit. 'spies (*speculatores*) of condemnation'.   17–18 the peasantry] The Latin word *pagani*, which Flemming translates 'the heathen'.   22 The text of the quotation is influenced by Pesh.

with purity before God; and even though she be righteous and pray for the wicked, her intercession for them will not be heard, but that for herself alone; for God makes trial of the hearts in judgement, and receives intercessions with discernment. But if they pray for those who have sinned and repent, their prayers will be heard. But those who are in sin, and do not repent, not only are they not heard when they pray, but they even call to remembrance their transgressions before the Lord.

[iv. 7] Wherefore, O bishops, fly and avoid such ministrations; for it is written: *There shall not go up upon the altar of the Lord (that which cometh) of the price of a dog, or of the hire of a harlot.* For if widows pray for fornicators and transgressors through your blindness, and be not heard, not receiving their requests, you will perforce bring blasphemy upon the word through your evil management, as though God were not good and ready to give.

Take good heed therefore that you minister not to the altar (p. 76) of God out of the ministrations of transgression. For you have no pretext to say, 'We do not know'; for you have heard that which the Scripture saith: *Depart from an evil man, and thou shalt not fear; and trembling shall not come nigh unto thee.* [iv. 8] But if you say: 'These are they alone who give alms; and if we receive not of them, from whence shall the orphans and widows and those in distress be provided?' God saith to you: 'To this end did you receive the gifts of the Levites, the firstfruits and offerings of your people, that you might be sustained and even have over and above, that you might not be constrained to receive from evil persons.' But if the Churches are so poor that those in want must needs be supported by such, it were better for you rather to be wasted with famine than to receive from evil persons.

Search out and make trial, therefore, that you may be receiving from the faithful, who communicate with the

---

10 Deut. xxiii 18.   20 Isa. liv 14.

13–14 be not heard, not receiving their requests] The sense suggests 'be not heard: whereas they do not receive', etc., but the punctuation and construction are against this.   24 be provided] lit. 'be ministered to': ὑπηρετηθήσονται *A C*.

Churches and conduct themselves well, (wherewithal) to nourish those in distress, and may not receive from those who are expelled from the Church until they are found worthy to be members of the Church. But if you are in want, tell the brethren, and let them treat together and give; and thus perform your ministrations in righteousness. [iv. 9] And teach your people and tell them that it is written: *Honour the Lord with (the fruits of) righteous labour, and with the chiefest of all your increase.* Wherefore, nourish and clothe those in want from the righteous labour of the faithful; and those things which are given by them, as we have already said, bestow for the ransom of the faithful; and redeem slaves and captives and prisoners, and those who are treated with violence, and those condemned by the mob, and those sentenced to fight with beasts, or to the mines, or to exile, and those condemned to the games. And let the deacons go in to those who are in distress, and let them visit each one and provide him with what he lacks.

[iv. 10] But if ever it should happen that you are constrained and receive unwillingly some pieces of money from any evil person, you shall not employ them for (the purchase of) food; but if they be few, spend them on firewood for yourselves and for the widows, lest a widow, receiving of them, be forced to buy her some food with them. And so, unsullied by iniquity, the widows will pray and receive from God all good things for which they ask and make petition, all of them (p. 77) together and each one severally: and you also will not be reproached with these sins.

7 Prov. iii 9.

---

3 expelled from the Church] ἀποσυναγώγων *AC* (see already p. 141). 12 ransom] lit. 'purchase', which is explained in S marg. by the word 'redemption'. Funk renders 'dispertite *in tempore* ad redemptionem', misreading *zebhna* as *zabhna* ('time'), and incorporating the marginal gloss. 13 treated with violence] ὑπηρεαζομένους *AC*. 14 by the mob] CH ('by the *demos*'): 'lawlessly' ('without *nomos*') S; but S marg. adds 'to the multitude'. 14-15 to fight with beasts] lit. 'to κυνήγιον'. 16 games] *ludi* transliterated. 24 unsullied by] I follow the reading of C: H gives much the same sense with a different verb: S has, without sense, 'not prevailing over', by corruption of the verb in C. Flemming and Funk attempt to render S.

CHAPTER XIX

That it is a duty to take care of those who for the name of Christ suffer affliction as Martyrs.

[v. 1] You shall not turn away your eyes from a Christian who for the name of God and for His faith and love is condemned to the games, or to the beasts, or to the mines; but of your labour and of the sweat of your face do you send to him
5 for nourishment, and for a payment to the soldiers that guard him, that he may have relief and that care may be taken of him, so that your blessed brother be not utterly afflicted. For let him that is condemned for the name of the Lord God be esteemed of by you as a holy martyr, an angel of God, or God
10 upon earth, even one that is spiritually clothed with the Holy Spirit of God; for through him you see the Lord our Saviour, inasmuch as he has been found worthy of the incorruptible crown, and has renewed again the witness of (His) passion. To those therefore who are bearing witness it is the duty of
15 all you the faithful to minister with care, and to refresh them out of your possessions through your bishop. But if there be a man who has nothing, let him fast, and that which would have been spent by him that day let him give for his brethren. But if thou art rich, thou must minister to them according to
20 thy power, or even give thy whole possession and redeem them from bonds; for they it is who are worthy of God, and the sons who perform His will; as the Lord has said: *Every*

---

22 Mt. x 32.

CHAP. XIX. *AC* places here ch. xxii (acc. to Syr.), on the upbringing of children; and certainly this is a more fitting place for it. Funk follows the arrangement of *AC*, so that in his edition the present chapter begins on p. 236, while ch. xxii begins on p. 230.   10-11 one that is... Spirit of God] δοχεῖον τοῦ ἁγίου πνεύματος *AC*.   16-18 But if... his brethren] εἰ δὲ οὐκ ἔχει τις, νηστεύσας τὸ τῆς ἡμέρας καὶ μερίσας τοῦτο ἐκταξάτω τοῖς ἁγίοις *AC*: cf. Hermas *Sim.* v 3. 7 ἐν ἐκείνῃ τῇ ἡμέρᾳ ᾗ νηστεύεις ... ἐκ τῶν ἐδεσμάτων σου ὧν ἔμελλες τρώγειν συμψηφίσας τὴν ποσότητα τῆς δαπάνης ἐκείνης τῆς ἡμέρας ... δώσεις αὐτὸ χήρᾳ ἢ ὀρφανῷ ἢ ὑστερουμένῳ. Comp. also Aristides *Apol.* xv (Syriac version) 'And if there is among them a man who is poor or needy, and they have no superfluity of necessaries, they fast two or three days that they may supply the needy with their necessary food.'

one that shall confess me before men, I also will confess him before my Father. And you shall not be ashamed to go to them where they are imprisoned. And when you do these things, you shall inherit everlasting life, for you become sharers of their martyrdom. For let us learn how our Lord said in the Gospel: *Come unto me, all ye blessed of my Father, inherit the kingdom which was prepared for you from before the foundations of the world. For I was hungry, and ye gave me to eat; and I was thirsty, and ye gave me to drink; I was a stranger, and ye gathered me; and I was naked, and ye covered me; I was sick, and ye visited me; and I was in prison, and ye came unto me. Then will the righteous answer and say: Our Lord, when saw we thee hungry, and gave thee to eat? or thirsty, and gave thee to drink?* (p. 78) *or naked, and covered thee? or sick, and did visit thee? or a stranger, and gathered thee? or in prison, and came unto thee? And he will answer and say to them: All that ye did to one of these little and mean ones, ye did it to me.* And then *shall they go into life everlasting.*

[v. 2] But if there be one who is called a Christian, and he fall away and be tempted by Satan, and be convicted of evil deeds and condemned for (his) deeds, whether of theft or murder: avoid such persons, lest any one of you be put on trial by those who seize him. For if one seize thee and question thee, and say to thee: 'Art thou also a Christian, like this man?' thou canst not deny that thou art a Christian, but must needs confess it. But thou wilt not be condemned as a Christian, but punished as a malefactor. For he asks thee whether thou art 'like this man': and thy confession is rendered void. But if thou deny, thou hast also denied the Lord. Therefore avoid them, that you may be without offence. But the faithful who are violently and unjustly seized and imprisoned as evildoers, or even bound, help (as) your members with abundant care and with much pains, that you may deliver them from the hand of evil men. But if any man come near to them and be seized with them, and for no offence suffer

6 Mt. xxv 34-40. 18 Mt. xxv 46.

DIDASCALIA APOSTOLORUM

affliction for his brother's sake, blessed is he in being called a Christian; for he has confessed the Lord, and he shall live before God. For if a man come near to those who are bound for the name of the Lord and be seized with them, he shall be blessed in being found worthy of such company.

[v. 3] And those again who are persecuted for the faith and pass *from city to city*, according to the Lord's command, do you receive and refresh; and when you receive them, rejoice, for you are made sharers of their persecution. For our Lord spoke concerning them in the Gospel thus: *Blessed are ye, when they shall persecute you and revile you for my name's sake.* For when a Christian is persecuted and bears witness and is slain for the faith, he becomes a man of God; and he is now no more persecuted by any man, for he has won him approval of the Lord. [v. 4] But if he deny, and say that he is not a Christian, he shall be called an offence; and (though) not persecuted by men, yet is he (p. 79) cast off by God for his denial; and he shall receive henceforth no portion with the saints in the kingdom everlasting, according to the Lord's promise, but his inheritance shall be with the ungodly. For the Lord God has said: *Whosoever shall deny me and my words before men, or shall be ashamed of me: I also will be ashamed of him, and will deny him before my Father who is in heaven, when I come with power and glory to judge the dead and the living.* And again you find it written: *Every one that loveth his father or his mother more than me, is not worthy of me; and every one that loveth his son or his daughter more than me, is not worthy of me; and every one that taketh not up his cross* rejoicing and glad *and cometh after me, is not worthy of me; and every one that shall lose his life for my sake, shall find it; and every one that shall*

---

7 Mt. x 23, xxiii 34.   10 Mt. v 11.   13 Cf. 1 Tim. vi 11, 2 Tim. iii 17.
21 Lk. ix 26, Mt. x 33.   24 Cf. Mt. xxiv 30, 2 Tim. iv 1.   25 Mt. x 37–39.   30 Mt. xvi 25 f.

---

17 not persecuted] H : S omits the negative: οὐχ ὑπ' ἀνθρώπων ἔτι μισούμενος, ἀλλ' ὑπὸ θεοῦ ἀπωσμένος *AC*.   24–25 *when I come ... living*]. With this we must compare the creed-passage at the end of the work (p. 258) 'who cometh with power and glory to judge the dead and the living'.   31 *life*] lit. 'soul', and so in the following lines.

save his life, by denying, *shall lose it. For what shall a man be profited if he acquire the whole world, and forfeit his soul? or what shall he give in exchange for his soul?* And again: *Fear not them that kill the body, but are not able to kill the soul; but fear me rather, that am able to destroy soul and body in hell.*

[v. 5] Now every one who learns any craft watches his master and sees how by his skill and his knowledge he executes the work of his craft; and he himself copies him and executes the work which he has set him, that he may not be ill spoken of by him. But if he abate anything of the (tasks) set him, he is not perfect. We, then, who have our Lord for master and teacher, why do not we imitate His teaching and His conversation? For He left riches and favour, and power and glory, and came thus in poverty; and moreover He parted with Mary His blessed mother, and with His brethren, and with His life itself, and endured persecution even unto the cross. And these things He endured for our sake, that He might redeem us, who are of the People, from the bonds of *the Second Legislation*, of which we have already spoken, and might redeem you also, who are of the Gentiles, from the worship of idols and from all ungodliness, and get you for an inheritance. If then He suffered thus for our sake, to redeem us who believe in Him, and was not ashamed, why do not we also imitate His sufferings, while He gives us endurance?—and this for our own sake,

---

4 Mt. x 28.

---

5 *fear me*, etc.] A striking alteration of the Gospel words, due no doubt to the author himself. 10–11 be ill spoken of] lit. 'hear badly from', i.e. κακῶς ἀκούειν. 12 perfect] BCS: 'a disciple' H. 19 from the bonds] + 'and from the guilt' H. of the Second Legislation] ܒܝܬ؟ ܕܚܒ؟ (BHS: C is wanting), i.e. lit. 'of house (*or* place) of trees', which is probably a corruption of something else. We should expect, on the analogy of other passages, 'from the bonds of the Second Legislation', and Flemming accordingly emends ܕܚܒܘܫܝܐ. But here there is the difficulty that Syr. nowhere else uses the one word *tenyāna* (= *secundatio*) for the Deuterosis, but always *tenyān nāmōsa* (*secundatio legis*), and it is hard to conceive how any scribe could have produced out of this the remarkable phrase now in the MSS. 20 of which we have already spoken] For a previous discussion of the Second Legislation see pp. 12–15.

that we may be delivered from the death of fire. For He endured for our sake, but we for our own sake. Or has our Lord any need that (p. 80) we should suffer for Him? Rather it is this alone that He desires, to make proof of the love of our faith, and of our free will. [v. 6] Let us then part with our parents and our kinsfolk, and with all that is in this world, and even with our life.

We must indeed pray that we *come not into temptation*; yet if we be called to martyrdom, let us confess when we are interrogated, and when we suffer let us endure, and when we are afflicted let us rejoice, and when we are persecuted let us not grieve; for so doing, not only shall we deliver ourselves from hell, but we shall also teach those who are young in the faith, and the hearers, to do the like: and they shall live before God. But if we fail in faith towards the Lord, and deny through the infirmity of the body—as our Lord said: *The spirit is willing and ready, but the body is weak*—we shall not only destroy ourselves, but shall kill also our brethren with us. For when they see our denial, they will think that they have been made disciples of an erring doctrine; and when they stumble, we shall render an account for them as well as for ourselves, every one of us, to the Lord in the day of judgement.

But if thou be taken and brought before the authority, and deny the hope that thou hast towards the Lord by thy holy faith, and thou be set at large to-day, but to-morrow fall sick of a fever and take to thy bed; or if thy stomach ail thee and retain no food, but vomit it out with grievous pains; or thou be afflicted with a disease of the belly, or with a disease in one of thy members; or thou bring up blood and bile from within thee by reason of dire disorders; or thou have an ulcer in one of thy members and be cut by the hands of physicians, and

---

8 Mt. xxvi 41 (cf. vi 13). 17 *Ibid.*

4–5 Rather ... free will] μόνον δὲ τὸ τῆς πίστεως ἡμῶν γνήσιον ἐπιζητεῖ καὶ αὐθαίρετον *AC*. 13–14 young in the faith ... hearers] i. e. neophytes and catechumens: τοὺς νεοφωτίστους ... καὶ τοὺς κατηχουμένους *AC*. 17 *willing and ready*] So Ephraim on the Diatessaron (Mösinger, p. 231): 'willing' *syr. sin.*: 'ready' *syr. vulg.* *weak*] lit. 'sick' or 'infirm'

die in manifold afflictions and torments: what then will thy denial have availed thee which thou hast denied, O man? For behold, thy soul has inherited pains and afflictions, and thou hast destroyed thy life for ever before God; and thou shalt burn and be tormented without respite everlastingly: even as the Lord has said: *Every one that loveth his life, shall lose it; and every one that shall lose his life for my sake, shall find it.* Now a Christian who denies, loves his life for a little while in this world, that he may not die for the name of the Lord God; but he has destroyed himself for ever in fire, for he has fallen of himself into Gehenna. For Christ has denied him, as He said in the Gospel: *Whosoever shall deny me before men, I also will deny him before my Father who is in heaven*; but those (p. 81) whom the Lord has denied they *put forth and cast into the outer darkness: and there is their weeping and their gnashing of teeth.* For He said: *Every one that loveth his life more than me, is not worthy of me.*

Let us be earnest then to commit ourselves to the Lord God; and if any man be found worthy of martyrdom, let him accept of it with joy, seeing that he has been counted worthy of so great a crown, and that his departure from this world is by martyrdom. For the Lord our Saviour has said: *There is no disciple better than his master: but every one shall be perfected as his master.* Now our Lord consented to all these His sufferings that He might save us; and He submitted to be beaten, and that men should blaspheme Him and spit in His face, and to drink vinegar and gall; and at last He endured even to be hanged upon the cross. Let us therefore, who are His disciples, be also His imitators. For if He bore and endured all things for us, even to the sufferings (of His passion), how much more ought we, for our own sakes, to be

---

6 Mt. x 39.   12 Mt. x 33.   14 Mt. viii 12, xxii 13.   16 Mt. x 37 (cf. Joh. xii 26).   22 Lk. vi 40.

2 O man] Flemming and Funk have strangely misread this simple vocative, taking 'O' for 'or' and treating 'man' *homo*, as if equivalent to 'any man': 'aut alii cuiquam' Funk, and Flemming to the same effect. 4 destroyed thy life] Cf. Hermas *Sim.* viii 6. 6, 7. 5, 8. 2.   6, 7 *life*] lit. 'soul', and so again at l. 17 below.

patient when we suffer? And we ought not to doubt; for so He has promised us, that if we should be burned with coals of fire, while we believe in our Lord Jesus Christ and in God His Father, the Lord God Almighty, and in His Holy Spirit, —to whom be glory and honour for evermore, Amen.—

CHAPTER XX

Concerning the Resurrection of the Dead.

[v. 7] God Almighty will raise us up through God our Saviour, as He has promised. And He will raise us up from the dead even as we are—in this form in which we now are, but in the great glory of everlasting life, with nothing wanting to us. For though we be cast into the depths of the sea, or be scattered by the winds like chaff, we are still within the world; and the whole world itself is inclosed beneath the hand of God. From within His hand therefore will He raise us up: as the Lord our Saviour has said: *A hair of your head shall not perish; but in your patience ye shall possess your souls.*

Now concerning the resurrection, and concerning the glory of the martyrs, the Lord spoke in Daniel thus: *Many that sleep in the breadth of the earth shall rise up in that day: some unto life everlasting, and some unto reproach and shame and dispersion. But they that understand shall shine as the luminaries which are in the heaven; and they that have been strengthened by the word, as the stars of heaven.* As (of) the sun, then, and the moon, (p. 82) the luminaries of heaven,

14 Lk. xxi 18 f.   18 Dan. xii 2 f. (LXX)

---

5 to whom ... Amen] This doxology is a mere parenthesis (comp. pp. 20, 156); the chapter heading has been inserted in the middle of a sentence, of which the apodosis comes with the first words of ch. xx. The words 'God Almighty will raise us up', etc., would be intolerably abrupt in the Syriac as the beginning of a new sentence.   18-23 *Many that sleep*, etc.] This quotation from Daniel follows the LXX, not the more widely used version of Theodotion. *A C* in the main conforms to Theodotion.

(such) glorious light has He promised to give to them *that understand*, and confess His holy name, and bear witness.

But not to the martyrs alone has He promised the resurrection, but to all men; for He speaks thus in Ezekiel: ¹ *The hand of the Lord came upon me: and the Lord brought me forth in the spirit, and set me in the midst of a valley: and it was full of bones. ² And he caused me to pass overagainst them: and they were many, and they were exceeding dry. ³ And he said unto me: Son of man, shall these bones live? And I said: Thou knowest, Lord Adonai. ⁴ And the Lord said unto me: Prophesy unto these bones, and say to them: Ye dry bones, hear the word of the Lord. ⁵ Thus saith the Lord Adonai unto these bones: Behold, I will cause the spirit to enter into you, and ye shall live; ⁶ and I will put sinews upon you, and will build up flesh upon you, and will clothe you with skin; and I will give the spirit in you, and ye shall live: and ye shall know that I am the Lord. ⁷ And I prophesied as he spake unto me. And as I prophesied, there was made a sound and a movement; and the bones drew nigh, bone unto bone. ⁸ And I saw that there came upon them sinews and flesh, and skin was stretched over them above: but there was no spirit in them. ⁹ And the Lord said unto me: Prophesy unto the spirit, and say: Thus saith the Lord Adonai: Come, spirit, from the four winds, and enter into these dead, and they shall live. ¹⁰ And I prophesied, as he spake unto me: and the spirit entered into them, and they lived: and they stood upon their feet in a great army. ¹¹ And the Lord said unto me: Son of man, these bones are the house of Israel; for they say: Our bones are dried up, and our hope is perished, and we are not. ¹² Thus saith the Lord Adonai: Behold, I open your graves, and I will bring you forth from thence, O my people, and will bring you in to the land of Israel; ¹³ and ye shall know that I am the Lord, when I shall open your graves, to bring up my people*

---

4 Ez. xxxvii 1-14.

---

6 *in the spirit*] 'in the way' Syr. (BS: CH have not the passage): ἐν πνεύματι LXX. No doubt ܒܐܘܪܚܐ is only a corruption of ܒܪܘܚܐ.

from the graves. ¹⁴ *And I will give my spirit in you, and ye shall live. And I will cause you to dwell in your land: and ye shall know that I am the Lord, that have spoken and have performed it.*

And all the inhabitants of the earth shall be silent, saith the Lord. And again by Isaiah He said: *All they that sleep and are dead shall rise; and all they that are in the graves shall awake: for thy dew is a dew of healing unto them. But the land of the wicked shall perish.* And many other things also He said by Isaiah and by all the prophets concerning the resurrection and the life everlasting, and concerning the glory of the righteous; and as touching the wicked also, concerning their dishonour and exposure and downfall, and concerning their undoing (p. 83) and overthrow and condemnation. For that which He said, *the land of the wicked shall fall*, He speaks concerning their body; because it is of the earth, and shall be reckoned unto the earth in dishonour. Because they served not God, they shall fall into fire and torment. And in the Twelve Prophets again He speaks thus: *Behold, ye wicked, and see, and understand marvels: and return to corruption. For I do a work in your days, the which if a man recount it unto you, ye will not believe.* Now these things, and many more than these, are spoken concerning those who believe not in the resurrection, and concerning those who deny God, and those who serve not God, and concerning transgressors of the law and the heathen; and when they shall see the glory of the faithful, they will be turned back to be destroyed in fire, because they believed not.

But we have learned and have believed; and by our Lord's resurrection from the dead is made sure to us the resurrection which God, who lies not, has promised us. For our Saviour, by rising Himself first, was made an earnest also of our resurrection. And those also who are called from the Gentiles, and even the heathen, read and hear concerning the resurrec-

---

1 Isa. xxvi 18.   2 Isa. xxvi 19.   15 Habak. i 5 (Acts xiii 41).

1-2 *And all . . . saith the Lord*] om. *AC*. There is some disorder here. The words 'saith the Lord' appear in LXX at the end of the foregoing passage from Ez. xxxvii, but 'And all . . . be silent' are from Isa. xxvi 18 and belong to the following quotation (see Lat.).   1 *shall be silent*] πεσοῦνται LXX (= Lat.).   2 And . . . He said] καὶ διὰ Ἡσαίου φησίν *AC* (after ὅτι ἐγὼ κύριος λελάληκα καὶ ποιήσω of the passage from Ez.): om. Lat. (*ut uid.*)   11 *shall fall*] So here, but at l. 5 above 'shall *perish*': πεσεῖται LXX.   19 spoken concerning] + 'infidelibus uel' Lat.   28 who are called] The participle must be read as passive, *kĕrēn* (cf. Lat.): the active would mean 'who read'.   29 and even the heathen] Not

[XXXIX] ... *dicit dominus.* *Sed cadent inhabitantes: et resurgent mortui, et exurgent qui in monumentis sunt: ros enim quod a te est, sanitas eis est: terra autem impiorum periet.* Multa quidem et alia ⟨tam⟩ per Eseiam quam et per alios pro-
5 fetas dicta sunt de resurrectione et uita permanente in gloria iustorum; et de impiis similiter, et infamia et aeuacuatione ruinae, et de absolutione et condemnatione. Id uero quod dictum est, *terra autem impiorum periet*: id est, corpus eorum, quod de terra est, cum turpitudine in terra deputabitur, propter
10 quod non coloerunt Deum, et in igne cum poena incadent. Nam et in duodecim profetis ita dictum est: *Uidete, contemptores, et respicite, et uidete mirabilia, et auertimini et segregamini: quoniam opus ego operor in diebus uestris, quod non creditis si quis enarrauerit uobis.* Et haec quidem, et ab his
15 pluriora, de infidelibus uel his qui non credunt de resurrectione dicta sunt, et de his qui abnegant et non coluerunt Deum, et de praeuaricatoribus et de gentilibus: quoniam uidebunt gloriam fidelium et auertentur ut depereant in igne infideles.

Nos uero credere didicimus per domini nostri resurrectionem
20 a mortuis, et nostram certam esse †repromissionem,† ⟨quam repromisit nobis⟩ et ipse qui non fallit Deus. Nam et ipse saluator pignus resurrectionis nostrae fuit, cum primus resurrexerit. Nam uos, qui ex gentibus uocati estis, scitis quoniam et gentiles de resurrectione futura legent et audiunt [XL] a

---

1 *dicit dominus*] Perhaps the conclusion of the passage from Ez. xxxvii (see note to Syr.); but possibly '⟨et per Eseiam iterum⟩ dicit dominus', or the like, is to be understood.   20–21 repromissionem ... et ipse] 'repromissione met ipse' Hauler.   We must certainly correct, with the help of Syr. and *AC*, 'resurrectionem ... et ipse'. So Funk, but with omission of 'et': (πιστεύομεν γίνεσθαι) τὴν ἀνάστασιν (καὶ ἐκ τοῦ κυρίου ἀναστάσεως) *AC*.

'(also) auch Heiden (waren)', as Flemming took it.   29 ff. read ... thus] The Syriac order is 'read and hear concerning the resurrection from the Sibyl that which is spoken and proclaimed to them thus'.

tion that which is spoken and proclaimed to them by the Sibyl thus: *When all things have been made dust and ashes, God Most High will allay the fire, even he that kindled it. And then again will God himself raise up the bones and the ashes of men, and will clothe them with their form. For he will raise up men as they were before: and then shall be the judgement, wherein God will judge in the world to come. And the wicked and the ungodly the earth will cover again; (but) the just and the righteous shall live in the living world. And God will give them spirit and grace and life: and then shall they all see one another.*

And not only by the Sibyl, brethren, was the resurrection preached to the Gentiles, but by the holy Scriptures also our Lord proclaimed beforehand, to the Jews and the heathen and Christians at once, and announced the resurrection of the dead which is to be for men; and even by a dumb bird, we mean the Phoenix, which is but one alone, by means whereof God gives us again abundant demonstration of the resurrection. For if he had a mate, many would be seen by men; but now one only is seen, once in five hundred years, which enters Egypt (p. 84) and comes to the altar which is called 'of the Sun', bringing cinnamon. And as he prays toward the East, a fire is kindled of itself and burns him up, and he is reduced to ashes. And from the ashes again there is formed a worm; and it grows in his form and becomes a perfect Phoenix. And then he departs and goes away whence he came.

If then by means of a dumb animal God shows us concerning the resurrection, we who believe in the resurrection and in the promise of God ought much more, as men deemed worthy

---

2 *Orac. Sibyll.* iv 179–185, 187, 189–190 (ed. Geffcken).

3 *Most High*] ἄφθιτος *AC*.   4 *raise up*] Added by the translator, as also 'and' before 'will clothe'.   5 *will clothe . . . their form*] μορφώσει *AC*.   7 *in the world to come*] (κρίνων) ἔμπαλι κόσμον *AC*: rendered as if ἔμπαλι were an adj.   9 *the living*] Added by the translator.   10 *one another*] ἑαυτούς *AC*.   16 For references to the Phoenix in classical and early Christian writers Funk's note may be consulted; here, in addition to 1 Clem. xxv, it is enough to mention Tertullian *de Resurrectione* xiii and Origen *c. Cels.* iv 98.   17 *gives us abundant demonstration*] lit. 'shows us richly': cf. *AC* φασὶ γὰρ ὄρνεόν τι μονογενὲς ὑπάρχειν, πλουσίαν τῆς ἀναστάσεως παρέχον τὴν ἀπόδειξιν. 26–27 *If then . . . the resurrection*] εἰ τοίνυν . . . διὰ τοῦ ἀλόγου ὀρνέου δείκνυται ἡ ἀνάστασις *AC*: cf. 1 Clem. xxvi 1 ὅπου καὶ δι' ὀρνέου δείκνυσιν ἡμῖν τὸ

DIDASCALIA APOSTOLORUM 173

Sybylla illis dictum et praedicatum sic: *Sed cum iam omnia puluis et cinus fuerint facta, et ignem †uitauerit† Deus immortalis, qui etiam accendit: ossa et cinerem ipse Deus iterum* [*est*] *uirorum formabit:* [*in*]*mortales autem iterum statuet, ut ante*
5 *erant. Et tunc iam iudicium erit ipso iudicante Deo, iudicans iterum saeculum. Et eos qui inpie peccauerunt, hos denuo cooperiet terra: quanti autem pie gesserunt, uiuent iterum in mundo, spiritum Deo dante simul et gratiam ipsis piis: omnes etenim tunc se uidebunt.*

10 Non solum ergo, carissimi, a Sybilla dictum est et manifestatum de resurrectione, sed et per sacras scripturas: nam dominus Iudaeis et gentilibus simul etiam Christianis in unum praeadnuntiauit praedicans eam quae a mortuis futura est hominum resurrectio. Nam et per mutum animal, id est per
15 foenicem, quod unicum est, manifestam nobis de resurrectione ostensionem Deus fecit. Nam si esset par aut multi, ipsi multi uelut fantasma uideri poterant hominibus: nunc autem uidetur, cum ingrediatur, quia solum est. Post quingentos enim annos ingreditur in Aegyptum ad eum locum qui uocatur Solis Ara,
20 portans cinnamomum, et orat contra orientem, et succenditur a se ipso et conburitur et fit cinis. De cinere autem fit uermis, et hic uermis crescens deformatur et fit iterum foenix perfectus: et tunc recedit denuo et pergit ibidem unde et uenit.

Si ergo et Deus per mutum animal ita [in] exemplum
25 [XLI] resurrectionis nobis ostendit, multo magis nos credentes resurrectioni et repromissioni Dei, etiamsi martyrium nobis

---

2 *uitauerit*] κοιμίσῃ *AC*. Can the word be a misreading of 'sedauerit'?
4 *uirorum*] ἀνδρῶν *AC*: 'uiuorum' cod.   *inmortales*] βροτούς *AC*.
Hauler and Funk adopt 'in mortales': I prefer to regard '*im*mortal' as the correction of a Latin scribe.   15 manifestam nobis de] 'manifestat nobis di' cod.   16 aut multi] om. Syr.   17 uelut fantasma] om. Syr., and perh. rightly: if the species were common, that would hardly tend to discredit the existence of the Phoenix.   19 locum] om. Syr., also *AC* (ἐπὶ τὸν λεγόμενον ἡλίου βωμόν).   24 in] Hauler and Funk adopt 'id'.
25 credentis cod.

μεγαλεῖον τῆς ἐπαγγελίας αὐτοῦ.   28 ought much more, etc.] In this sentence it has been impossible to follow the involved order of the Syriac clauses, but in other respects the translation is nearly literal.

of so great glory that we should receive an incorruptible crown in the life everlasting, to rejoice, if martyrdom come to us, in the great grace and in the honour and glory of martyrdom for God, and to accept of it joyfully with all our soul, and to believe in the Lord God who will raise us up in glorious light. As in the beginning God commanded by a word, and the world was made, and said: *Let there be light*, and night and day, and heaven and earth and sea, and birds and living creatures of the sea, and creeping things of the earth and four-footed beasts, and trees; and everything was made by His word and established in its nature, as the Scripture has said: these works themselves, which came into being through the obedience which they rendered Him, bear witness to God who made them that by Him they were made from that which was not; and they also show a sign of the resurrection. As then He made every thing, so will He the more rather quicken and raise up man, who is of His own forming. For if from that which was not He fashioned and established the world, much easier is this, that from that which is He should quicken and raise up man, who is the formation of His hands: even as also, in the human seed, He clothes man in the womb with a form and causes him to grow.

If then He raises up all men,—as He said by Isaiah: *All flesh shall see the salvation of God*,—much more will He quicken and raise up the faithful; and (yet more) again will He quicken and raise up the faithful of the faithful, who are the martyrs, and establish them in great glory and make them His counsellors. For to mere disciples, those who believe in Him, He has promised a glory as of the stars; but to the martyrs He has promised to give an everlasting glory, as of the luminaries which fail not, with more abundant light, that they may be shining for all time.

7 Gen. i 3 ff.   23 Isa. xl 5, lii 10.   29 Cf. Dan. xii 3.

5 who will] Or 'that He will': 'quia' Lat.   12 which came into being] om. Lat.: prob. an explanatory addition.   15 As then, etc.] Cf. Aphraates Hom. viii 6 (*de Resurrectione*) 'For in the beginning God created Adam, from the dust He formed him and raised him up. But if, when Adam was not, He made him from nothing, how much easier is it now that He should

superuenerit, quasi qui talem digni sumus adsequi gloriam ut coronam portemus incorruptam in uita aeterna, gaudentes ad tam magnum hoc donum et dignitatem gloriae Dei, id est ad martyrium, properemus, ac libenter illud cum gaudio
5 suscipiamus, credentes domino Deo, quia per gloriam suam clarificatos resuscitauit nos. Sicuti in principio Deus praecipiens uerbo mundum construxit dicens: *Fiat lumen*, dies, nox, caelum, terra, mare, uolatilia, natatilia, repentia et quadrupedia, arbusta, et uniuersa per uerbum eius creata sunt
10 et deformata, sicuti et scriptura significat: et ipsa creatura per oboedientiam testimonium Deo, qui ea fecit, perhibet de eo quod facta sunt ex non constitutis, resurrectionem significantia. Sicuti ergo omnia fecit, ita et hominem, qui et plasma eius propria est, multo magis uiuificans resuscitauit.
15 Si enim ex non constitutis mundum construxit, facilius ex constitutis hominem, cum sit plasma eius, uiuificans resuscitauit, sicuti et in semine hominem deformans in utero perfectum reddet.

Si igitur omnes homines resuscitat, ut dicit per Eseiam:
20 *Quoniam uidebit omnis caro salutarem Dei*, multo magis saluat ⟨et⟩ uiuificat fideles suos; et iterum fidelium fideliores constitutos martyres, in maiori gloria fortiores suscitans [XLII] consiliarios adoptauit sibi et saluabit eos. Quoniam eis quidem, qui simpliciter discipuli eius fideles sunt, gloriam stillarum
25 habere eos pollicitus est: martyribus uero luminarium non deficientium gloriam aeterni luminis fulgentem per omne tempus ⟨se⟩ praestaturum repromisit.

6 resuscitauit] With *u* for *b*: and twice again below.   10 et ipsa] I understand that the apodosis begins here: cf. Syr.   creatura] 'these works' Syr. The Gk. may have been κτίσματα, which would account for the fluctuation between sing. and plur. in the following verbs, and for the neuter plur. 'ea .. facta sunt'.   20-21 saluat ⟨et⟩] Unless we should read 'saluans'.   23 adoptauit] With *u* for *b*.

raise him up: for lo, he is but sown in the earth.'   29 has promised] sc. in Dan. xii 3, quoted above at p. 167.

As disciples (p. 85) of Christ, therefore, let us believe that we shall receive from Him all the good things which He has promised us in the life everlasting; and so let us imitate all His teaching and His patience. For as touching His birth from a virgin, and His coming, and the will of His passion, we have assurance through His holy Scriptures, even as the prophets foreannounced and foretold all things concerning His coming, and all have been accomplished and established in our hearts: for even the demons, trembling before His name, lauded His advent. Concerning those, therefore, which have come to pass of the things we have already mentioned, you also have believed and have been fully assured; but we yet more, who were with Him and have seen Him with our eyes, and have eaten with Him, and have been made the associates and witnesses of His coming. As touching also His great and unspeakable gifts which He is yet to give us, according as He has promised, let us believe and hope that we shall receive them; for (by this) is all our faith put to the proof, if we believe in (those) His promises which are yet to be (fulfilled).

If then we are called to martyrdom for His name, and go forth from the world confessing (Him), we shall be pardoned all sins and offences, and shall be found pure. For He spoke in David concerning the martyrs thus: *Blessed are they whose iniquity is forgiven, and whose sins are covered. Blessed is the man to whom the Lord shall not impute his sins.* [v. 8] Blessed therefore are the martyrs, and clear of all offences; for they have been removed and taken away from all iniquity: as He said in Isaiah of Christ and of His martyrs: *Behold, the righteous (man) is perished, and there is none that understandeth; and godly men are taken away, and no man layeth it to heart. For the righteous is gathered up from the presence of evil: and his burial shall be in peace.* [v. 9] Now these things are said of those who bear witness for the name of Christ.

9 Cf. Ja. ii 19.   13 Cf. Acts x 41, 1 Joh. i 1.   24 Ps. xxxi (xxxii) 1 f.
29 Isa. lvii 1 f.

---

8 established] Or 'verified'.   22 confessing (Him)] lit. 'with confession'.

Sicut discipuli ergo fideles Christi omnia credamus ab eo nos accepturos quae repromissa nobis sunt bona in uitam aeternam, si imitati doctrinam eius et patientiam fuerimus. De generatione enim eius quae per uirginem fuit, et de aduentu eius et
5 uoluntate passionis persuasimur per diuinas scripturas, quomodo profetae omnia praenuntiabant de aduentu eius, de quibus manifestum est nos persuasos cordibus confortari : sicuti et demones, trementes nomen eius, magnificabant aduentum eius. De his uero quae iam fluxerunt, de quibus et
10 praediximus, et uos persuasi estis : nos enim abundantius, ⟨qui⟩ perspeximus et conuersati sumus cum eo et concibauimus, et participes et testes aduentus eius fuimus. Ea uero quae futura sunt de repromissionibus eius magna et inenarrabilia dona, accipi sperantes credimus : omnis enim fidis nostra in hoc est,
15 cum probemus omnes repromissiones eius et credimus ueras esse eas.

Nam et si ad martyrium uocati in confessione nominis eius exierimus de hoc mundo, innocentes inueniemur et purgati ab omni delicto et ab omni peccato, quoniam dicit in Dauid de
20 martyribus ita : *Beati quorum remisse sunt* ⟨*iniquitates*⟩ . . .

10 enim] We expect 'autem'.   ⟨qui⟩] With Syr.   11 conciuauimus cod.   19 delecto cod.

But again, sins are *forgiven* by baptism also to those who from the Gentiles draw near and enter the holy Church of God. Let us inquire also, to whom sins are *not imputed*. To such us Abraham and Isaac and Jacob and all the patriarchs, as also to the martyrs. Let us hear then, brethren, for the Scripture saith : *Who shall boast himself and say : I am clear of sins? Or who shall be confident and say: I am innocent?* And again : *There is no man pure of defilement: not though his life be but one day.* To every one therefore who believes and is baptized his (p. 86) former sins have been *forgiven* ; but after baptism also, provided that he has not sinned a deadly sin nor been an accomplice (thereto), but has heard only, or seen, or spoken, and is thus guilty of sin. But if a man go forth from the world by martyrdom for the name of the Lord, *blessed* is he; for brethren who by martyrdom have gone forth from this world, of these *the sins are covered*.

CHAPTER XXI

Concerning the Pascha and the Resurrection of Christ our Saviour.

[v. 10] Wherefore, a Christian ought to keep himself from vain speech and from words of levity and profanity. For not even on Sundays, in which we rejoice and make good cheer, is it permitted to any one to speak a word of levity or one alien to religion : as our Lord also teaches us in the Psalm by David, saying thus: *And now, ye kings, understand; and be*

---

6 Prov. xx 9.   8 Job xiv 4 f.   22 Ps. ii 10–12.

10–11 but after baptism] Comp. Hermas *Mand.* iv 3. 1 ff.   11 provided that] C : S has 'not', which does not construe: H has shortened and altered the passage. On the meaning of the word see note to p. 55, l. 24.   13 But if, etc.] Cf. Hermas *Sim.* ix 28. 3 ὅσοι ποτὲ ἔπαθον διὰ τὸ ὄνομα ἔνδοξοί εἰσι παρὰ τῷ θεῷ, καὶ πάντων τούτων αἱ ἁμαρτίαι ἀφῃρέθησαν, ὅτι ἔπαθον διὰ τὸ ὄνομα τοῦ υἱοῦ τοῦ θεοῦ.   CHAP. XXI. The headline is in the margin of S, together with the note 'Pay well attention here'. Similar calls to attention appear twice again in the margins of this chapter, addressed, it would seem, to scribes rather than to the reader.

DIDASCALIA APOSTOLORUM

instructed, all ye judges of the earth. Serve the Lord with fear, and rejoice unto him with trembling. Give ye heed to discipline, lest the Lord be angry, and ye perish from the way of justice: for his wrath will shortly be kindled against you. Blessed are all they that trust on him. We must conduct our festivals and our rejoicings, then, with fear and trembling; for a faithful Christian, it saith, must not sing the songs of the heathen, nor have anything to do with the laws and doctrines of strange assemblies; for it may happen that through (their) songs he will make mention also of the name of idols, which God forbid that it should be done by the faithful; [v. 11] for the Lord by Jeremiah upbraids certain folk and speaks thus: *They have left me, and have sworn by them that be no gods.* And again He saith: *If Israel will return, let him return unto me, saith the Lord; and if he will put away his abominations out of his mouth, and will fear before my face, and swear, As the Lord liveth.* And again He saith: *I will take away the name of idols out of your mouth.* And by Moses again He saith to them: *They have provoked me to jealousy by that which is no god; and with their idols they have angered me.* And in all the Scriptures (p. 87) He speaks of these things.

[v. 12] And not by idols only is it not lawful for the faithful to swear, but neither by the sun, nor by the moon; for the Lord God speaks by Moses thus: *My people, if ye shall see the sun and the moon, ye shall not be led astray by them, and ye shall not serve them: for these have been given you for light upon the earth.* And by Jeremiah again He saith: *Ye shall not learn according to the ways of the gentiles; and ye shall not fear the signs of heaven.* And by Ezekiel He speaks thus: *And he brought me in to the court of the house of the Lord, between the*

---

13 Jer. v 7.   14 Jer. iv 1 f.   17 Cf. Hos. ii 17 (19), Zech. xiii 2.
19 Deut. xxxii 21.   24 Deut. iv 19.   26 Cf. Gen. i 15.   27 Jer. x 2.
29 Ez. viii 16-18.

8 have anything to do with] lit. 'come near to'.   9 for it may happen, etc.] ἐπεὶ συμβήσεται αὐτῷ διὰ τῆς ᾠδῆς εἰδώλων μνημονεύειν ὀνόματα δαιμονικά *AC*.   24–26 the sun ... and ye shall not] H: the words have fallen out in S: μὴ ἰδὼν τὸν ἥλιον καὶ τὴν σελήνην καὶ τοὺς ἀστέρας πλανηθεὶς προσκυνήσῃς αὐτοῖς *AC*. The verse is quoted by Irenaeus *Haer.* III vi 4.

porch and the altar. *And I saw there men whose backs were toward the temple of the Lord, and their faces toward the east: and they were worshipping the sun. And the Lord said unto me: Son of man, is this a light thing to the house of Judah to do these abominations which they do here, that they have filled the earth with iniquity, and have turned again to provoke me to anger? And they are become as scoffers: but I will deal (with them) in wrath; and mine eye shall not spare, and I will not have mercy. And they shall cry in mine ears with a loud voice, and I will not hear them.* You see, our beloved, how sternly and bitterly sentence is passed on those who worship the sun or swear thereby, that the Lord should *deal in His wrath.* Therefore it is not lawful for a believer to swear, neither by the sun nor by any other of the signs of heaven or the elements; nor to make mention with his mouth of the name of idols; nor to utter a curse out of his mouth, but rather blessings and psalms and (words from) the dominical and divine Scriptures, which are the firm foundation of our faith: and especially in the days of the Pascha, wherein all the faithful throughout the world fast; as our Lord and Teacher said when they asked Him: *Why do John's disciples fast, but thine fast not? And he answered and said to them: The sons of the bridechamber cannot fast, as long as the bridegroom is with them. But the days will come when the bridegroom shall be taken away from them: and then they shall fast in those days.* But now by His working is He with us, but visibly He is absent, because He has ascended to the heights of heaven and sat at the right hand of His Father.

[v. 13] Wherefore, when you fast, pray and intercede for

---

21 Mk. ii 18-20 (Mt. ix 14 f., Lk. v 33-35).   27 Cf. Mk. xvi 19.

---

1 *porch*] *kesṭrōma* (i.e. καταστρωμα), as Pesh.   5 *that they*] lit. 'and they'.   8 '*and mine eye shall not spare*] From S marg.: H omits all after 'filled the earth with iniquity', but quotations are frequently curtailed in this MS.   18-20 in the days of the Pascha ... fast] Cf. Tertullian *de Ieiunio* 2 'Certe in euangelio illos dies ieiuniis determinatos putant, in quibus ablatus est sponsus, et hos esse solos legitimos ieiuniorum Christianorum'.

them that are lost; as we also did when our Saviour suffered. [v. 14] For while He was yet with us before He suffered, as we were eating the Passover with Him, He said to us: *To-day, in this night, one of you will betray me.* (p. 88) And we said unto Him, each one of us: *Is it I, Lord?* And he answered and said to us: *He that putteth forth his hand with me into the dish.* And Judas Iscariot, who was one of us, rose up and went his way to betray Him. Then our Lord said to us: *Verily I say unto you, a little while and ye will leave me; for it is written: I will strike the shepherd, and the lambs of his flock shall be scattered.* And Judas came with the scribes and with the priests of the people, and betrayed our Lord Jesus.

Now this was done on the fourth day of the week. For when we had eaten the passover on the third day of the week at even, we went forth to the Mount of Olives; and in the night they seized our Lord Jesus. And the next day, which was the fourth of the week, He remained in ward in the house of Caiaphas the high priest. And on the same day the chiefs of the people were assembled and took counsel against Him. And on the next day again, which was the fifth of the week, they brought Him to Pilate the governor. And He remained again in ward with Pilate the night after the fifth day of the week. But when it drew on (towards day) on the Friday,

3 Mk. xiv 30: Mt. xxvi 21–23 (Mk. xiv 18–20). 7 Cf. Joh. xiii 30.
8 Joh. xvi 32: Mt. xxvi 31, Mk. xiv 27.

1 as we also did, etc.] Comp. *Gosp. of Peter* 7 ἐπὶ δὲ τούτοις πᾶσιν ἐνηστεύομεν καὶ ἐκαθεζόμεθα πενθοῦντες καὶ κλαίοντες [cf. Mk. xvi 10 γενομένοις πενθοῦσι καὶ κλαίουσιν] νυκτὸς καὶ ἡμέρας ἕως τοῦ σαββάτου. 3 *To-day, in this night*] From Mk. xiv 30. 7 And Judas, etc.] It is not evident whether the author intended to place the exit of Judas before or after the Institution. Funk understood him to mean that Judas was present at the Eucharist; but the author of *AC* (whether interpreting *Didasc.* or following his own opinion) took the other view; and so Aphraates Hom. xii 6, 7 (but not Ephraim, *Com. in Diatess.*, ed. Mösinger p. 221). 9 *a little while*] lit. 'a little other', which is the *syr. sin.* rendering of ἔτι μικρὸν χρόνον at Joh. xii 35. The next words, 'ye will leave me', depend on Joh. xvi 32. 13 Now this, etc.] On the author's strange chronology for Holy Week and his treatment of the paschal fast, see the Introduction. He is followed in the main by Epiphanius, *Haer.* lxx 10–12, who cites several clauses, not verbatim but *ad sensum*, with more or less free paraphrase, as I think Funk has shown. The whole passage is printed and discussed by Funk in his second vol., pp. 4 ff. 23 drew on] The verb answers to ἐπιφώσκειν.

they accused him much before Pilate; and they could show nothing that was true, but gave false witness against Him. And they asked Him of Pilate to be put to death; and they crucified Him on the same Friday.

He suffered, then, at the sixth hour on Friday. And these hours wherein our Lord was crucified were reckoned a day. And afterwards, again, there was darkness for three hours; and it was reckoned a night. And again, from the ninth hour until evening, three hours, (reckoned) a day. And afterwards again, (there was) the night of the Sabbath of the Passion.— But in the Gospel of Matthew it is thus written: *At even on the sabbath, when the first day of the week drew on, came Mary Magdalene and the other Mary to see the tomb. And there was a great earthquake: for an angel of the Lord came down and rolled away the stone.*—And again (there was) the day of the Sabbath; and then three hours of the night after the Sabbath, wherein our Lord slept. And that was fulfilled which He said: *The Son of man must pass three days and three nights in the heart of the earth,* as it is written in the Gospel. And again it is written in David: *Behold, thou hast set my days in measure.* Now because those days and nights came short, it was so written.

1 Mk. xv 3.   11 Mt. xxviii 1 f.   18 Mt. xii 40.   20 Ps. xxxviii (xxxix) 6.

---

5 the sixth hour] The next sentence appears to imply that our Lord had been some hours upon the cross *before* the sixth hour (cf. Mk. xv 25), when the darkness began. Or did the author compute that the journey to Calvary and the fastening of Jesus to the cross occupied two or three hours? Otherwise the words 'wherein our Lord was crucified' can only be referred to His trial and sentence. In this computation of the three days and three nights that the Son of Man was 'in the heart of the earth' (see l. 18), no reason is given for the inclusion of the two periods before the death and burial. For the similar attempt of Aphraates to define the three days and nights, see Additional Notes.   11 But in the Gospel of Matthew, etc.] Nowhere else does the author appeal by name to any N. T. book, and I have little doubt that this passage is an interpolation: it interrupts the author's computation here most awkwardly, and I suspect that it originally stood as a marginal note to p. 183, ll. 1-2 below.   12-13 *Mary Magdalene and the other Mary*] The text has by error 'Mary and the other Mary, Magdalene'.   20 *Behold*, etc.] Ps. xxxviii 6, not lxxxviii 46, to which Flemming and Funk refer.

In the night, therefore, *when the first day of the week drew on*, He appeared to *Mary Magdalene and to Mary* (p. 89) *the daughter of James*; and in the morning of the first day of the week He went in to (the house of) Levi; and then He appeared also to us ourselves. And He said to us, teaching us: 'Are ye fasting for Me these days? or have I any need that ye should afflict yourselves? But it is for your brethren that ye have done this; and do ye the same in these days when ye fast, and on the fourth of the week and on the Friday always, as it is written in Zechariah: *The fourth fast, and the fifth fast*, which is the Friday. For it is not lawful to you to fast on the first of the week, because it is My resurrection; wherefore the first of the week is not counted in the number of the days of the Fast of the Passion, but they are counted from the second day of the week, and are †five† days. Wherefore, *The fourth fast, and the fifth fast, and the seventh fast, and the tenth fast shall be to the house of Israel.* Fast then from the second day of the week, six days wholly, until the night after the Sabbath; and it shall be reckoned to you as a week.

---

1 Mt. xxviii 1, 9 (cf. Joh. xx 1, 14).   4 Cf. *Gosp. of Peter* 14.
10 Zech. viii 19.   15 Zech. viii 19.

---

3 *daughter of James*] See p. 133 and note, also 148.   4 went in to ... Levi] There can hardly be a doubt that this comes from the *Gospel of Peter* c. 14, where we read ἐγὼ δὲ Σίμων Πέτρος καὶ Ἀνδρέας ὁ ἀδελφός μου λαβόντες ἡμῶν τὰ λίνα ἀπήλθαμεν εἰς τὴν θάλασσαν· καὶ ἦν σὺν ἡμῖν Λευεὶς ὁ τοῦ Ἀλφαίου, ὃν κύριος ... Here the fragment ends: the next words were probably ἐκάλεσεν ἐπὶ τὸ τελώνιον καθήμενον, or the equivalent (Mk. ii 14). Peter and Andrew, then, have with them Levi, who formerly entertained Jesus and his disciples in his house. Why is he with them now, if not again to receive them into his house—there to see the risen Lord? So I venture to reconstruct the story underlying the above statement in *Didasc.* That Levi's house was in Galilee, not in Jerusalem, appears not to have troubled the author.   and then] Still, I surmise, in Levi's house.
10–11 *the fourth* ... Friday] See again l. 16: the author's application of this text of Zech. to the weekly fasts on Wednesday and Friday is far-fetched and obscure. In Zech. 'fourth', 'fifth', etc., refer of course to the months, and apparently to those named in connexion with the capture and destruction of Jerusalem (2 Kings xxv, Jer. lii).   15 five] Probably read 'six', as in l. 18: the fast is from Monday to Saturday inclusive. 18 wholly] Or 'completely'. At p. 189, where the same word occurs, *AC* has ὁλόκληρον. There it denotes a fast *from all food* on the Friday and Saturday, but here it must mean six *full days*.

But *the tenth*,—because the beginning of My name is Yod,—wherein was made the inception of the fasts. But (fast) not after the custom of the former People, but according to the new testament which I have appointed you: that you may be fasting for them on the fourth day of the week, because on the fourth of the week they began to destroy their souls, and apprehended Me.—For the night after the third of the week belongs to the fourth of the week, as it is written: *There was evening and there was morning, one day*. The evening therefore belongs to the following day: for on the third of the week at even I ate My Pascha with you, and in the night they apprehended Me.—But fast for them also on the Friday, because thereon they crucified Me, in the midst of their festival of unleavened bread, as it is said of old in David: *In the midst of their festivals they set their signs, and they knew not*.

'And be ye constant in fasting during these days always, and especially you who are of the Gentiles. For because the People was not obedient, I delivered them (the Gentiles) from blindness and from the error of idols and received them: that through your fast and theirs who are of the Gentiles, and your service during those days, when you pray and intercede for the error and destruction of the People, your prayer and intercession may be accepted before My Father who is in heaven, (p. 90) as though from one mouth of all the faithful on earth; and (that) all things which they did unto Me may be forgiven them. For this cause also I have already said to you in the Gospel: *Pray for your enemies*, and: *Blessed are they that mourn*, over the destruction of them that believe not.'

Know therefore, our brethren, that (as regards) our fast which we fast in the Pascha, it is on account of the disobedience of our brethren that you are to fast. For even though they hate you,

2 ff. Cf. *Didache* viii 1.   8 Gen. i 5.   14 Ps. lxxiii (lxxiv) 4.
27 Cf. Mt. v 44, Lk. vi 27 : Mt. v 4.

---

1 *the tenth*] Here the 10th of the month, and the Monday, as is explained later (see pp. 187, 188).   2 inception] Or 'dedication': sc. the day on which the lamb was selected (cf. p. 189).   But (fast) not, etc.] Comp. *Didache* viii 1 αἱ δὲ νηστεῖαι ὑμῶν μὴ ἔστωσαν μετὰ τῶν ὑποκριτῶν· ... ὑμεῖς δὲ νηστεύσατε τετράδα καὶ παρασκευήν. The relation of these two passages is discussed in *J. T. S.* xxiv 151 f.: Jan. 1923.

yet ought we to call them brethren; for we have it written in Isaiah thus: *Call them brethren that hate and reject you, that the name of the Lord may be glorified.* For their sake therefore, and for the judgement and destruction of the (holy) place, we ought to fast and to mourn, that we may be glad and take our pleasure in the world to come; as it is written in Isaiah: *Rejoice, all ye that mourn over Zion*; and again He saith: *To comfort all them that mourn over Zion: instead of ashes, the oil of gladness; and instead of a spirit afflicted with pain, a vesture of glory.* [v. 15] We ought then to take pity on them, and to have faith and to fast and to pray for them. For when our Lord came to the People, they did not believe Him when He taught them, but put away His teaching from their ears. Therefore, because this People was not obedient, He received you, the brethren who are of the Gentiles, and opened your ears that your heart might hear; as our Lord and Saviour Himself said by the prophet Isaiah: *I appeared unto them that asked not after me, and I was found of them that sought me not; and I said, Behold, I am here, to a people that called not (upon) my name.* Now of whom did He speak thus? Was it not of the Gentiles, because that they had never known God, and because that they were serving idols? But when our Lord came to the world and taught you, you believed, you who have believed in Him, that God is one; and they also who are worthy shall believe, until the number is filled up of them that are to be saved, *a thousand thousand, and ten thousand times ten thousand,* as it is written in David.

But concerning the People, who believed not in Him, He said thus: *I spread forth my hands all the day long to a people that obey not and resist, and walk in a way that is not good, and go after their sins: a people that is provoking before me.* [v. 16]

---

2 Isa. lxvi 5.   7 Cf. Isa. lxvi 10.   Isa. lxi 2 f.   17 Isa.
lxv 1.   23 Hermas *Mand.* i 1.   24 Cf. 1 Clem. ii 4, lix 2.
26 Cf. Ps. lxvii (lxviii) 18, Dan. vii 10.   29 Isa. lxv 2 f.

---

16 that your heart might hear] lit. 'unto the hearing of your heart': διὰ τὴν ὑπακοὴν τῆς καρδίας ὑμῶν AC (the context being quite altered). 23–24 believed ... that God is one] Cf. Hermas *Mand.* i 1 πρῶτον πάντων πίστευσον ὅτι εἷς ἐστὶν ὁ θεός.   27 as ... in David] So also AC.

See, then, that the People provoked our Lord in that they believed not in Him. Wherefore he saith: *They provoked the holy Spirit; and he was turned to enmity unto them.* And again (p. 91) He speaks otherwise of them by Isaiah the prophet: *Land of Zebulun, land of Naphtali, the way of the sea, beyond Jordan, Galilee of the nations, a people that sitteth in darkness: ye have seen a great light; and they that sit in darkness and in the shadow of death, light is risen upon them. They that sit in darkness* He said concerning those who have believed in our Lord Jesus from (among) the People. For by reason of the blindness of the People a great darkness was round about them. For they saw Jesus, but that He is the Christ they knew not; and they understood Him not, neither from the writings of the prophets nor from His works and His healings. But to you of the People who have believed in Jesus we say: Learn how the Scripture bears witness to us and saith, *they have seen a great light.* You then who have believed in Him *have seen a great light,* even Jesus Christ our Lord; and they also shall see who are (yet) to believe in Him. But *they that sit in the shadow of death* are you who are of the Gentiles; for you were *in the shadow of death,* because you had set your hope on the worship of idols, and knew not God. But when Jesus Christ our Lord and Teacher appeared to us, *light rose upon you,* for you beheld and set your hope on the promise of the kingdom everlasting; and you have departed from the customs and practices of (your) former error, and no more serve idols as you were wont to serve them, but have already believed and been baptized in Him: and *a great light is risen upon you.*

Thus then, because the People were not obedient, they were made darkness; but the hearing of the ear of you who are of

---

2 Isa. lxiii 10.   5 Isa. ix 1 f., Mt. iv 15 f.   31 Ps. xvii (xviii) 45.

3 *he was turned*] 'they were turned' text (BS): ἐστράφη LXX *AC*. 4 otherwise] i. e. in a different strain: 'elsewhere' Flemming and Funk; but the adverb has not that sense to my knowledge, and the ordinary meaning is very suitable here.   31 the hearing of the ear] i. e. the ready obedience: from Ps. xvii 45 εἰς ἀκοὴν ὠτίου ὑπήκουσέν μοι.

the Gentiles was made light. Wherefore, do you pray and intercede for them, and especially in the days of the Pascha, that by your prayers they may be found worthy of forgiveness, and may return to our Lord Jesus Christ.

[v. 17] It behoves you then, our brethren, in the days of the Pascha to make inquiry with diligence and to keep your fast with all care. And do you make a beginning when your brethren who are of the People keep the Passover. For when our Lord and Teacher ate the Passover with us, He was betrayed by Judas after that hour; and immediately we began to be sorrowful, because He was taken from us. By the number of the moon, as we count according to the reckoning of the believing Hebrews, on the tenth of the moon, on the second day of the week, (p. 92) *the priests and elders of the people assembled and came to the court of Caiaphas the high priest; and they took counsel to apprehend Jesus and put him to death: but they feared, saying: Not in the festival, lest the people make a tumult*; for all men *were hanging upon Him*, and *they held him for a prophet* on account of His miracles of healing which He did among them.

But *Jesus was* that day *in the house of Simon the leper*, and we together with Him, and He related to us that which was about to happen to Him. But Judas went out privily from us, thinking that he would evade our Lord, and went to the house of Caiaphas where the chief priests and elders were assembled, and said to them: *What will ye give me, and I will betray Him to you* when I have found an occasion? *But they appointed*

---

14 Mt. xxvi 3–5.   18 Lk. xix 48.   19 Mt. xxi 46.   21 Mt. xxvi 6.
26 Mt. xxvi 15.

---

7 And do you make a beginning, etc.] Cf. Epiphan. *Haer.* lxx 10 ὁρίζουσι γὰρ ἐν τῇ αὐτῇ Διατάξει οἱ ἀπόστολοι, ὅτι ὑμεῖς μὴ ψηφίζητε, ἀλλὰ ποιεῖτε ὅταν οἱ ἀδελφοὶ ὑμῶν οἱ ἐκ περιτομῆς, μετ' αὐτῶν ἅμα ποιεῖτε. On this see Funk vol. ii, p. 7, who rightly concludes that Syr. preserves the original text, while Epiphan. has paraphrased for his own purposes. It may be observed for one thing that the author of *Didasc.* does not employ οἱ ἐκ περιτομῆς for Jewish converts, but regularly 'those who are from the People' (οἱ ἐκ τοῦ λαοῦ).   13 on the tenth, etc.] Cf. *AC* v 14. 1 (Funk, p. 271) ἤρξαντο γὰρ τὴν κατὰ τοῦ κυρίου βουλὴν ποιεῖσθαι δευτέρᾳ σαββάτων μηνὶ πρώτῳ. See also below, p. 188, ll. 26 ff.

and gave him thirty pieces of silver. And he said to them: 'Make ready young men armed, because of His disciples, that if He go forth by night to a desert place I may come and lead you'. And they made ready the young men and prepared to seize Him. And Judas *was watching, when he might find him an occasion to betray him.*

But by reason of the multitudes of all the people, from every city and from all the villages, who were coming up to the temple to keep the Passover in Jerusalem, the priests and elders took counsel and commanded and appointed that they should keep the festival straightway, that they might seize Him without disturbance. For the inhabitants of Jerusalem were engaged with the sacrifice and the eating of the Passover; and moreover, all the people that were without were not yet come, for they had deceived them as to the days. That they might be convicted before God of erring utterly in all things, therefore they anticipated the Passover by three days, and kept it on the eleventh of the moon, on the third day of the week. For they said: 'Because the whole people is gone astray after Him, now that we have an occasion let us seize Him; and then, when all the people are come, let us put Him to death before all, that this may be known openly, and all the people may turn back from after Him.'

And so in the night when the fourth day of the week drew on, (Judas) betrayed our Lord to them. But they made the payment to Judas on the tenth of the month, on the second day of the week; wherefore they were accounted by God as though on the second day of the week they had seized Him,

---

5 Mt. xxvi 16.

12-13 were engaged with, etc.] This must refer to Tuesday the 11th of Nisan. 15 had deceived them] i. e., apparently, by not notifying them of the anticipation of the Passover. 16-17 therefore they anticipated, etc.] Similarly Epiphan. *Haer.* li 26 προέλαβον γὰρ καὶ ἔφαγον τὸ πάσχα, ὥς φησι τὸ εὐαγγέλιον ... ἔφαγον οὖν τὸ πάσχα πρὸ δύο ἡμερῶν τοῦ φαγεῖν, τουτέστι τῇ τρίτῃ ἑσπέρας, ὅπερ ἔδει τῇ πέμπτῃ ἑσπέρας: and he says this Tuesday was the 11th of the moon. 26 on the tenth] See also p. 187, l. 13. 28 on the second day of the week they had seized Him] B (in text) S marg.: H reads 'they had seized Him', then omitting 'because ... put Him to death'. B and S marg. certainly give the original text.

because on the second of the week they had taken counsel to seize Him and put Him to death; and they accomplished their malice on the Friday: as Moses had said concerning the Passover, thus : *It shall be kept by you* (p. 93) *from the tenth until the fourteenth*: *and then all Israel shall sacrifice the passover.*

[v. 18] Therefore you shall fast in the days of the Pascha from the tenth, which is the second day of the week; and you shall sustain yourselves with bread and salt and water only, at the ninth hour, until the fifth day of the week. But on the Friday and on the Sabbath fast wholly, and taste nothing. [v. 19] You shall come together and watch and keep vigil all the night with prayers and intercessions, and with reading of the Prophets, and with the Gospel and with Psalms, with fear and trembling and with earnest supplication, until the third hour in the night after the Sabbath; and then break your fasts. For thus did we also fast, when our Lord suffered, for a testimony of the three days; and we were keeping vigil and praying and interceding for the destruction of the People, because that they erred and confessed not our Saviour. So do you also pray that the Lord may not remember their guilt against them unto the end for the guile which they used against our Lord, but may grant them a place of repentance and conversion, and forgiveness of their wickedness.

For he who was a heathen and of a foreign people, Pilate

4 Ex. xii 6.   25 ff. Cf. *Gosp. of Peter* 1.

7 Therefore, etc.] ἐν ταῖς ἡμέραις οὖν τοῦ πάσχα νηστεύετε, ἀρχόμενοι ἀπὸ δευτέρας μέχρι τῆς παρασκευῆς καὶ σαββάτου, ἐξ ἡμέρας, μόνῳ χρώμενοι ἄρτῳ καὶ ἁλὶ καὶ λαχάνοις καὶ ποτῷ ὕδατι . . , τὴν μέντοι παρασκευὴν καὶ τὸ σάββατον ὁλόκληρον νηστεύσατε *AC.* Epiphan. *Haer.* lxxv 6, referring to the Διατάξεις τῶν ἀποστόλων, asks καὶ περὶ τῶν ἐξ ἡμερῶν τοῦ πάσχα πῶς παραγγέλλουσιν μηδὲν ὅλως λαμβάνειν ἢ ἄρτου καὶ ἁλὸς καὶ ὕδατος ; A fast of six days before Easter is mentioned by Dionys. Alex. (*Ep. Canon.*, Routh iii 229). Irenaeus speaks of a fast of one, two, or more days (*ap.* Euseb. *H. E.* v 24). The only fast of obligation known to Tertullian (*de Ieiun.* 2) and Hippolytus (*Apost. Trad.*, Hauler p. 116) was confined to Friday and Saturday before Easter.   17 For thus, etc.] Cf. *Gosp. of Peter* 7, and see p. 181 l. 1. 25 etc. For he who, etc.] Cf. *Gosp. of Peter* 1 τῶν δὲ Ἰουδαίων οὐδεὶς ἐνίψατο τὰς χεῖρας, οὐδὲ Ἡρώδης οὐδὲ εἷς τῶν κριτῶν αὐτοῦ. καὶ βουληθέντων νίψασθαι ἀνέστη Πιλᾶτος. καὶ τότε κελεύει Ἡρώδης ὁ βασιλεὺς παρ⟨αλημ⟩φθῆναι τὸν κύριον, εἰπὼν αὐτοῖς ὅτι· ὅσα ἐκέλευσα ὑμῖν ποιῆσαι αὐτῷ, ποιήσατε.

the judge, did not consent to their deeds of wickedness, but *took water and washed his hands, and said: I am innocent of the blood of this man*. But the People answered and said: *His blood be upon us, and upon our children*; and Herod commanded that He should be crucified; and our Lord suffered for us on the Friday. Especially incumbent on you therefore is the fast of the Friday and of the Sabbath; and likewise the vigil and watching of the Sabbath, and the reading of the Scriptures, and psalms, and prayer and intercession for them that have sinned, and the expectation and hope of the resurrection of our Lord Jesus, until the third hour in the night after the Sabbath. And then offer your oblations; and thereafter eat and make good cheer, and rejoice and be glad, because that the earnest of our resurrection, Christ, is risen. And this shall be a law to you for ever, unto the end of the world. For to those who have not believed in our Saviour He is dead, because their hope in Him is dead; but to you who believe, our Lord and Saviour is risen, because your hope in Him is immortal and living for ever.

Fast then on the Friday, because thereon the People killed themselves in crucifying our Saviour; and on the Sabbath also, because it is the sleep (p. 94) of our Lord; for it is a day which ought especially to be kept with fasting: even as blessed Moses also, the prophet of all (things touching) this matter, commanded. For because he knew by the Holy Spirit and it was commanded him by Almighty God, who knew what the People were to do to His Son and His beloved Jesus Christ,— as even then they denied Him in the person of Moses, and said: *Who hath appointed thee head and judge over us?*—therefore he bound them beforehand with mourning perpetually, in that he set apart and appointed the Sabbath for them. For they deserved to mourn, because they denied their Life, and laid

---

2 Mt. xxvii 24.   4 Cf. *Gosp. of Peter* 1.   29 Ex. ii 14.

7 the vigil] Cf. Tertullian *ad Uxor.* ii 4 'Quis denique sollemnibus paschae abnoctantem securus sustinebit?'   18 because your hope, etc.] ὅτι ἡ εἰς αὐτὸν ἐλπὶς ἀθάνατος ζωὴ καὶ αἰώνιος *AC*.   27 His Son and His beloved] HS marg.: 'His Son His beloved' S.   28 as they ... Moses] S ('Him' from S marg.); 'in the person of' is lit. 'through': 'as they denied Moses' H.   32 because.they] Or 'who'.

hands upon their Saviour and delivered Him to death. Wherefore, already from that time there was laid upon them a mourning for their destruction.

[v. 20] But let us observe and see, brethren, that most men in their mourning imitate the Sabbath; and they likewise who keep Sabbath imitate mourning. For he that mourns kindles no light: neither do the People on the Sabbath, because of the commandment of Moses; for so it was commanded them by him. He that mourns takes no bath: nor yet the People on the Sabbath. He that mourns does not prepare a table: neither do the People on the Sabbath, but prepare and lay for themselves the evening before; because they have a presentiment of mourning, seeing that they were to lay hands on Jesus. He that mourns does no work, and does not speak, but sits in sorrow: so too the People on the Sabbath; for it was said to the People concerning the mourning of the Sabbath thus: *Thou shalt not lift thy foot to do any work, and thou shalt speak no word out of thy mouth.* Now who testifies that the Sabbath is a mourning for them? The Scripture testifies, and saith: *Then shall the people lament, family over against family: the family of the house of Levi apart, and their women apart; the house of Judah apart, and their women apart*: even as, after the mourning of Christ until now, on the ninth of the month of Ab (August) they come together and read the Lamentations of Jeremiah

---

6 Cf. Ex. xxxv 3.   11 Cf. Ex. xvi 29.   16 Isa. lviii 13 (LXX).
19 Zech. xii 12 f.

---

16 *Thou shalt not*, etc.] οὐκ ἀρεῖς τὸν πόδα σου ἐπ' ἔργῳ, οὐδὲ λαλήσεις λόγον ἐν ὀργῇ ἐκ τοῦ στόματός σου Isa. lviii 13 (LXX). The reference is supplied by Funk; Flemming took the words to be from an apocryphal source; and so Resch p. 298. 18–19 that the Sabbath ... The Scripture] B H, S marg. 23 month of Ab] Cf. Josephus *Bell. Iud.* vi 4. 5 (as to the destruction of the temple by the Romans) τοῦ δ' ἄρα κατεψήφιστο μὲν τὸ πῦρ ὁ θεὸς πάλαι, παρῆν δ' ἡ εἱμαρμένη χρόνων περιόδοις ἡμέρα δεκάτη Λώου μηνός, καθ' ἣν καὶ πρότερον ὑπὸ τοῦ τῶν Βαβυλωνίων βασιλέως ἐνεπρήσθη. On the dates '9th' or '10th' see *Jewish Encyclop. s.v.* 'Ab'. Comp. St. Jerome *In Sophon.* i 15 f. 'Uideas in die quo capta est a Romanis et diruta Ierusalem uenisse populum lugubrem, confluere decrepitas mulierculas et senes pannis annisque obsitos ... Congregatur turba miserorum ... plangere ruinam templi sui populum miserum', etc. (quoted by Schürer).

and wail and lament. Now nine represents *Theta*; but *Theta* denotes God. For God therefore they lament, even for Christ who suffered—rather, on account of God our Saviour, but over themselves and their own destruction. Does any man lament, brethren, except he have a grief? Therefore do you also mourn for them on the day of the Sabbath of the Pascha (p. 95) until the third hour in the night following; and thereafter, in the Resurrection of Christ, rejoice and make good cheer for their sake, and break your fast; and the surplus of your fast of six days offer to the Lord God. And let those of you who have abundance of worldly possessions minister diligently to those who are poor and needy and refresh them, that the reward of your fast may be received.

Wherever, then, the Fourteenth of the Pascha falls, so keep it; for neither the month nor the day squares with the same season every year, but is variable. When therefore that People keeps the Passover, do you fast; and be careful to perform your vigil within their (feast of) unleavened bread. But on the first day of the week make good cheer at all times; for he is guilty of sin, whosoever afflicts his soul on the first of the week. And hence it is not lawful, apart from the Pascha, for any one to fast during those three hours of the night between the Sabbath and the first of the week, because that night belongs to the first of the week; but in the Pascha alone you are to fast these three hours of that night, being assembled together, you who are Christians, in the Lord.

---

1 represents *Theta*] The same unexpected order again at p. 216, l. 15, where see also Lat. 17-18 perform your vigil, etc.] φάσκουσι γὰρ (sc. the Apostles) τὴν ἀγρυπνίαν φέρειν μεσαζόντων τῶν ἀζύμων Epiphan. *Haer.* lxx 10. *Didasc.* would appear to mean that the Saturday before Easter day should be the first Saturday after the Jewish Passover. The Christian fast is fixed to the days of the week—Monday to Saturday—so that the days may coincide with those of the week in which Christ suffered. Thus the Passover is an index only to the date of the Pascha *week*: there is no question here of Quartodecimanism, only of the date of Easter. The Quartodecimans observed 'the 14th of the first month, on whatever day (of the week) it might fall' (Hippolytus *Philos.* viii 18). 19-20 for he is guilty of sin, etc.] ἔνοχος γὰρ ἁμαρτίας ἔσται ὁ τὴν κυριακὴν νηστεύων *AC*: ὁ κακῶν ἑαυτοῦ τὴν ψυχὴν ἐν κυριακῇ ἐπικατάρατός ἐστι τῷ θεῷ Epiphan. *Haer.* lxx 11 (referring to the Διατάξεις of the Apostles). *AC* and Epiphan. modify *Didasc.* in different ways. 26 you ... in the Lord] lit. 'you Christians who are in the Lord' (HS): but 'assemble in the Lord' is the natural expression.

CHAPTER XXII
That Children should be taught Crafts.

[iv. 11] And teach your children crafts that are agreeable and befitting to religion, lest through idleness they give themselves to wantonness. For if they are not corrected by their parents, they will do those things that are evil, like the
5 heathen. Therefore spare not to rebuke and correct and teach them; for you will not kill them by chastising them, but rather save them alive: as our Lord also teaches us in Wisdom, saying thus: *Chasten thy son, that there may be hope for him: for thou shalt strike him with a rod, and deliver his*
10 *soul from Sheol.* And He saith again: *Whosoever spareth his rod, hateth his son.* Now our rod is the Word of God, Jesus Christ: even as Jeremiah also saw Him (as) *an almond rod.* Every man accordingly who spares to speak a word of rebuke to his son, hates his son. Therefore teach your sons the word
15 of the Lord, and punish them with stripes, and bring them into subjection from their youth by your word of religion. (p. 96) And give them no liberty to set themselves up against you their parents; and let them do nothing without your counsel, lest they go with those of their own age and meet
20 together and carouse; for in this way they learn mischief, and are caught and fall into fornication. Now, whether this happen to them without their parents, their parents themselves will be accountable before God for the judgement of their souls; or whether again by your licence they are un-

---

6 Cf. Prov. xxiii 13.   8 Cf. Prov. xxix 17.   9 Prov. xxiii 14.
10 Prov. xiii 24.   12 Jer. i 11 f.

CHAP. XXII. *AC* places this chapter earlier (see p. 161).   11-12 Jesus Christ] '(even) of Jesus Christ' Nau, Flemming, Funk: but the Syriac construction seems to require that the name be taken in apposition to 'the Word'.   12 *an almond rod*] Jer. i 11-12: the prophet sees an almond (*shāked*) rod; the Lord says 'Thou hast seen well, for I am watching (*shōked*) over my words to perform them' (so the Heb.). But this word-play is lost in the Gk., and so it is probable that our author goes to the passage only for the connexion of 'rod' with the 'word' of God.

disciplined and sin, you their parents will likewise be guilty on their account before God. Therefore be careful to take wives for them, and have them married when their time is come, lest in their early age by the ardour of youth they commit fornication like the heathen, and you have to render an account to the Lord God in the day of judgement.

CHAPTER XXIII
On Heresies and Schisms.

[vi. 1] Before all things beware of all abominable and evil and bitter heresies, and fly from them as from a blazing fire, and from those who adhere to them. For if when a man makes a schism, he condemns himself to fire together with those who go astray after him, how much more if one go and sink himself in the heresies. For know this, that if any of you covet the primacy and dare to make a schism, he shall inherit the place of Korah and Dathan and Abiram, he and they that are with him, and with them he shall be condemned to fire. For even the adherents of Korah were Levites, and ministered in the tabernacle of witness; but they coveted the primacy, and desired the high priesthood; and they began to speak evil of the great Moses, because, said they, he is married to a heathen woman—*for he had an Ethiopian wife*—and is defiled with her; and many others, and they of the following of Zimri, who committed fornication with the Midianite women, are with him. And the people, said they, that are with him are defiled; and his brother Aaron, too, was the author of idolatry, who made for his people the molten and graven image. [vi. 2] And they spoke evil of Moses, [vi. 3]

14 Nu. xvi 1 ff.   20 Nu. xii 1.   22 Nu. xxv 1 ff.

12 sink himself] The same verb as at p. 66, l. 2, where *AC* reads συμποδισθήσεται.   20 *Ethiopian*] 'Kushite' Syr. The complaint was made by Aaron and Miriam, not by Korah, etc.   22 Zimri] The incident referred to occurred long after the rebellion of Korah.

who wrought so many mighty works and signs from God for the People; who did these excellent and marvellous works for their benefit; who brought the ten plagues upon the Egyptians; who divided the Red Sea that the waters stood up as a wall on this side and on that, and caused the People to pass over as in (p. 97) the dry desert, and drowned their enemies and them that evil entreated them, and all that were with them; who made sweet for them the fountain of water, and brought them forth streams from the flinty rock, so that they drank and were satisfied; who brought them down manna from heaven, and with the manna gave them also flesh; who gave them a pillar of fire by night for light and guidance, and a cloud by day for a covert, and in the desert stretched forth the hand to them for the dispensation of the Law, and gave them the Ten Words of God. And they spoke evil against the friend and good servant of the Lord God, as men glorying in righteousness, and boasting of holiness, and making a show of purity, and in hypocrisy making a display of service.

And thus, as puritans and sticklers for holiness, they said: 'Let us not be polluted with Moses and the people that is with him, because they are defiled.' And there rose up two hundred and fifty men, and they (Korah, &c.) led them astray to forsake the great Moses, that (men) might suppose concerning them that they were giving God more glory and ministering to Him more zealously. For among that multitude of the people aforesaid but one censer of incense was offered to the Lord God; but they who were in the schism, two hundred and fifty men with their leaders, offered each one a censer of incense, two hundred and fifty censers, as though forsooth they were far more religious and pure and zealous than Moses and Aaron and the people that was with them. But the more numerous ministry of those in the schism availed them nothing, but *fire was kindled from before the Lord, and devoured them;* and those two hundred and

34 Nu. xvi 35.

1–15 For a similar passage see p. 220.

fifty men were burned up, holding the censers in their hands. And the earth opened her mouth and swallowed up Korah and Dathan and Abiram, and their tents and their vessels, and all that were with them: and they went down alive to Sheol unto punishment. And thus were the error-leaders of the schism swallowed up by the earth; and those two hundred and fifty men who went astray were burned with fire while the whole people beheld it. But the most of the people the Lord spared, among whom were many sinners, whom the Lord would judge each according to his works. And the most of the people He spared; but those who supposed that they were pure and holy, and performing a better ministry, the fire devoured, because that they were in the schism. *And the Lord said* (p. 98) *to Moses and to Aaron: Take the censers of brass from the midst of the burning, and make (of) them fine plates, and overlay the altar therewith; that the children of Israel may see, and no more do so. And scatter the strange fire there; because it hath sanctified the censers of (them that were) sinners in their souls.*

Let us regard therefore and see, beloved, the end of the schismatics, what befell them. For though they should appear pure and holy and chaste, their last end is given unto fire and burning everlasting. Let this then inspire you with fear, that even the fire of the schismatics was judged with fire: not because it *sanctified the censers*, but because they *in their souls* sanctified them; that is, forasmuch as the fire was performing its work, they also supposed in their heart, and *in their souls*, that their censers were holy. For it behoved the fire, which was employed for the ministry of transgression and the provocation of God, not to obey them but to cease from its operation, or to be quenched, and not to devour or burn or consume that which was put upon it. But now, because it did not the will of the Lord God, but obeyed the schismatics, therefore it

2 Nu. xvi 32 f.   13 Nu. xvi 36–38.

17 *scatter*] σπεῖρον LXX. Here and at p. 197, l. 1 BS, by misplacement of two diacritical points, have a verb that yields no sense: I therefore correct ܘܕܪܝ to ܘܕܪܝ. H omits the present clause, but at p. 197, l. 1 has correctly 'scatter'.

was said: *And scatter also the strange fire there*; that is, With fire the Lord judgeth the fire.

[vi. 4] If therefore upon those schismatics, who supposed that they were glorifying God, this threat and judgement was laid, what will happen to these heretics who blaspheme Him? Do you then, when you see from the Scriptures with the eyes of faith the plates of brass laid over the altar, beware of making schisms. For the adherents of Korah, Dathan and Abiram were made a monument and example of the destruction of schismatics; and every one who imitates them shall perish even as they. As men therefore who believe and know, keep yourselves far from schisms, and go not near them in any wise: as Moses said concerning them to the people: *Separate yourselves from among these stubborn men, and come not near to any thing that is theirs, lest ye perish with them in all their sins.* And when the anger of the Lord had burned against the schismatics, it is written that the people fled from them, and said: *Lest the earth swallow us* also (p. 99) with them. So then do you also, as men contending for their lives, flee from schisms; and those who would do any such thing reject, for you know the place of their condemnation.

[vi. 5] But as for heresies, be unwilling even to hear their names, and defile not your ears (with them); for not only do they in no wise glorify God, but they verily blaspheme against Him. Wherefore, the heathen are judged because they have not known, but the heretics are condemned because they withstand God: as also our Lord and Saviour Jesus said:

2 Cf. Isa. lxvi 16.   14 Nu. xvi 26.   18 Nu. xvi 34.

---

2 With fire the Lord judgeth the fire] See also p. 196, l. 24 above. B and S have in the margin this comment: '*With fire the Lord judgeth the fire*: because fire came out from before the Lord and burned up those who offered incense without authority'. As the author appears to treat the phrase as a Scriptural saying, we may compare Isa. lxvi 16 ἐν γὰρ τῷ πυρὶ κυρίου κριθήσεται πᾶσα ἡ γῆ, where Heb. has 'for with fire the Lord will judge'. 24–25 against Him] B and S have in the margin here 'Hence the Lord has no pleasure in the prayers of heretics nor in their petitions and praises.' 25 the heathen are judged, etc.] Cf. Hermas *Sim.* iv 4 οἱ μὲν γὰρ ἁμαρτωλοὶ καυθήσονται, ὅτι ἥμαρτον καὶ οὐ μετενόησαν· τὰ δὲ ἔθνη καυθήσονται, ὅτι οὐκ ἔγνωσαν τὸν κτίσαντα αὐτούς.

There shall be heresies and schisms: and again: *Woe unto the world because of scandals. For it must needs be that scandals and schisms come: yet woe to the man by whom they come.*

Then indeed we did but hear, but now we have also seen, even as the Scripture declares by Jeremiah saying: *Defilement is gone forth in all the earth.* Now these *defilements*, of heresies, *are gone forth*; and they have come about for the persuasion of our hearts, and for the confirming of our belief that those things which were foretold are true; for behold, they have come to pass and are accomplished. For all the working of the Lord our God has passed from the People to the Church through us the Apostles; and He has withdrawn Himself and left the People, as it is written in Isaiah: *He hath left his people the house of Jacob*; and: *Jerusalem is deserted, and Judah is fallen. And their tongues are (busy) with iniquity, and they obey not the Lord*; and: *I will leave (my) vineyard*; and: *Behold, your house is left to you desolate.*

He has left that People, therefore, and has filled the Church; and He has accounted her a mountain of habitation, and throne of glory, and lofty house, as He said in David: *The mount of the Lord is a mountain of fatness, a mountain of peaks. What think ye of the mountain of peaks? It is the mountain which the Lord hath chosen him to dwell therein: the Lord shall abide therein for ever.* You see then how He

---

1 Cf. 1 Cor. xi 19.   1 Mt. xviii 7.   5 Jer. xxiii 15.   13 Isa. ii 6.
14 Isa. iii 8.   16 Cf. Isa. v 6.   17 Mt. xxiii 38.   20 Ps. lxvii (lxviii) 16–17.

---

1 *There shall be heresies and schisms*] Cf. Justin *Dial.* 35 εἶπε γάρ· ... καὶ· ἔσονται σχίσματα καὶ αἱρέσεις. See Resch p. 100 and Ropes p. 96. Funk thinks that the saying arose out of 1 Cor. xi 19 in conjunction with Mt. xxiv 11, 24.   3 *and schisms*] Added under influence of the previous saying, and perhaps only by the translator.   5 declares] lit. 'delivers'. 5–6 *Defilement ... Now these*] B S marg.; but the particle marking the beginning of a quotation is left before 'defilements' in l. 6. The words are perhaps a marginal addition: cf. *AC* ἐκ γὰρ τῆς κακίας τῶν αἱρεσιωτῶν ἐξῆλθεν μόλυσμα ἐπὶ πᾶσαν τὴν γῆν, ὥς φησιν Ἱερεμίας ὁ προφήτης. H has changed and shortened.   20–21 *The mount*, etc.] ὄρος τοῦ θεοῦ ὄρος πῖον, ὄρος τετυρωμένον, ὄρος πῖον. ἵνα τί ὑπολαμβάνετε, ὄρη τετυρωμένα; LXX. The word rendered 'peaks' is from Pesh., which simply transliterates the Heb. It is connected with a root signifying coagulation (hence τετυρωμένον); but in Syriac there is a noun from the same root which means an eyebrow, also the brow of a hill (Lk. iv 29). Our author takes the last words, ὄρη τετυρωμένα, as accusative.

saith to others: *What think ye?* even to those who err (in thinking) that there are other churches: for one is she that is the mountain of God's sanctuary. And by Isaiah He said again: *In the last days the mountain of the house of the Lord, the God of Jacob, shall be established on the top of the mountains, and higher than the hills;* (p. 100) *and all nations shall look unto it; and many peoples shall go and say: Come, let us go up to the mountain of the Lord, and to the house of the God of Jacob; and he shall teach us his way, and we will go therein.* And again He said: *There shall be signs and wonders in the midst of the people from the Lord of Sabaoth, and him that dwelleth in Mount Zion.* And again by Jeremiah He said: *A high throne is our sanctuary.* As then He left the People, so did He leave their temple to them desolate; and He rent the veil, and took away from it the Holy Spirit, and shed Him upon them that believed from among the Gentiles, as He said by Joel: *I will pour out of my spirit upon all flesh.* For He took away the Holy Spirit, and the power of the word, and all the ministry from that People, and set it in His Church.

Now in like manner did Satan also, the tempter, depart from that People and come against the Church. And he now no longer tempts that People, because by their evil works they have fallen into his hands, but he has set about to tempt the Church and to exercise his agency in her. And he has raised up against her afflictions and persecutions, and blasphemies and heresies and schisms. [vi. 6] Formerly indeed, in that time, there were heresies and schisms in that People; but now Satan by his evil agency has driven forth (some) that were of the Church, and has made heresies and schisms.

4 Isa. ii. 2 f.   10 Isa. viii 18.   13 Jer. xvii 12.   14 Mt. xxiii 38.   17 Joel ii 28.

10–11 *in the midst of the people*] ἐν τῷ οἴκῳ Ἰσραήλ LXX (*AC* omits the passage).   15 from it] i. e., possibly, from the People, not the temple: ἀπ' αὐτῶν *AC*.

[vi. 7] Now the beginning of heresies was on this wise. Satan clothed himself in a certain Simon, one that was a magician and his minister of old; and when we, by the gift of the Lord our God and by the power of the Holy Spirit, were working miracles of healing in Jerusalem, *and by the laying on of our hand the fellowship of the Holy Spirit was given* to those who drew nigh (to the faith), then *he offered* us much *money*, and desired that, as he had deprived Adam of the knowledge of life through eating of the tree, so by the gift of money he might deprive us also of the gift of God, and might take captive our minds with the bestowal of possessions, to the end that we should barter away and give to him for money the power of the Holy Spirit. Hereupon were we all stirred up; then Peter looked upon Satan, who was dwelling in Simon, and said to him: *Thy money go with thee to perdition: but thou shalt have no part in this word.*

[vi. 8] (p. 101) But when we had divided the whole world into twelve parts, and were gone forth among the Gentiles into all the world to preach the word, then Satan set about and stirred up the People to send after us false apostles for the undoing of the word. And he sent out from the People one whose name was Cleobius, and joined him to Simon, and others also after them. [vi. 9] Now the party of Simon followed hard upon me Peter, and came to corrupt the word. And when he was in Rome he disturbed the Church much and subverted many; and he even made a show as though he would fly. And he was capturing the Gentiles, moving them by the power and agency of his magic arts. And on a certain

---

5 Acts viii 18 f.   15 Acts viii 20 f.   18–19 Cf. Mk. xvi 15.

---

5 in Jerusalem] So in the *Actus Petri cum Simone* (ed. Lipsius c. 23), whereas in Acts viii the scene of Simon's activity is Samaria. *AC* corrects *Didasc.* on this point.   17–18 But...twelve parts] om. *AC*. Cf. the opening of the *Acta Thomae* (Gk. and Syr.), and *Apost. Ch. Order* i.   On the whole subject see Lipsius *Die apocr. Apostelgesch.* i 11 ff. (1883).   21–22 And he sent...to Simon] καὶ προεβάλοντο Κλεόβιόν τινα καὶ παρέζευξαν τῷ Σίμωνι *AC*. Cleobius is coupled with Simon by Hegesippus (Eus. *H. E.* iv 22), and in the apocryphal Ep. of the Corinthians.   In the recently published *Epist. Apostolorum* (ed. Schmidt, p. 25) Simon's associate is Cerinthus. 26 and subverted many] πολλοὺς ἀνατρέπων καὶ ἑαυτῷ περιποιούμενος *AC*

[XLIII] ... ⟨pecuniam⟩ multam *optulit* nobis cupiens, sicuti Adam per degustationem ligni scientiae a ligno uitae [eum] alienauit, ita et nos per dationem paecuniae a datione Dei uoluit circumuenire, et per pecuniam mentem nostram occupare, ut
5 commutantes detraheremus illi uirtutem sancti spiritus pro pecunia. Sed cum omnes in hoc moti fuissemus, intendens Petrus ad propinquum Simonis diabolum dixit: *Pecunia tua tecum erit in interitum: non enim erit tibi participatio neque sors in hoc uerbo.*

10 Cum autem diuidissemus inter nos duodecim uncias saeculi et exiuimus ad gentes ut in omni mundo praedicaremus uerbum, tunc inspirauit diabolus et concitauit plebem ut mitterent post nos pseudoapostolos ad intaminationem uerbi. Et optulerunt de populo Cleouium quendam et iunxerunt eum Simoni, et postea
15 iterum alios post illos. Simon ergo, et qui cum eo erant, post uestigia mea Petri sequebantur seducentes populum. Et cum uenisset Romam, ualde depopulatus est ecclesiam multos de-⟨e⟩xhortans et adoptans sibi, et gentiles seducebat magicis

1-3 sicuti ... alienauit] Syr. somewhat differently, with this order: 'that as Adam through eating of the tree he had deprived of the knowledge of life': comp. *AC* ὡς τὸν Ἀδὰμ τῇ γεύσει τοῦ ξύλου τῆς κατ' ἐπαγγελίαν ἀθανασίας ἐστέρησεν, (οὕτως κτλ.). Evidently '*tree* of life' has been introduced by the Latin translator. 5 detraheremus] For 'distraheremus': 'distrahere', 'to sell', has already occurred at p. 5 l. 16, and in both places *AC* has the verb ἀποδίδωμι. Funk's emendation here, '[de]traderemus', is therefore not required. 17-18 deexhortans] ἀνατρέπων *AC*.

(cf. Lat.). 26-27 and ... would fly] om. *AC* (= Lat.). 27-28 And ... magic arts] τὰ δὲ ἔθνη ἐξιστῶν μαγικῇ ἐμπειρίᾳ καὶ δαιμόνων ἐνεργείᾳ *AC*. Cf. *Actus Petri cum Simone* 5 'omnes enim qui in me crediderunt dissoluit astutia sua et energia sua Satanas, cuius uirtute se adprobat esse' (sc. Simon); and 6 'magico carmine adque sua nequitia hinc inde omnem fraternitatem dissoluit'.

day I went and saw him flying in the air; then I stood still, and said: 'By the power of the name of Jesus I cut off thy powers.' And he fell and broke the ankle-bone of his foot. And then many turned back from him; but others, worthy of him, continued with him. And thus was that his heresy first established. And by other false prophets beside was the enemy working.

[vi. 10] And they all had one law †upon earth†, that they should not employ the Torah and the Prophets, and that they should blaspheme God Almighty, and should not believe in the resurrection. And in other respects they were teaching and disturbing (men) with many opinions. For many of them taught that a man should not marry, saying that if one did not marry, this was holiness; and in the name of holiness they were commending the tenets of their heresies. Others again of them taught that a man might not eat flesh, saying that no one might eat any thing wherein there is a soul. But others said that one was bound to abstain from swine's flesh only, but might eat those things which the Law pronounces clean, and that he should be circumcised according to the Law. And some taught this, and some that, causing contentions and disturbing the Churches.

CHAPTER XXIV

On the ordering of the Church: showing also that the Apostles came together for the correction of abuses.

[vi. 11] Now already we had rightly preached the holy word of the Catholic Church; and we returned once more to come to the Churches, and found men occupied (p. 102) with other opinions.

---

1 flying, etc.] Cf. *Act. Pet. c. Sim.* 32.   3 broke ... his foot] lit. 'was broken at', etc.: συντρίβεται τὸ ἰσχίον καὶ τῶν ποδῶν τοὺς ταρσοὺς *AC*: 'fregit crus in tres partes' *Act. Pet. c. Sim.* 32.   8 upon earth] ἐπίσης *AC* (= Lat.), which the translator read as ἐπὶ γῆς. 8–11 that they ... resurrection] Similarly in the apocryphal Ep. of the

operationibus et uirtutibus: sicuti in una die procedens uidi illum per aera uolantem, et ferebatur. Et subsistens dixi: 'In uirtute sancti nominis Iesu excido uirtutes tuas'; et sic ruens femur pedis sui fregit. Multi quidem tunc abscesserunt ab eo; alii autem, qui digni illo fuerunt, manserunt cum ipso. Et tunc prima illa fixa est [XLIV] haeresis illius: et per ceteros pseudoapostolos operatus est diabolus.

Et erat quidem illis omnibus aequaliter lex decreta, et ut profetas non utantur, et ut patrem Deum blasfemarent, et resurrectionem non credant: cetera autem diuers[a]e per doctrinas suas inspergebant. Alii enim multos docebant non debere nubere, dicentes quia qui non nubet castitatem studeret; ⟨et⟩ per castitatem sensus suos ad haeresim detulerunt. Alii iterum ex ipsis neque carnem sumere docebant, dicentes ea que animam habent non debere manducari. Alii autem dicebant a sola porcina carne debere se abstinere, ea uero quae in lege sunt munda debere manducare, et secundum legem circumcidi. Alii uero aliter docentes seditiones faciebant et ecclesias depraedabant.

Nos autem, qui rectum catholicae ecclesiae uerbum ante praedicaueramus, reuertebamur iterum ad ecclesias: et inueniebamus illos ad alias uoluntates fuisse praeuentos. Alius qui-

9 profetas] νόμῳ καὶ προφήταις (μὴ χρᾶσθαι) *AC* (cf. Syr.). patrem] παντοκράτορα *AC* (= Syr.). 10 cetera] 'uetera' cod. 13 per ... detulerunt] ἵν' ὡς σεμνοί τινες τὴν πονηρὰν αὐτῶν γνώμην ὡς ἀξιόπιστον παραδεχθῆναι ποιήσωσιν *AC*, but evidently with some alteration. 20 rectum] τὸν ἱερὸν καὶ εὐθῆ *AC* (cf. Syr.). 22 praeuentus cod.

Corinthians: 'non debere, inquiunt, uatibus credi, neque esse Deum ⟨omnipotentem⟩, neque esse resurrectionem carnis'. 9 employ] lit. 'minister with'. There is probably no need to correct the verb with Lagarde and Flemming; it occurs again in this phrase (but in the passive) at p. 204, l. 12. 14 in the name of] lit. 'through' (so Lat.). holiness] Often for 'chastity' in Syriac. 17 wherein ... a soul] ἔμψυχον no doubt: cf. Epiphan. *Haer*. xlvii 1 ἔμψυχα βδελύσσονται (the Encratites); and comp. Hegesippus (Euseb. *H. E*. ii 23) οὐδὲ ἔμψυχον ἔφαγε (sc. James the brother of the Lord). 20–21 And some taught ... that] lit. 'et alii aliter docebant'. 23–24 of the Catholic Church] τῆς εὐσεβείας *AC*: but cf. Lat. 25 men] lit. 'them' (masc.).

For some forsooth were observing holiness; and some abstained from flesh and from wine, and some from swine's flesh; and they were observing (some or other) of all the bonds which are in the Second Legislation.

[vi. 12] When therefore the whole Church was in peril of falling into heresy, all we the twelve Apostles came together to Jerusalem and took thought what should be done. And *it seemed good to us, being all of one accord*, to write this Catholic Didascalia for the confirming of you all. And we have established and set down therein that you worship God Almighty and Jesus Christ and the Holy Spirit; that you employ the holy Scriptures, and believe in the resurrection of the dead; and that you make use of all His creatures with thanksgiving; and that men should marry: for He saith in Proverbs: *Of God is a woman betrothed to a man*; and in the Gospel again our Lord saith: *He that created from the beginning the male, said that he created also the female. Therefore a man shall leave his father and his mother, and shall cleave to his wife: and they two shall be one body. What therefore God hath coupled, let not man separate.* But sufficient for the faithful is the circumcision of the heart, (which is) spiritual, as He said by Jeremiah: *Light you a lamp, and sow not among thorns. Be circumcised unto the Lord your God, and circumcise the foreskin of your heart, ye men of Judah.* And again in Joel He saith: *Rend your hearts, and not your garments.* And as for baptism also, one is enough for you, even that which has perfectly forgiven you your sins. For Isaiah said not (only) *Wash*, but *Wash, and be cleansed*.

Now we had much questioning, as men contending for life; and not we the Apostles only, but also the people, together with James the bishop of Jerusalem, who is our Lord's brother after the flesh, and with his presbyters and deacons and all the Church. For also some days before, *certain men had come*

---

7 Cf. Acts xv 25.   13 Cf. 1 Tim. iv 3.   15 Prov. xix 14.   16 Mt. xix 4-6, Gen. ii 24.   22 Jer. iv 3 f.   25 Joel ii 13.   28 Isa. i 16.
33 Acts xv 1 ff.

5-6 When ... heresy] ' of falling into heresy ' is lit. ' that heresy should happen to her ': ἀλλ' ἐπεὶ τότε αὕτη ἡ αἵρεσις [ἰσχυροτέρα πρὸς πλάνην]

DIDASCALIA APOSTOLORUM

dem castitatem studebat, alius autem a carne et uino se abstinebat, alius iterum a porcina: et quanta ex uinculis secundationis legis erant obseruabant.

Quapropter, cum uniuersa ecclesia periclitaretur et haeresis facta esset, conuenientes nos duodecim apostoli in unum in Hierosolyma, tractauimus quid deberet fieri; et *placuit nobis* scribere *unum sentientibus* catolicam ⟨hanc Doctrinam⟩...

---

7 ⟨hanc Doctrinam⟩] As at p. 211, l. 3, below : τὴν καθολικὴν ταύτην διδασκαλίαν AC (vi 14. 1, Funk p. 335, which corresponds to the present passage).

ἔδοξεν εἶναι, καὶ τῆς ἐκκλησίας ὅλης κινδυνευούσης AC.   10–11 worship... the Holy Spirit] θεὸν παντοκράτορα . . . σέβειν μόνον καὶ προσκυνεῖν διὰ Ἰησοῦ Χριστοῦ τοῦ κυρίου ἡμῶν ἐν τῷ παναγίῳ πνεύματι AC (vi 14. 2), clearly with alteration so as to introduce the author's favourite form of doxology : S marg. adds 'the Father' after 'God' and 'His Son' after 'Jesus'.   16–17 *He that created... the female*] The exact order is 'He that created from the beginning the male, and the female He said that He created.'. In *syr. cur.* we find 'He that made the male from the beginning, also the female He made, and said : Therefore', etc. : *syr. sin.* omits 'from the beginning' and 'and said'. Possibly in both *syr. sin.* and *Didasc.* Syr. the allusion to Gen. ii 24 was not recognized, so that καὶ εἶπεν formed a difficulty.   20–21 But sufficient... spiritual] ἀρκεῖσθαι δὲ πιστοῖς τὴν τῆς καρδίας περιτομὴν ἐν πνεύματι AC (vi 14. 5).   22 *Light you a lamp*] As Pesh. and Heb. : νεώσατε ἑαυτοῖς νεώματα LXX.   23–24 *the foreskin of your heart*] τὴν σκληροκαρδίαν ὑμῶν LXX : but τὴν ἀκροβυστίαν τῆς καρδίας ὑμῶν AC. Quoted also in *Ep. Barnab.* ix 5 (τὴν σκληροκαρδίαν), and Iren. *Haer.* IV xxvii 1 ('duritiam cordis').

down from Judaea to Antioch, and were teaching the brethren, (saying): Except ye be circumcised and conduct yourselves according to the law of Moses, and keep yourselves clean from meats, and all the rest, *ye cannot be saved; and they had much conflict and questioning.* And when the brethren of Antioch knew that we were all assembled and come to make inquiry of these matters, they sent to us (p. 103) certain men (that were) believers and had knowledge of the Scriptures to learn concerning this question. *And when they were come to Jerusalem, they related to us* the controversy which they had in the Church of Antioch. *And there rose up certain (men) who had believed from the sect of the Pharisees, saying: Ye ought to be circumcised and to keep the law of Moses.* And others also were crying out and saying in like manner. Then I *Peter rose up and said to them: 'Men, brethren, ye yourselves know that from the first days when I was among you, God made choice that by my hands the gentiles should hear the gospel and believe. And God, who proveth the hearts, gave witness of them*; for to Cornelius, a certain centurion, there had appeared an angel and told him of me; and he sent for me. But when I was ready to go to him, it was shown me concerning the Gentiles that they were about to believe, and concerning all meats. For I ⁹ *had gone up to a housetop to pray;* ¹¹ *and I saw the heavens opened, and a certain vessel, that was tied by its four corners, being lowered and let down upon the earth;* ¹² *and there were therein all manner of fourfooted beasts and creeping things of the earth and fowls of the heaven.* ¹³ *And there came to me a voice*

---

9 Acts xv 4.   11 Acts xv 5.   14 Acts xv 7 f.   18 Cf. Acts x 1 ff.
22 Acts x 9–16 (xi 4–10).

---

2 *and conduct yourselves*] Or 'and converse': as if representing καὶ . . . περιπατῆτε of Cod. Bezae. The verb does not mean 'to walk' in the literal sense, though it would be a natural rendering of περιπατεῖν in the ethical sense.   11 *certain*] H, S marg.: 'those who' S.   24 *and a certain vessel*, etc.] καὶ τέσσαρσιν ἀρχαῖς δεδεμένον σκεῦός τι ὡς ὀθόνην λαμπρὰν καὶ καθιέμενον ἐπὶ τῆς γῆς *AC*: '(et uidit caelum apertum) ex quattuor principiis *ligatum* uas quodam et linteum *splendidum*' Cod. Bez. lat. (at Acts x 11). This passage may suggest that the author of *AC* used a 'Western' text of Acts: it hardly proves that the author of *Didasc.* did so. On this question see further p. 208 and note.

saying: Simon, arise, slay and eat. ¹⁴ But I said: God forbid, Lord, for I have never eaten any thing defiled and profane. ¹⁵ And there came to me again another voice, the second time, saying: What God hath made clean, do not thou make profane. ¹⁶ Now this was done thrice: and the vessel was taken up to heaven. Thereupon *I bethought me, and understood the word of the Lord, how that He had said: Rejoice, ye gentiles, with the people,* and that everywhere He had spoken of the calling of the Gentiles; and I rose up and went my way. And when I was entered into his house and had begun to speak the word of the Lord, the Holy Spirit lighted down upon him and upon all the Gentiles that were there present. God, then, *hath given the Holy Spirit to them even as to us, and hath made no distinction between us and them in the faith, and he hath cleansed their hearts. Now therefore, why tempt ye God, that ye should lay a yoke upon the necks of the disciples which neither our fathers nor we were able to bear? But by the grace of our Lord Jesus Christ we believe that we shall be saved even as they also.* For our Lord came and released us from those bonds, and said: *Come unto me, all ye that toil and are laden with heavy burdens, and I will give you rest.* (p. 104) *Take my yoke upon you, and learn of me; for I am gentle and lowly in heart: and ye shall find rest unto your souls. For my yoke is pleasant, and my burden is light.* If then our Lord has released and unburdened us, why will ye lay snares for your own selves?'

¹³ *Then all the people was silent; and I James answered and said: Men, brethren, hear me.* ¹⁴ *Simon hath told how formerly God said that he would choose him out a people from the gentiles to his name:* ¹⁵ *whereunto agree the words of the prophets, as it is written:* ¹⁶ *Hereafter will I raise up and build the tabernacle of David, that is fallen; and the ruins thereof*

---

6 Acts xi 16.   7 Deut. xxxii 43 (Rom. xv 10).   11 Acts xi 15.   12 Acts xv 8–11.   20 Mt. xi 28–30.   26 Acts xv 13–29.

---

7 *Rejoice*, etc.] *AC* substitutes other texts.   24–25 unburdened us] lit. 'lightened from us'.   25 lay snares for] or 'put halters upon': the same verb and noun as in 1 Cor. vii 35, where the Gk. is οὐχ ἵνα βρόχον ὑμῖν ἐπιβάλω.

will I build and raise up; [17] that the residue of men may seek the Lord, and all the gentiles upon whom my name is called, [18] saith the Lord who maketh known these things from everlasting. [19] Wherefore I say, that no man vex them that turn to God from among the gentiles, [20] but that word be sent them on this wise: that they abstain from evil (practices), and from idols, and from that which is sacrificed, and from that which is strangled, and from blood. [22] Then we *the apostles* and the bishops *and the elders, together with the whole church,* thought it well to choose out men from amongst them and send them ⟨to Antioch⟩ in company with Barnabas and Paul, who were come thence. And we chose and appointed *Judas, who was called Barsabbas, and Silas, notable men among the brethren,* [23] *and wrote by them as followeth:—The apostles and elders and brethren to the brethren who are of the gentiles in Antioch and Syria and Cilicia, greeting.* [24] *Forasmuch as we have heard that some have troubled you with words, that they might corrupt your souls, whom we sent not:* [25] *we have determined, being all assembled together, to choose out and send men unto you with our beloved Barnabas and his companions,* whom ye sent (hither). [27] *And we have sent Judas and Silas, who themselves will tell you of these things by word* (of mouth). [28] *For it hath seemed good to the Holy Spirit, and to us, that no further burden be laid upon you, save that ye abstain from* (these) *necessary things:* [29] *from that which is sacrificed, and from blood, and from that which is strangled, and from fornication. And from these keep yourselves, and do well. Fare ye well.*

[vi. 13] Now the epistle we sent; but we ourselves remained

6-8 *abstain . . . from blood*] ἀπέχεσθαι ἀπὸ τῶν ἀλισγημάτων τῶν ἐθνῶν, εἰδωλοθύτου καὶ πορνείας καὶ αἵματος καὶ πνικτοῦ *A C*. The only peculiarity in Syr. is the substitution (from *v.* 29) of εἰδωλοθύτων (rendered 'from that which is sacrificed') for τῆς πορνείας. But J. H. Ropes thinks that the position of καὶ πνικτοῦ in *A C*—at the end, instead of before καὶ τοῦ αἵματος— indicates that this term was absent from the Gk. of *Didasc.*, and supplied by *A C*; and he expresses the opinion that 'the text of the quotations from Acts in the Didascalia was originally completely "Western", and has been occasionally modified by our Syriac translator' (*The Acts of the Apostles*, 1926, pp. cxcv-vi). The grounds for so large a conclusion appear to me insufficient: Ropes makes no mention of Lat., which begins again (p. 209) just in time to include Acts xv 29 and has there no more trace of the

[XLV] ... ²⁹ *ut abstineatis uos ab idolis immolato, et a sanguine, et a suffocatione, et a fornicatione : a quibus custodientes uos bene agite. Ualete.*

Et epistulam quidem transmisimus [ei], et ipsi aliquantos

---

4 ei] Hauler prints 'ei⟨s⟩': om. *AC* (= Syr.).

Western text than Syr.; moreover, he has not remarked that *Didasc.* twice quotes the Golden Rule in the negative form (see pp. 4, 145), but in a text quite different from that of Cod. Bezae in Acts xv 20, 29. 13 *Barsabbas*]. 'Barnabas' Syr., which may well be only a scribe's slip : Βαραββᾶν Cod. Bezae. 24–26 *abstain . . . from fornication*] ἀπέχεσθαι εἰδωλοθύτου καὶ αἵματος καὶ πνικτοῦ καὶ πορνείας *AC*. 28 ff. τὴν μὲν οὖν ἐπιστολὴν ἐξαπεστείλαμεν, αὐτοὶ δὲ ἐν ἱκαναῖς ἡμέραις ἐν Ἱεροσολύμοις ἐπεμείναμεν ἅμα συζητοῦντες πρὸς τὸ κοινωφελὲς εἰς διόρθωσιν *AC*, omitting here the mention of 'the Catholic Didascalia' which follows in Syr. and Lat.

in Jerusalem many days; and we were consulting and ordering together those things which were for the advantage of all the people, and writing also this Catholic Didascalia.

CHAPTER XXV

(p. 105) *Showing that the Apostles returned once more to the Churches and set them in order.*

Now the decision which we reached with counsel and thought concerning those who have already gone astray, we have thus affirmed and established. And we will return yet again and go to the Churches a second time, as in the beginning of the preaching, and will confirm the faithful that they may avoid the offences aforesaid, and may not receive those who come deceitfully in the name of apostles, but may know them by the changeableness of their words and by the performance of their works. For these are they of whom our Lord said: *There shall come unto you men having on the clothing of lambs, but inwardly ravening wolves: and by their fruits ye shall know them. Beware of them therefore. Now there shall arise false Christs and lying prophets, and lead many astray; and by reason of manifold iniquity the love of many shall wax cold. But he that shall endure unto the end, the same shall be saved.*

[vi. 14] Now let those who have not erred, and those also who repent of their error, be left in the Church. But as for those who are still held fast in error and repent not, we have decreed and enjoined that they be put forth from the Church and be separated and removed from the faithful, because they are become heretics; and that the faithful be commanded wholly to avoid them, and not to communicate with them either in speech or in prayer. For these are enemies and

---

13 Mt. vii 15 f.   15 Mt. xxiv 11-13, 24.

---

4 decision] lit. 'mind', or 'purpose'.   reached with counsel and thought] lit. 'consulted and thought out'.   6 affirmed] S: 'sent' H (by change of a diacritical point).   8 that they may] H: 'and they will' S.   19 those who] +'sustinuerint et' Lat., and rightly (cf. l. 18).

dies in Hierusolymis remansimus simul [et] conquirentes de communi utilitate ad emendationem, nec non etiam catholicam hanc Doctrinam scribentes.

Et tractatum consilii nostri aduersus eos qui nunc errauerunt ⟨...; et⟩ statuimus redire iterum ⟨ad⟩ ecclesias, sicuti in principio [fuerunt] praedicationis, et secundia⟨re⟩ et confortare fideles abstinere se a praedictis scandalis, et non suscipere eos qui false sub nomine apostolorum uenient, cognoscentes eos per commutationem uerborum et ab actione operarum suarum. Quoniam hii sunt de quibus dixit dominus: *Uenient ad uos in indumentis ouium, ab intus autem sunt lupi rapaces: ex fructibus eorum cognoscitis eos. Adtendite uobis: exsurgent enim pseudochristi et pseudoprofetae et seducent multos. Et quoniam abundabit iniquitas, refrigescet caritas multorum. Qui autem sustenuerit in finem, hic saluus erit.*

Qui sustinuerint et non fuerint peruersi, et qui a peruersione penituerint, permitti in ecclesia, eos uero qui iam tenti sunt in peruersione et non penitentur, eici decreuimus et separari a fidelibus, quoniam heretici facti sunt, et praecipi fidelibus omni modo abstinere ab ipsis et neque per uerbum neque per orationem communicare illis. Hii enim sunt aduersarii [XLVI]

---

1 et] om. *AC* (= Syr.).   4–5 Et tractatum ... redire] I assume that a new clause begins here, as in Syr.; but possibly 'et tractatum ... errauerunt' should go with the preceding. If my punctuation be right, something like 'firmauimus et' must have fallen out after 'errauerunt' (cf. Syr.: *AC* gives no help).   6 secundia⟨re⟩] so Hauler: om. Syr. (unless there be some connexion with 'a second time', just before). 14 *abundabit*] Perhaps for 'abundauit'.   *refrigescit* cod.

spoilers of the Church; for concerning these our Lord commanded us and said to us: *Beware of the leaven of the Pharisees and of the Sadducees*; and: *Into the cities of the Samaritans ye shall not enter*. Now *the cities of the Samaritans* are those of the heresies, which go in a perverse way, concerning which He said in Proverbs: *There is a way which men think right: but the end thereof leadeth to the bottom of Sheol*. These are they concerning whom our Lord sternly and bitterly gave sentence and said: *It shall not be forgiven them, neither in this world nor in the world to come*. For as regards the People, who believed not in Christ and laid hands upon Him, it is against the Son of Man, on whom they laid hands, that they blaspheme; and our Lord said: *It shall be forgiven them*; and again our Lord said of them: *My Father, they know not what they have done, nor what they speak: if it be possible, forgive them*. And as for the Gentiles again, it is against the Son of Man also that they blaspheme, by reason of (p. 106) the cross; and for these there shall come forth forgiveness. For to those who have believed, from the People or from the Gentiles, forgiveness of their evil works has been granted through baptism; as the Lord Christ said: *Wherefore I say unto you: All sins and blasphemies shall be forgiven to men: but blasphemy against the Holy Spirit shall not be forgiven, neither in this world nor in the world to come. And every one that shall say a word against the Son of Man, it shall be forgiven him; but every one that shall say (it) against the Holy Spirit, it shall not be forgiven him, neither in this world nor in the world to come*. But those who blaspheme the Holy Spirit, those who lightly and in hypocrisy blaspheme God Almighty, those heretics who receive ⟨not⟩ His holy Scriptures, or receive them ill, in hypocrisy with blaspheming, who with evil words blaspheme the Catholic Church which is the receptacle of the Holy Spirit: it is they who, before the judgement to

---

2 Mt. xvi 6.   3 Mt. x 5.   6 Prov. xiv 12.   9 Mt. xii 32.
13 Mt. xii 32.   14 ?(cf. Lk. xxiii 34, Mt. xxvi 39, 1 Tim. i 7).   21 Mt. xii 31 f.

---

13 *It shall be forgiven them*] Referring to Mt. xii 32, as below.   14 *My Father*, etc.] This strange quotation has occurred already at p. 52, where

et contrarii ecclesiae. De his nobis fidelibus praecipiens dominus dixit: *Adtendite a fermento Farisaeorum et Sadduceorum*, et: *In ciuitate Samaritanorum nolite ingredi.* Haec enim sunt ciuitates Samaritanorum, id est heresis peruerso itinere ambulantes, de quibus in Prouerbiis dixit dominus: *Est uia quae uidetur aput homines recta esse, posteriora uero eius ueniunt ad intimum inferni.* Hii sunt de quibus amare et durissime statuit dominus: *Non illis dimittitur, neque in hoc saeculo neque in futuro.* Quoniam populus, non credens Christo [est] et manus iniciens, in filium hominis ingeretur, eum blasfemans: et dixit dominus, *dimittitur illis.* Et iterum de illis dominus dicit: *Pater, ne⟨c⟩ quid fecerant ne⟨c⟩ quid dicunt sciunt: si possibile est, remittes illis.* Similiter et gentes filium hominis et crucem negant, sed et his remissio fluxit. His uero, qui siue de plebe siue de gentibus crediderunt, per baptismum remissio de pessimis operibus data est, sicuti dixit dominus Iesus: *Propterea dico uobis, Omne peccatum et blasfemia remittetur hominibus: icumque autem dixerit uerbum aduersus spiritum sanctum, non illi remittetur, neque in hoc saeculo neque in futuro.* Hii ergo ⟨qui spiritum⟩ sanctum blasfemant, qui omnipotentem Deum apertissime cum hypocrisi blasfemant, id est heretici, qui[a] sacras scripturas eius non suscipiunt, ⟨aut⟩ qui male cum subdolositate in blasfemio suscipiunt ea⟨s⟩, qui catholicam ecclesiam, quae est [XLVII] susceptorium sancti spiritus, in detractationibus blasfemant: hii sunt qui ante

---

3 *in ciuitate*] εἰς πόλιν Mt. x 5 : 'in ciuitates' is adopted by Hauler and Funk. 6 *posteriora*] 'per seriora' cod. : τὰ τελευταῖα LXX. 9 est] Either omit or correct to 'sed'. 10 ingeretur] Probably for 'ingeritur'. It is not obvious why Hauler and Funk prefer to read 'ingerebat'. 11-12 *nec quid fecerant nec quid*] Cf. Syr. : 'ne quid . . . ne quidquid' cod. ; but the second 'quid' of 'quidquid' begins a new line, which is enough to account for the repetition. 12 *remittes*] Possibly for 'remittas'. 19 ⟨qui spiritum⟩] Cf. Syr. Hauler and Funk restore only 'spiritum'. 21 ⟨aut⟩] Cf. Syr. Funk restores 'uel': οἱ τοὺς θείους λόγους ἀρνούμενοι ἢ μεθ' ὑποκρίσεως προσποιούμενοι δέχεσθαι *AC*.

Lat. is not extant. *they have done*] 'fecerant' Lat.: 'they do' at p. 52. 15 *if*] 'but if' at p. 52. 21 *Wherefore*, etc.] The shorter form of this quotation in Lat. is perhaps the original. 28 lightly] lit. 'hastily': 'apertissime.' Lat. 29 ⟨not⟩] From Lat.

come and before ever they can make a defence, are already condemned by Christ. For that which He said, *It shall not be forgiven them*, is the stern sentence of condemnation which goes forth for them.

And when we had ordained and affirmed and set down (these things) together with one accord, we set forth to go each one to his former province, confirming the Churches. For those things which were foretold have been fulfilled, and the hidden wolves are come, the *false Christs and lying prophets* have appeared. And this is evident and manifest, that when the times draw near and the Advent is at hand, there will be yet many more and worse than these: from whom the Lord God will deliver you.

Those then who have repented of the error of (their) godless apostasy we have healed with much admonition and with the word of doctrine (and) exhortation, and have made them whole and have suffered them to remain in the Churches; but those who are smitten unto death with the perverse word of error, and for whom there is no cure, we have driven out, that they may not contaminate the holy Catholic Church, the pure Church of God: that (the evil) may not creep like a leprosy and travel to all like a putrid gangrene, but that, pure and without stain or blemish or scar the Church may remain sound unto the Lord God. And these things we so do in every place and in every city, and throughout the whole world; and we have given (our) testimony, and have left this Catholic Didascalia justly and rightly to the Catholic Church for a memorial and for the confirming of the faithful.

---

9 Mt. xxiv 24, Mk. xiii 22.   23 Cf. Eph. v 27.

---

4 goes forth] The present tense is indicated by the pointing, but perh. the perfect should be read: cf. Lat.   18 ff. but those, etc.] τοὺς δὲ ἀνιάτως ἔχοντας ἐξεβάλομεν τῆς ποίμνης, ἵνα μὴ ψωραλέας νόσου μεταδῶσιν καὶ τοῖς ὑγιαίνουσιν ἀρνίοις, ἀλλὰ καθαρὰ καὶ ἄχραντα, ὑγιῆ καὶ ἄσπιλα διαμείνῃ κυρίῳ τῷ θεῷ *AC*, with considerable abridgement.   19 of error] + 'magis autem sine uerbo peruersione' Lat.: corresponding words have prob. fallen out in Syr.   22 putrid] I conjecture that ܠܐܒܐ (an unknown form) may cover the Gk. σηπεδών. S marg. has a noun which means 'white lead': H substitutes 'the sore of'.   26-27 this Catholic

iudicium futurum sine excusatione a Christo iam nunc condemnati sunt. Quod enim dicit, *non illis remittetur*, sententia ⟨est⟩ condemnationis quae illis exiit.

Et haec statuentes et unum sentientes egressi sumus unus-
5 quisque iterum ad priorem sortem adquaestus sui confirmantes ecclesias. Quoniam ea quae praedicta sunt inpleta sunt, et occulti lupi adfuerunt, et *falsi Christi et falsi profetae* manifesti facti sunt; procedente autem tempore et fine saeculi adpropinquante pluriores et pessimiores erunt: de quibus
10 eripiet uos dominus Deus.

Eos uero qui intellexerunt in ea quae sine Deo est peruersio, in multa correptione e⟨t⟩ uerbo doctrinae et obsecratione sanantes incolumes in ecclesia dimisimus. Eos autem qui mortaliter laesi sunt in uerbo peruersionis, magis autem
15 sine uerbo peruersione, cum insanabile haberent uulnus, eiecimus, ut neque inquinent electam sanctam catholicam ecclesiam Dei, neque uelut scauia transeat aut serpeat putredo et omnes maculet, sed munda et sine macula et incolumis ecclesia permaneat domino Deo. Et haec per ciuitates omnes
20 in uniuersam terram fecimus, relinquentes hanc catholicam Doctrinam dign[a]e et iust[a]e ecclesiae catholicae ad commemorationem confirmationis credentibus contestati.

2 *illis*] With Syr., and Lat. at p. 213, l. 8 above: 'talis' cod., though Hauler marks the first two letters as uncertain. ⟨est⟩] With Syr. 3 quae] 'quia' cod. 8 Procedente, etc.] Is this an echo of *Didache* xvi 3, ἐν γὰρ ταῖς ἐσχάταις ἡμέραις πληθυνθήσονται οἱ ψευδοπροφῆται? 15 sine uerbo] i. e. ἀλόγῳ. 22 contestati] ' and we have given testimony' (placed at the beginning of the clause) Syr.: Lat. appears to mean '(thus) delivering our testimony'. *AC* has εἰς μνημόσυνον ἐπιστηρισμοῦ τοῖς πεπιστευκόσι θεῷ, then altering.

Didascalia] τήνδε τὴν καθολικὴν διδασκαλίαν *AC*. justly and rightly] ἀξίως καὶ δικαίως *AC*. Comp. Hippol. *in Dan.* lib. ii c. 29 ἀξίως κ. δικαίως, and lib. iii c. 4 ἀξίαν κ. δικαίαν—neither in any liturgical context.

CHAPTER XXVI

(p. 107) *On the bonds of the Second Legislation of God.*

[vi. 15] But you who have been converted from the People to believe in God our Saviour Jesus Christ, do not henceforth continue in your former conversation, brethren, that you should keep vain obligations, purifications and sprinklings and baptisms and distinction of meats; for the Lord has said to you: *Remember not the former things;* and: *Behold, I make all things new: the which I now declare, that ye may know them. And I will make in the desert a way.* Now *deserts* the Churches formerly were, in which there is now a highway and the knowledge of religion, (a way) wherein there is no erring, but new and evident, even Jesus Christ and all His dispensation which was from the beginning. For you know that He gave a simple and pure and holy law, (a law) of life, wherein our Saviour set His name. For whereas He spoke the Ten Words, He signified Jesus: for Ten represents Yod; but Yod is the beginning of the name of Jesus. Now concerning the Law the Lord testifies in David, saying thus: *The law of the Lord is without blemish, and converting souls.* And many other things are said on this wise everywhere; for in completion of the writings of the Prophets the Lord spoke at the end by Malachi the Angel and said thus: *Remember the law of Moses the servant of the Lord, how he commanded you*

---

6 Isa. xliii 18, 19.   18 Ps. xviii (xix) 8.   21 Mal. iv 6.

4 purifications] + ἀφορισμῶν AC (= Lat.).   7 *which I now declare*] ἃ νῦν ἀνατελεῖ LXX (= Lat.), but ἀνατελῶ cod. ℵ*.   8 Now *deserts*, etc.] Irenaeus similarly comments on the same passage: 'Now a *wilderness* and a *waterless place* was at first the calling of the Gentiles' (*Apost. Preaching* c. 89, trans. J. A. Robinson: cf. also *Haer.* IV lv 5).   11 new and evident] om. Lat.   13 of life] = σωτήριον AC.   15 for Ten represents Yod] Cf. Lat., and compare p. 192, l. 1.   16-17 Now... saying thus] om. Lat., and apparently AC.   19-20 in completion, etc.] Comp. the 'Muratorian Fragment' l. 78 f. 'inter profetas completum numero'.   21 the Angel] See again p. 254: τοῦ προφήτου AC. In Irenaeus *Haer.* IV xxix 5 and xxxiv 2, where the Latin has 'in duodecim prophetis Malachias' and 'in prophetis Malachias', the Armenian version

Qui autem conuertentur de populo ut [XLVIII] credant
Deo et saluatori nostro Iesu Christo, iam priorem conuersationem non tenea⟨n⟩t obseruantes uincula uana et purificationes
et segregationes et asparsiones baptismi et escarum discre-
5 tiones, quoniam dicit uobis dominus: ⟨Ne⟩ *mementote anti-
quorum*, et: *Ecce facio noua, quae nunc exorientur, et scietis.
Et dabo in deserto uiam*. Desertae ante erant ecclesiae, in
quabus modo diuina et sine errore uia religionis Christiane
firmata est. Cognoscentes igitur dominum Iesum Christum
10 et uniuersam eius dispensationem quae a principio facta est,
scitote quia dedit legem simplicem quondam, salubrem,
sanctam, in qua et saluator proprium nomen infixit. Decalogum enim proferens significauit Iesum: ·I· enim iota significat, iota autem initium nominis est Iesu. *Lex* ergo *domini
15 inrepraehensibilis, conuertens animas*: et alia multa ubique sic
dictum est; nam et in conpletione scripturarum profeticarum
iam in fine per Malaciam loquens, qui nuncupatur et angelus,
dominus ita dixit: *Mementote legis Moysi pueri mei, quomodo*

4–5 decretiones cod. 8 Christiane] om. Syr. (*AC* omits the clause).
9 ff. Cognoscentes, etc.] γνόντες γὰρ [θεὸν διὰ] Ἰησοῦ Χριστοῦ καὶ τὴν σύμπα-
σαν αὐτοῦ οἰκονομίαν ἀρχῆθεν γεγενημένην, ὅτι δέδωκεν νόμον ἁπλοῦν ... καθαρόν,
σωτήριον, ἅγιον, ἐν ᾧ καὶ τὸ ἴδιον ὄνομα ἐγκατέθετο *AC*: Syr. differently.
11 quondam] om. *AC* Syr.: possibly 'quandam' should be read.
17 nuncupatur et] So Hauler restores: 'nuncputaret' cod. At p. 255, l. 7
we find 'qui nuncupatus est'. Syr. omits 'who is (was) called' here, but
has the words at p. 254. 18 *pueri mei*] 'the servant of the Lord' Syr.:
ἀνθρώπου τοῦ θεοῦ *AC*: τοῦ δούλου μου LXX.

has 'the angel' for 'Malachias'. Clem. Alex. (*Strom.* i §§ 122, 127, 129,
135) similarly speaks of ὁ ἐν τοῖς δώδεκα ἄγγελος. In 4 Esdras i 40 we have
'Malachiae, qui et angelus Domini uocatus est' (see Dr. J. A. Robinson's
note on p. 47 of his ed. of the *Apost. Preaching* of Irenaeus). It may be
added that in an Old Lat. list of the O. T. books, given in c. xiv of the *Inst.
diu.* of Cassiodorus (perh. to be ascribed to Pope Hilarus), Malachi
appears as 'Malachim qui et angelus': and so in the list in Codex
Amiatinus, taken from Cassiodorus' *codex grandior* of the Old Lat. (see
an article on 'The Codex Amiatinus and Cassiodorus' by Dom John
Chapman, in *Rev. Bénéd.* for April–July, 1926, pp. 139 ff.).

commandments and judgements. And our Saviour also, when He cleansed the leper, sent him to the Law, and said to him: *Go, show thyself to the high priests, and offer the gifts of thy cleansing, as Moses commanded, for a testimony unto them*; that He might show that He does not undo the Law, but teaches what is the Law and what the Second Legislation. For He said thus: *I am not come to undo the law, nor the prophets, but to fulfil them.* The Law therefore is indissoluble; but the Second Legislation is temporary, and is dissoluble. Now the Law consists of the Ten Words and the Judgements; to which (Law) Jesus bore witness and said thus: *One Yod letter shall not pass away from the law.* Now it is the Yod which passes not away from the Law, even that which may be known from the Law itself through the Ten Words, which is the name of Jesus. But the *letter* is the extension of the wood of the cross. And in the mount also Moses and Elias appeared with our Lord: that is, the Law and the Prophets.

[vi. 16] The Law then consists of the Ten (p. 108) Words and the Judgements, which God spoke before that the People made the calf and served idols. For also that it is called the Law, (is) truly on account of the Judgements. This is the simple and light Law, wherein is no burden, nor distinction of meats, nor incensings, nor offerings of sacrifices and burnt offerings. In this Law accordingly He shows concerning the dispensation of the Church and concerning the uncircumcision of the flesh only. For He spoke concerning sacrifices thus:

---

3 Mt. viii 4.   7 Mt. v 17.   11 Mt. v 18.   15 Cf. *Didache* xvi 6.

3 *to the high priests*] τῷ ἀρχιερεῖ *AC* (= Lat.): '*high* priest' here is peculiar.   5–6 but teaches what is the Law] With Lat.: om. H: 'but teaches the Second Legislation' S (by error of one word).   11–12 *One Yod letter shall not pass away*] Leaving ἡ μία κεραία unrepresented. This curious rendering is found in *syr. sin.* and Aphraates (see Burkitt's note *in loc.*, and also his vol. ii, p. 117); it affords clear proof of our translator's familiarity with one of the older Syriac versions of the Gospels, and is the more remarkable here because it does not fit with the author's commentary: for this the 'Yod' and the 'letter' have to be treated as separate entities.   12 it is the *Yod*] So Lat. The Syr. text as pointed in H and S would more naturally be read 'Now that Yod which', etc.; but this would create a grammatical difficulty in what follows.   15–16 the extension of the wood of the cross] 'of the cross' is doubtless an explanatory addition due to the translator: Lat. certainly preserves the original form of the expression,

DIDASCALIA APOSTOLORUM 219

uobis dedit praecepta et iustitias. Et saluator similiter, cum mundaret leprosum, ad legem eum transmisit dicens : *Pergens ostende te principi sacerdotum, et offer munus purgationis tuae, sicuti praecepit Moyses, in testimonium illorum.* ⟨Ut ostendat⟩
5 quoniam non distruo legem, sed doceo quid sit lex et quid secundatio legis, dicit: *Non ueni distruere legem neque* [XLIX] *profetas, sed adinplere.* Lex ergo est indestructibilis, secundatio autem legis temporalis. Lex uero est decalogus et iudicia, sicuti testimonium praebet Iesus dominus dicens:
10 *Iota, id est unus apex, non transiet a lege.* Iota quidem est, quod non transiet a lege: iota autem significatur per decalogum, nomen Iesu. Apex uero signum est extensionis ligni. Nam et Moyses et Helias erant cum domino in montem, id est lex et profetae.

15 Lex ergo est decalogus et iudicia, quae antequam uitulum faceret populus et idololatriaret locutus est dominus. Nam lex uocata est specialiter propter iudicia. Lex autem haec simplex est et leuis, non habens onerantes parationes escarum neque sacrificia neque conbustionum oblationes. In hac lege de
20 ecclesia et de preputio dicit, sed dispensatione[m] solummodo dicit de sacrificiis ita : *Si facis mihi altarem, de terra facies*

---

4 ⟨Ut ostendat⟩] Cf. Syr., which however suggests that 'ut ... legis' should be read with what precedes, and that 'enim' should further be supplied after the following 'dicit', thus: '*in testimonium illorum,* ut ostendat quoniam ... secundatio legis ; dicit enim'.   6 dicat cod.   *uene* cod.   9 praebet] For the more usual 'perhibet', and so again p. 251, l. 15.   10 *id est*] I can offer no explanation of this except that the translator may have read ἤτοι for ἤ.   18 onerantes parationes] Perh. emend 'onera neq(ue) separationes' (cf. Syr.).   20 solummodo] Cf. the 'only' in Syr.: 'solam modo' cod.

---

reproducing the σημεῖον ἐκπετάσεως of *Didache* xvi 6 (see *J. T. S.* xxiv 152–3: Jan. 1923). Syr. has omitted 'sign' ('ātha') owing, probably, to the presence of the cognate word 'letter' ('āthūtha').   18 consists of] lit. 'is'.   19 Judgements] sc. the δικαιώματα in Ex. xxi (see p. 14 before). 21 on account of the Judgements] i. e., as I understand, the expressly legal enactments in Ex. xxi justify the extension of the term 'law' to the Decalogue in ch. xx.   23 nor incensings] om. Lat.   24–26 concerning the dispensation of the Church ... thus] It is possible that Syr. has missed the construction and sense of the original here, cf. Lat.

If thou shalt make me an altar, make it of earth: but if of stones, thou shalt make it of whole and unwrought, and not of wrought stones. Forasmuch as thou hast laid an iron (tool) upon it, thou hast also polluted it: not (as speaking) concerning ⟨the axe, but concerning⟩ the iron of the knife which is the physician's knife, with which he circumcises the foreskin. Wherefore He does not say, ' Make for me ', but, *If thou shalt make an altar*. He did not impose this as a necessity, but showed what was about to be. For God had no need of sacrifices; as neither of old was it commanded Cain and Abel, but they of their own accord presented offerings: and their offering achieved a brother's murder. And Noah likewise offered, and was blamed. Wherefore He signified here: ' If thou desire to sacrifice, whereas I need it not thou sacrificest unto me.'

So then the Law is easy and light, †of no weak voice†. But when the People denied God, who by Moses visited them in their afflictions, who wrought signs by his hand and through his rod, who smote the Egyptians with the ten plagues and divided the Red Sea in two, who led them in the midst of the sea on dry land as in the desert, who drowned their enemies and them that hated them, who with wood made sweet the fountain of the bitter waters of Marah, who made water to flow for them in abundance from the rock: that they might be satisfied, who with a pillar of cloud and a pillar of fire over-

---

1 Ex. xx 24 f., Deut. xxvii 5.

1 *If thou shalt make*, etc.] ἐὰν δὲ ποιήσῃς μοι θυσιαστήριον, ἐκ γῆς ποιήσεις μοι αὐτό *AC*, omitting the rest. This is a strange perversion of Ex. xx 24, where the command to make an altar (of earth) is absolute. 3-4 *Forasmuch ... polluted it*] τὸ γὰρ ἐγχειρίδιόν σου ἐπιβέβληκας ἐπ' αὐτοὺς καὶ μεμίανται Ex. xx 25 : οὐκ ἐπιβαλεῖς ἐπ' αὐτὸ σίδηρον Deut. xxvii 5. The explanation of the following difficult comment is to be found, I believe, in the fact that the author has both these passages in mind and has fused their wording.   *an iron (tool) upon it*] This is from Deut. : in Ex. the Heb. has 'sword', which LXX render ἐγχειρίδιον : Ex. has also ἐπ' αὐτούς, sc. λίθους.   5 ⟨the axe, but concerning⟩] Cf. Lat. Something of the kind is clearly wanting. Although the texts of both Syr. and Lat. are in confusion, yet from a comparison of the two the general sense becomes clear: the iron (σίδηρος, *ferramentum*) forbidden is not that of any instrument for cutting stone (*bipennis* Lat.), but that of the surgical knife used in circumcision (ἐγχειρίδιον, *manuale*). Thus our author extracts from the passage a prohibition both of altar (with sacrifice) and circumcision.

illud: si autem ex lapidibus, non facies illos secatos: quoniam ferramentum tuum immisisti [inerit] in eo, maculatum est; non ergo in bipenn[a]e †faciest†, sed de manuale, quod est medicinale ferramentum, quod et circumcidit praeputium. Non autem dixit ⟨'Fac', sed *Si*⟩ *facis altarem*: non inposuit necessitatem, sed quod futurum erat †alteraret†. Non enim sacrificia aegebat dominus: sed quoniam et antea Cain et Abel, cum non fuissent postulati, a semet ipsis ostiam offerunt, et oblatio eorum internecionem fraternam operata est; et Noe similiter, sed repraehensus est: propterea hic dicit: 'Si sacrificare desideras, [L] cum non indigeam, sacrifica.'

Haec ergo sinplex et leuis et facillima lex est. Sed cum populus Deum denegasset, qui per Moysetem in tribulatione ipsorum uisitauerat illos, qui signa in uirga et manu fecit, qui Aegyptios decem plagarum poena percussit, qui rubrum mare diuisit in separationibus, qui transduxit illos in medio aquae sicut in desertum aridam, qui inimicos et aduersarios eorum submersit, qui Myrram amarissimam fontem per lignum indulcauit, qui de petra rupis produxit illis ad saturitatem aquam, qui per columnam ignis et per columnam nubis adumbrabat eos et

2 *inerit*] The explanation of this superfluous verb would seem to be that the translator, or a scribe, began to write 'inerit in eo macula'. 3 facies] Prob. to be omitted, with Syr. The verb left to be understood may be 'maculatum est', or (if 'in' should have the sense of 'de' following) 'dicit'. 5 ⟨'Fac', sed *Si*⟩] οὐκ εἶπεν· ποίησον, ἀλλ'· ἐὰν ποιήσῃς *AC*, cf. Syr. 6 alterare] It may seem obvious to suggest 'altare' for this, but I suspect corruption of some finite verb like 'monstrauit': 'showed' Syr. 17 aridam] Following the gender of ἔρημος. 20 adumbrauat cod.

9–10 had no need of sacrifices] Cf. Irenaeus *Haer.* IV xxix 1, xxxi 2 (*fin.*). 12 achieved a brother's murder] Cf. 1 Clem. iv 7 ὁρᾶτε, ἀδελφοί, ζῆλος καὶ φθόνος ἀδελφοκτονίαν κατειργάσατο. 13 and was blamed] For this there is no authority in the Bible. 13–15 If thou desire, etc.] εἰ θύειν ἐπιθυμεῖς, οὐ δεομένῳ μοι θῦε *AC*. 16 easy] The change of one letter (*pĕshīṭa* for *pĕshīḳa*) would give 'simple' (= Lat.). of no weak voice] lit. 'not little-voiced': 'facillima' Lat. 18–19 by his hand and through his rod] ἐπὶ χειρὸς καὶ ῥάβδου *AC*. 18–25 For a similar passage see pp. 194–5.

shadowed and guided them, who brought them down manna from heaven, and gave them flesh from the sea, who ordained the Law for them in the mount: Him they denied and said: *We have no God to go before us; and they made them a molten calf and worshipped it* and sacrificed to a graven image.

Therefore the Lord was angry; and in His hot anger—(yet) with the mercy of His goodness—He bound them with the Second Legislation, and laid heavy burdens upon them, and a hard yoke (p. 109) upon their neck. And He says now no longer: *If thou shalt make*, as formerly; but He said: 'Make an altar, and sacrifice continually', as though He had need of these things. Wherefore He laid upon them continual burnt offerings with a necessity, and caused them to abstain from meats by means of distinctions of meats. For from that time were animals discerned, and clean and unclean flesh; from that time were separations, and purifications, and baptisms, and sprinklings; from that time were sacrifices, and offerings, and tables; from that time were burnt offerings, and oblations, and shewbread, and the offering up of sacrifices, and firstlings, and redemptions, and he-goats for sin, and vows, and many other things marvellous. For because of manifold sins there were laid upon them customs unspeakable; but by none of them did they abide, but they again provoked the Lord. Wherefore He yet added to them by the Second Legislation a blindness worthy of their works, and spoke thus: *If there be found in a man sins worthy of death, and he die, and ye hang him upon a tree; his body shall not remain the night upon the tree, but ye shall surely bury him the same day: for cursed is every one that is hanged upon a tree*; that when Christ should come they might not be able to help Him, but might suppose that He was guilty of a curse. For their blinding therefore was this spoken, as Isaiah said: *Behold, I show my righteousness, and thine evils: and they shall not help thee at all.* For the Lord

---

4 Cf. Ex. xxxii 1, 8.   10 Cf. Ex. xx 24 f., Deut. xxvii 5 f.
25 Deut. xxi. 22 f., cf. Gal. iii 13.   32 Isa. lvii 12.

2 flesh from the sea] i. e. the quails blown up 'from the sea' (Nu. xi 31).
13 with] lit. 'and' (cf. Lat.).   15 and clean and unclean flesh] Or

ducebat, qui de caelo mannam eis praebuit et de mare carnem dedit eis, qui de monte[m] legem dedit eis: hunc denegauerunt dicentes: *Non habemus Deum qui praecedat nos. Et fecerunt uitulum fusilem et adorauerunt eum,* et sacrificauerunt sculptili.
5 Propterea iratus est dominus et in furore irae suae, cum misericordia bonitatis suae, alligauit illos in secundatione legis et obstrictione o⟨ne⟩ris et in duritia catenae. Itaque non iam dixit, *Si facies,* sed dixit: 'Fac altarem, et sacrifica incessanter', quasi qui talia egeret, 'et conbure frequenter'. Et necessita-
10 tem inposuit illis, et ab escis separauit eos. Ex tunc descretiones escarum, ex tunc animalia munda⟨e⟩ et inmundae carnis significantur, ex tunc segregationes et purificationes et baptisma et asparsio, ex tunc sacrificia . . .

7 oneris] Cf. Syr.   9 egerit cod.   11 munda⟨e⟩] Cf. Syr.

possibly 'and flesh of that which is clean and that which is unclean'. 30 to help Him] So Syr. (H S). The verb is the same as in the following quotation (ὠφελήσει LXX). Funk puts, without note, 'eum agnoscere'; Flemming renders 'zu ihm halten', but gives the literal sense in his notes. I see no way but to translate the text.

judged them with a just judgement, and dealt thus with them because of their wickedness, and hardened their heart like Pharaoh's; as the Lord said to them by Isaiah: *Hearing ye shall hear, and shall not understand; and seeing ye shall see, and shall not know. For the heart of this people is waxed gross; and their eyes they have shut, and their ears they have stopped, that they may not be converted: lest at any time they should see with their eyes, and hear with their ears.* And in the Gospel again He said: *This people's heart is waxed gross; and their eyes they have shut, and their ears they have stopped, lest at any time they should be converted. But blessed are your eyes that see, and your ears that hear.* For you have been released from the bonds, and relieved of the Second Legislation, and set free from bitter slavery, and the curse has been taken off and put away from you.

[vi. 17] For the Second Legislation was imposed for the making of the calf and for idolatry. But you through baptism have been set free from idolatry, and from the Second Legislation, which was (imposed) on account of idols, you have been released. For in the Gospel (p. 110) He renewed and fulfilled and affirmed the Law; but the Second Legislation He did away and abolished. For indeed it was to this end that He came, that He might affirm the Law, and abolish the Second Legislation, and fulfil the power of men's liberty, and show forth the resurrection of the dead. For even before His

---

2 Cf. Joh. xii 40, Ex. iv 21, etc.   3 Isa. vi 9 f., Acts xxviii 26 f.
9 Mt. xiii 15 f.

2 and hardened their heart] Comp. also p. 230, l. 30. Flemming and Funk render 'and their hardness of heart', but the noun-form which this presupposes does not occur.   24 the power of men's liberty] Cf. Iren. *Haer.* IV xxviii ' Haec ergo, quae in seruitutem et in signa data sunt illis, circumscripsit nouo libertatis testamento', and again 'tanquam qui et libertatis potestatem acceperimus'.   24–25 show forth the resurrection] Cf. *Ep. Barnab.* v 6 ἵνα καταργήσῃ τὸν θάνατον καὶ τὴν ἐκ νεκρῶν ἀνάστασιν δείξῃ, which is copied by Hippolytus in the eucharistic prayer of his *Apost. Trad.* 'ut mortem soluat . . . et resurrectionem manifestet': see also *Philos.* x 33 καὶ ἀνάστασιν ἐφανέρωσεν, and Iren. *Apost. Preaching* 38 'And He manifested the resurrection, Himself becoming the first-begotten of the dead': in the *Acts of John* c. 109 we find τὴν δειχθεῖσαν ἡμῖν διά σου ἀνάστασιν.

coming He foretold His coming through the prophets, and
together with His coming He signified also the disobedience
of the People, and preached the undoing of the Second Legislation; as He said by Jeremiah: *Why bring ye me frankin-*
cense from Sheba, and cinnamon from a far country? Your
burnt offerings are not acceptable unto me, and your sacrifices
delight me not. And again He said: *Bring together your burnt*
offerings with your sacrifices, and eat flesh. For I gave you no
command, when I brought you out from the land of Egypt,
neither concerning burnt offerings nor concerning sacrifices.
Yea, verily, in the Law He gave no command, but in the bonds
of the Second Legislation, after that they had served idols.
And again by Isaiah also He said: *To what purpose is the*
multitude of your sacrifices unto me? saith the Lord. I am
sated with burnt offerings of rams; and the fat of lambs and

---

4 Jer. vi 20.   7 Jer. vii 21 f.   13 Isa. i 11-14.

1-2 and together with His coming] Flemming and Funk mistranslate here through reading the prep. '*am*, ' with ', as the subst. ' people '.
2-3 the disobedience of the People] lit. 'the People, that it was disobedient'.
4 This and the following text from Jerem. are quoted near together in Iren. *Haer.* IV xxix 3, where the same problem is being handled.
11 Yea] '*ēn*, defectively for '*eyn*, and not to be read 'if', as Flemming took it.

the blood of oxen I desire not. And when ye come to see my face, who hath required these things at your hands? Trample my courts no more. If ye will bring me fine flour, it is a vain oblation; and your new moons and your sabbaths and solemn days are rejected of me: your fasts and your restings are not acceptable unto me, and your festivals my soul hateth. And in all the Scriptures He speaks thus; and through the sacrifices He abolishes the Second Legislation; for, as we have already said, it is in the Second Legislation that sacrifices are prescribed.

If, then, even before His coming He made known and revealed His coming, and the disobedience of the People, and spoke of the abolition of the Second Legislation, much more, being come, did He fully and completely abolish the Second Legislation. For He did not use sprinklings, or baptisms, or other wonted rites; nor did He offer sacrifices or burnt offerings, or any thing that it is written in the Second Legislation to offer. And what else did He (hereby) signify but the abolition of the Second Legislation? as also He loosed you and called you from the bonds, and said: *Come unto me, all ye that toil and are laden with heavy burdens; and I will give you rest.* Now we know that our Saviour did not say (this) to the Gentiles, but He said it to us His disciples from among the Jews, and brought us out from burdens and a heavy load.

Those therefore who do not (p. 111) obey Him, that He may lighten and deliver them from the bonds of the Second Legislation, obey not God, who has called them to come forth unto

---

20 Mt. xi 28.

---

15 For He did not use, etc.] The author of *AC* took exception to this, and removed the negatives: καὶ γὰρ καὶ περιετμήθη καὶ ἐρραντίσθη, θυσίας τε προσήνεγκεν καὶ ὁλοκαυτώσεις καὶ τοῖς ἄλλοις ἐθισμοῖς ἐχρήσατο (with other changes in the context).   16 wonted rites] lit. 'customs', though S has, by a slight transcriptional error, 'festivals' (H omits the context). 19-20 He loosed you and called you] H (= Lat.): om. S, but clearly by error (cf. p. 14 'For He set loose from those bonds and thus called... and said: *Come unto me*, etc.). We may compare Irenaeus *Haer.* IV xvi (as to Sabbath) 'Uindicabat enim semen eius Dominus, soluens a uinculis et aduocans ad salutem'; and III x .'Aduocabat autem omnes homines plangentes, et ... soluebat eos a uinculis'.

[LI] . . . *nolo, etsi ueniatis ut uideam uos. Quis enim exquisiuit haec de manibus uestris? Calcare atrium meum non adponitis adhuc. Si adferatis mihi similaginem, uanum: incensum abominatio mihi est: numenias uestras et sabbata et*
5 *diem magnam non suffero: ieiunium et uacationem et ferias uestras odit anima mea.* Et in omnibus scripturis conuenienter dicens despicit per sacrificia secundationem: sacrificia enim, sicuti praediximus, de secundatione scripta sunt.

Si ergo et ante aduentum eius †libertatem† eius et incredu-
10 litatem populi et destructionem secundationis †significaturus conrigit,† cum uenisset ipse †omnipotens† secundationem destruxit. Neque enim asparsionibus neque aliis consuetudinibus usus est, neque sacrificia optulit neque holocausta neque quanta ad secundationem legis offerri scripta erant: quid aliut nisi distructionem
15 secundationis faciens? et nos suluit uocans de uinculis et dicens: *Uenite ad me, omnes qui laboratis et onerati estis, et ego uos repausabo.* Agnoscimus ergo quoniam saluator noster non gentibus sed nobis, qui ex Hebreis discipuli eius fuimus, dicebat, et a labore et ab oneratione nos eduxit.

20 Qui autem non ei obaudiunt ut releuentur et de uinculis secundationis legis exeant, et domino non credunt, qui vocat eos ad solutionem et remissionem et refrigerium, et semet ipsos

---

4 *incensum . . . mihi est*] om. *AC* (= Syr.). 7 despicit] ἀπαναίνεται *AC*. 9 libertatem] Certainly correct to 'aduentum', with Syr. (cf. also p. 224, l. 25 f.). Lat. represents παρρησίαν, for παρουσίαν, the word in *AC* just before. Funk keeps 'libertatem', and substitutes 'hominis' for 'eius'. 10–11 significaturus conrigit] This is kept by Funk, though it is quite impossible. To begin with, we may adopt 'significat' out of the first word; then we must make what we can of the remaining 'urusconrigit' (the final *t* may be *s*, Hauler says). This group must be quite corrupt, or else a misreading of the palimpsest: Syr. reads here 'much more (being come)', and *AC* πολλῷ μᾶλλον (ἐλθών). Is not, or was not, therefore the reading simply 'multo magis'? 11 omnipotens] 'fully and completely' Syr., which may be a double rendering of παντελῶς (*AC* has altered at this point). I have no doubt that the word in Lat. should be read 'omnimodis' or 'omnimodo'. 14 offerri] 'offeris' cod.

release and rest and refreshment; and they bind themselves with the heavy burdens of the Second Legislation, which are of no avail. [vi. 18] For our Lord and Saviour Himself, who gave the Law and the Second Legislation, bears witness concerning the Law that it is life to them that keep it; ⟨but⟩ concerning the Second Legislation He testifies and shows that it is a bond and a blindness. For He everywhere makes a distinction; and He bears witness to the Law, and admonishes and commands us that we be under the Law: for every one who is not under law is lawless. And therefore He thus bears witness to the Law: *In the law of the Lord shall be his pleasure, and in his law will he meditate day and night. Not so the wicked.* We see then, beloved, how the righteous are declared blessed on account of righteousness and the keeping of the Law. But *not so the wicked*; for they have no pleasure either in the righteous or in the Law, and they do not mediate therein. Wherefore He calls 'the wicked' those who do not converse according to the Law. For in the Gospel also He affirms the Law, and calls and brings us out from ⟨the burden of the bonds and from the Second⟩ Legislation. But that the Law is other than the Second Legislation, in David likewise He shows by a distinction, speaking thus: *Let us sever their cords, and loose their yoke from us.* You see how the Holy Spirit speaks as it were out of the mouth of the world and reveals its thought, and says that the Law is a 'yoke', but the Second Legislation 'cords'. For the Law is a yoke, because like the plough-yoke of oxen it is laid upon the former People and upon the present Church of God; even as now in the Church it is upon us who are called from the People, and upon you who from among the Gentiles have obtained mercy: it has

5 Cf. Rom. x 5, Lev. xviii 5.   11 Ps. i 2.   22 Ps. ii 3.   23 Cf. Acts iv 25.

---

8 admonishes] The verb usually means to convict or confute, and Lat. has 'conuincens'.   10 lawless] lit. 'iniquitous', but here for παράνομος (*AC*).   14 righteousness] I have removed a suffix which would require us to translate 'the righteousness', sc. of the Law.   19-20 ⟨the burden ... Second⟩] Supplied from Lat. The text reads 'and from the Law He calls us', etc.   But that] 'And' text: 'quia uero' Lat.   23-25 You see

ligant honeribus secundationis non bonis. Ipse enim dominus Deus, qui legem et secundationem illis dedit, in lege quidem perhibet testimonium, uitam esse in ea his qui [LII] utuntur eam; secundationem autem manifestat uinculum esse cecitatis.
5 Ubique enim disting⟨u⟩it, legi testimonium perhibens et conuincens, et in lege quidem nos esse iubet: omnis enim qui non est sub lege, †inlege† est. Propterea testimonium perhibet legi ita: *Sed in lege domini uoluntas eius, et in lege eius meditabitur die et nocte. Non sic impii.* Uidemus, fratres, iustos quidem
10 beatificari per ipsum in iustitia et in legis conuersatione: *non* autem *ita impios*, neque enim sunt iusti neque consentiunt legi neque meditantur eam. Ergo 'impios' illos dixit qui non utuntur lege. Nam et in euangelio confirmat legem; de uinculorum autem onere et de secundatione prouocans nos educit. Quia
15 uero aliut est ⟨lex et aliut⟩ secundatio, et in Dauid destinguens dicit: *Dirumpamus uincula ipsorum, et proiciamus a nobis iugum eorum.* Uidete quomodo spiritus sanctus tamquam ex sono unius uocis dicit, et populi cogitatum adnuntians adserit 'iugum' quidem esse legem, 'uincula' autem secundationem. 'Iugum'
20 ergo legem hancpropter dicit, quia ueluti iugus boum inposita est tam super priorem populum quam etiam super ecclesiae populum: sicuti et modo in ecclesia est tam super nos, qui de populo uocati sumus, quam super uos, qui de gentibus misericordiam estis consecuti. Utrosque igitur in idipsud congregat

2 in lege] We expect 'de lege', or 'legi' (cf. Syr., and l. 5 below). 7 inlege] Cf. *AC* (vi 23. 7) πανταχοῦ γὰρ ἐννόμους ἡμᾶς εἶναι βούλεται, ἀλλ' οὐχὶ παρανόμους. So 'inlege' may be for παράνομος, as 'sub lege' is for ἔννομος. 10 conuersatione] Syr. ('keeping') would suggest 'conseruatione'. 15 ⟨lex et aliut⟩] From Syr., which has the same construction, 'other is the Law and other the Second Legislation'. 17–18 ex sono (sonu cod.) unius uocis] This does not yield a very satisfactory sense. In Syr. 'out of the mouth of *the world*' is naturally referred to the ἔθνη, λαοί, etc., of the psalm (*vv.* 1–2). I can only suggest that 'unius uocis' may be a misreading of 'uniuersi', or 'uniuersali'. populi cogitatum] 'its (sc. the world's) thought' Syr. 21 pupolum cod.

... its thought] Syr. by itself gives a good sense, but there is difficulty in harmonizing it with Lat. It may be noted that the author appears to have in mind Acts iv 25 ff., where Ps. ii 1, 2 is introduced with the words ὁ τοῦ πατρὸς ἡμῶν διὰ πνεύματος ἁγίου στόματος Δαυεὶδ παιδός σου εἰπών. 27 plough-yoke] So B: 'snare-yoke': simply 'iugus' Lat.

gathered and held us both together in one accord. But He well calls the Second Legislation ' bonds '; for when the People served idols, there was added to them the weight of the Second Legislation. For the bonds were justly imposed, as it befell the People then; but the Church has not been bound. For to Ezekiel He explains and makes known that the Law of life is one, but the second Law, of death, is another; for He spoke thus: *I brought them forth from the land of Egypt, and brought them into the wilderness, and gave them my commandments, and made known to them my judgements: that if a man should do them, he might live* (p. 112) *by them.* And afterwards, upbraiding them because they had sinned and had not kept the Law of life, He repeats to them and saith thus: *I have given them commandments that are not good, and judgements whereby they may not live.* Now the judgements which do not give life are those of the bonds. Hence also the word aforesaid in the Second Legislation was for the blinding of a blind people, to wit: *Cursed is every one that is hanged upon a tree.* For thus did they think of Him who gives and distributes blessings to them that are worthy, that He is under a curse. Wherefore, (because) they knew Him not, even after the signs that were done by Him in the world: when He suffered, justly in accordance with their works that word was set down for the blinding of the People; and it was a bar that they might not believe and be saved. Whence also by Isaiah He speaks thus: *Who is blind, but my servants? and the servants of God are blinded. And I have brought out a blind people, that have eyes, and see not: and their ears also are deaf.* For by this word, because of their works, their eyes were blinded, and their ears made deaf like Pharaoh's. Hence with this word the Second Legislation also was imposed, which Moses appointed. And it is the Second Legislation that He called *judgements that are not good*; and it cannot save alive.

---

8 Ez. xx 9–11. 14 Ez. xx 25. 18 Deut. xxi 23. 26 Isa. xlii 19.
27 Isa. xliii 8.

5-6 For to Ezekiel, etc.] For a remarkable parallel to this and some other passages of *Didasc.* in Aphraates Hom. xv 7-8 see Additional Notes.

et gubernat. 'Uincula' autem merito uocauit secundationem; nam quoniam ad idololatriam conuersus est populus, ideo illis secundatio ad onerationem . . .

---

1 Uincula autem] 'isi ncultum cum' Hauler: but later he verified the above conjecture (see Funk *Didasc. et Const. Apost.* vol. i p. xi note 1).

---

7 the second Law] Not the usual rendering of δευτέρωσις in Syr.   14 *I have given*, etc.] Quoted also by Irenaeus *Haer*. IV xxvi 1 in his discussion of the Law: 'At ubi conuersi sunt in uituli factionem . . . aptam concupiscentiae suae acceperunt reliquam seruitutem, a Deo quidem non abscindentem, in seruitutis autem iugo dominantem eis: quemadmodum et Ezechiel propheta causas talis legis datae reddens ait: Et post concupiscentiam cordis sui erant oculi eorum; et ego dedi eis praecepta non bona, et iustificationes in quibus non uiuent in eis.' See also p. 14 before and note.   21 (because) . . . not] Reading ܠܐ for ܠ of the text. 22–23 when He suffered] To be taken with the following: it was when Christ was hanged on the cross that the words took effect.   24 was a bar] lit. 'hindered'.   29 this word] sc. Deut. xxi 23, as above.

They therefore who bring upon themselves those things which were imposed for the worship of idols, shall inherit the Woes; for *Woe to them that prolong their sins as a long rope, and their iniquity as the band of a heifer's yoke.* For the yoke of the bonds is the *heifer's yoke*—the bonds of the ⟨Second⟩ Legislation (now) upon the People, which like *a long rope* is laid upon them by reason of other men's sins which from former times and generations they bring upon themselves. Every one who strives to be under the ⟨Second⟩ Legislation becomes guilty of the calf-worship; for the Second Legislation was imposed for nothing else but for idolatry. For the bonds were decreed because of idolatry; they therefore who regard them are bondsmen and idolaters. Wherefore, every

---

3 Isa. v. 18.   9 Cf. Gal. v 3.

2-3 the Woes] The plur., if correct, will refer to the series of Woes in Isa. v 18-20.   4 *a heifer's yoke*] Or 'the yoke of a cart'. The words for 'heifer' and 'cart' have the same consonants in Hebrew and Syriac; but the author is using the LXX, which has δαμάλεως.   5-6 the ⟨Second⟩ Legislation] The text has simply 'the Law' (*nāmōsa*); but the *deuterosis* is clearly meant, and we must supply ⟨*tenyān*⟩ *nāmōsa*. The same note applies again at l. 9 below.

one who binds himself becomes guilty of the Woe, and ought likewise to profess idolatry. Now one who is such asserts also the curse against our Saviour; for if thou uphold the Second Legislation, thou also assertest the curse against our Saviour, and thou art held fast in the bonds and made guilty of the Woe—an enemy of the Lord God.

Cease therefore, beloved brethren, (p. 113) you who from among the People have believed, yet desire (still) to be tied with the bonds, and say that the Sabbath is prior to the first day of the week because that the Scripture has said: *In six days did God make all things; and on the seventh day he finished all his works, and he sanctified it.*

We ask you now, which is first, Alaf or Tau? For that

---

10 Ex. xx 11, Gen. ii 2 f.

---

3 the curse] sc. that in Deut. xxi 23, already spoken of. 10 *In six days*, etc.] A combination of Ex. xx 11 with Gen. ii 2–3. Compare *Ep. Barnab.* xv 3 τὸ σάββατον λέγει ἐν ἀρχῇ τῆς κτίσεως· καὶ ἐποίησεν ὁ θεὸς ἐν ἓξ ἡμέραις τὰ ἔργα τῶν χειρῶν αὐτοῦ, καὶ συνετέλεσεν ἐν τῇ ἡμέρᾳ τῇ ἑβδόμῃ καὶ κατέπαυσεν ἐν αὐτῇ, καὶ ἡγίασεν αὐτήν. We shall presently find some further coincidences with *Barnab.* xv in our author's treatment of the Sabbath.

(day) which is the greater is that which is the beginning of the world, even as the Lord our Saviour said by Moses: *In the beginning God created the heaven and the earth. But the earth was invisible and unshapen.* And again He said: *And there was one day*: and as yet the seventh day was unknown. But what say you? Which is greater, that which had come into being, and existed, or that which was yet unknown, and of which there was no expectation that it should come to be? But again we ask you: Are your last children blessed, or the firstborn? as the Scripture also saith: *Jacob shall be blessed among the firstborn*; and: *My son, my firstborn (is) Israel*; and: *Every male that openeth the womb of his mother is blessed to the Lord.*

But that we may make you firm in the faith, hear ye. The first day and the last are equal; for learn how you find it written, that *In his kingdom the day of the Lord is as a thousand years: the day of yesterday which is past; and as a watch of the night.* (One day therefore is a thousand years in the kingdom of Christ, wherein also will be the judgement. For *a watch of the night*) He said concerning the judgement, which is a dark prison to them that are condemned. A day therefore is to be revealed in which the sun will stand in his mid-course, and the moon likewise, following the sun. For He said: *Behold, I make the first things as the last, and the last as the first*; and: *The last shall be first, and the first*

---

2 Gen. i 1 f. 4 Gen. i 5. 10 ? (cf. Ecclus. xxxvi 14).
11 Ex. iv 22. 12 Lk. ii 23 (cf. Ex. xiii 2, 12). 16 Cf. 2 Pet. iii 8,
Ep. Barnab. xv 4: Ps. lxxxix (xc) 4. 22 Cf. Habak. iii 11, *Ep. Barnab.*
xv 5. 24 Cf. *Ep. Barnab.* vi 13. 25 Mt. xx. 16.

---

4 *invisible*] lit. 'not known': ἀόρατος LXX. The Syriac verb 'to know' often bears, in the passive, the sense of appearing, as in the common phrase 'plain ('known') and manifest'. Hence in ll. 5, 7 below 'unknown' is no variant to 'necdum ... manifestato', 'necdum manifestatum' in Lat. 10 *Jacob*, etc.] The quotation has not been identified, but comp. Ecclus. xxxvi 14 Ἰσραὴλ ὃν πρωτογόνῳ ὡμοίωσας. 13 *blessed*] So also Lat.: ἅγιον in Lk. ii 23, and ἁγιάζειν in Ex. xiii 2, 12. 16 *In His kingdom*] om. Lat. (but apparently implied there in the comment). The words perhaps do not belong to the quotation. 16–17 *the day ... a thousand years*] Cf. 2 Pet. iii 8; also *Ep. Barnab.* xv 4 ἡ γὰρ ἡμέρα παρ' αὐτῷ χίλια ἔτη. αὐτὸς δέ μοι μαρτυρεῖ λέγων· ἰδοὺ ἡμέρα κυρίου

DIDASCALIA APOSTOLORUM

[LIII] . . . . est, principium saeculi est. Similiter per Moysetem dominus Deus dicit: *In principio fecit Deus caelum et terram. Terra autem erat inuisibilis et inconposita.* Et post haec infert et dicit: *Et factus est dies unus*, necdum septimo manifestato. Quid ergo maius esse suspicatur? id quod iam factum est et constat, aut id quod necdum manifestatum est et nec speratur quia futurum est? Et adhuc aliut interrogamus uos: filii uestri nouissimi natu benedicti sunt, aut primitiui? quoniam et scriptura dicit, quod *Iacob inter primitiuos benedictus est*; et: *Filius primogenitus mihi Istrahel*; et: *Omne masculum aperiens matricem matris benedictum domino.*

Ut autem uos confirmemus in fide, audite, si prima dies et nouissima aequales sunt. Quomodo itaque, discite: inuenietis scriptum, quoniam *Dies domini ut mille anni: dies hesternus qui transiit, et custodia nocturna.* Dies unus ergo mille anni in regno Christi, in quo et iudicium erit. *Custodiam* enim *nocturnam* iudicium significat, quod est poena tenebrarum his qui condemnati sunt. Dies ergo manifestatur, cum medium cursum incipit habere sol, similiter et luna, quia secuta erit: nam id dictum est: *Ecce facio prima sicut nouissima, et nouissima sicut prima*; et: *Erunt nouissimi primari⟨i⟩, et*

---

13 si] om. Syr., and perh. rightly.   14 Hauler and Funk punctuate 'Quomodo? Itaque discite'.   15 quoniam]+'in His kingdom' Syr. (and cf. Lat. at l. 17).   17–18 Custodiam . . . significat] i. e. perhaps 'Custodiam enim nocturnam (dicendo) iudicium significat (cf. Syr.); but Funk corrects to 'custodia . . . nocturna'.   22 et: *Erunt*] Hauler prints '*ita e*runt'; but his note shows that this is mere conjecture: I follow Syr. (and so Funk).

ἔσται ὡς χίλια ἔτη. In our text the saying displaces the first half of Ps. lxxxix 4. See Resch p. 288.   18–20 (One day . . . *the night*)] From Lat.: the omission in Syr. is plainly accidental.   21–22 A day therefore, etc.] Cf. *Ep. Barnab.* xv 5 καὶ ἀλλάξει τὸν ἥλιον καὶ τὴν σελήνην καὶ τοὺς ἀστέρας, τότε καλῶς καταπαύσεται ἐν τῇ ἡμέρᾳ τῇ ἑβδόμῃ. Comp. Aphraates Hom. xiii 13 'But let us keep the Sabbath of God . . . that we may enter into the Sabbath of rest, wherein the heaven and the earth keep Sabbath and all creatures pause and rest'.   24–25 Behold . . . *as the first*] Cf. *Ep. Barnab.* vi 13 λέγει δὲ κύριος· ἰδοὺ ποιῶ τὰ ἔσχατα ὡς τὰ πρῶτα, and Hippol. *in Dan.* lib. iv c. 37 ἔσονται γὰρ τὰ ἔσχατα ὡς τὰ πρῶτα. See Resch pp. 167–8.

last; and: *Remember no more the former things, and let them not come to your mind. Behold, I make things new, which now shall be revealed*; and: *In those days and in that time they shall no more say: The ark of the covenant; neither shall it come to mind, nor be visited, nor any more be made.* But 5 the Sabbath itself is counted even unto the Sabbath, and it becomes eight (days); thus an ogdoad is (reached), which is more than the Sabbath, even the first of the week.

Wherefore, brethren, every day is the Lord's; for the Scripture has said: *The earth is the Lord's with the fullness* 10 *thereof: the world that is under heaven, and all that dwell therein.* For if God willed that we should be idle one day for six, first of all the patriarchs and righteous men, and all they that were before Moses, would have remained idle (upon it), and God Himself also with all His creatures. But now 15 all (p. 114) the governance of the world is carried on ever continually; and the spheres do not cease even for a moment from their course, but at God's command (their universal and perpetual motion proceeds.) For if He would say: *Thou shalt be idle, and thy son, and thy servant, and thy maidservant,* 20 *and thine ass*, how does He (continue to) work, causing to

---

1 Isa. xliii 18 f.   3 Jer. iii 16.   10 Ps. xxiii (xxiv) 1.   19 Cf. Ex. xx 10, Deut. v 14.

5-6 But the Sabbath itself, etc.] At p. 234 above it was argued that the first day of the week is greater than the Sabbath, as being the first of all days. With that and the present passage comp. Justin *Dial.* 41 μία γὰρ τῶν σαββάτων, πρώτη μένουσα τῶν πασῶν ἡμερῶν, κατὰ τὸν ἀριθμὸν πάλιν τῶν πασῶν ἡμερῶν τῆς κυκλοφορίας ὀγδόη καλεῖται, καὶ πρώτη οὖσα μένει.   6 even unto] 'ad' Lat. The Syr. is lit. 'upon' or 'over'.   7 is (reached)] lit. 'becomes' (= γίνεται).   8 more than] Or 'better than', which also may be the sense intended by Syr.: 'super' Lat. Flemming translates this sentence: 'Aber eben der Sabbat wird zur Woche hinzugezählt, und (es) ergibt acht (Tage). Die Zahl Acht also ist das, was über die Woche hinausreicht, der Sonntag'. It is better not to introduce the word 'week' here: the idea is that if you count from Sabbath to Sabbath *inclusively*, you get the number 8: but 'the 8th day' is the first of the week (as in Justin, just above, and *Ep. Barnab.* xv 9). The author is proving that the Christian Sunday is greater than the Jewish Sabbath.   13 the patriarchs, etc.] Cf. Justin *Dial.* 27 ἢ καὶ τοὺς πρὸ Μωυσέως καὶ 'Αβραὰμ ὠνομασμένους δικαίους ... μήτε τὰ σάββατα φυλάξαντας, διὰ τί οὐκ ἐδίδασκε ταῦτα ποιεῖν; Comp. Iren. *Haer.* IV. xxvii 2 'Sed et reliqua autem omnis multitudo eorum qui ante Abraham fuerunt iusti, et eorum patriarcharum qui ante Moysem fuerunt, et sine his quae praedicta sunt

primarii nouissimi; et: *Nolite recordare antiqua et cogitare: ecce facio noua, quae nunc orientur*; et: *In diebus illis et in tempore illo non dicent* [LIV] *adhuc: Arca testamenti sancti Istrahel: non ascendit in corde nec uisitabitur iam.* Sed et
5 ipse sabbatus intra se cum resupputatur, sabbatum ad sabbatum, fiunt octo dies: octaua igitur ⟨fit⟩, quae super sabbatum est, una sabbati.

Unde, fratres, omnes dies domini sunt; dicit enim scriptura: *Domini est terra et plenitudo eius, orbis terrarum et uniuersi
10 inhabitantes in ea*. Si itaque uolebat Deus post sex dies uacare nos, primum utique patriarchae et qui ante Moysetem fuerunt iusti omnes uacassent, aut forte et ipse Deus cum uniuersa creatura. Nunc autem uniuersa dispensatio—quod dicit Grecus oeconomia—mundi semper gubernatur: subinde
15 non cessantibus elementis nec punctum horae a motione sueta, uniuersa et perennis motio eorum ex praecepto domini fit. Si autem, *Uacabis tu*, inquid, *et filius tuus et puer tuus et ancilla tua et subiugale tuum*, quomodo ipse operatur pariens,

---

6 ⟨fit⟩] From Syr.   13–14 quod dicit Graecus oeconomia] Cf. again p. 255, l. 18 'quod dicit Graecus fotisma'; and in the translation of the *Apost. Trad.* of Hippolytus 'quod dicit Graecus antitypum . . . quod dicit Graecus similitudinem' (Hauler p. 112), 'quod dicitur Graece apoforetum' (Hauler p. 114). This is one of several indications that the translations in the Verona palimpsest are all from the same hand.
15 elementis] 'emolumentis' cod. The corresponding Syriac word (*mauzĕlātha*), which I have rendered 'spheres', denotes the heavenly bodies, and probably translates στοιχεῖα.

(sc. circumcision and Sabbath) et sine lege Moysi iustificabantur', also Aphraates Hom. xiii 8 'These righteous fathers did not observe the Sabbath, but they were justified by faith'.   15 But now, etc.] Cf. Justin *Dial.* 29 ἐπειδὴ καὶ ὁ θεὸς τὴν αὐτὴν διοίκησιν τοῦ κόσμου ὁμοίως καὶ ἐν ταύτῃ ἡμέρᾳ πεποίηται καθάπερ καὶ ἐν ταῖς ἄλλαις ἁπάσαις.   18–19 ⟨their . . . proceeds⟩] Supplied from Lat.

generate, and making †the winds to blow†, and fostering and nourishing us His creatures? On the Sabbath day He causes (the winds) to blow, and (the waters) to flow, and (thus) works. But this (the Sabbath) has been set as a type for the times, even as many other things have been set for a type. The Sabbath therefore is a type of the (final) rest, signifying the seventh thousand (-years). [vi. 19] But the Lord our Saviour, when He was come, fulfilled the types and explained the parables, and He showed those things that are life-giving, and those that cannot help He did away, and those that cannot give life He abolished.

And not only in His own person did He show this, but He wrought also by the Romans; and He overthrew the temple, and caused the altar to cease, and made an end of sacrifices, and all the commands and bonds that are in the Second Legislation He abolished. For the Romans also hold the Law, but they refuse the Second Legislation: therefore is their dominion strong. Thou, therefore, who desirest to-day to be under the Second Legislation, whilst the Romans rule thou canst not perform aught that is written in the Second Legislation. For thou canst not stone the wicked, nor kill idolaters, nor discharge the ministry of sacrifices, nor perform the libations and sprinklings ⟨with the ashes⟩ of a heifer; nor canst thou fulfil aught else of those things which are in the Second Legislation, nor observe them. For it is written: *Cursed is every one that keepeth not these words to do them*; and this is a thing impossible, to fulfil the Second Legislation

---

23 Nu. xix 9 f.: cf. Heb. ix 13. 26 Deut. xxvii 26, Gal. iii 10.

---

1 making the winds to blow] 'prouidens' Lat. Compare with this passage the *Odes of Solomon* xvi 12 f. 'And He rested from His works: and the created things run their courses, and work their works, and they know not how to stand still or to be idle'; and Aphraates Hom. xiii (*de Sabbato*) 3 'But we see that (on the Sabbath) the sun travels on, and the moon proceeds, and the stars run, and the winds blow, and the clouds fly', etc.   2–3 causes ... to flow] Without the Gk. original it is difficult to trace connexion here between Syr. and Lat.   5 a type] Cf. Iren. *Haer.* IV xxvii 1 'In signo ergo data sunt haec' (sc. circumcision and Sabbath); see also *ibid.* 2, and Justin *Dial.* 21.   6–7 rest ... seventh thousand (-years)] Cf. *Ep. Barnab.* xv 4 ὅτι ἐν ἑξακισχιλίοις

prouidens, nutriens, gubernans nos et creationes suas, et in die sabbatis †oculum circumeunt† mouentia se omnia, et operantur? Sed haec ad tempus ad formae similitudinem facta sunt: nam et hoc similitudo est septimanae requietionis, 5 septimum [et] milesimum annum significans. Dominus uero noster et saluator ueniens et similitudines impleuit et parabolas ostendit, et ea quae saluant docuit, et ea quae nihil iuuant destruxit, et ea quae non saluant soluit; non solum per semet ipsum docens, sed et per Romanos inspirans: et 10 templum [LV] deposuit, altare cessare faciens et sacrificia destruens, et omnia quae in secundatione praecepta erant uincula destruens. Nam et Romani legem utuntur, secundationem autem praetermiserunt: propterea et ⟨imperium eorum⟩ confirmatum est. Tu autem, si hodie sub secundatione de-15 sideras esse, Romanis imperantibus quae sunt secundationis facere non potes: neque enim lapidare malignos, neque interficere idololatras, neque ministeria sacrificiorum facere, neque uitulae cinus in asparsione facere, neque aliut quicquam de his que sunt secundationis conplere, sed nec contingere illa. 20 Scriptum est enim: *Maledictus omnis qui non inmanet in uerbis libri huius, ut faciat ea.* Inpossibile autem est, cum in dispersione inter gentes sitis, ut secundationem inplere

---

2 oculum] This cannot be right, and in fact Hauler marks every letter as uncertain. The *s* at the end of 'sabbatis' probably belongs to the following group of letters, which therefore may have been 'secula'. The next word, 'circumeunt', appears also to be doubtful; but 'saecula circumeunt' would give a tolerable sense. Another possible suggestion would be 'circulum circumeunt'.   9 inspirans] 'He wrought' Syr.: both perhaps rendering ἐνεργῶν.   13 (imperium eorum)] From Syr.

ἔτεσιν συντελέσει κύριος τὰ σύμπαντα... οὐκοῦν, τέκνα, ἐν ἓξ ἡμέραις, ἐν τοῖς ἑξακισχιλίοις ἔτεσιν συντελεσθήσεται τὰ σύμπαντα, and xv 8 οὐ τὰ νῦν σάββατα (ἐμοὶ) δεκτά, ἀλλὰ ὃ πεποίηκα, ἐν ᾧ καταπαύσας τὰ πάντα ἀρχὴν ἡμέρας ὀγδόης ποιήσω, ὅ ἐστιν ἄλλου κόσμου ἀρχήν. See also Hippolytus *in Dan.* lib. iv c. 23 δεῖ οὖν ἐξ ἀνάγκης τὰ ἑξακισχίλια ἔτη πληρωθῆναι, ἵνα ἔλθῃ τὸ σάββατον, ἡ κατάπαυσις, ἡ ἁγία ἡμέρα κτλ. The same idea of the Sabbath as a type of the final 'requietio Dei' underlies Iren. *Haer.* IV xxvii 1, V xxx 4, and possibly also a passage in the *Apost. Trad.* of Hipoplytus (Hauler p. 119) in which he speaks of Christ's death on the cross as the ushering in of a new day: 'Unde incipiens dormire, principium alterius diei faciens, imaginem resurrectionis conpleuit.' The world was to end with the sixth millennium, after that was to follow the resurrection and κατάπαυσις, the true Sabbath of God.   23 ⟨with the ashes⟩] See Lat.

while dispersed among the Gentiles. Wherefore, every one that touches it falls under a curse, and binds himself, and inherits a Woe; and he asserts the curse against our Saviour, and as an enemy of God he is condemned.

But if thou follow Christ, thou shalt inherit the blessings. For *there is no disciple better than his master*: but when thou conformest to Him, through the Gospel thou conformest to the Law, and thou wilt entirely avoid the Second Legislation: even as the Lord Himself, who gave the kingdom to men, declared also that His commands ought justly to be kept; for in every age there is of right a legislation (given). Now having the Gospel, [thou conformest to the Law,] the renewal of the Law and the seal, beyond (p. 115) the Law and the Prophets seek nothing else. For the Second Legislation is undone, but the Law is made firm. And those who would be without the Law, against their will come under the Law; for He said in the Law: *Thou shalt not kill*; but if a man kill, he is condemned by the law of the Romans, and he comes under the Law. But if you follow and conform to the truth of the Church and the power of the Gospel, your hope in the Lord shall not be frustrated.

[vi. 20] Do you therefore avoid all heretics, who follow not the Law and the Prophets, and obey not Almighty God, but are His enemies; and who abstain from meats, and forbid to

---

5 Cf. 1 Pet. iii 9. 6 Mt. x 24. 17 Ex. xx 13.

---

3 the curse] Referring to Deut. xxi 23 (see p. 230). 7 through the Gospel] This might be taken with what precedes ('conformest to Him through the Gospel'); but in *AC* the paragraph begins ἑπόμενοι οὖν Χριστῷ τὰς εὐλογίας κληρονομήσωμεν, νόμῳ καὶ προφήταις διὰ τοῦ εὐαγγελίου στοιχήσωμεν. Lat. may be defective and in part corrupt. 11 of right] Or perhaps 'a suitable'; but the expression is usually adverbial. 12 having] lit. 'while you have'; and 'seek', at the end of the sentence, is also 2nd pers. plur. The following words, 'thou conformest to the Law', are therefore probably a repetition by error from ll. 7–8. 14 nothing else] i.e., as I understand, nothing else than the Gospel: *not* (as the position of the words might suggest) than the Law and the Prophets. The sense I take to be: 'Having the Gospel, ... seek nothing else (beside it) beyond the Law and the Prophets'— excluding only the Second Legislation. 21 be frustrated] lit. 'fall'.

possitis. Unde, cum eam contingere coeperis, sub maledicto incides, et conlegando temet ipsum uae possidebis, et optinebis maledictum quod aduersum saluatorem est, ⟨et⟩ tamquam Deo resistens condemnaberis.

5 Sequens uero Christum benedictiones possidebis. *Non est discipulus super magistrum*: hoc oportet nos sequi, et †nomine euangelico† contentos esse, et a secundatione omni modo nos abstinere: sicuti ipse dominus, cum regnum homin⟨ib⟩us conmitteret, et cognosceret quod iuste deberent custodiri prae-
10 cepta ipsius, secundum tempora et leges definitionis fecit. Habentes itaque euangelium, recapitu-[LVI]lationem et uerticem legis, signaculum quod plus est a lege ⟨et⟩ a profetis, †ut euangelio† nolite nihil aliud querere. Secundatio enim destructa est, lex autem confirmata est: et qui uolunt esse sine
15 lege, inuiti sub lege sunt. In lege dicit: *Non occides*; si quis ergo interfecerit, a lege per Romanos condemnatur, et sub lege est. Si ecclesiasticam uero regulam et euangelicam formam utamur et contenti ei simus, et spes nostra in domino non diminuabitur.

20 Obseruate igitur uos ab omni ⟨h⟩eretico, qui legem non utuntur neque profetas, et Deo omnipotenti non credentes inimicantur, et abstinent[es] se a cibis et prohibent nubere, et

2-3 et optinebis ... est, ⟨et⟩] So Funk: 'et optinebis maledictum; quod aduersum saluatorem es[t]' Hauler (but wrongly: cf. pp. 232, 243, 251). Syr. gves the true meaning.   4 condemnaueris cod. (*u* for *b*).
6 hoc] Read 'hunc' (?): cf. Syr.   6-7 nomine euangelico] The last two letters of 'nomine' are marked by Hauler as uncertain, and are said to be '*in rasura*'. I therefore suggest 'norma (*or* forma) euangelica': compare 'et euangelicam formam utamur et contenti ei simus' at ll. 17-18. Syr. appears to represent νόμῳ διὰ τοῦ εὐαγγελίου (cf. *AC*, there quoted).
7 contentos esse] στοιχήσωμεν *AC*, and Syr. ('conformest to') may well represent this verb.   9 cognosceret] 'declared' (lit. 'made known') Syr., which suggests γνωρίζειν as the Gk. verb.   iuste] 'iusti' cod., which Hauler keeps, altering 'custodiri' to 'custodire': but cf. Syr.
10 leges definitionis] Read 'legis definitiones' (?).   11-12 recapitulationem et uerticem] 'renewal' (only) Syr. Perhaps Lat. is a double rendering of ἀνακεφαλαίωσιν.   12-13 legis, signaculum ... nolite] The punctuation is a matter of uncertainty, and must depend on the reading adopted.   ut euangelio] om. Syr. With the punctuation provisionally adopted above I should emend 'ab (= apart from) euangelio'. These words may have been inserted in Lat. to avoid an apparent exclusion of the Gospel.

marry, and believe not in the resurrection of the body; who moreover will not eat and drink, but would fain rise up demons, unsubstantial spirits, who shall be damned everlastingly and punished in unquenchable fire. Fly and avoid them therefore, that you may not perish with them.

[vi. 21] But if there be any who are precise and desire, after the Second Legislation, to observe the wonted courses of nature and issues and marriage intercourse: first let them know that, as we have already said, together with the Second Legislation they affirm the curse against our Saviour and condemn themselves to no purpose. And again, let them tell us, in what days or in what hours they keep themselves from prayer and from receiving the Eucharist, or from reading the Scriptures—let them tell us whether they are void of the Holy Spirit. For through baptism they receive the Holy Spirit, who is ever with those that work righteousness, and does not depart from them by reason of natural issues and the intercourse of marriage, but is ever and always with those who possess Him, and keeps them; as the Lord said in Proverbs: *If thou sleep, he keepeth thee; and when thou awakest, he will speak with thee.* And in the Gospel also our Lord said: *Every one that hath, there shall be given to him, and shall be added unto him; but from him that hath not, even that which he thinketh he hath shall be taken away.* To those therefore who have, yea, it shall be added unto them; but from those

---

20 Prov. vi 22.   22 Lk. viii 18 (Mt. xiii 12, xxv 29, Mk. iv 25).

1–3 who moreover ... spirits] ἐσθίειν καὶ πίνειν μὴ βουλόμενοι, δαιμόνια δὲ ἄσαρκα φαντζόμενοι ἐκ νεκρῶν ἀναστήσεσθαι *AC* (cf. Lat.).   6 are precise] *mezdahrīn*, meaning take heed, are cautious: παρατηρούμενοι *AC*. The observances here condemned are actually prescribed in *Hom. Clem.* vii 8 ἡ δὲ ὑπ' αὐτοῦ ὁρισθεῖσα θρησκεία ἐστὶν αὕτη· ... ἀπὸ κοίτης γυναικὸς λούεσθαι, αὐτὰς (sc. γυναῖκας) μέντοι καὶ ἄφεδρον φυλάσσειν. 11–15 let them tell us, etc.] λεγέτωσαν ἡμῖν, εἰ ἐν αἷς ὥραις ἢ ἡμέραις ἔν τι τούτων ὑπομείνωσιν παρατηροῦνται προσεύξασθαι ἢ εὐχαριστίας μεταλαβεῖν ἢ βιβλίου θιγεῖν, καὶ ἐὰν συνθῶνται, δῆλον ὡς τοῦ ἁγίου πνεύματος κενοὶ τυγχάνουσιν *AC*.   12–13 keep themselves from prayer] lit. 'keep to pray', here in the sense of 'avoid': παρατηροῦνται *AC*.   14 let them tell us] om. Lat.: a resumption to relieve the construction—unless it be for δῆλον ὡς (*AC*).   22–23 *and shall be added unto him*] So (for καὶ περισσευθήσεται) *syr. cur.* at Mt. xiii 12, and *syr. vulg.* (*cur.* and *sin.* are wanting) at Mt.

resurgere in carne nolunt, tamquam nolentes manducare et bibere, sed demones uolunt resurgere spiritales in fantasmis: quique condemnabuntur in perenni igne in aeternum, et ibi iudicabuntur. Fugite ergo ab ipsis, ut non simul cum eis pereatis.

Si qui uero obseruantes secundum secundationem custodiunt consuetudinaria †naturaliter† seminis sui cursus et adproximationes mulierum : primum quidem cognoscant, sicuti praediximus, quoniam ex secundatione quod aduersum saluatorem est maledictum uan[a]e confirmant ad propriam condemnationem : postea dicant, in quibus horis aut diebus obseruant ne orentur aut eucharistiam percipiant aut librum contingant, [LVII] quoniam a sancto spiritu euacuati sunt. Per baptismum enim sanctum spiritum accepimus, qui cum his qui iuste conuersantur semper est et obseruat illos, †mulieri†⟨nun⟩quam separatur propter naturale meatum et conmixtionem, sed semper adest et custodit eos qui illum possident; sicuti in Prouerbiis dicit dominus : *Cum autem dormis, custodiat te; et cum surge[n]s, adloquatur te.* Et iterum in euangelio similiter dicit dominus : *Omni habenti dabitur, et abundabit: ab eo autem qui non habet, et quod se sperat habere tolletur ab eo.* Ergo his qui habent, additur illis : ab his

---

1 nolunt] 'uolunt' cod.   3–4 quique ... iudicabuntur] οἴτινες καταδικασθήσονται δι' αἰῶνος ἐν τῷ αἰωνίῳ πυρί *AC*.   7 naturaliter] 'of nature' Syr.: (ἔθιμα) ἰουδαϊκά *AC*. Probably read 'naturalia et': the Gk. must have been (ἔθιμα) φυσικά.   7–8 adproximationes] πλησιασμούς *AC*.   12 orentur] For this and some other rare deponents cf. A. Souter *The earliest Latin Commentaries on the Epistles of St Paul* (Oxford, 1927) p. 92 n. 2.   15 et observat illos] om. Syr. The words seem redundant, anticipating 'et custodit eos' just after.   mulieri ⟨nun⟩quam] So Hauler, and Funk and Flemming offer no suggestion; but every letter of 'mulieri' is dotted as uncertain by Hauler, and we must surely correct this word to 'et ab illis (*or* eis)' : cf. Syr.   21 *sperat*] We have already had 'sperare' in the sense of 'putare' (p. 89, l. 4), and it recurs in this context several times.

---

xxv 29 : also added at Lk. viii 18 in *syr. cur.*, after 'shall be given unto him'. Cf. Mk. iv 24 μετρηθήσεται ὑμῖν, καὶ προστεθήσεται ὑμῖν. *AC* omits the quotation.

who think that they have not, even that which they think they have shall be taken away.

For if thou think, O woman, that in the seven days of thy flux thou art void of the Holy Spirit; if thou die in those days, thou wilt depart empty and without hope. But if (p. 116) the Holy Spirit is always in thee, without (just) impediment dost thou keep thyself from prayer and from the Scriptures and from the Eucharist. For consider and see, that prayer also is heard through the Holy Spirit, and the Eucharist through the Holy Spirit is accepted and sanctified, and the Scriptures are the words of the Holy Spirit, and are holy. For if the Holy Spirit is in thee, why dost thou keep thyself from approaching to the works of the Holy Spirit? as those who say: *Whosoever sweareth by the altar, sinneth not; but whosoever sweareth by the gift that is upon it, sinneth.* As our Lord said: *Fools and blind, whether is greater, the gift, or the altar that sanctifieth the gift? Every one therefore that sweareth by the altar, sweareth by it, and by all that is upon it. And every one that sweareth by the temple, sweareth by it, and by him that dwelleth therein. And every one that sweareth by the heaven, sweareth by the throne of God, and by him that sitteth thereon.* If therefore thou possess the Holy Spirit, but keep thyself from His fruits so that thou approach not to them, thou also shalt hear from our Lord Jesus Christ: 'Fool and blind, whether is greater, the bread, or the Spirit that ⟨sanctifieth the bread?' Therefore, if the Holy Spirit⟩ thou possessest: fool, thou keepest vain observances. But if the Holy Spirit is not in thee, how canst thou work righteousness? For the Holy Spirit continues ever with those who possess Him; but from whom He departs, to him an unclean

---

14 Mt. xxiii 18–22.

10 accepted and] om. Lat.   12 why] 'uane, inaniter' Lat.   26 ⟨sanctifieth... Holy Spirit⟩] Supplied from Lat. I assume that the words were omitted in Syr. by homoeoteleuton.   27 fool] 'uana' Lat.: Syr. has mistaken a neuter plur. for a fem. sing.   27–29 But... righteousness] 'Si habes sanctum spiritum, quid est quod obseruas?' Lat. It looks as if Syr. and Lat. had each missed out a clause here, so that the original is to be got by combining these two readings, i.e. by reading the sentence in Lat. before that in Syr.   30 He departs]+'longe est

DIDASCALIA APOSTOLORUM

autem qui sperant se in aliquibus diebus non habere, et id quod in aliis diebus sperant se habere tollitur ab ipsis. Si enim speras te, o mulier, in septem diebus in sessione fuisse et a sancto spiritu uacuatam; si defuncta fueris in diebus
5 illis, uacua et sine spe ibis. Si autem spiritum habes semper, ab oratione uero et gratiarum actione et a libris subterfugis, cogita, quia et oratio per sanctum spiritum suscipitur, et gratiarum actio per sanctum spiritum sanctificatur, et libri, cum sancti spiritus sonus sint, sancti sunt. Si ergo in te habes
10 sanctum spiritum, uane, inaniter obseruas sancti spiritus operas tangere, sicuti et hii qui dicunt: *Quicumque iurauerit in altare, nihil est: qui autem iurauerit in dono eius quod desuper est, debet.* Quibus dixit dominus: *Stulti et caeci, quid est maius, munus, aut altare quod sanctificat munus? Qui ergo iurauerit*
15 *in altare, iurat in illo et in omnibus* [LVIII] *quae sunt super ipsud. Et qui iurauerit in templo, iurat in eo et in habitante in illo. Et qui iurauerit in caelo, iurat in throno Dei et in eo qui super ipsum sedet.* Si itaque sanctum spiritum possides, fructos uero eius contingere obseruas, et audies similiter a
20 domino Deo Christo: 'Stulta et caeca, quid est maius, panis, aut sanctus spiritus qui sanctificat panem?' Ergo si spiritum sanctum possides, uana obseruas et uana custodis. Si habes sanctum spiritum, quid est quod obseruas? Sanctus enim spiritus possidentibus se semper adest, et ab his a quibus re-
25 cesserit longe est semper. Si autem ab aliquo sanctus spiritus uel uno die recesserit, in hunc mox inmundus spiritus ingre-

1–2 in aliquibus diebus, *and* in aliis diebus] om. Syr. The words may be a gloss, added to explain an apparent inconsistency. 3–4 in septem... uacuatam] εἰ γὰρ νομίζεις, ὦ γύναι, ἑπτὰ ἡμέρας ἐν ἀφέδρῳ οὖσα τοῦ ἁγίου πνεύματος κενὴ τυγχάνειν *AC* (cf. Syr.). 22–23 Si habes... obseruas?] See note to Syr. ll. 27–29. 25–26 longe... recesserit] om. Syr., to which see note.

semper. Si autem ab aliquo sanctus spiritus uel uno die recesserit' Lat., which perhaps should be supplied in Syr.: *AC* has the sentence thus: τὸ γὰρ ἅγιον πνεῦμα τοῖς κεκτημένοις αὐτὸ ἀεὶ παράμονόν ἐστιν, [ἕως ἂν ὦσιν ἄξιοι,] καὶ ὧν ἂν χωρισθῇ, τούτους ἐρήμους καθίστησιν καὶ τῷ πονηρῷ πνεύματι ἐκδότους. This appears to support the shorter text of Syr., but at this point *AC* is condensing a good deal. Cf. Hermas *Mand.* v 2. 7 εἶτα ὅταν ἀποστῇ (τὸ τρυφερὸν πνεῦμα) ἀπὸ τοῦ ἀνθρώπου ἐκείνου οὗ κατοικεῖ, γίνεται ὁ ἄνθρωπος ἐκεῖνος κενὸς ἀπὸ τοῦ πνεύματος τοῦ δικαίου, καὶ τὸ λοιπὸν πεπληρωμένος τοῖς πνεύμασι τοῖς πονηροῖς κτλ.

spirit joins himself. *For the unclean spirit, when he is gone out from a man, departeth and goeth about in waterless places—* that is, men who go not down into the water (of baptism)—*and when he hath found him no rest, he saith: I will return to my former house, whence I came out. If therefore he come and find it empty and swept and garnished, then he goeth and taketh with him seven other spirits worse than himself, and they come and dwell in that man; and his last state is made worse than the first.*

Learn now, why, when the unclean spirit is gone out, he finds him no rest in any place: because every man soever is filled with a spirit, one with the Holy Spirit, and one with an unclean spirit. A believer is filled with the Holy Spirit, and an unbeliever with an unclean spirit: and his nature does not receive an alien spirit. He therefore who has withdrawn and separated himself and departed from the unclean spirit by baptism, is filled with (p. 117) the Holy Spirit; and if he do good works, the Holy Spirit continues with him, and he remains fulfilled; and the unclean spirit finds no place with him, for he who is filled with the Holy Spirit does not receive him. For all men are filled with their own spirit; and the unclean spirits depart not even a little from the heathen, while yet they are heathens, even though they imagine that they do good works; for there is no other power whereby the unclean spirit may depart save by the pure and holy Spirit of God. Thus, then, when he has nowhere found him a place to enter, he returns and comes to him from whom he went forth; because one who is filled with the Holy Spirit does not receive him.

Thou then, O woman, according as thou sayest, ⟨if⟩ in the

---

1 Mt. xii 43-45.

11–13 because ... unclean spirit] πᾶς δὲ ἄνθρωπος ὁ μὲν τῷ πνεύματι πεπλήρωται τῷ ἁγίῳ, ὁ δὲ τῷ ἀκαθάρτῳ, καὶ οὐχ οἷόν τε φυγεῖν αὐτῶν ἑκάτερον *AC.* The whole paragraph is strongly reminiscent of Hermas *Mand.* v 2. 5–7.   14–15 his nature ... spirit] 'ingressum non suscipit alieni spiritus' Lat.   He therefore, etc.] πᾶς δὲ βεβαπτισμένος κατὰ ἀλήθειαν τοῦ μὲν διαβολικοῦ πνεύματος κεχώρισται, τοῦ δὲ ἁγίου πνεύματος ἐντὸς καθέστηκεν· καὶ ἀγαθοεργοῦντι μὲν παραμένει τὸ πνεῦμα τὸ ἅγιον, πληροῦν αὐτὸν σοφίας καὶ συνέσεως, καὶ τὸ πονηρὸν πνεῦμα οὐκ ἐᾷ αὐτῷ πλησιάσαι, ἐπιτηροῦν αὐτοῦ τὰς ἐφόδους *AC.*   20–21 for he ... receive him] om. Lat.   23 they

ditur, sicuti dixit dominus: *Cum exierit inmundus spiritus ab homine, circuit per ⟨in⟩aquosa loca*—id est per eos qui non sunt baptizati homines—*et cum non inuenerit refrigerium, dicit: In domum meam reuertar priorem, unde exii. Si ergo ueniens inuenerit uacantem et mundatum, tunc uadit et adpraehendit secum alios septem spiritus maligniores se, et uenientes habitabunt in hominem illum: et fiunt nouissima hominis illius peiora prioribus.*

Quare ergo, cum egressus fuerit inmundus spiritus, nusquam requiem inuenit, discite: quoniam omnis homo repletus est, fidelis quidem de sancto spiritu, infidelis autem de inmundo, et ingressum non suscipit alieni spiritus. Qui uero per baptismum reiecit et deposuit et liberatus est ab inmundo spiritu, sancto repletur. Si itaque bonum operatus fuerit, permanet in illum spiritus sanctus, et manet repletus, et inmundus locum non inuenit. Quia omnes homines a propriis spiritibus pleni sunt, et non recedent [LIX] a gentilibus †inspirationibus† paenitus, quamdiu gentiles permanent, etiamsi bonum faciant: nulla est ⟨enim⟩ alia curatio, ut abscedat ab eo spiritus inmundus, nisi per sacram purgationem et sanctum baptismum. Ita ergo, cum non possit ingredi nusquam, reuertetur ad eum qui illum reiecit et deposuit: qui autem repletus est sancto spiritu, non illum suscipit.

Tu autem, o mulier, sicuti dicis, etiamsi in diebus sessionis tuae

---

17 inspirationibus] 'Added above the line by the hand of a corrector, apparently', says Hauler. But should not the correction be read 'inmundi spiritus'? so Syr., and so the context suggests. 19 (enim)] From Syr. curatio] 'power' or 'authority' Syr. (usually for ἐξουσία). 20 nisi ... baptismum] 'save by the pure and holy Spirit of God' Syr.—a quite unaccountable variant. 23 succipit cod.

imagine that] om. Lat. 29 ff. Thou then ... unclean spirits] σὺ οὖν, ὦ γύναι, καθὼς λέγεις, εἰ ἐν ταῖς ἡμέραις τῆς ἀφέδρου κενὴ τυγχάνεις τοῦ ἁγίου πνεύματος, τοῦ ἀκαθάρτου πεπλήρωσαι *AC*. I have supplied 'if' from *AC* and Lat.

days of thy flux thou art void, thou shalt be filled with unclean
spirits. For when the unclean spirit returns to thee and finds
him a place, he will enter and dwell in thee always: and then
will there be entering in of the unclean spirit and going forth
of the Holy Spirit, and perpetual warfare. Wherefore, O foolish
(women), these misfortunes befall you because of your imaginings; and because of the observances which you keep, and
on account of your imaginings, you are emptied of the Holy
Spirit and filled with unclean spirits: and you are cast out from
life into the burning of everlasting fire. But again I will say
to thee, O woman: In the seven days of thy flux thou
accountest thyself unclean according to the Second Legislation: after seven days, therefore, how canst thou be cleansed
without baptism? But if thou be baptized for that which
thou supposest, thou wilt undo the perfect baptism of God
which wholly forgave thee thy sins, and wilt be found in the
evil plight of thy former sins; and thou shalt be delivered
over to eternal fire. But if thou be not baptized, according to
thine own supposition thou remainest unclean, and the vain
observing of the seven days has availed thee nothing, but is
rather hurtful to thee; for according to thy supposition thou
art unclean, and as unclean thou shalt be condemned.

Be thus minded therefore concerning all those who observe
issues and the intercourse of marriage; for all these observances
are foolish and hurtful. For if, when a man use matrimony, or
blood come forth from him, he be baptized, let him also wash
his couch: and he will have this labour (p. 118) and vexation
incessantly; he will be baptizing and will be washing his
clothes and his couch, and will be able to do nothing else.
Now if thou be baptized from an issue and from marriage
intercourse according to the Second Legislation, thou owest it

---

3 he will ... always] om. Lat. In this paragraph there are several
points of difference between Syr. and Lat. which are difficult to account
for.   6 misfortunes befall you] lit. 'happenings happen to you':
Lat. differently.   13–15 after seven ... supposest] Lat. very
differently.   14–15 But if ... of God] Flemming renders
'Und wenn du dich badest, so lösest du durch das, was du glaubst,
die vollkommene Taufe Gottes auf'. This is possible, but gives an
inferior sense.   18 But ... not baptized] 'tamquam non baptizata'

uacua sis, ab inmundo repleris spiritu: conuertitur enim in te et
inuenit locum uacantem: et erit in sempiternum in te inmundi
et mundi spiritus ingressus et egressus et perpetuum bellum.
Unde stulta quae talis est suspicio a uobis speratur: et ex eo
5 quod tales obseruationes custoditis, per suspicionem uacatio in
uobis a sancto spiritu erit et repletio ab inmundo: et ita erit
uitae reiectio et conbustio aeterna. Dicito mihi uero postea,
o mulier: septem diebus tuae suspurgationis uel sessionis tuae
inmunda tibi eris secundum secundationem, et inueniris post
10 septem dies tamquam non baptizata: et purgaris aut baptizaris,
ut uidearis quasi mundata, et quod est perfectum purgationem
peccatorum cum non inueneris, aeternae igni daris tamquam
non baptizata. Secundum enim tuam suspicionem inmunda
permanes, et nihil tibi prodest septem dierum uana abstinentia,
15 sed †contrario et† nociua: quia per conscientiam inquinata es,
et sicuti coinquinata condemnaris.

Haec igitur super omnes cogitate qui seminum [LX]
cursus et adproximationes mulierum obseruant: nam quae
tales sunt obseruationes omnes stultae et nociuae sunt. Si
20 enim cursum seminis quis passus et adproximans mulieri
baptizetur, et stratum suum lauet: et erit illi hoc fatigatio,
numquam deficiens a baptismo et a lauatione rerum et a stratu
suo: et nihil aliut poterit agere. Si enim post seminis cursum
et conmixtionem secundum secundationem baptizaris, necesse

4 Unde stulta ... speratur] Hauler and Funk take this as a question;
but the 'Wherefore' in Syr. is not interrogative, but equivalent to 'therefore'. As the text stands 'stulta' must be taken with 'suspicio', but
'stulte' (adv.) would fit the construction better.   5 vagatio cod.
15 sed ... nociua] Read 'sed e contrario est nociua' (?).

(with the preceding clause) Lat.   29 clothes] Or 'vessels' (but
'clothes' at p. 250, l. 4): 'rerum' Lat., perh. from σκευῶν.

also to be baptized when thou treadest upon a mouse : and thou shalt never be clean. For even as to the shoes of thy feet, with the skin of dead (animals) and with the hides of those that are sacrificed thou art shod ; and as to clothes also, with the wool of the like (animals) thou art clothed. And if thou tread upon a bone, or enter a tomb, thou oughtest to be baptized : and thou shalt never be clean. And thou wilt undo the baptism of God, and thou renewest thy offences, and art found in thy former sins, and affirmest the Second Legislation, and takest upon thee the idolatry of the calf,—for if thou take upon thee the Second Legislation, take also idolatry, for because of idolatry the Second Legislation was imposed,—and the former sins of others, *as a long rope, and as the band of a heifer*, thou drawest and bringest upon thee. Moreover, thou bringest upon thee the Woe ; for when thou affirmest the Second Legislation, thou consentest to the curse against our Saviour ; and thou settest at naught Christ the King, who distributes blessings to them that are worthy. Wherefore thou shalt inherit a curse ; for *every one that shall curse a man is cursed* [*and every one that blesseth is blessed*]. To what curses, therefore, and to what judgement or to what condemnation shall they be delivered who affirm a curse against our Saviour and our Lord and our God !

[vi. 22] Wherefore, beloved, flee and avoid such observances : for you have received release, that you should no more bind yourselves ; and do not load yourselves again with that which

---

13 Isa. v 18.   19 Cf. Nu. xxiv 9.

---

1 a mouse] Here doubtless should follow the sentence 'And if . . . baptized' at ll. 5-6 below (cf. Lat.).   4 sacrificed] sc. to idols : rendering εἰδωλοθύτων, as at p. 208, l. 7 (see also Lat.).   8 of God] 'sacratissimum' Lat. (prob. θεῖον).   16 consentest to the curse] See pp. 230, 240 : Deut. xxi 23 is again referred to.   16-18 and thou . . . worthy] Cf. Lat. : Syr. omits the second allusion to the curse. 19-20 *and . . . blessed*] om. Lat., and rightly.

te est et hoc facere, ut etiam si suricem calcaueris baptizeris; et si ossum morticinum †aut pellem aut ossuum uulneratum† et monumentum tetigeris, debes baptizari: et numquam exis mundus. Nam et calciamenta, de mortuis animalibus et ab
5 idolis immolatis pellibus calciaris; et uestes, de similibus lanis co⟨o⟩periris: et nunquam poteris mundari; et sacratissimum baptismum infirmas, et renouas delicta tua, et in peccatis tuis prioribus inueniris, et secundationem confirmas, et in te recipies et uituli idololatriam. Suscipi⟨en⟩s enim secundationem, in te
10 recipis et idololatria⟨m⟩, propter quam secundatio posita est: et aliena et uetustissima peccata *ut funiculam longam et ut* †*legis uinculum iugum et lorum* [*et iugum*]† ipse tibi induces, et uae adtrahes. Secundationem confirma⟨n⟩s, etiam in maledicto quod aduersus saluatorem fuit consentis; et id, quod contra
15 benedictionem et qui benedictiones diuidit dignis Christum, maledictum est, testimonium praebens maledictiones possidebis. Si *qui*[*s*] enim *maledicit, maledictus est,* qualium maledictionum et qualium et quantarum condemnationum [LXI] rei erunt qui saluatoris nostri domini Dei maledictum laudant?

20 Unde fugite a talibus obseruationibus, dilectissimi, et cum acceperitis solutionem ⟨uosm⟩et ipsos nolite conligare, et

2 aut ... uulneratum] These words are not represented in Syr.: they seem quite corrupt, but may be only marginal or other jottings incorporated by the scribe. 4–5 ab idolis immolatis] So cod. (see Hauler's note), and rightly. Hauler alters 'ab idolis' to 'a uitulis'; but the Gk. was certainly ἀπ' εἰδωλοθύτων (see p. 209, l. 1). The sentence means 'thou art shod with skins (taken) from dead animals and from those sacrificed to idols'. 7 delecta cod. 8 confirmas, et in te recipies] Hauler prints 'in te recipies et confirmas et', but in his note he suggests the above correction (from Syr.): the note also shows that the correction was probably intended to be made in the MS. itself. At all events it is the *secundatio* that is 'affirmed', and idolatry that is 'taken upon' the Judaizer. 11 *ut*] 'et' cod. 12 *legis ... et iugum*] Another confused passage, resting on Isa. v 18 ὡς σχοινίῳ μακρῷ, καὶ ὡς ζυγοῦ ἱμάντι δαμάλεως. Probably some marginal jottings have been brought into the text. 14 id] For 'ei': it must refer to 'maledictum'. Translate: 'and, giving testimony to (= upholding) that curse which is against the blessing and (against) Him that distributes blessings to them that are worthy, even Christ, thou shalt inherit curses'. 16 praebens] See p. 219, l. 9 and note. 21 ⟨uosm⟩et ipsos] Perhaps only '⟨m⟩etipsos' is to be restored: see p. 253, l. 1, and already p. 125, l. 11.

our Lord and Saviour has lifted from you. And do not observe these things, nor think them uncleanness; and do not refrain yourselves on their account, nor seek after sprinklings, or baptisms, or purification for these things. For in the Second Legislation, if one touch a dead man or a tomb, he is baptized; but do you, according to the Gospel and according to the power of the Holy Spirit, come together even in the cemeteries, and read the holy Scriptures, and without demur perform your ministry and your supplication to God; and offer an acceptable Eucharist, the likeness of the royal body of Christ, both in your congregations and in (p. 119) your cemeteries and on the departures of them that sleep—pure bread that is made with fire and sanctified with invocations—and without doubting pray and offer for them that are fallen asleep. For they who have believed in God, according to the Gospel, even though they should sleep, they are not dead; as our Lord said to the Sadducees: *Concerning the resurrection of the dead, have ye not read that which is written: I am the God of Abraham, and the God of Isaac, and the God of Jacob? And he is not the God of the dead, but of the living.* And Elisha the prophet also, after he had slept and was a long while (dead), raised up a dead man; for his body touched the body of the dead and quickened and raised it up. But this could not have been were it not that, even when he was fallen asleep, his body was holy and filled with the Holy Spirit.

For this cause therefore do you approach without restraint

15–16 Cf. Joh. xi 25.   17 Mt. xxii 31–33.   21 4 Reg. xiii 21.

1 lifted] lit. 'lightened'.   And do not, etc.] The passage in *AC* corresponding to the rest of this paragraph is vi 30 (Funk p. 381). 2–3 and do not ... their account] om. Lat.   3 seek after] + ἀφορισμούς *AC* (= Lat.).   6 but do you, etc.] For the rest of the paragraph *AC* has the following: ἀπαρατηρήτως δὲ συναθροίζεσθε ἐν τοῖς κοιμητηρίοις, τὴν ἀνάγνωσιν τῶν ἱερῶν βιβλίων ποιούμενοι ... καὶ τὴν ἀντίτυπον τοῦ βασιλείου σώματος Χριστοῦ δεκτὴν εὐχαριστίαν προσφέρετε ἔν τε ταῖς ἐκκλησίαις ὑμῶν καὶ ἐν τοῖς κοιμητηρίοις, καὶ ἐν ταῖς ἐξόδοις τῶν κεκοιμημένων ... οἱ γὰρ θεῷ πεπιστευκότες, ἐὰν καὶ κοιμηθῶσιν, οὐκ εἰσὶν νεκροί· λέγει γὰρ ὁ σωτὴρ τοῖς Σαδδουκαίοις (etc.) ... καὶ γὰρ Ἐλισσαῖος ὁ προφήτης μετὰ τὸ κοιμηθῆναι αὐτὸν νεκρὸν ἤγειρε ... ἔψαυσεν γὰρ τὸ σῶμα αὐτοῦ τῶν Ἐλισσαίου ὀστέων, καὶ ἀναστὰς ἔζησεν· οὐκ ἂν δὲ ἐγεγόνει τοῦτο, εἰ μὴ ἦν τὸ σῶμα Ἐλισσαίου ἅγιον.
10 royal] Syr. reads here 'the likeness of the body the kingdom of Christ'; but by merely prefixing the genitive particle and reading '*of*

a domino et saluatore releuati ⟨uos⟩met ipsos nolite onerare.
Sed penitus nolite obseruare et sperare tales esse inquinationes
et quaerere segregationes aut asparsiones aut baptismas aut
purgationes. Secundum secundationem ⟨enim post⟩ tanctionem
monumenti uel mortui, et baptizantur: uos uero, secundum
euangelium et secundum sancti spiritus uirtutem, et in memo-
riis congregantes uos et sacrarum scripturarum facite lectionem
et ad Deum praeces indesinenter offerite, et eam quae secundum
similitudinem regalis corporis Christi est regalem eucharistiam
offerte tam in collectis uestris quam etiam in coemiteriis et in
dormientium exi[ni]tione: panem mundum praeponentes, qui
per ignem factus est et per inuocationem sanctificatur, sine
discretione orantes offerite pro dormientibus. Qui enim Deo
crediderunt, secundum euangelium, etiamsi mortui fuerint, non
sunt mortui; sicuti dominus et saluator noster dicit Sadduceis:
*De resurrectione mortuorum non legistis quod scriptum est,
quoniam Ego sum Deus Abraham et Deus Isac et Deus Iacob?
Non est Deus mortuorum, sed uiuorum.* Nam et Eliseus
profeta, cum dormisset †uetustissimum iam† mortuum suscitauit: tetigit enim corpus eius corpus [LXII] defuncti et
suscitauit illud. Numquam uero hoc fuisset, nisi corpus illius
qui dormierat sanctum fuisset et repletum sancto spiritu.

Unde ergo eos qui requiescunt sine obseruatione tangentes

---

4 ⟨enim post⟩ So Funk supplies from Syr.   6–7 memoriis] κοιμητηρίοις
AC (= Syr.).   The word denotes mortuary chapels: for other examples
see the Benedictine Index to St. Augustine's works.   8 indesinenter]
ἀπαρατηρήτως *AC*: 'without demur' (lit. 'murmuring') Syr.   9 rega-
lem] δεκτήν *AC* (= Syr.): 'regalem' is repeated from 'regalis' just before.
10 collectis] ἐκκλησίαις *AC*: 'congregations' (often for συναγωγή) Syr.
11 exinitione] ἐξόδοις *AC*.   panem] 'omnem' cod.   14 mortui
fuerint] κοιμηθῶσιν *AC* (= Syr.).   Lat. may be influenced by recollection of
'etiamsi mortuus fuerit' in Joh. xi 25.   15 dominus et saluator
noster] ὁ σωτήρ *AC*: 'our Lord' Syr.   19 uetustissimum iam] Cf. Syr.:
it was Elisha who was 'a long while' dead.

---

the kingdom', we get the equivalent of an adjective: βασιλείου *AC*
(= Lat.).   13 invocations] So pointed in Syr.: sing. Lat.   14 pray] B:
'and pray' S, ungrammatically: H omits the context.   15–16 according
to the Gospel] lit. 'as in the Gospel'.

to those who are at rest, and hold them not unclean. In like manner also you shall not separate those (women) who are in the wonted courses; for she also who had the flow of blood was not chidden when she touched the skirt of our Saviour's cloak, but was even vouchsafed the forgiveness of all her sins. And when ⟨your wives⟩ suffer those issues which are according to nature, have a care that, in a manner that is right, you cleave to them; for you know that they are your members, and do you love them as your soul: as it is written in the Twelve Prophets, ⟨in⟩ Malachi who was called the Angel: *The Lord hath borne witness between thee and the wife of thy youth, whom thou hast left, thy partner, and she the wife of thy covenant. And did not he make her? and they* (fem.) *are the residue of his spirit. And ye have said: What else doth God seek but pure seed? Give heed in your spirits: and the wife of thy youth thou shalt not leave.* Wherefore, a woman when she is in the way of women, and a man when an issue comes forth from him, and a man and his wife when they consort and rise up one from another: let them assemble without restraint, without bathing, for they are clean. But if a man should corrupt and defile another's wife after baptism, or be polluted with a harlot, and rising up from her should bathe in all the seas and oceans and be baptized in all the rivers, he cannot be made clean.

Do you therefore, our beloved, avoid all such foolish observances, and come not near them. And be careful to abide (p. 120) in the wedded company of one wife, and to keep your

---

3 Mt. ix 20 ff.   10 Mal. ii 14 f.

4 our Saviour's] σωτηρίου *AC*.   6-7 And when ... nature] καὶ φυσικῶν μὲν φαινομένων ταῖς γυναιξίν *AC* (cf. Lat.). The words 'which are according to nature' are from H (ܡܨ̈ܠ ܐ̈): BS have the (here meaningless) adverbial expression ܡܨ̈ܠ ܐ̈?? from the adj. 'clean.' Flemming has attempted to translate S.   10 Malachi ... the Angel] See p. 216 and note.   14 *spirit*] 'spirits' text, as Pesh.   16 ff. Wherefore, etc.] ἀνὴρ οὖν καὶ γυνή, νομίμῳ γάμῳ συνερχόμενοι καὶ ἀπ' ἀλλήλων ἐγειρόμενοι, ἀπαρατηρήτως προσευχέσθωσαν· καὶ μὴ λουσάμενοι καθαροί εἰσιν. ὃς δ' ἂν ἀλλοτρίαν γυναῖκα ὑποφθείρας μιάνῃ ἢ συμμιανθῇ πόρνῃ, ἀναστὰς ἀπ' αὐτῆς, οὐδ' ἂν τὸ πέλαγος ὅλον καὶ τοὺς ποταμοὺς πάντας ἀπολούσηται, καθαρὸς εἶναι δυνήσεται *AC* (Funk p. 379 ll. 24 ff.). It is to be observed that *AC* omits 'after baptism', which seemed perhaps to imply too severe a doctrine as to post-baptismal forgiveness.   25 and come not near them] om. Lat.   And be careful] After this some words may be wanting: see Lat.

nolite abominari; et quod in consuetudinibus est, it nolite segregare. Nam et ea quae fluctum patiebatur, cum tetigisset salubrem fimbriam, non est repraehensa, sed tum sanata perfectam remissionem peccatorum meruit. Itaque, cum naturalia
5 profluunt uxoribus uestris, nolite conuenire illis, sed sustinete eas et, scientes propria membra esse, diligite sicut proprias animas: sicuti et in Malachia, qui nuncupatus est angelus, in duodecim profetis scriptum est: *Quoniam dominus contestatus est inter medium ⟨te et inter medium⟩ mulierem iuuentutis tuae,*
10 *quam dereliqui⟨s⟩t⟨i⟩: et ipsa particeps tua: et non alius fecit: et reliquum spiritus eius. Et dixistis: Quid aliut quaerit dominus, nisi semen? Et custodite in spiritu vestro, et mulierem iuuentutis tuae ne derelinquas.* Et mulier ergo cum in menstruis est, et uir cum in cursu seminis, et uir et mulier legibus
15 ad nuptias conuenientes et ab alterutrum exurgentes, sine obseruatione et non loti orent, et mundi sunt. Quicumque autem alienam uxorem sollicitans inquinauerit post inluminationem,—quod dicit Graecus fotisma,—aut iterum coinquinatus meretrici exsurrexeris ab ea, etiamsi omne pelagum uel omni-
20 bus fluminibus lotus fueris, mundus esse non poteris.

Cauete ergo, carissimi fratres, eas quae tales sunt [LXIII] stultas obseruationes, et ea quae inmortalitatem praestant pertinaces ⟨estote⟩ sectari, custodientes in uno coniugio corpus

---

3 tum sanata] om. Syr.: τοὐναντίον δὲ ἰάσατο αὐτήν *AC* (omitting the forgiveness of sins). 3–4 perfectam] So Funk emends: 'tectam' cod., according to Hauler. 5 nolite conuenire illis] *AC* has here (οἱ ἄνδρες) μὴ συνερχέσθωσαν προνοίας ἕνεκεν τῶν γεννωμένων: 'have a care that, in a manner that is right (= *secundum quod iustum est*), you cleave to them' Syr.—which seems more in the spirit of the author. Possibly Lat. and *AC* are independent 'improvements'. 12 *custodire* cod. 18 quod ... fotisma] See p. 237 and note. 19–20 exsurrexeris (*and following verbs*)] In 3rd sing. *AC* (= Syr.). 19 omne pelagum] Keeping the Gk. construction τὸ πέλαγος ὅλον ... ἀπολούσηται (*AC*). 23 sectari] 'et cari' Hauler: but on consulting the MS. again, at a friend's suggestion, he verified the conjecture 'sectari' (see Funk vol. i p. xi note 1). Funk supplies 'estote', which is necessary. coniugium cod.

bodies unspotted and unsullied; that you may receive life, that you may be partakers of the kingdom of God, and that you may receive that which the Lord God has promised, and may have rest for evermore.

[vi. 23] Now with many other demonstrations similar to these we might the more clearly declare to you the Didascalia; but not to extend and prolong the writing, already we conclude the discourse and lay it aside, lest by reason of the severity of the truth the teaching of our discourse should remain but a short time with you. Wherefore, take not amiss those things which have been said; for our Lord and Saviour also spoke with severity to those who were worthy of condemnation, and said: *Take and cast them into the outer darkness: there shall be weeping and gnashing of teeth*; and: *Depart from me, ye cursed, into everlasting fire, which my Father hath prepared for the evil one and his angels.* That the word is likened to fire and a sword, He has said also in Jeremiah: *Behold, my words go forth as fire, and as iron that cutteth stone*—yet sword and fire and †constraint†, not to those who hearken to the truth, but (He means) that word which the People heard not with pleasure when our Lord and Teacher reproved them; for they were unwilling to hearken to it because they esteemed it hard like iron. For they hearkened not to that which He said to them, for He appeared to them to speak harshly and severely. Wherefore He said to them: *Why call ye me Lord, Lord, and that which I say ye do not?*

13 Mt. xxv 30.   14 Mt. xxv 41.   18 Jer. xxiii 29.   26 Lk. vi 46.

---

5 ff. *AC* omits the whole of this paragraph.   8 discourse] lit. 'word' (and so l. 9).   9–10 should remain ... with you] 'ad satietatem uobis fiat' Lat. Syr. has confused κόρος with καιρός.   15–16 *which my Father hath prepared*] So also Lat. '*Didasc.*' should therefore be added to the Greek authorities for this 'Western' reading: it is not found in *syr. sin.*, Aphraates or *syr. vulg.* (*syr. cur.* is wanting).   18 *Behold*, etc.] Verbally as Pesh.; and hence Syr. does not help to illustrate the interesting text of Lat. The following commentary, however, implies the 'uerbum' of Lat.   19 yet sword] An obscurely worded comment, resembling that on Ex. xx 24 at p. 220 above.   constraint] ἀνάγκη transliterated: 'securis' Lat., to which see note.   22 to it] 'to Him' text: the pronoun in the original must have referred to λόγος.   23–24 hearkened not] 'non faciebant audientes' Lat., which is supported by the following quotation from Lk. vi 46.

uestrum inmaculatum et absque inquinatione, ut participes inmortalitatis et regni Dei †et communionis† efficiamini, et promissionem domini Dei accipientes requiescatis in saecula saeculorum.

5 Et per pluriores et similes manifestationes adhuc habentes uobis clariorem facere doctrinam, cum ampliaretur scriptura, hic alicubi iam deponimus uerbum, ut non per seueriorem ueritatem ad satietatem uobis fiat doctrinae nostrae sermo. Unde nolite grauiter ferre de his quae dicta sunt; nam et ipse dominus et
10 saluator noster cum seueritate respondens his qui digni erant condemnatione, dixit: *Tollite illos et mittite in tenebras exteriores; et ibi erit fletus et stridor dentium*; et: *Abite a me, maledicti, in ignem aeternum, quem praeparauit pater meus diabolo et angelis eius*. Et ⟨quod⟩ ignis et gladii operas facit uerbum,
15 et per Hieremiam dicit: *Uerbum domini sicuti secure cedens lapidem, et ignis perambulans et consumens*. Gladius ergo et ignis et securis ⟨non⟩ est audientibus ueritatem, uerbum ⟨autem⟩ quod populus non libenter audiuit cum argueretur a domino et magistro nostro: sed non crediderunt, sperantes esse sicut est
20 ferrum et ignis, eo quod non faciebant audientes quae ab eo dicebantur: dura enim illis uidebantur uerba ipsius. Sic itaque dicebat illis: *Quid[e] me dicitis, Domine, domine, et non facitis quae dico?*

---

1 particeps cod.   2 et ... communionis] καὶ κοινωνοὶ τῆς βασιλείας τοῦ θεοῦ *AC* (cf. Syr.).   14–16 Et ... *lapidem*] We must here compare Iren. *Haer.* V xvii 4 ὅτι δὲ ἀξίνῃ ἔοικεν ὁ λόγος τοῦ θεοῦ Ἰωάννης ὁ Βαπτιστής φησι περὶ αὐτοῦ· ἤδη δὲ ἡ ἀξίνη πρὸς τὴν ῥίζαν τῶν δένδρων κεῖται. Ἱερεμίας δὲ ὁμοίως φησίν· ὁ λόγος κυρίου ὡς πέλεκυς κόπτων πέτραν. This quotation from Jeremiah agrees exactly with the first part of the text in Lat. But the LXX have (according to cod. A) οὐκ ἰδοὺ οἱ λόγοι μου ὥσπερ φλέγον πῦρ, λέγει κύριος, ὡς πέλεκυς κόπτων πέτραν; Irenaeus omits the first clause, about 'fire', because he does not require it; but why should the author of *Didasc.* alter the Bible text by inverting the order of the clauses about 'fire' and 'axe', and also write (like Irenaeus) ὁ λόγος κυρίου? The answer seems to be that he is using Irenaeus; and this is also suggested by the manner in which the quotation is introduced.   14 operas facit] 'is likened to' Syr., which is more natural (cf. ἔοικεν in Irenaeus).   17 securis] Syr. has the Gk. word ἀνάγκη, which is quite unsuitable.   ⟨non⟩] From Syr.   ⟨autem⟩] From Syr. After this 'significat' is probably to be understood.   18 populum cod.   19 sperantes] = 'putantes': see notes at pp. 89, 243.

And so in like manner this our writing also appears to some to speak harshly and severely by reason of its truth. For if we had written indulgently for the gratification of men, many would grow weak and melt away from the faith, and we should be guilty of their blood. For as a physician, when he has not been able to conquer and heal an ulcer with drugs and fomentations, comes to a severer remedy and to surgical cuttings, that is to iron and cauteries, by which alone the physician is able to overcome and conquer (the sore) and presently heal the sick man: even so is the word; to those who hear and do it it is as a compress and an emollient and a plaster, but by those who hear and do it not it is esteemed as iron and fire.

Now to Him who is able to open (p. 121) the ears of your hearts to receive the †incisive† words of the Lord through the Gospel and the teaching of Jesus Christ the Nazarene, who was crucified in the days of Pontius Pilate, and slept, that He might announce to Abraham and to Isaac and to Jacob and to all His saints the end of the world and the resurrection that is to be for the dead; and rose from the dead, that He might show and give to us, that we might know Him, a pledge of the resurrection; and was taken up to heaven by the power of God His Father and of the Holy Spirit, and sat on the right hand of the throne of God Almighty upon the Cherubim; to Him who cometh with power and glory to judge the dead and the living: to Him (be) dominion and glory and majesty and kingdom, and to His Father and to the Holy Spirit: who was, and is, and abideth, both now and unto all generations and ages. Amen.

13-15 Cf. Rom. xvi 25, 2 Mac. i 4.

---

3 indulgently] So by a very slight correction: 'humaniora' Lat. 5 guilty] H: om. BS. 6 ulcer] σηπεδών transliterated. 7 a severer remedy] lit. 'severity', or 'cruelty'. and ... cuttings] om. Lat. 11 it is] 'and it is' text. compress ... plaster] The first and third words are σπληνίον and μάλαγμα transliterated. 14 incisive] lit. 'sharp': τὰ διηκονημένα AC (= Lat.). Funk observes that Syr. presupposes derivation from διακονάω. 18 the end] H: 'at the end' BS. 20 to us, that we might know Him] Or possibly 'to us who shall know Him' (BS): 'to those who have known Him' H: ἡμῖν (simply) AC. 24-25 dead ... living] The almost invariable order in early Syriac writings (see p. 163 above): yet H has here 'living ... dead'. 26 and to ... the Holy Spirit] 'patri et filio' Lat., no doubt rightly.

[LXIV] Similiter ergo et scriptura nostra quibusdam uidetur seuerissima esse propter ueritatem suam. Si enim scripsissemus humaniora ad gratiam hominibus, multi a fide potuissent debilitari, et nos rei pro eis eramus. Sicuti ergo medicus non
5 diu tenere sapiens putridinem per medicamina et emplastros, sed ad acutiorem uenit curationis medellam, id est ad ferrum et cauteria, per que sola optinet infirmitatem et sanat eum: similiter uerbum domini, his quidem qui audiunt illum et faciunt emplaster et cataplasma et malacma est, his uero qui
10 audiunt et non faciunt ferrum et ignis esse uidetur.

Ipsi ergo qui potens est aperire aures cordis uestri, ut suscipiatis quae ministrata sunt eloquia domini per euangelium et per doctrinam Iesu Christi Nazoreni, qui crucifixus est sub Pontio Pilato et dormiuit, ut euangelizaret Abraham et Isac et Iacob
15 et sanctis suis uniuersis tam finem saeculi quam resurrectionem qua⟨e⟩ erit mortuorum, et exurrexit a mortuis ut ostendat et det notis suis pignus resurrectionis, et in caelis susceptus per uirtutem Dei et spiritus eius, et sedenti[s] ad dextram sedis omnipotentis Dei super cherubin, qui ueni[un]t cum uirtute et gloria iudicare
20 uiuos et mortuos: ipsi est potentia et gloria et magnitudo et regnum, patri et filio, qui erat, et est, et erit, et nunc ⟨et⟩ in generationes generationum et in omnia saecula saeculorum. Amen.

17 notis suis] Hauler suggests 'nobis' for 'notis' (ἡμῖν AC); but cf. Syr. It may be surmised that τοῖς γνωρίμοις αὐτοῦ stood in the Greek original: 'notis' in any case must not be removed. 19 ueniunt] ἐρχομένου AC. 20–21 ipsi ... patri et filio] We are reminded of the peculiar formula in the doxologies of the *Apost. Trad.* of Hippolytus: 'per quem tibi gloria ... patri et filio cum sancto spiritu'.

Of this remarkable creed-doxology the following version is given in AC: τῷ οὖν δυναμένῳ ἀνοῖξαι τὰ ὦτα τῶν καρδιῶν ὑμῶν εἰς τὸ καταδέχεσθαι τὰ διηκονημένα τοῦ θεοῦ λόγια διά τε τοῦ εὐαγγελίου καὶ διὰ τῆς διδασκαλίας Ἰησοῦ Χριστοῦ τοῦ Ναζωραίου, τοῦ σταυρωθέντος ἐπὶ Ποντίου Πιλάτου [καὶ Ἡρώδου] καὶ κοιμηθέντος καὶ ἀναστάντος ἐκ νεκρῶν καὶ [πάλιν] ἐρχομένου ἐπὶ συντελείᾳ τοῦ αἰῶνος μετὰ δόξης καὶ δυνάμεως πολλῆς, καὶ τοὺς μὲν νεκροὺς ἀνεγείροντος, τῷ κόσμῳ δὲ τέλος ἐπάγοντος, [ἑκάστῳ δὲ τὰ πρὸς ἀξίαν ἀπονέμοντος·] τῷ δόντι ἡμῖν ἀρραβῶνα τῆς ἀναστάσεως ἑαυτὸν καὶ εἰς οὐρανοὺς ἀναληφθέντι διὰ τῆς δυνάμεως τοῦ θεοῦ καὶ πατρὸς αὐτοῦ ἐπ' ὄψεσιν ἡμετέραις τοῖς συμφαγοῦσιν αὐτῷ καὶ συμπιοῦσιν ἐπὶ ἡμέρας τεσσαράκοντα μετὰ τὸ ἀναστῆναι αὐτὸν ἐκ νεκρῶν, καὶ καθεσθέντι ἐκ δεξιῶν τοῦ θρόνου τῆς μεγαλωσύνης τοῦ παντοκράτορος θεοῦ ἐπὶ τῶν χερουβίμ, τῷ : . . δι' οὗ τὸ σέβας καὶ ἡ μεγαλωσύνη καὶ ἡ δόξα τῷ παντοκράτορι θεῷ καὶ νῦν καὶ εἰς τοὺς αἰῶνας· ἀμήν. The passage which I have omitted will be found to have no bearing on the text of *Didasc.*

ADDITIONAL NOTES

p. 4 ll. 24 f. 'But for men who obey God there is one law, simple and true and mild,—without question (*zētēma*), for Christians,—this' (Syr. codd. BCS).

'Eis autem hominibus qui obediunt Deo una lex est sinplex, uera, sine quaestione Christianis constituta, ita' (Lat.).

τοῖς δὲ ὑπηκόοις θεῷ ἀνθρώποις εἷς νόμος θεοῦ ἁπλοῦς, ἀληθής, ζῶν οὗτος ἐνυπάρχει (*AC*).

A negative form of the Golden Rule follows. The third adjective, 'mild' (*bassīma*), is omitted by cod. H of Syr. and is absent from Lat., while *AC* has in its place ζῶν. It is rejected by Flemming and Funk. The next words in Syr., 'without question, for Christians', are omitted in *AC* and corrupted in Syr. cod. H, but guaranteed as genuine by the support of Lat. How are we to explain them? In Syr. and Lat. they read like a parenthesis containing some sort of play upon the last preceding adjective. In Lat., however, where the last adjective is 'uera', there is nothing to suggest them and we get the impression that some key-word is wanting. But the preceding adjective in Syr. (*bassīma*) is the regular equivalent of χρηστός in the sense of gentle or pleasant; and hence, if codd. BCS give us the original reading of Syr., the translator must have had before him a Greek text which ran: 'one law, simple and true and *chrēstos*,—without question, for *Christians*'; and we recall at once the familiar passages of Suetonius and Tertullian: 'Iudaeos impulsore *Chresto* assidue tumultuantes Roma expulit' (*Claud.* 25), and: 'Christianus uero, quantum interpretatio est, de unctione deducitur. Sed et cum perperam *Chrestianus* pronuntiatur a uobis (nam nec nominis certa est notitia penes uos), de suauitate uel benignitate conpositum est' (*Apol.* 3). Lactantius also notes the error of those who 'immutata littera *Chrestum* solent dicere' (*Inst. diu.* iv 7).

If χρηστός did not stand in the original *Didascalia* here, I see no satisfactory explanation of the following reference to 'Christians'; and a later insertion of the equivalent adjective in MSS. of the Syriac version seems equally inexplicable: it could only be set down as an amazingly happy accident. It is to be observed also that *AC* does not really support Lat. here as against Syr. It has with Syr. a third adjective, though a different one; and the substitution of another word admits of a reasonable explanation, for *AC* then omits the next words with the reference to 'Christians'. Why? Probably, I venture to suggest, because the compiler of *AC* did not care to make the Apostles responsible for a false derivation of 'Christian'. A similar motive, or perhaps the impossibility of reproducing the original word-play, may have determined the Latin translator to disregard χρηστός in his version. As for Syr. cod. H, its omission of the equivalent word may seem significant as supporting Lat.; but if we remember the general character of this MS. its evidence here will carry less weight, and especially as its text at this point is 'editorial', and seems also to be corrupt. It has the clause 'there is one law', etc., thus:

ܣܘ ܘܗ ܒܥܕܒܐ ܠܥܕܒܐ ܩܪܫܝܠܐ ܕܫܪܝܪܐ ܘܒܠ ܠܐܘ ܕܠܐ ܬܥܒܕ ܫܘܐܠܐ
ܠܟܪܣܛܝܢܐ.

'there is one law, simple and true: and I say (mean), that thou shalt not cause questions to Christians'.

In Syriac 'I say' is used for *id est*; but the 'and' before it here is quite irregular, and is apt to suggest that there was a third adjective to follow, which the scribe carelessly passed over. Thus we should probably translate: 'simple and true and..'.(?): I mean', etc.

For *bassīma* = χρηστός the following examples will suffice. The derived subst. *bassīmūtha* twice stands in Syr. for χρηστότης in the Prayer of Manasseh, and it stands for τὸ χρηστόν in Rom. ii 4. The adj. renders χρηστός in Lk. vi 35 and Eph. iv 32. Above all it translates χρηστός in Mt. xi 30 (*syr. sin., cur., vulg.*, Aphraates, *Didasc.* Syr. 2/2); and this text is one that is constantly in our author's mind when (as probably here) he is contrasting the light and easy yoke of Christ with the burden and hard yoke of the *Deuterosis* or 'Second Legislation'.

I have added this note because much more is involved than the inclusion or exclusion of a single word. If the adjective *bassīma* comes to us from the Syriac translator, it is almost certain that we have here another indication of the early associations of the *Didascalia*.

p. 14 l. 17. 'God's promise of everlasting life': lit. 'the promise of God of everlasting life'. So CS; but BH, and also *AC*, omit 'of God'.

p. 37 l. 16. After 'often' probably supply 'brethren' (vocative) with H, which is doubtless right in reading ܐܚܝ̈ for ܐܬܝ̈. (So Flemming.)

p. 58 ll. 20 f. 'a restrainer of sins and an example and encourager of righteousness': (χρὴ γὰρ τὸν ἐπίσκοπον) καὶ τῶν ἁμαρτιῶν κωλυτὴν (διὰ τῆς νουθεσίας γίνεσθαι) καὶ τῆς δικαιοσύνης σκοπόν *AC*. This shows that the word ܕܡܘܬܐ is to be read *dĕmūtha*, 'likeness' or 'example', not *dĕ-mauta*, 'of death', as previous translators have taken it (sc. 'a restrainer of sins and *of death* and an encourager', etc.).

p. 61 l. 11. '*fient*' is no doubt corrupt for '*ferent*'.

p. 66 ll. 1–2. 'or will be sunk in the heresies': ἢ εἰς αἱρέσεις συμποδισθήσεται *AC*. Did Syr. misread here, and again at p. 194 l. 12, συμποντισθήσεται?.

p. 72 l. 8. After the words 'and led him away to Babylon' (2 Chron. xxxiii 11) cod. H. adds 'in a *zodion* of brass'. This is a mere editorial addition similar to others which appear in H; but we may endeavour to trace its history and thereby illustrate the story in the *Didascalia*.

ADDITIONAL NOTES 263

Anastasius Sinaita (saec. vii) gives the following account of Manasseh :[1]

Φασὶ γὰρ ἀρχαῖοι τῶν ἱστοριογράφων ὅτι ἀπενεχθεὶς Μανασσῆς ὁ βασιλεὺς Ἰσραὴλ ὑπὸ Χαλδαίων αἰχμάλωτος ἐν Βαβυλῶνι τῆς Περσίδος κατεκλείσθη εἰς ζῴδιον χαλκοῦν ὑπὸ βασιλέως Περσῶν· καὶ ἔσω ὢν ἐν τοιούτῳ ζῳδίῳ προσηύξατο μετὰ δακρύων τὴν προσευχὴν τῆς ᾠδῆς αὐτοῦ. καὶ προστάξει καὶ φιλανθρωπίᾳ θεοῦ διερράγη τὸ ζῴδιον· καὶ ἐξῆλθεν ὁ Μανασσῆς καὶ ἐσώθη ὑπὸ ἀγγέλου θεοῦ εἰς Ἱερουσαλήμ, κἀκεῖ ἐτελεύτησεν ἐν μετανοίᾳ καὶ ὁμολογήσει.

It is evident that the story told in *Didasc.* could not have been the source of this. There Manasseh is delivered only from his chains, which are melted from him by a flame of fire. Even H does not mention his deliverance from the *zodion*, which shows clearly enough that this feature is foreign to the *Didasc.* account. We get nearer to Anastasius in the Targum on 2 Chron. xxxii 10–13, which is to the following effect :

10 ' And the Lord spake to Manasseh and to his people and testified unto them by the hand of the prophets, and they hearkened not. 11 And the Lord brought against them the captains of the army of the king of Assyria ; and they seized Manasseh with handcuffs and bound him with chains of brass, and carried him away to Babylon. And the Chaldees made a mule (מולוות) of brass and bored it all over with small holes, and shut him up in the midst of it, and applied fire round about him. 12 And when he was in distress, he besought all the idols that he had made, but got no help, for there was no profit nor honour in them. And he prayed before the Lord his God, and humbled himself exceedingly before the God of his fathers. 13 And (as) he prayed before Him, straightway all the angels which are appointed over the doorways of prayer in heaven went and shut on his account all the doorways of prayer and all the windows and lattices of heaven, to the end that his prayer might not be received. And forthwith the pity of the Lord of the world was moved, whose right hand is held out to receive sinners who return to His worship and who break the evil disposition of their heart by repentance. And He made a lattice and a breach in heaven beneath the throne of His glory, and moved the world by His word ; and the mule (מולאת) was burst, and (Manasseh) went out thence. And a wind (*or* spirit) came forth from beneath the wings of the Cherubim and blew him by the decree of the word of the Lord, and he returned to his kingdom to Jerusalem. And Manasseh knew that the Lord He is God, who did those signs and wonders with him ; and he repented with all his heart before the Lord, and left all his idols and served them not.'[2]

[1] *In psalmum vi.* Migne *P. Gr.* lxxxix 1104 B.
[2] With this we must compare the *Apocalypse of Baruch* (said to have been written in the latter half of the first century A. D.) c. 64 : 'On this account Manasseh was at that time named " the impious ", and finally his abode was in fire. For though his prayer was heard with the Most High, finally, when he was cast into the brazen horse and the brazen horse was melted, it served as a sign unto him for the hour. For he had not lived perfectly [*translate rather*: " For he was not saved finally "], for he was not worthy—but that thenceforward

This is more circumstantial than the account in Anastasius, but there is a general agreement. The '*zodion*' of Anastasius leaves the shape of the image undetermined, which would be natural enough in a Greek version of the story; while the 'angel' in Anastasius might be an adaptation of 'the word (*or* Word) of the Lord' in the Targum.

In the *Chronicon* of Bar-Hebraeus (ed. Bedjan p. 24) we find the following:

'After Hezekiah, Manasseh his son: 55 years. And in his 13th year he killed Isaiah the prophet by sawing him in two with a saw. And for this God rejected him and delivered him into the hands of the Assyrians. And when they had led him into captivity, they bound him with hard irons and put him in a *zodion* of brass in Nineveh. And when affliction was sore upon him, he turned himself to the God of his fathers and offered a sincere repentance, and prayed the famous Prayer. And God answered him, and he was delivered and returned to Jerusalem. And the image of four faces, which he had made, he put out of the temple and cleansed it (the temple), and he cast away the idols.'

Bar-Hebraeus's chief source here would appear to be the *Historiarum Compendium* of Cedrenus,[1] which states that Manasseh was led captive to Nineveh by king Merodach, was there bound with chains of brass, and made a 'sincere repentance'; being sent back to Jerusalem, he overthrew the idolatrous shrines and cleansed (ἥγνισε) the temple. The murder of Isaiah by sawing him in two is also mentioned, and the four-faced image[2] (τετραπρόσωπον εἴδωλον); but nothing is said of the *zodion*. This last feature Bar-Hebraeus would seem to have derived from some Greek version of the story similar to that found in Anastasius.

We have already seen that the additional words in cod. H do not fit with the rest of the story as told in the *Didascalia*; and the passages just quoted will show, I think, that the words touch another line of tradition. It is unnecessary to go further and discuss the question whether the '*zodion*' was a mule (as in the Targum), a horse (as in *Baruch*), or a brazen bull like that in which the Sicilian tyrant Phalaris roasted his victims.

p. 78 ll. 2-4. 'nor spending ... as your own'. I corrected the text here according to *AC* and Lat. The correction is supported by C and H, which, however, still omit a necessary negative.

he might know by whom finally he should be tormented' (Charles, *Pseudepigrapha* ii p. 515).

[1] Migne *P. Gr.* cxxi 228.
[2] Bar-Hebraeus might have introduced this detail from the Syriac version of 2 Chron. xxxiii 7: 'and he set the image of four faces, which he had made, in the house of the Lord'. On the traditions about this image see S. Landersdorfer, *Der Βάαλ τετράμορφος und die Kerube des Ezechiel* ('Studien zur Geschichte und Kultur des Altertums', ix 3: Paderborn, 1918). The *Apoc. of Baruch* (*loc. cit.*) says that Manasseh made an image of *five* faces, four looking to the four winds, and one on the top 'as an adversary to the zeal of the Mighty One'.

ADDITIONAL NOTES

p. 81 l. 8. 'from all your people'. I have translated here from a slight, and quite unconscious, emendation ܡܢ ܟܠܗ ܥܡܟܘܢ. The text (BHS) has 'from all that (are) with you' (ܡܢ ܟܠ ܕܥܡܟܘܢ): but compare pp. 81 l. 11 and 82 l. 1, also p. 80 l. 10.

p. 92 ll. 9 f. 'and wait for the glorious promise': καὶ ἔνδοξον ... ἐπαγγελίαν ἀπεκδεχομένους *AC*. For 'promise' Syr. (BHS) has ܡܠܟܐ, which in BS has the vocalization *malkā* indicated, i.e. 'king'. I have suggested in the note that the word may be *melkā*, because the corresponding verb means 'to promise' as well as 'to counsel'; but I can find no instance of the subst. except in the sense of 'counsel' or 'advice', and so perhaps we should emend to *mulkānā*, the usual word for 'promise'. So Flemming: Nau and Funk render 'king', which is unsuitable.

p. 112 ll. 30 f. 'whether there be any accusation against him also'. *AC* has more suitably 'whether this be the first (person) whom he has accused' (εἰ πρῶτον τούτου κατηγορεῖ). With a slight change (ܐܦ݂ܠܐ for ܐܦ݂ܠܗ) Syr. would mean 'whether also he has (formerly) *brought* an accusation against the same (person)', which is somewhat nearer to *AC*. Flemming proposes a more drastic emendation, but with nearly the same result.

p. 122 l. 21. 'But if' is from H: om. BS.

p. 122 l. 30. '⟨whether of the same district⟩'. This is supplied from l. 13 before and *AC* Lat. I had not observed that the words are represented in H in the form 'whether a son of thine own congregation'—a different rendering of ἢ ἐγχώριος from that at l. 13.

p. 133 l. 16. 'the Lord God, Jesus Christ': so BS: 'Jesus Christ' (only) H.

p. 138 ll. 24 f. 'apart from that which is commanded them': BS: + 'by the bishop' H, which goes with Lat. 'citra consilium aut imperium episcopi'. *AC* has δίχα γνώμης τοῦ διακόνου. The 'citra consilium' of Lat. must be from δίχα γνώμης, which requires a following genitive.

p. 160 l. 24. 'unsullied' (see note *in loc.*): ܠܐ ܛܡܐܝܢ C; ܠܐ ܛܡܐܝܢ H; ܠܐ ܛܡܐܢ BS.

p. 181 ff. In his twelfth Homily, on the Passover or Pascha, Aphraates treats of the date of the Paschal festival. His argument is in places very obscure, and it is difficult to know what we are to conclude from it. But there appear to me to be strong reasons for connecting this Homily with the 21st chapter of the *Didascalia*, which also treats of the Pascha. There are no doubt essential differences between the two: Aphraates has nothing of the strange chronology for Holy Week which we find in the *Didascalia*, and the Easter fast is mentioned by him only incidentally towards the end. Yet there is a seeming inconsequence about the treatment in both documents which is curiously similar, and in one point there is a positive coincidence which can hardly be accidental. In each, near the beginning of the discussion, and without any manifest reason, the author goes off into a proof that our Lord did truly, according to His saying in the Gospel, 'pass three days and three nights in the heart of the earth', and in each this follows immediately after a notice of the Last Supper and of the departure of Judas. The three days and nights are not obtained by quite the same method, for Aphraates makes them three nights and days, beginning his count earlier than does the author of the *Didascalia*; but both include periods previous to the death of our Lord, and both reckon the three hours of darkness and the ensuing hours of light as a night and a day; and at this point there is much similarity in the language. I give here a translation of the relative portion of the Homily:

'Now the minds of simple and ignorant men are much disturbed about this great day of the Festival, how they are to know and observe it. But the true Lamb was our Saviour, *of one year, without blemish*; as the prophet said concerning Him: *There was no iniquity in him, neither was guile found in his mouth.* ....

'For our Saviour ate the Passover with His disciples in the accustomed night of the Fourteenth; and the sign of the Passover He performed in truth[1] for His disciples. After Judas was gone out from them, *He took bread and blessed and gave to his disciples, and said: This is my body: take, eat of it, all of you. And also over the wine he so blessed, and gave to his disciples, and said: This is my blood, the new testament, which for many is shed for the forgiveness of sins. This,* said He, *do ye in remembrance of me, when ye are assembled.* Before our Lord was seized He said these things; and our Lord rose up from where He had performed the Passover and given His Body to be eaten and His Blood to be drunk, and went with His disciples to that place where He was seized.

'Now one whose body is eaten and his blood drunk[2] is reckoned with the dead. For our Lord with His own hands gave His Body to be eaten, and before He was crucified He gave His Blood to be drunk. And He was seized in the night of the Fourteenth, (and judged) until the sixth hour. And at the time of the sixth hour they condemned Him and caused Him to ascend (the cross) and crucified Him.[3] Now while they were judging Him He did not speak, and He gave no answer, it saith, to His judges. For He might have spoken and given an answer; but the thing was not possible that one reckoned with the dead should speak. And from the sixth hour till the ninth there was darkness; and He delivered up His spirit to His Father at the ninth hour. And He was with the dead in the night when the 15th drew on, the night of the Sabbath and the whole day (thereof), and three hours on the Friday. And in the night when the first of the week drew on, at the time at which He had given His Body and His Blood to His disciples, He rose from the dead.

---

[1] That is, apparently, He celebrated the true Passover, of which the Jewish Passover was the sign or type.

[2] So by a simple and convincing emendation (ܐܟܣ for ܐܟܠ) suggested by Professor Burkitt, without which the text would read 'who has eaten his body and drunk his blood'.

[3] Compare the obscure passage in *Didasc.* p. 182 ll. 5–6.

ADDITIONAL NOTES

'Show us now, O wise man, what are the three days and three nights that our Saviour was with the dead. For we see that there were the three hours of the Friday, and the night when the Sabbath drew on, and the whole day (of the Sabbath): and in the night of the first of the week He arose. Define me these three days and three nights, where they are. For see, He was (with the dead) but one complete day and night. Yet was it truly as our Saviour said: *As Jonah the son of Mattai was in the belly of the fish three days and three nights, so shall the Son of Man be in the heart of the earth.* Now from the time that He gave His Body to be eaten and His Blood to be drunk there were three days and three nights, thus:

'*The hour*, it saith, *was night* when Judas went out from them and they, His eleven disciples, ate our Lord's Body and drank His Blood: behold now one night, that in which the Friday drew on. And until the sixth hour they judged Him: behold one day and one night. And (there were) the three hours wherein there was darkness, from the sixth hour to the ninth, and three hours after the darkness: behold two days and two nights. And (there was) the complete night when the Sabbath drew on, and the whole day of the Sabbath. There were fulfilled accordingly to our Lord three days and three nights with the dead; and in the night of the first of the week He rose from the dead.'

The following scheme will show the relation of Aphraates to the *Didascalia* in this matter of the days and nights:

Didascalia.	Aphraates.
1. { Trial, etc. (1st day) Three hours of darkness (1st night).	1. { Night before trial (1st night).[2] Trial (1st day).
2. { Three hours of light (2nd day) Night before Sabbath (2nd night).	2. { Three hours of darkness (2nd night). Three hours of light (2nd day).
3. { The Sabbath (3rd day). Three hours after Sabbath (3rd night).	3. { Night before Sabbath (3rd night). The Sabbath (3rd day).

p. 182 l. 5. 'at the sixth hour' (ܫܥܐ ܫܬ). Flemming and Funk translate 'for six hours', which would mean from the third to *the ninth*. But this is contrary to Syriac usage, as may be seen by referring to Mk. xv 34, 'at the ninth hour', where the construction is exactly the

---

[1] The following lines offer a very close parallel to *Didasc.* p. 182 ll. 5-11 and 15-19.

[2] As Aphraates places the resurrection at an hour corresponding to that of the Last Supper (that is, three hours earlier than the author of the *Didascalia*), he has to find his three *nights* by beginning earlier and counting in the night of the arrest. This is the only real difference between the two computations: the *days* in both are the same.

same. Nor does it remove the apparent difficulty of this sentence in relation to the next : 'And these hours in which our Lord was crucified (not 'was hanging on the cross', as Flemming takes it) were reckoned a day'. So far we are not taken beyond the sixth hour, after which followed the darkness, i. e. the first '*night*'. We must, I think, understand the verb 'was crucified' here as including the whole preliminary action from the third to the sixth hour; and so apparently the author of *AC* took it : ἕκτῃ μὲν ὥρᾳ σταυρώσαντες αὐτόν, τρίτῃ δὲ ὥρᾳ τὴν ἀπόφασιν δεξάμενοι τὴν περὶ αὐτοῦ (Funk p. 275 l. 27).

p. 184 l. 12. After 'apprehended Me' B and S marg. add 'Do you fast (upon) it': CH are wanting. The words seem redundant after ll. 4–5 before, and I have omitted them as a gloss (and so Flemming).

p. 190 l. 12. 'And then offer your oblations; and thereafter eat and make good cheer'. Flemming translates : 'Und dann bringt eure Opfergaben dar : und nun esset und seid guter Dinge'; quoting which (p. 288) Achelis remarks : 'This is the Eucharist, which accordingly still had the form of a meal'. But this seems to rest on a slight ambiguity in the German, viz. in the word 'nun'. The Syriac ܡܟܝܠ, 'hereafter', 'thereafter', 'henceforth', 'thenceforth', may often be rendered 'now' (*iam*), but only with reference to some point (in the past or future) which is assumed to have been passed; it has not a contemporaneous sense (*simul*). Here the fixed point is the conclusion of the Easter fast, marked by the celebration of the Eucharist at the third hour of the night following the Saturday. *AC* makes the sense clear : προσενέγκατε τὴν θυσίαν ὑμῶν ... καὶ λοιπὸν ἀπονηστεύετε, εὐφραινόμενοι κτλ. (Funk p. 293). The Syriac word would be an exact rendering of λοιπόν here, which therefore need not be suspected. The passage, then, tells us nothing about the Eucharist except that it marks the end of the fast. It is merely what we are told in the *Apostolic Tradition* of Hippolytus : 'Nemo in Pascha, antequam oblatio fiat, percipiat' (Hauler p. 116).

p. 193 ll. 11 f. As this is the only passage in the *Didascalia* which speaks of Christ as 'the Word', and as other translators have taken it differently, it is necessary to justify the rendering I have given. I have said in the note : 'the Syriac construction seems to require that the name [Jesus Christ] be taken in apposition to "the Word".' I think I might have said that the grammar and the sense absolutely require this, for there is really no other way of taking the Syriac :

ܡܕܡ ܕܝܢ ܕܡܢ ܐܝܬܘܗܝ ܐܝܟܢܐ ܕܚܙܝܗܝ ܝܪܡܝܐ ܦܐܪܐ ܚܠܝܐ ܗܘ ܕܡܠܬܗ ܕܐܠܗܐ.

Flemming renders this : 'Unser Stock aber ist das Wort Gottes, (nämlich) Jesu Christi, wie auch Jeremias eine Haselrute sah', and Funk is to the same effect. But there is no justification for taking the name 'Jesus Christ' as a genitive in apposition to 'of God' : for this the genitive particle would need to be repeated. The first clause can only be grammatically rendered : ' Now our rod is the Word of God, (even) Jesus Christ'. Then in the second clause the objective suffix to the verb 'saw' cannot be pleonastic, referring to the object 'rod'; the position of the verb at the end of the clause forbids this: it must refer back to 'Jesus Christ': 'even as Jeremiah saw *Him* (as) an almond (*or* hazel) rod'. And the grammatical rendering gives a good sense, which the other does not : what Jeremiah saw was not just an almond rod, but the Word of God under that figure.

p. 197 l. 8. After 'of making schisms' B and S marg. add 'and of falling into schisms', for which H has 'and you shall not fall into judgement'. I have omitted the additional words as a gloss, but perhaps they are to be retained in one or other of the two forms. Flemming adopts them as in B and S marg.

p. 198 ll. 5–7. '*Defilement* ... Now these *defilements* of heresies'. See footnote *in loc.* H reads here : ' *There is gone forth in all the earth the heathenism* (or *impiety*) of heresies', which looks like an attempt to improve upon the shorter text of S, without knowledge of S marg. The word 'heathenism' is that in the Syriac Bible here (Jer. xxiii 15).

p. 202 ll. 12–17. Compare Iren. *Haer.* I xviii 'Nubere autem et generare a Satana dicunt esse. Multi autem ex iis, qui sunt ab eo [sc. the followers of Saturninus of Antioch], et ab animalibus abstinent, per fictam huiusmodi continentiam seducentes multos'. Hippolytus reproducing this passage (*Philos.* vii 28) has ἐμψύχων for 'animalibus'. Cf. also Hippol. *Philos.* viii 20 : 'abstaining from things which have a soul (ἐμψύχων), drinking water, and forbidding to marry' (of the Encratites).

p. 228 l. 27. 'The plough-yoke', lit. 'the yoke of the plough'. This is the reading of B. For 'of the plough' S has 'of the snare (*or* noose)'. This is difficult, and وفسا (S) is probably a corruption of وفمل (B). C and H are wanting.

p. 230 (*et passim*). The following passage from Aphraates, Hom. xv ('On distinction of meats'), might easily be mistaken for an excerpt from the *Didascalia*.

' And Jeremiah said : *I have left my house, I have given the beloved of my soul into the hand of her enemies* (xii 7). . . . And by the prophet Ezekiel He distinguished and showed them, because of their contentiousness, and gave them various sacrifices and oblations, if haply by means of these they might be restrained from their sins. He had already said to them : *I gave them commandments and made known to them judgements* (xx 11); and then He said: *I gave them commandments that are not good, and judgements whereby they may not live; and I have defiled them with their gifts, when they offer oblations* (xx 25 f.). . . . For behold, for thy sins He gave thee oblations and made for thee a distinction of meats.[1] Of what oblations, pray, and judgements did Ezekiel say: *That*

---

[1] Cf. p. 222 ll. 12–14.

whosoever doeth them may live by them? and of which did he say : *I gave you commandments that are not good, and judgements whereby ye may not live?* The lifegiving commandments and judgements are those which were written before, and the just and righteous judgements which He set before them are the holy Ten Commandments [1] which He inscribed with His hands and gave unto Moses to teach them. But when they had made the calf [2] and turned away from following Him, then did he give them *commandments and judgements that are not good*—oblation, and purification for leprosy and flux and menstruation and childbearing, and that none should touch a dead man, or a tomb, or (dead) bones,[3] or them that have been slain, and that they should offer an oblation for every sin and every human defilement. . . . Out of the Law they cannot be justified, as the Apostle saith : *No man is justified out of the law : but he that doeth the things that are written therein shall live by them* (Gal. iii 11 f.).[4] But it is manifest that no man can do them, and that he is unable to keep them. And our Lord also, seeing that they were heavy, called us and said to us:[5] *Come unto me, ye that toil and are laden with burdens, and I will give you rest. And take my yoke upon you; for my yoke is light and pleasant* (Mt. xi 28-30). We thank the Mercy that hath taken from us the hard yoke, the heavy yoke, and hath given us His own, light and pleasant.'

p. 238 ll. 5-7. Add to the references in the notes 'Iren. *Haer.* V xxxiii 2' ('Haec sunt in regni temporibus, hoc est in septima die, quae est sanctificata, in qua requieuit Deus ab omnibus operibus quae fecit, quae est uerum iustorum sabbatum, in qua non facient omne terrenum opus'— a clear reference to the seventh millennium as the true Sabbath of God). Also V xxviii 3 ('Etenim dies Domini quasi mille anni ; in sex autem diebus consummata sunt quae facta sunt : manifestum est quoniam consummatio ipsorum sextus millesimus annus est ').

p. 254 l. 10. 'who was called the Angel : *The Lord hath*', etc. I have here made a slight correction of the text, which has : 'who was called the Angel of the Lord : *He hath*', etc. But 'the Lord' belongs to the quotation, so that the genitive prefix before it must be removed.

p. 258 l. 3. 'indulgently'. The correction referred to in the note consists in reading ܡܒܣܡܐܝܬ for ܡܪܣܡܐܝܬ. To the latter adverb no suitable meaning can be attached, and Payne Smith says it is probably corrupt : it is from a verb which means 'to cause to flow'.

---

[1] Cf. pp. 14 ll. 1-4, 218 ll. 18-20, 224 ll. 16-17.
[2] See the last three references.   [3] Cf. pp. 250-52.
[4] Cf. p. 238 l. 26, where the previous verse (Gal. iii 10) is used.
[5] Cf. pp. 14 ll. 9 ff., 226 ll. 19 ff.

INDEX LOCORUM

An asterisk (*) signifies an allusion, or possible allusion, only. Brackets denote that the passage is parallel or secondary to another. The Psalms are numbered as in the Septuagint.

Genesis
i 1-2 : 234
   3 : 174
   5 : 184, 234
  15 : 179*
ii 2-3 : 232
  24 : (204)
iv 7 : 53
ix 6 : 106
  25 : 44
xxvii 29 : (6), (144)

Exodus
ii 14 : 190
iv 21 : 224*
  22 : 234
vii 1 : 92
xii 6 : 189
xiii 2 : (234)
  12 : (234)
xvi 8 : 93
  29 : 191*
xix 5-6 : (86)
xx 10 : 236*
  11 : 232
  13 : 240
  17 : 4
  24-5 : 220, 222*
xxi 17 : 94
xxii 28 : 92
xxiii 8 : 105
  15 : 100
xxxii 1 : 222
  8 : 222
xxxv 3 : 191*

Leviticus
xviii 5 : 228*
xix 18 : (101)
  27 : 10
xxi 17 : 32
xxvi 23-4 : 109*
  27-8 : 109*

Numbers
xii 1 : 194
  14 : 53
xiv 2 : (93)
xvi 1 ff. : 194*
  26 : 197
  32-3 : 196
  34 : 197
  35 : 195
  36-8 : 196
xviii 1 : 56
  1-32 : 82
xix 9-10 : 238*
xxiv 9 : 6, 144, 145, 250
xxv 1 ff. : 194

Deuteronomy
i 16 : 114*
  17 : 105
iv 19 : 179
v 14 : 236
  21 : 4
vi 4 : 37
  5 : (100)
xvi 19 : (105)
xix 15 : (102)
  17 : 111*
xxi 22-3 : 222
  23 : 230
xxiii 18 : 159
xxiv 16 : 43
xxv 4 : 80
xxvii 5 : 220, 222*
  26 : 238
xxviii 37 : 74*
xxix 19 : 74
xxxii 21 : 179
  43 : 207

1 Samuel (1 Reg.)
viii 10-17 : 94

1 Kings (3 Reg.)
viii 46 : 55

2 Kings (4 Reg.)
xiii 21 : 252*
xxi 1-17 : 66
  18 : 74
  19-20 : 76*

2 Chronicles (2 Paral.)
vi 36 : (55)
xxxiii 1-13 : (66)
  11 : 72
  12-13 : 72
  13 : 72, 74
  18 : 72*
  20 : 74

Job
xiv 4-5 : 55, 178

Psalms
i 2 : 228
ii 3 : 228
  7 : 93
  10-12 : 178
iv 5 : 116
vi 6 : 42
xvii 26 : 109*
  45 : 186
xviii 8 : 216
xxiii 1 : 236
xxxi 1-2 : 176
xxxviii 6 : 182
l 6 : 55
lxv 12 : 98
lxvii 16-17 : 198
  18 : 185
  34 : 120
lxviii 34 : 98
lxxiii 4-5 : 184
  19 : 43
lxxxix 4 : 234

Proverbs
iii 9 : 160
v 1-14 : 18
  22 : 43

Proverbs (cont.):		Isaiah (cont.):		Ezekiel	
vi	6–8 : 129	v	6 : 198	v	7 : 126
	8 : 145		18 : 232, 250	viii	16–18 : 179
	8–11 : 129		20 : 106	xiv	9 : 74
	14 : 113		23 : 106		12–14 : 43
	22 : 242	vi	9–10 : 134, 224	xvi	47 : 127
vii	1–27 : 16	viii	18 : 199	xviii	1–32 : 44
	11 : 134	ix	1–2 : 186	xx	9–11 : 230
ix	13–18 : 24	xxvi	18 : 170		25 : 230
x	12 : 32*		19 : 170	xxxiii	1–6 : 36
	18 : 145	xxvii	11 : 128		7–9 : 37
xi	22 : 24	xxix	13 : 100		10 : 63
	25–6 : 96	xl	5 : 174		10–11 : 42
xii	4 : 23, 24	xlii	7 : 98		12–19 : 50
	28 : 116		19 : 230	xxxiv	1–31 : 56
xiii	24 : 193	xliii	8 : 230		3 : 78
xiv	12 : 212		18–19 : 216, 236		4 : 62, 64
xv	1 : 32	xlv	9–10 : 100		5 : 64
	17 : 158	xlix	9 : 98		16 : 62, 63
xviii	3 : 24	lii	5 : 26		17 : 60
xix	14 : 204		10 : 174	xxxvii	1–14 : 168
xx	9 : 178	liii	2–6 : 81		
	22 : 6		11 : 150		
xxi	9 : 24, 28		12 : 81	Daniel	
	19 : 24, 28	liv	14 : 159	vii	10 : (185)
xxii	10 : 108	lvii	1–2 : 176	xii	2–3 : 167
xxiii	13 : 193*		12 : 222		3 : 174*
	14 : 193	lviii	6 : 55, (64), 114, 116	xiii (Susanna) : 114*	
xxvi	2 : 145		7 : 131		
	17 : 114		13 : 191	Hosea	
xxvii	25–6 : 35	lix	7–8 : 66	i	10 : 96
xxix	17 : 193	lxi	2–3 : 185	ii	17 (19) : 179*
xxxi	10–31 : 22		10 : 86	iv	9 : 36
		lxiii	10 : 186		
		lxv	1 : 185		
Wisdom			2–3 : 185	Joel	
iv	7 : 66	lxvi	2 : 30	ii	13 : 204
			5 : 185		28 : 199
			10 : 185		
Ecclesiasticus			16 : 197*		
vii	25 : 152*			Habakkuk	
xi	3 : 129*			i	5 : 170
xxxiv	10 : 38*	Jeremiah		ii	11 : 234*
xxxvi	14 : 234*	i	11 : 193		
		ii	11 : 127		
		iii	16 : 236	Zechariah	
Tobit		iv	1–2 : 179	viii	16 : 106, 114*
iv	15 : 4*, 145*		3–4 : 204		19 : 183
		v	7 : 179	xii	12–13 : 191
		vi	20 : 225	xiii	2 : 179*
Isaiah		vii	21–2 : 225		
i	7 : 152	viii	4–5 : 43		
	11–14 : 225	x	2 : 128, 179	Malachi	
	16 : 204	xvii	12 : 199	iv	16 : 216
	17 : 106, 114	xxiii	15 : 198	xi	14–15 : 254
ii	2–3 : 199		29 : 256		
	6 : 198	xxiv	9 : 74*		
iii	8 : 198				

INDEX LOCORUM

2 Maccabees
i 4 : 258*

Prayer of Manasseh
7₂

From unknown sources
72^{8-11}; 74^{5-13}; 76^{2-7}; 109^{8-5}; 128^{6}; 152^{11-12}; 234^{10}; 234^{24}; (cf. 32^{26}; 234^{16})

St. Matthew
- iv 15-16 : 186
- v 4 : 184
  - 5 : 30
  - 7 : 30
  - 8 : 32
  - 9 : 30, 111
  - 11 : 163
  - 11-12 : 38
  - 17 : 218
  - 18 : 218
  - 20 : 98
  - 22 : 93, 116
  - 23-4 : 116
  - 27-8 : 4
  - 44 : 6, (144), 184
- vi 1 : 143
  - 2 : 144
  - 3 : 110, 143
  - 10 : 118
  - 12 : 66
  - 13 : 165*
  - 14-15 : (106)
  - 19 : 154
  - 20 : 100, 138
  - 21 : 136
- vii 1 : 101
  - 2 : 106, 112, 210
  - 3 : 53
  - 5 : 53
  - 6 : 133
  - 15-16 : 210
- viii 4 : 218
  - 12 : 166
- ix 2 : 64
  - 11-12 : (104)
  - 12 : 64
  - 14-15 : (180)
  - 20 : 254*
- x 5 : 128, 212
  - 10 : 78*
  - 12 : 117

St. Matthew (cont.):
- x 12-13 : 144
  - 23 : 163
  - 24 : 240
  - 28 : 164
  - 32 : 161
  - 33 : (163), 166
  - 37 : 166
  - 37-9 : 163
  - 39 : 166
- xi 15 : 37
  - 28 : 14, 226
  - 28-30 : 98, 207
- xii 30 : 118, 124
  - 31-2 : 212
  - 32 : 212
  - 36-7 : 28
  - 40 : 182
  - 43-5 : 246
- xiii 12 : (242)
  - 14-15 : (134)
  - 15-16 : 224
- xv 4 : 94
  - 8 : (100)
- xvi 6 : 212
  - 19 : 96*
  - 25-6 : 163
- xvii 20 : 134
- xviii 6 : 54*
  - 7 : 198
  - 10 : 54
  - 12 ff. : 63*
  - 15-16 : 102
  - 16-17 : 102
  - 17 : 103
  - 18 : 40, 55, 96*
  - 19 : 134
  - 21 : 110, 111
  - 22 : 111, 117
- xix 4-6 : 204
  - 19 : 101
  - 21 : 98
- xx 19 : 234
  - 26-8 : 148
- xxi 13 : 54
  - 21 : 134
  - 46 : 187
- xxii 10 : 118
  - 13 : 166
  - 21 : 110
  - 31-3 : 252
- xxiii 18-22 : 244
  - 34 : 163
  - 38 : 198, 199
- xxiv 11-13 : 210
  - 24 : 210, 214
  - 30 : 163*
- xxv 29 : (242)
  - 30 : 256
  - 33 : 110*

St. Matthew (cont.):
- xxv 34-40 : 162
  - 41 : 256
  - 46 : 162
- xxvi 3-5 : 187
  - 6 : 187
  - 15 : 187
  - 16 : 188
  - 21-3 : 181
  - 31 : 181
  - 39 : 52*, 212*
  - 41 : 165
- xxvii 24 : 190
  - 56 : 148
- xxviii 1 : 182, 183
  - 9 : 183*

St. Mark
- ii 16-17 : 104
  - 18-20 : 180
- iv 25 : (242)
- v 34 : (64)
- x 52 : (64)
- xii 30 : 100
  - 41-4 : 138
- xiii 22 : (214)
- xiv 18-20 : (181)
  - 27 : (181)
  - 30 : 181
- xv 3 : 182
- xvi 15 : 200*
  - 19 : 180*

St. Luke
- ii 23 : 234
- iii 13 : 103
  - 22 : 93*
- iv 18 : 64
  - 24 : 122
- v 30-1 : (104)
  - 33-5 : (180)
- vi 23 : (38)
  - 27 : 6, 184
  - 28 : 6, 144
  - 37 : (101), 106
  - 37-8 : 66
  - 40 : 166
  - 41-2 : (53)
  - 46 : 256
- vii 50 : (64)
- viii 18 : 242
  - 48 : (64)
- ix 26 : 163
- x 5 : (117)
  - 7 : 78*
  - 16 : 60, 93
  - 27 : 100

St. Luke (*cont.*):
xii	33 : (98),(100)
	48 : 56
xiv	11 : 32
xv	4 ff. : 63*
xvi	9 : 154
xvii	3 : 102*
	19 : (64)
xviii	14 : 32
xix	1 ff. : 103*
	46 : (54), 187
xx	25 : (110)
xxi	18–19 : 167
xxiii	34 : 52*, 212*

St. John
vii	24 : 114*
viii	3–11 : 76
x	1, 16 : 120*
xi	25 : 252*
xii	26 : 166*
	36 : 6*, 93*, 110*
	40 : 224*
xiii	4–5 : 150
	14–15 : 150*
	30 : 181*
xvi	32 : 181*
xx	1 : 183*
	14 : 183*

Acts
iv	25 : 228*
viii	18–19 : 200
	20–1 : 200
x	1 ff. : 206*
	9–16 : 206
	41 : 176
xi	4–10 : (206)
	15 : 207
	16 : 207
xiii	41 : (170)
xv	1 ff. : 204
	4 : 206
	5 : 206
	7–8 : 206
	8–11 : 207
	13–29 : 207
	25 : 204
xxviii	26–7 : (134), (224)

Romans
ii	24 : (26)
vii	2–3 : 131*
viii	17 : 2*

Romans (*cont.*):
x	5 : 228*
xv	10 : (207)
xvi	25 : 258*

1 Corinthians
vi	1 ff. : 110*
vii	32 : 136*
	34 : 136*
	39 : 131*
ix	9 : (80)
xi	3 : 20*
	19 : 198*

2 Corinthians
| xiii | 13 : 2* |

Galatians
iii	10 : 238*
	13 : (222)
iv	9 : 93*
v	3 : 232*
vi	2 : 8*

Ephesians
iii	6 : 2*
iv	26 : 116
v	9 : 6*
	22–3 : 20
	27 : 214*

Philippians
| iii | 19 : 136* |

1 Thessalonians
| v | 5 : 6*, 93* |

2 Thessalonians
| iii | 10 : 129 |

1 Timothy
i	7 : 52*, 212*
ii	4 : 118
iii	2 : 28, 32, 56, 78
	2–3 : 32
	3 : 76
	4 : 32
	4–5 : 32*

1 Timothy (*cont.*):
iii	6 : 32
	8 : 35, 113, 148
iv	3 : 204
v	9 : 130
	18 : 78*, (80)
vi	11 : 163*

2 Timothy
ii	22 : 28
iii	17 : 163*
iv	1 : 163*

Titus
| i | 7 : 28, 76, 78 |

Hebrews
| ix | 13 : 238* |

James
i	12 : 38*
ii	2 : 122*
	19 : 176*

1 Peter
i	2 : 2
	17 : 2*
ii	9 : 86
	24 : 81*
iii	9 : 145, 240*
	14 : 38*
iv	4 : 38*
	8 : 32
	10 : 78*

2 Peter
| iii | 8 : 234* |
| | 9 : 118* |

1 John
| i | 1 : 176* |

Apocalypse
| xxi | 2 : (86) |

Agrapha
38^{18}; 78(?); 101^6; 198; 234

GENERAL INDEX

Ab (August), Jewish lamentation on the 9th of, 191 n.
Abraham, lxxxii, 236 n., 259.
Achelis, Hans, v, xxiii, xxxvi, xxxvii n., xl, xli, xlii, lii, lv, lvi, lxix, lxxii, lxxvi–lxxviii, lxxxvi n., lxxxviii n., lxxxix, xci, 96 n., 268.
Acta Pauli, lxxviii.
Acts of John, 224 n.
Acts of Judas Thomas, l, lxxxviii, 146 n., 200 n.
Acts of Peter, lxxix.
Actus Petri cum Simone (*ed.* Lipsius), 200 n., 201 n., 202 n.
Advent, Second, 214.
Agape, xliv, liii, liv, 88–91, 123 n.
Agrapha, lxxxiii, lxxxviii, 38 (l. 18), 101 (l. 6).
— *see also* Index Locorum (p. 271) *and* Resch, Ropes.
Aleppo, lxxxix.
Altar, 220, 222.
— *see also* Widow.
Ambrose, St., xix.
Amon, son of Manasseh, lxx, 74, 76.
Anastasius Sinaita, 263, 264.
Angel, *see* Elijah, Malachi, Confessor.
Anicetus, Pope, liii n., 123 n.
Anna, 130.
Antioch, lxxxviii.
Aphraates, xvii, xviii, xxxii n., xlviii, lxxiv, lxxv, lxxviii, lxxxvii, 54 n., 67 n., 88 n., 102 n., 106 n., 116 n., 117 n., 181 n., 182 n., 218 n., 230 n., 235 n., 237 n., 238 n., 256 n., 262, 265–7, 269.
Apocalypse, 72 n , 86 n.
Apocalypse of Baruch, 263 n., 264 n.
Apocrypha, lxxv–lxxix.
Apocryphal Epistle of the Corinthians, lxxviii, lxxxiii, 200 n., 202 n., 203 n.
Apology of Aristides, 161 n.
Apostolic Church Order, xiv n., xviii, lxxxiv, lxxxv, 30 n., 31 n., 33 n., 87 n., 93 n., 130 n., 149 n., 200 n.
Apostolic Constitutions, xx–xxi *et passim*.
Apostolic Preaching (St. Irenaeus), 36 n., 44 n., 130 n., 216 n., 217 n., 224 n.
Apostolic Tradition (St. Hippolytus), xviii, xxvii, xli, li, liii, lxxxiii, lxxxix, 89 n., 91 n., 123 n., 189 n., 224 n., 237 n., 239 n., 259 n., 268.

Athanasius, St., lxxxiv, 158 n.
Audiani, lxxxvii.
Augustine of Hippo, St., lviii, 253 n.

Baptism, xlviii–l, lxxxviii, 38, 178, 242, 247, 254.
— not to be administered by women, 142.
— one only, 204, 248.
— ritual of, xlix, l, 146, 147.
Baptisms, ceremonial, 216, 248–51, 254.
Bar-Hebraeus, xvi n., lxxxiv, 264.
Barnabae Epistola, lxiii, lxxix, 4 n., 35 n., 132 n., 205 n., 224 n., 233 n., 234 n., 235 n., 236 n., 238 n.
Bartlet, J. Vernon, xxi, 133 n.
Bathing, 14, 26, 126, 191.
Baumstark, A., xvi n.
Beard, not to be shaven, 10.
Benedict, St., 33 n., 149 n.
Bishop, 28–119 *passim*.
— conducts public worship, xl.
— dispenses alms and offerings, 78, 81, 88, 131.
— 'high priest', 86.
— judge of accusations against brethren, 101–8.
— judge in other causes between Christians, 109–19.
— mediator between God and the faithful, 80, 86, 92, 98.
— merciful to penitents, 40–77.
— not to be judged, 98, 100.
— nothing to be done without, 88, 92.
— people's 'father after God', 86, 93.
— power to bind and loose, 55, 96.
— preaches, admonishes, rebukes, 37–40.
— 'priest and mediator', 98.
— qualifications, xxxviii, xxxix, 28–36.
— represents God, 55, 86, 88, 90, 92.
— supported by offerings of the faithful, 78–101.
— visiting, lii, liii, 122, 123.
Books of the heathen prohibited, 12.
Burkitt, F. C., l n., lxxiv n., lxxv n., 54 n., 106 n., 116 n., 218 n., 266 n.

Cain, 220.
Callistus, Pope, liv.
Canons of Hippolytus, lxxxiv–lxxxvii.

Catechumens ('hearers'), 38, 39, 165, cf. 103 n.
Catholic, see Church, Didascalia.
Cedrenus, 264.
Cerinthus, 200 n.
Chapman, John, 217 n.
Cherubim, 258.
Children, upbringing of, 152-7, 193, 194.
Chrēstos; possibly a play on χρηστός and Χριστιανός, 4, 5 n.
Christ; divine epithets coupled with Name, 2, 63, 76, 77, 118, 133, 149, 150, 151, 167, 216, 217, 245, 250, 251.
— 'High Priest', 86.
— our pattern, 81.
— sole approach to God, 90.
— spoke through Moses, 4.
— virgin birth, 176.
— the Word of God, xlv, 193, 268, 269.
'Christians', derivation of term, 261.
Church, 'beloved daughter of the Lord God', 108, 127.
— a body, 107, 124.
— duty of assembling in, 124-9.
— a fold, 120.
— the 'Great', 86, 87.
— 'Holy Catholic', 2, 3, 80, 81, 85, 86, 108, 112, 118, 127, 202, 203.
— one only, 199.
— ordering of places in, 119-24.
— 'receptacle of the Holy Spirit', 212, 213.
— typified by tabernacle 'of witness', 80.
— 'your mother', 127.
Circumcision, 202, 204, 218-21.
Clement of Alexandria, lxxxiii, xci, 17 n., 33 n., 101 n., 109 n., 217 n.
Clement of Rome, Pope, lxx, lxxx, 17 n., 26 n., 33 n., 106 n., 119 n., 147 n., 172 n., 221 n.
Clementine Homilies, lxxxiii n., lxxxiv-lxxxvi, 6 n., 242 n.
Cleobius, xxxii, lxxviii, lxxxiii, 200, 201.
Codex Borgianus (B), xii, xv, xvi, xxiv.
Codex Cantabrigiensis (C), xvi, xxiii.
Codex Harrisianus (H), xiii-xvi, xxiii, xxiv.
Codex LV (53), Verona, xviii.
Codex Sangermanensis (S), xi-xvi, xxiv.
Codex (Vatican), xvi n.
Coelesyria, lxxxix.
Confessor, esteemed as 'Angel of God', 161.

Confessor, see also Martyrs.
Conflate reading in AC, 67 n.
Creed, 163 n., 258.
Cup of the Agape (?) and visiting bishop, 122, 123.
Curse against Christ, 222, 230, 232, 240, 242, 250.
Cursing prohibited, 144, 145.
Cyprian, St., xlv, xlix, liii, 123 n.
Cyril of Jerusalem, St., xlix.

Daniel, quoted according to LXX, 167.
Day, Jewish, counted from evening, 184, 192.
Deacon, agent of the bishop, xl, xli, 109.
— duties of, 148-51.
— holds place of Christ, 88, 90.
— number proportionate to community, 148.
— proclamation in church by, 117.
— two at Mass and services, xli, 120-3.
Deaconess, appointment and duties, xlii, lxxxviii, 146-8.
— symbol of Holy Spirit, 88.
Dead, defilement from contact with, 250, 252.
— Eucharist offered for, 252.
Decade, 86.
— see also Yod.
Decalogue ('Ten Words'), lx, lxi, lxiii, lxvi-lxviii, lxxxii, 4, 14, 86, 218.
— see also Law.
Decius, xc, xci.
Demiurge, lxvii.
Demons, incorporeal, 242, 243.
— tremble at name of Christ, 176.
Deuterosis, xxxiv, xxxv, li, lvii-lxix, lxxxi, lxxxix, 12-15, 34, 98, 164, 204, 216-53, 261.
— abolished by Christ, 224-6.
— imposed for idolatry, 14, 224, 225, 232, 250.
— see also Law.
Diatessaron (Tatian), 165 n., 181 n.
Didache, xx, xxvii-xxix, xxxvii, xxxviii, lxxix, lxxx, 4 n., 6 n., 11 n., 30 n., 31 n., 35 n., 79 n., 86 n., 98 n., 100 n., 109 n., 131 n., 154 n., 155 n., 156 n., 158 n., 184 n., 218 n., 219 n.
Didascalia, author, xci.
— 'Catholic', 2.
— date, lxxxix-xci.
— the document, xxvi-lxxxvii.
— place, lxxxvii-lxxxix.
— text, xi ff.
— theology, xlv-xlviii.

GENERAL INDEX

Didascalia, title, xxvii, xxviii, 204, 205, 210, 211, 214, 215.
— unity, xxvi–xxxviii.
Diocletian, xc.
Dionysius of Alexandria, St., xxxvii, xxxviii, lxxxiii, 189 n.
Discipline of the Secret, *cf.* 143.
Doxology, 4 (l. 9), 20 (l. 13), 156 (l. 16), 258.
Dress, of men, 10.
— of women, 23.

East, prayer towards, 119.
Easter, date of, 187, 192.
— *see also* Fast, Pascha.
Edessa, lxxxix.
Elijah, 130 n.
Elisha's dead body 'filled with the Holy Spirit', xlviii n., 252.
Encratism, *see* Tatianism.
Ephraim, St., lxxiv, lxxvii, lxxxvii, 165 n., 181 n.
Epiclesis, lii.
Epiphanius, St., lviii, lix, lxv n., lxxxiv, lxxxvii, 3 n., 10 n., 79 n., 181 n., 187 n., 188 n., 189 n., 192 n., 203 n.
Eucharist, l–liv, 94, 100, 116, 120, 122, 123, 242, 266, 267.
— 'likeness of the Royal Body of Christ', 252, 253.
— offered at Easter after 3rd hour on Saturday night, 190.
— offered for the dead, 252.
— replaces sacrifices of Old Law, 86.
— sanctified by the Holy Spirit, 244.
— sanctified by invocation, 252.
— visiting bishop to be invited to offer, lii, liii, 122, 123.
Eusebius of Caesarea, liii n., lix, lxxi, lxxxviii, xc, xci, 17 n., 123 n., 189 n., 200 n., 203 n.
Ezekiel, 269.
— author's text of, 37 n., 45 n., 56 n., 57 n., 58 n., 59 n., 60 n.

Fairs of the heathen, 126, 128.
Fast, Paschal, xxxi, xxxii, lxxxvii, 178–92, 265, 268.
— — called 'Fast of the Passion', 183.
— — concluded at 3rd hour of Saturday night, 189, 190, 192.
— — determination of date, 187, 192.
— — more rigorous on Friday and Saturday, 189.
— — six days (Monday to Saturday), 183.
Fast, weekly, on Wednesday and Friday, 183, 184.
Fasting imposed for penance, 52.

First day of the week, day of rejoicing, 183, 192.
— — fasting forbidden, 183, 192.
— — *see also* Lord's Day, Sunday.
Flemming, J., vi, xiii n., xiv, xvii, xxiii–xxv, xxviii, 10 n., 34 n., 53 n., 54 n., 66 n., 96 n., 118 n., 123 n., 128 n., 132 n., 143 n., 144 n., 156 n., 158 n., 160 n., 164 n., 166 n., 171 n., 182 n., 186 n., 191 n., 193 n., 203 n., 223 n., 224 n., 225 n., 236 n., 243 n., 248 n., 254 n., 261, 262, 265, 267, 268, 269.
Forgiveness of sins, liv–lvi, 40–77, 101–108.
— — after baptism, 38, 178, 254.
— — through martyrdom, 178.
— — *see also* Penitents.
Funk, F. X., vi, xvi n., xx–xxiv, xxvi, xxviii, xxxvi, xxxviii, li n., lxxi n., lxxxiii, lxxxiv, lxxxv n., lxxxvi n., lxxxviii n., lxxxix, 3 n., 5 n., 8 n., 41 n., 68 n., 69 n., 97 n., 102 n., 109 n., 110 n., 118 n., 128 n., 132 n., 134 n., 135 n., 139 n., 143 n., 144 n., 146 n., 158 n., 160 n., 161 n., 166 n., 171 n., 173 n., 181 n., 182 n., 186 n., 187 n., 191 n., 193 n., 198 n., 201 n., 205 n., 213 n., 223 n., 224 n., 225 n., 227 n., 231 n., 235 n., 241 n., 243 n., 249 n., 252 n., 253 n., 254 n., 255 n., 258 n., 261, 265, 267, 268.

Gallienus, xc, xci.
Games ('ludi'), those condemned to, 160, 161.
Gehenna, 36.
Gelasius I, Pope, lii n.
Gibson, Mrs. Dunlop, vi, xiii, xvi, xxii–xxiv.
Golden Rule, 4, 145, 261.
Gospel according to the Hebrews, lxxii, lxxvii, lxxxviii, 88 n.
'Gospel of Matthew', 182.
Gospel according to Peter, lxxv, lxxvi, lxxxii n., lxxxviii, xci, 181 n., 183 n., 189 n., 190 n.

Hair, treatment of, 10, 23.
Ham, curse of, 44.
Hand, imposition of, by widows, 138, 140.
— — in baptism, 93, 146.
— — in ordination, 32.
— — in reconciling penitents, 56, 104, 107.
Hand, left, *see* Heathen.
Harnack, Adolf, xxxvi, xxxvii, lxv n., lxvi n., lxxxix.
Harris, Rendel, xiii.

Hauler, Edmund, xix, xxv, xxvi, xxviii, li n, liii n., 3 n., 5 n., 27 n., 29 n., 41 n., 51 n., 69 n., 87 n., 89 n., 91 n., 95 n., 97 n., 99 n., 135 n., 139 n., 149 n., 151 n., 171 n, 173 n., 189 n., 209 n., 211 n., 213 n., 215 n., 217 n., 227 n., 231 n., 235 n., 237 n., 239 n., 241 n., 243 n., 247 n., 249 n., 251 n., 255 n., 259 n., 268.
Hearers, *see* Catechumens.
Heathen, books of, 12.
— called men 'of the left hand', 110, 143.
— Christian men must not go to law before, nor admit as witnesses, 109, 110.
— example quoted to shame Christians, 90, 126.
— festivals of, 35, 126, 128.
— must not know what is done in church, 143.
— songs of, 179.
Hebrews. *see* Gospel.
Hegesippus, lxxxiii, 17 n., 200 n., 203 n.
Heresies, 197–205.
— called 'cities of the Samaritans', 128, 212.
Heretics, 210–15.
Hermas, xlviii, lxxix, 17 n., 42 n., 48 n., 73 n., 79 n., 114 n., 116 n., 131 n., 154 n., 155 n., 156 n., 161 n., 166 n., 178 n., 185 n., 197 n., 245 n., 246 n.
— *cf. especially* 154–7.
Herod, gives command for Our Lord's crucifixion, 190.
Hippolytus, St., xviii, xix n., xxvii, xli, xlv, xlix, li, liii, liv, lxxxiii, lxxxix, 14 n., 89 n., 91 n., 123 n., 189 n., 192 n., 215 n., 224 n., 235 n., 237 n., 239 n., 259 n., 268, 269.
Hody, H., lvii n., lix.
Holy Spirit, *see* Spirit.
Holy Week chronology, xxxii, lxxvii, 181–92, 265–8.
Holzhey, C., xxxvii, lxxxiii.

Ignatius of Antioch, St., xxxix, lii, lxxvii, 27 n., 88 n., 89 n., 91 n., 102 n.
Imposition, *see* Hand.
Iota, *see* Yod.
Irenaeus, St., lii, liii, lxiii, lxiv, lxxxi, lxxxii, xci, 14 n., 17 n., 36 n., 44 n., 102 n., 106 n., 123 n., 130 n., 179 n., 205 n., 216 n., 217 n., 221 n., 224 n., 225 n., 226 n., 231 n, 236 n., 238 n., 239 n., 257 n., 269, 270.

James, Dr. M. R., lxxvi n., lxxviii n.

James, St., 'bishop of Jerusalem', 204.
Jeremiah, 126, 256, 257, 269.
— quotations wrongly attributed to, 100, 126.
— *see* Lamentations.
Jerome, St., xl n., lii, lviii, lix, lxxvii, lxxviii, 191 n.
Jerusalem, 183 n., 200 n., 204, 264.
'Jew', signifies 'confession', 126.
Jewish observances, 242–55.
— — on Sabbath, 191.
Jews, 126 n., 180–92 *passim*.
— prayed for during Paschal Fast, 184, 187.
— to be called 'brethren', 184–5.
John the Evangelist, St., xlv, lxxxv.
Josephus, Flavius, 191 n.
Judas, 44, 181, 188.
Judgement, causes to be heard on Mondays, 111.
— dispensed by bishop, 40–77, 101–15.
— presbyters and deacons to assist, 111.
— Roman methods, 115.
— *see* Law.
Justin Martyr, St., xlv, lxxix–lxxxi, xci, 17 n., 36 n., 93 n., 100 n., 198 n., 236 n., 237 n., 238 n.

Korah, Dathan, and Abiram, examples of schismatics, 194–7.

Lactantius, 261.
Lagarde, Paul de, xi–xiii, xxi, xxii, xxiv, 203 n.
Lamentations of Jeremiah, read by Jews on 9th Ab, 191, 192.
Landersdorfer, S., 264 n.
Laodicea, Council of, liii.
Law, Old, lvi–lxix, lxxxi.
— — consists especially of 'The Ten Words and the Judgement', 14, 15, 218, 219.
— — distinguished from 'Deuterosis' or 'Second Legislation', 12–15, 34, 216–18, 222, 224, 228, 238, 240.
— — respected by Romans, 238.
Lector, xli, xlii, 90.
Letter of Ptolemaeus to Flora, lxv–lxvii.
Levi, visited after Resurrection, 183.
Logos doctrine, xlv.
Lord's Day, 124.
— — *see also* First Day of the week, Sunday.
Lordship, 109 n., 129 n.

Malachi, 'the Angel', 216, 254.
Manasseh, xxix, liv, lxx, lxxvi, lxxxiv, lxxxviii, 68–76, 262–4.

GENERAL INDEX

Manasseh, apocryphal traditions, 72, 74.
— *see also* Prayer of Manasseh.
Marcion, lxiv, lxvii.
Marcionism, xxxiii n.
Marriage, 152, 194, 202, 204.
— second lawful, third unlawful, 131.
Martyrs and martyrdom, 161-78.
Mary, Blessed Virgin, 142, 164.
Mary, 'daughter' of James, 133, 148, 183.
Mary, sister of Moses, 53, 194 n.
Matthew, St., 103.
Meats, distinction of, 216, 218, 222.
Medical language, xci, 104, 105, 107, 165, 166, 258.
Melito of Sardis, St., 17 n.
Memoriae (mortuary chapels), 253.
Millennium, seventh, 238, 270.
Mines, those condemned to, 160, 161.
Mishna, lvii, lviii.
Mistranslations in the Syriac, 12, 38, 76, 124, 134, 152, 154.
Moses, 4, 130 n., 195, 236 n.
Mouse, 250.
Mule of brass, Manasseh enclosed in, 72 n., 262 ff.
Muratorian Fragment, 216 n.
Mustard, the Word likened to, 132.

Name of Jesus connected with Decalogue by initial letter, 86, 216-18.
Names of benefactors, not to be disclosed by widows, 143.
— — to be told to widows, that they may pray for them, 131.
Names of idols (demons), not to be spoken, 179, 180.
Narsai, xlix n., 146 n.
Nau, F., vi, xv, xxii-xxiv, xxviii, xxxvi, xxxvii n., lxxx n., 34 n., 193 n., 265.
Nazarenes, lxxxix.
Nebuchadnezzar, 15 n.
Nestle, Eberhard, 80 n.
Nicaea, Council of, lvi n.
Nineveh, 264.
Nisan, 188 n.
Noah, 'blamed' for offering sacrifice, 220.
Novatian, lxxxix.
Novatianism, xxxvi, xxxvii, lxxxix.

Oblations, non-eucharistic, li.
Odes of Solomon, 74 n., 238 n.
Offerings to a bishop, xliii, xliv.
Opus imperfectum in Matthaeum, lxxxiv, 68 n., 72 n., 74 n., 75 n., 76 n., 110 n.
Origen, lix, lxxxiii, 172 n.

'Pagani', 158 n.
Painters of pictures, 158.
Papias, lviii, lxxi, lxxii.
Part-offering, 80 n.
Pascha, Christian, 180-92.
— — *see* Easter, Fast.
Passover, Jewish, 181, 187, 192.
— — anticipated by 3 days in year of Crucifixion (being kept on Tuesday, 11th of month), 188.
Penance, *see* Forgiveness of sins.
Penitents, reconciliation of, 56, 104.
Pericope de adultera, xxix, lv, lxxi, lxxvii, 76.
Peter, Gospel of, see Gospel of Peter.
Phoenix, lxxx, 172.
Pilate, exonerated, 189, 190.
Polycarp, St., xliv, liii n., lxxx, 27 n., 89 n., 123 n.
Prayer of Manasseh, 262, 68 n., 72.
Presbyter, xxxix, xl, 86, 88, 90, 91 n.; 96, 111, 119, 122, 140.
— appointed by bishop, 96.
— councillor of bishop, xxxix, xl, 90, 91 n., 96.
— overshadowed by deacon, xl n.
— represents Apostles, 88, 90.
— sits with bishop, 119.
Prophets, *see* 'Twelve Prophets'.
Proverbs, Book of, cited by this title, 114, 116, 145, 204, 212, 242.
— *see also* Wisdom.
Ptolomaeus (his letter to Flora), lxv-lxviii.

Quartodecimans, lxxxvii, 192 n.
Quaestiones ueteris et noui testamenti, xl n.

Raca (= 'empty'), 93.
Regula S. Benedicti, 149 n.
Resch, Alfred, xcii, 27 n., 33 n., 39 n., 52 n., 79 n., 101 n., 152 n., 191 n., 198 n., 235 n.
Resurrection, 167-77, 202, 204, 224, 242.
— to 'show forth' the, 224.
Rigorism opposed, liv-lvi.
Robinson, C., xliii n.
Robinson, J. Armitage, vii, xliii n, lxii, lxiv n., lxxv n., 44 n., 130 n. 216 n., 217 n.
Roman methods of judgement, 115.
— officials, 158.
Romans used as God's instruments, 238-41.
Ropes, James H., xcii, 39 n., 52 n., 79 n., 198 n., 208 n.
Rufinus of Aquileia, lix.

Sabbath, lxxx, lxxxi, lxxxviii.
— day of mourning for Jews, 190-1.
— type of seventh millennium, 236.
— *see also* Saturday.
Sacraments, xlv, xlviii–lvi.
Sacrifices abolished by Christ, 226, 238.
— prescribed in 'Second Legislation', 222, 226.
— not prescribed in 'The Law'; 218–23, 225.
Saturday, Holy, vigil on, 189, 190, 192.
Schürer, lvii, lix, 191 n.
'Second Legislation', see *Deuterosis*.
Serapion, lii.
Shoes, 10, 23, 250.
Sibyl, xxxi, 172.
Sibylline Oracles, lxxix, 172 n.
Silas, 208.
Simon Magus, xiv n., xxxii, lxxviii, lxxix, lxxxiii, 200, 202.
Sin, 'deadly', 178.
— *see also* Forgiveness.
Snake lying upon treasure, fable of, 154.
Solis Ara, 173.
Solomon, *see* Odes of Solomon.
Songs of heathen forbidden, 179.
Spirit, 'alien', 246-7.
Spirit, Holy, xlv–xlviii, lxvii, lxxxviii, 2, 20, 88, 94, 161, 242.
— — blasphemy against, 212.
— — Christians filled with, 246.
— — Elisha's dead body filled with, 252.
— — Eucharist sanctified by, 244.
— — given in baptism, 93, 104.
— — in doxology, 20 (l. 13), 156 (l. 17), 167 (l. 4), 259 n.
— — represented by deaconess, 88.
— — witness with Father and Son, 102.
— — worshipped with Father and Son, 204.
Statutes of the Apostles, xvi n., xli n., xlii n., liii n.
Subdeacon, servant of deacon, xli, xlii, 96.
Suetonius, 261.
Sunday, lxxx, lxxxi, 134, 178.
— *see also* First Day of the Week, Lord's Day.
Susanna, 114.

Tabernacle, type of Church, 80.
Targum, lxx, lxxxviii, 72 n., 128 n., 263.
Tatianism, xxxiii n., 202–4, 240–2, 269.
Tertullian, xlv, xlvi n., xlix, li n., lii, liv, 38 n., 89 n., 172 n., 180 n., 189 n., 190 n., 261.
Testament, New, lxx–lxxv.
— Old, lxix, lxx.
Testamentum Domini, xiv n.
Theatre, 126–8.
Theodotion, lxix, 59 n., 60 n., 167 n.
Theta (θ), mystical meaning of, 192.
Throne, bishop's, 119.
Tomb, defiles by contact, 250, 252.
Torah, lviii, lxxix.
Turner, C. H., xix n., xx n.
'Twelve Prophets', collective formula of citation, 36, 170, 254.

Valerian, xc.
Vigil, *see* Saturday.
Virgins, order of, not mentioned, xli, xliv.

'Western' readings, lxxiii, 93, 206 n., 201 n., 256.
Widows, xlii–xliv, liv, 130–45, 156–60.
— age limit, xliii, 130.
— duties of, xliv.
— fast, pray for, and lay hands on sick, 138–40.
— forbidden to teach, 132–3.
— not to be supported by gifts from evil persons, 156–60.
— represent the Altar of God, 88, 133, 134, 143, 156.
Wilmart, A., xix n., lxxiv.
'Wisdom', Book of Proverbs cited as, 16, 22, 24, 28, 35, 43, 96, 108, 193.
Women, forbidden to baptize, 142.
— forbidden to teach, 132, 133.
— instructions to, 20–8.
Word of God, *see* Christ.

Yod, mystical link between The Decalogue and Jesus, 86, 184, 216–19.
— *see also* Name.

Zodion (ζῴδιον), Manasseh enclosed in brazen, 72 n., 262–4.

www.ingramcontent.com/pod-product-compliance
Lightning Source LLC
Chambersburg PA
CBHW071232290426
44108CB00013B/1379